# INTERNATIONAL TRADE IN SERVICES

# INTERNATIONAL TRADE IN SERVICES

## NEW TRENDS AND OPPORTUNITIES FOR DEVELOPING COUNTRIES

*Olivier Cattaneo, Michael Engman, Sebastián Sáez, and Robert M. Stern, Editors*

THE WORLD BANK
Washington, D.C.

1818 H Street NW
Washington, DC 20433
Telephone: 202-473-1000
Internet: www.worldbank.org
E-mail: feedback@worldbank.org



1 2 3 4 13 12 11 10



ISBN: 978-0-8213-8353-7
eISBN: 978-0-8213-8354-4
DOI: 10.1596/978-0-8213-8353-7

**Library of Congress Cataloging-in-Publication Data**

International trade in services : new trends and opportunities for developing countries / edited by Michael Engman ... [et al.].

p. cm.
Includes bibliographical references and index.
ISBN 978-0-8213-8353-7—ISBN 978-0-8213-8354-4 (electronic)
1. Service industries—Developed countries. 2. International trade. I. Engman, Michael, 1976 -
HD9989.D44I588 2010
382'.45—dc22

2010017084

Cover image: "Purple Door," by Ahmed Abushariaa, 2005, courtesy of the World Bank Art Program.
Cover design by Tomoko Hirata/World Bank.

# CONTENTS


| | | |
|---|---|---|
| | About the Editors and Contributors | xiii |
| | Foreword | xv |
| | Acknowledgments | xvii |
| | Abbreviations | xix |
| 1 | Assessing the Potential of Services Trade in Developing Countries: An Overview<br>*Olivier Cattaneo, Michael Engman, Sebastián Sáez, and Robert M. Stern* | 1 |
| 2 | Increasing Labor Mobility: Options for Developing Countries<br>*Sherry Stephenson and Gary Hufbauer* | 29 |
| 3 | Legal Services: Does More Trade Rhyme with Better Justice?<br>*Olivier Cattaneo and Peter Walkenhorst* | 67 |
| 4 | Health without Borders: International Trade for Better Health Systems and Services<br>*Olivier Cattaneo* | 99 |
| 5 | Market Structure, Liberalization, and Trade: The Case of Distribution Services<br>*Julian Arkell* | 141 |
| 6 | Building Empires Overseas: Internationalization in the Construction Services Sector<br>*Michael Engman* | 177 |
| 7 | Exporting Information Technology Services: In the Footsteps of India<br>*Michael Engman* | 219 |

8 Accounting Services: Ensuring Good Governance, Financial Stability, and Economic Growth through Trade 263
*Olivier Cattaneo and Peter Walkenhorst*

9 Engineering Services: How to Compete in the Most Global of the Professions 293
*Olivier Cattaneo, Linda Schmid, and Michael Engman*

10 Understanding Trade in Environmental Services: Key Issues and Prospects 319
*Nora Carina Dihel*

Index 349

## Boxes


| | | |
|---|---|---|
| 2.1 | Extent of Temporary Labor Migration | 31 |
| 3.1 | Some Key Facts about Legal Services | 69 |
| 3.2 | Growth and Investment Have Created a Viable Market for Legal Services in Developing Countries | 70 |
| 3.3 | The Four Modes of Supply for Legal Services | 72 |
| 3.4 | Using Foreign Legal Consultants to Facilitate Trade | 78 |
| 3.5 | Self-Regulation Often Results in Cartelization of the Legal Profession | 81 |
| 3.6 | Professional Bodies Play a Prominent Role in Legal Skill Development | 82 |
| 3.7 | Cost Pressures Force Clients to Rethink Their Approach to Legal Services | 86 |
| 3.8 | Negotiating Mutual Recognition Agreements Can Facilitate Trade in Legal Services | 87 |
| 3.9 | Negotiating Fast-Track Visa Procedures to Facilitate Crossborder Movement | 89 |
| 4.1 | Case Study: Remedying Health Shortages through Trade under Modes 4 and 2, Oman | 105 |
| 4.2 | Case Study: Remedying Health Shortages through Trade under Mode 3, India | 108 |
| 4.3 | Case Study: Travel and Health Industries Commingling, Thai Airways | 114 |
| 4.4 | Case Study: Exports of Offshore Medical Transcription Services, the Philippines | 115 |
| 4.5 | Case Study: Exports under Mode 2, ASEAN | 118 |
| 4.6 | Case Study: Exports under Mode 4, Tunisia | 122 |
| 4.7 | Case Study: Mitigating the Distributive and Other Adverse Effects of Trade in Health Services, Thailand | 124 |
| 4.8 | Case Study: SWOT Analysis, Health Services Trade, Morocco | 127 |
| 4.9 | Case Study: Regulatory Audit for Health Services, Tunisia | 129 |
| 4.10 | Seizing Opportunities in the United Kingdom: The Case of South Africa | 131 |
| 4.11 | Case Study: A Successful Government-Led Strategy to Develop Medical Tourism, Cuba | 132 |
| 5.1 | Principal Activities in the Distribution Sector | 142 |
| 5.2 | Estimates of the Economic Scope of the Distribution Sector | 143 |
| 5.3 | Selected Developing-Country Experiences in the Distribution Service Sector | 146 |
| 5.4 | Examples of Multinational Retailers with Foreign Affiliates | 148 |
| 5.5 | Regulatory Reform in the Retail Sector | 156 |
| 6.1 | The Main Characteristics of the Construction Service Sector | 178 |
| 6.2 | What Do Construction Services Cover? | 180 |
| 6.3 | Facilitating the Administration of Building Permits | 197 |

| | | |
|---|---|---|
| 6.4 | Chinese Construction Companies Dominate the Infrastructure Market in Africa | 198 |
| 6.5 | Enhancing Transparency: World Bank Guidelines on Notification and Advertising | 199 |
| 6.6 | Initiatives to Prevent Corruption in Construction Projects | 201 |
| 6.7 | Homegrown Champions Exporting Construction Services | 208 |
| 7.1 | Egypt as an Emerging Offshore Location for IT Services | 224 |
| 7.2 | The Value of Securing an Anchor Investor | 227 |
| 7.3 | Raising Internet Connectivity in Africa | 233 |
| 7.4 | NIIT: A Private Initiative to Train Personnel for IT Service Careers | 236 |
| 8.1 | The Four Modes of Supply of Accounting Services | 266 |
| 8.2 | Affiliations of Developing-Country Accounting Firms with the Big Four | 268 |
| 8.3 | Examples of Domestic Regulations That May Impede Trade in Accounting Services | 271 |
| 8.4 | Price Controls: Legitimate Policy Objectives and Adverse Effects | 272 |
| 8.5 | International Accounting and Auditing Standards | 274 |
| 8.6 | Reports on the Observance of Standards and Codes | 277 |
| 8.7 | An Example of a Regional Agreement on the Mutual Recognition of Qualifications | 279 |
| 8.8 | Investing in Education to Meet International Standards: The Case of Zambia | 280 |
| 9.1 | Definition of Engineering Services | 294 |
| 9.2 | The Four Modes of Supply of Engineering Services | 298 |
| 9.3 | An Example of Trade Success: Tunisian Engineering Firms | 300 |
| 9.4 | The Contribution of Regionalism to Integration in the Engineering Service Trade | 308 |
| 9.5 | Addressing the Fears Associated with Trade Opening: Accompanying Measures | 309 |
| 9.6 | Articulating Microstrategies and Macrostrategies | 311 |
| 10.1 | What Do Environmental Services Cover? | 320 |
| 10.2 | Explaining the Growth Potential of Environmental Markets: The Environmental Market Development Model | 325 |
| 10.3 | Case Study: Trade in Environmental Services, Mexico, 2001–06 | 327 |
| 10.4 | The Participation of Developing Countries in Environmental Services | 328 |
| 10.5 | Market Challenges Faced by Environmental Service Firms at Home | 336 |

## Figures

| | | |
|---|---|---|
| 1.1 | The Expanding Role of the Trade in Services in the World Economy, 1977–2007 | 3 |
| 1.2 | Trade, by Region, 2007 | 4 |
| 1.3 | Trade in Services, by Region, 2007 | 5 |

1.4 Worker Remittances Received, by Region, 2007 5
2.1 Provisions on Mode 4 in FTAs between Developed and Developing Countries 55
3.1 Exports of Legal Services from Selected Countries, 2001–07 79
4.1 Foreign Professionals Working in the Public Health Sector, Oman, 2003 105
4.2 Omani Patients Treated Abroad, 2006 106
4.3 Health: A Sector with Strong Potential for Outsourcing 114
4.4 A Definition of Medical Travel 116
4.5 Relative Size of Medical Traveler Segments 117
4.6 Mergers and Acquisitions in the Health and Social Services Sector 120
6.1 Construction Services: Mean Gross Value Added in GDP, 75 Countries 178
6.2 Construction Services: Market Share by Sector 179
6.3 Exports of Construction Services, Selected Economies 184
6.4 Commercial Presence of Large International Contractors in Foreign Markets 186
6.5 Number of Procedures Involved in Dealing with Construction Permits 189
6.6 Number of Days Required to Deal with Construction Permits 190
6.7 Cost of Dealing with Construction Permits 191
7.1 Offshoring = International *In*sourcing + International *Out*sourcing 221
7.2 A. T. Kearney's Global Services Location Index 228
7.3 Indian IT Workers in the United Kingdom 238
8.1 The Rising Global Revenues of Accounting Firms 264
9.1 Top 500 Engineering Design Firms by Revenue and Type of Work, 2008 297
9.2 Comparative Student Enrollments in Engineering, Selected Countries 305
10.1 Position of World Regions or Countries in the Environmental Market Development Model, 2000 325

## Tables

1.1 The Scope of Services Covered in the GATS 7
1.2 Modes of Supply and the GATS 8
1.3 Analytical Structure for the Description of Sectoral Barriers to a Service 24
1.4 Six Efficient Regulatory Principles and Related Good Regulatory Practices 26
2.1 The Magnitude of Service Trade through the Temporary Movement of Labor (Mode 4) 31

| | | |
|---|---|---|
| 2.2 | Quantitative Estimates of Gains from Increased Labor Mobility | 33 |
| 2.3 | Agreements between the United States and Developing Countries | 40 |
| 2.4 | Agreements between Canada and Developing Countries | 42 |
| 2.5 | Agreements between the EU and Developing Countries | 46 |
| 2.6 | Agreements between Japan and Developing Countries | 48 |
| 2.7 | Agreements between Australia, New Zealand, and Developing Countries | 51 |
| 2.8 | BLAs with Developing-Country Partners: Government Programs for Temporary Workers | 58 |
| 3.1 | Trade in Legal Services, 2007 | 73 |
| 3.2 | Importance of Trade under the Different Modes of Legal Service Supply | 74 |
| 3.3 | Trade in Legal Services: The Example of Morocco | 75 |
| 3.4 | Examples of Offshorable Legal Services | 80 |
| 3.5 | Frequently Encountered Restrictions on Legal Practice by Foreigners | 83 |
| 3.6 | Typical Cost Structure of a Law Firm | 85 |
| 3.7 | Law Firm Investments to Create Intangible Assets | 88 |
| 3.8 | Uruguay Round Commitments on Legal Services | 91 |
| 3.9 | A Checklist of Questions on Trade-Related Aspects of Legal Services Reform | 93 |
| 4.1 | What Are the Modes of Trade in the Health Sector? | 101 |
| 4.2 | Who Is the Exporter? Who Is the Importer? | 104 |
| 4.3 | Export Revenues and Patient Profile, Three ASEAN Countries | 118 |
| 4.4 | Comparative Costs of Surgical Procedures | 119 |
| 4.5 | African Physicians Practicing in Canada and the United States | 121 |
| 4.6 | Tunisian Exports under Mode 4, 2004 | 122 |
| 4.7 | Health Services Trade, Morocco | 127 |
| 4.8 | Regulatory Audit, Tunisia | 129 |
| 4.9 | Restrictions on Health Services Trade Listed by Morocco in the United States–Morocco Free Trade Agreement | 136 |
| 5.1 | Stores Owned by European Retail Roundtable Members, Developing Countries | 148 |
| 5.2 | International Footprint of Five European Retail Groups, 2008 | 148 |
| 6.1 | Major Exporters and Importers of Construction Services, 2005 | 183 |
| 6.2 | Procedures, Time, and Costs Involved in Building a Warehouse, Russian Federation, 2008 | 193 |
| 6.3 | Procedures, Time, and Costs Involved in Building a Warehouse, Kenya, 2008 | 195 |
| 6.4 | Commitments by WTO Members in Construction and Related Engineering Services | 202 |
| 6.5 | Number of Measures in Construction and Related Engineering Services | 203 |

| | | |
|---|---|---|
| 6.6 | A Checklist of Questions on Trade-Related Aspects of Construction Service Reform | 211 |
| 7.1 | Major Exporters and Importers of Computer Services, 2006 | 223 |
| 7.2 | A. T. Kearney's Index Metrics | 229 |
| 7.3 | Information and Communication Technology Performance Indicators | 231 |
| 7.4 | A Checklist of IT Service Questions for Policy Makers | 245 |
| 7A.1 | Computer and Related Services: UNCPC Descriptions of the GATS Sectoral Classification List Entries | 250 |
| 7A.2 | Information and Communication Technology Infrastructure Indicators | 252 |
| 8.1 | Exports of Accounting and Consulting Services, 2007 | 265 |
| 8.2 | The Big Four Global Accounting Firms, 2007 | 267 |
| 8.3 | Examples of Offshored Accounting Services | 269 |
| 8.4 | Optimal Levels of Negotiation for the Trade in Accounting Services | 272 |
| 8.5 | Use of International Financial Reporting Standards, Selected Developing Countries | 275 |
| 8.6 | Influences on Accounting Firms and Services | 281 |
| 8.7 | Restrictions on the Trade in Accounting Services | 284 |
| 8.8 | Initiatives to Improve the Environment for Accounting Firms | 286 |
| 9.1 | Trade in Architectural, Engineering, and Other Technical Services, Selected Economies, 2006 | 296 |
| 9.2 | Leading Engineering Firms, 2005 | 299 |
| 9.3 | Best Practices in Business Services: Mutual Recognition Agreements in Engineering | 313 |
| 9.4 | A Checklist of Questions on Trade-Related Aspects of Engineering Service Reform | 315 |
| 10.1 | The Global Environmental Industry, by Segment, 2002 | 323 |
| 10.2 | Evolution of the Global Environmental Industry, by Region or Country, 2000–06 | 324 |
| 10.3 | Trade in Environmental Services, Mexico, 2001–06 | 327 |
| 10.4 | The Operation of Environmental Service Firms Abroad | 329 |
| 10.5 | A Checklist of Questions on Trade-Related Aspects of Environmental Service Reform | 342 |

# ABOUT THE EDITORS AND CONTRIBUTORS

**Editors**

Olivier Cattaneo: Development Research Group, World Bank, and Research Associate, Groupe d' Economie Mondiale de Sciences Po, Paris.

Michael Engman: Economist, Finance and Private Sector Development, Africa Region, World Bank.

Sebastián Sáez: Senior Trade Economist, International Trade Department, Poverty Reduction and Economic Management, World Bank.

Robert M. Stern: Professor of Economics and Public Policy (Emeritus), Gerald R. Ford School of Public Policy, University of Michigan, Ann Arbor.

**Contributors**

Julian Arkell: Consultant, Officer of the Order of the British Empire, 1992, and Honorary Associate, Royal Institution of Chartered Surveyors, London 1991.

Nora Carina Dihel: Economist (Trade), Poverty Reduction and Economic Management Network (PREM 2), Africa Region, World Bank.

Gary Hufbauer: Reginald Jones Senior Fellow, Peterson Institute for International Economics, Washington, DC.

Linda Schmid: Independent Trade Policy and Development Consultant; formerly Trade in Services Officer, International Trade Centre, Geneva.

Sherry Stephenson: Adviser, Migration Policy, and Head of Institutional Relations, Organization of American States.

Peter Walkenhorst: Manager, Development Research Department, African Development Bank.

# FOREWORD

*What is trade in services? How does it take place?* The examples that typically come to mind include communication technologies, transportation such as shipping and aviation, and financial and banking services. But the term in fact encompasses a much broader range of service industries, spanning engineering, construction, legal, healthcare, media, consulting, and distribution, among others. The advancement in information and communications technologies has further propelled the expansion of trade in services. Technological progress has essentially transformed business practices, reducing the cost, increasing the speed, improving the quality, and expanding the range of available services that can now be traded across borders. Consequently, trade in services has now expanded both in breadth—to encompass more professions and industries—and in geographical reach, made possible through business process outsourcing and offshoring practices.

As services continue to evolve alongside technological improvements, information technology services in particular—even emerging areas such as environmental consulting and engineering services—are increasingly contributing to developing countries' export diversification and economic development strategies. This volume highlights those service industries that developing countries worldwide have been able to develop given their respective comparative advantages. Case studies are provided on how India, Malaysia, and Thailand export complex medical procedures; Morocco and Tunisia provide a range of legal, engineering, and accounting services to Europe based on historical and cultural ties; Argentina, Brazil, China, the Arab Republic of Egypt, India, and Turkey have competitive companies that provide construction services; and in the distribution services sector, companies in Chile, Mexico, and South Africa are big players in their respective regions.

Beyond describing the trends of trade in services, *International Trade in Services* also addresses the complex policy issues related to this topic, because services trade liberalization remains one of the most complicated and controversial issues in trade policy making. For trade in goods, liberalization is primarily about eliminating tariffs and nontariff barriers at the border. Services liberalization not only requires the elimination of discriminatory barriers that affect both services and service providers, but also addresses a host of nontrade measures geared to the protection of health, environment, public order, and morals, and other issues related to competition and consumer protection. These measures have legitimate policy objectives but often become difficult to distinguish from protectionist policies when it comes to services trade. This specific issue is one of the most challenging policy issues for the cross-border trade in services.

*International Trade in Services* also provides an assessment of how policy makers can further bolster their service industries by leveraging the changes prompted by technological advancements. The book provides policy recommendations that include the reduction of barriers to services trade across all sectors and the promotion of health- and environment-related development policies that should be promoted in parallel with a burgeoning services market. The first recommendation is considered the most important, because it focuses on the need to ensure trade openness, which helps ensure the access to services and promotes the quality of services provision through foreign and domestic competition. Moreover, the issue of temporary movement of labor is another focus of this book, given that it is one of the most important means of service exports for developing countries. This is an issue that is considered technically complex and politically sensitive because of its political and security implications. The book examines mechanisms that have been used by various countries to liberalize the temporary movement of persons and concludes that regardless of the negotiating forum—multilateral, regional, or bilateral—the policy making results on temporary movement of labor are, so far, modest and limited to a small range of categories. However, it proposes alternative ways to move forward that require further analysis by countries and relevant international organizations, including the World Bank.

It is our hope that this book will serve as a basis for further discussions, a catalyst for new research on this topic, and a guide for economic policy analysis in the area of services in developing countries around the world.

Otaviano Canuto<br>
Vice President<br>
Poverty Reduction and Economic Management<br>
World Bank

# ACKNOWLEDGMENTS

This volume concludes a long process begun in 2006, and deeply rooted in Africa, to develop a methodology for assessing the potential of services trade opening in developing countries. It draws on the first holistic services trade study conducted by Aaditya Mattoo and Lucy Payton in Zambia. Their work revealed the potential of services trade for the least developed countries, not only in the so-called backbone services, such as telecommunications and financial services, but also in services sectors so far untradable because they lacked the technology or because they were traded almost exclusively by wealthy countries (such as professional services). *International Trade in Services* covers the first attempts to conduct sectoral services trade diagnostic studies in Northern Africa by a team conducted by Olivier Cattaneo, Ndiame Diop, and Peter Walkenhorst—hence the many examples in this volume that refer to this region.

The editors wish to thank the authors of the individual chapters and the many individuals who contributed to this project. In particular, they would like to acknowledge the research conducted by Linda Schmid, which has profoundly shaped some of the original chapters, and the leading role of Peter Walkenhorst in the early stages of the project. They would also like to thank Nora Carina Dihel, Ana Margarida Fernandes, and Claudia Nassif, who have reviewed this volume and closely worked with the team throughout the editing process. To mention only a few, Mireille Cossy, Massimo Geloso-Grosso, Daria Goldstein, Will Martin, Richard Messick, Maurice Schiff, and Ronald Steenblik provided valuable comments on individual chapters. Thibaud Delourme provided research assistance for chapter 2.

Finally, this project would not have been possible without the continuous support and guidance of the World Bank management team, in particular Mona Haddad and Bernard Hoekman. The editors are also grateful to Anita Nyajur for her outstanding help in the formatting of the manuscript.

The editors would like to thank Susan Graham, Stephen McGroarty, and Andrés Meneses, from the World Bank´s Office of the Publisher, for managing the editorial services and the design, production, and printing of the book.

This project was supported in part by the governments of Finland, Norway, Sweden, and the United Kingdom through the Multidonor Trust Fund for Trade and Development.

# ABBREVIATIONS

| | |
|---|---|
| ASEAN | Association of Southeast Asian Nations |
| BLA | bilateral labor agreement |
| BV | business visitor and salesperson |
| CSS | contractual services supplier |
| EPA | Economic Partnership Agreement (European Union) |
| EU | European Union |
| FDI | foreign direct investment |
| FTA | free trade agreement |
| GATS | General Agreement on Trade in Services (World Trade Organization) |
| GDP | gross domestic product |
| ICT | intracorporate transferee |
| IFRS | international financial reporting standard |
| IP | independent professional |
| IT | information technology |
| NAFTA | North American Free Trade Agreement |
| OECD | Organisation for Economic Co-operation and Development |
| ROSC | Reports on the Observance of Standards and Codes (International Monetary Fund–World Bank) |
| RTA | regional trade agreement |
| UNCTAD | United Nations Conference on Trade and Development |
| WTO | World Trade Organization |

*Note:* All dollar amounts are U.S. dollars (US$) unless otherwise indicated.

1

# ASSESSING THE POTENTIAL OF SERVICES TRADE IN DEVELOPING COUNTRIES: AN OVERVIEW

*Olivier Cattaneo, Michael Engman, Sebastián Sáez, and Robert M. Stern*

The potential of the trade in services has remained largely overlooked and untapped by developing countries. A number of reasons could be evoked, including the widespread and persistent idea that services, as opposed to goods, are nontradable. In recent decades, technological obstacles to trade in services have been removed. Because of the technological gap between developed and developing countries, the impression has persisted, however, that the service trade is the privilege of the countries of the Organisation for Economic Co-operation and Development and that there is nothing or little of value in this trade for the poorest countries. Recent research and evidence have proven this to be erroneous: any country, including the least developed, can join the club of service trade exporters and benefit from increased market opening (Mattoo and Payton 2007). Of course, not all countries have the same potential, and the benefits of opening could be overshadowed by the associated costs. Often, success is conditioned by the adoption of complementary reforms that could become too costly in countries with limited budgetary and human resources. The sequencing of reforms also matters. Thus, it is necessary to assess carefully the trade and development potential of trade opening in different service sectors before building castles in the air: not every single developing country can become a service hub (for transport, back-office functions, tourism, and so on) even if the idea is attracting an increasing number of developing countries around the world.

The objective of this book is to provide a methodological framework for assessing the trade potential of individual countries in selected service sectors. The book also provides recommendations for those governments that have assessed the trade potential of their countries in given sectors or sets of sectors and that have decided to open their markets or promote their exports. It suggests complementary reforms that will maximize the benefits and minimize the costs of opening and, in short, ensure that trade potential translates into the attainment of development objectives.

While a holistic assessment of the service trade and of development potential is useful, the diversity of services is such that the analysis naturally takes place at the sectoral level. This book therefore focuses on sectoral recommendations. It looks at both the old and the new. By the old, we mean those service sectors that have long existed and have been the focus of the attention of the development community, but have rarely been analyzed through the lens of trade. For example, justice reforms often focus on judicial access, but hardly ever on the role of trade in providing access to better lawyers and, hence, better justice; health reforms hardly ever include a chapter on trade liberalization, despite the potential importance of foreign investment or international movements of health personnel to supply access to better treatments. By the new, we mean service sectors that are emerging and in which trade has long been restrained, mostly for technological reasons, for example in information technology (IT) or the environment. This book seeks to raise awareness of the trade potential of these service sectors, rather than of more traditional service sectors such as finance, telecommunications, and transport (the backbone services) that have already been studied at length. The selected service sectors are accounting, construction, distribution, engineering, environmental, health, IT, and legal services.

This book is designed, accordingly, for experts in nontrade sectors, so as to advance the understanding of how trade can improve the domestic supply of services and, for trade specialists, so as to enhance the understanding of relevant specific characteristics of the selected sectors. It focuses on concrete experiences and on approaches in the expansion of the service trade that have been fruitful in developing countries. Each chapter identifies trends in international integration, highlights the effects of the service trade on the domestic economy, and proposes policy initiatives that can help the private sector take advantage of the opportunities that service trade offers. The operational framework that is set out should guide analysts and policy makers toward efficient and successful practices. Options for facilitating labor mobility are also emphasized, given the particular relevance of this mobility to developing-country exports in most of the sectors.

## Why Services?

The service sector is key to economic growth, export competitiveness, and poverty reduction. The trade in services has grown more rapidly than the trade in goods, and, as noted in figure 1.1, the share of the trade in services in overall trade has been increasing for much of the last three decades. Together, the European Union and the United States still account for over 60 percent of service exports in the world, but India may soon be exporting more services than goods, and the business service exports of Brazil, China, and India have been growing by well over 10 percent every year for the last decade. Within the trade in services, commercial services such as financial services, communication services, and business and professional services have emerged as particularly dynamic. The service sector currently comprises more than two-thirds of the world economy: 72 percent of the gross domestic product (GDP) in high-income countries, 53 percent in middle-income countries, and 46 percent in low-income countries (WDI Database). There is a positive relationship between economic prosperity and the economic weight of the service sector that reflects the great urbanization process of modern times.

International trade in services adds approximately 12 percent to global GDP. As a share of GDP, traded services have added, on average, 13 percent of GDP in

**Figure 1.1.** The Expanding Role of the Trade in Services in the World Economy, 1977–2007

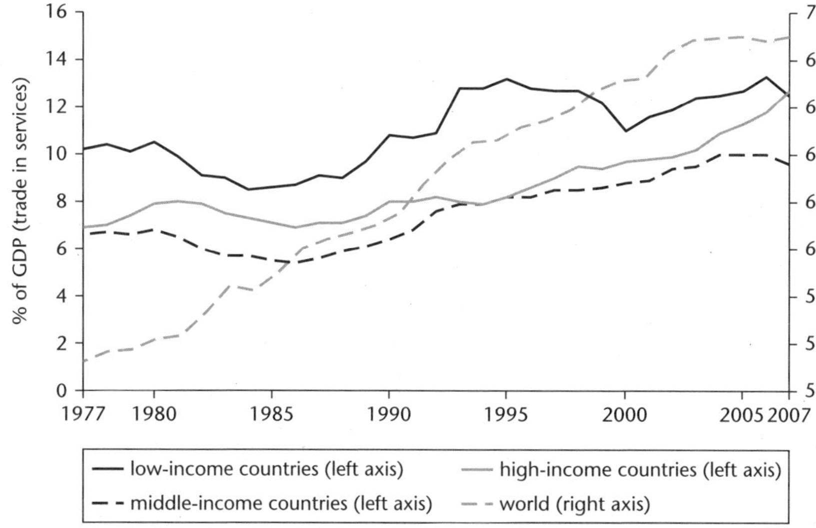


*Source:* WDI Database.

**Figure 1.2.** Trade, by Region, 2007

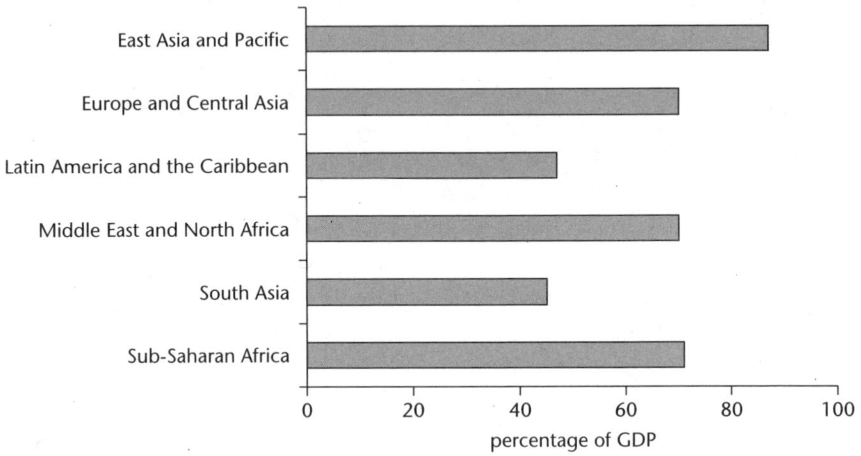


*Source:* WDI Database.

low-income countries and high-income countries alike and 10 percent in middle-income countries. The trade in services is an essential contribution to the economy in several countries. It comprised, for example, more than 50 percent of GDP in 18 of the 159 countries and customs territories that reported data for 2005. It is striking that all 18 countries, except Lebanon, Liberia, and Luxembourg, are islands.

Current data sources on the trade in services are improving, but still fail to capture the true extent of trade in some sectors and countries. Although the trade in goods represents the largest share in international flows, the trade data that are available for developing countries by region (noted in figures 1.2 and 1.3), including at the firm level, indicate that total trade and the trade in services were sizable as a percentage of GDP in 2007 in several of the regions shown. Worker remittances received as a share of GDP in 2007 are shown in figure 1.4 and are also sizable, especially in the Middle East and North Africa and in South Asia.

The stakes for the liberalization of services are substantial in the current round of multilateral trade negotiations, and this needs to be recognized especially because most of the attention has thus far been focused on the liberalization of agriculture and manufactured goods rather than services. Indeed, most service liberalization around the world has been achieved unilaterally and has been driven by a purely domestic agenda rather than a trade agenda.

Service trade liberalization does not stop and, often, does not even start at the border. Governments might have single ministries for agriculture or industry, but they have multiple technical ministries for transport, tourism, telecommunications,

**Figure 1.3.** Trade in Services, by Region, 2007

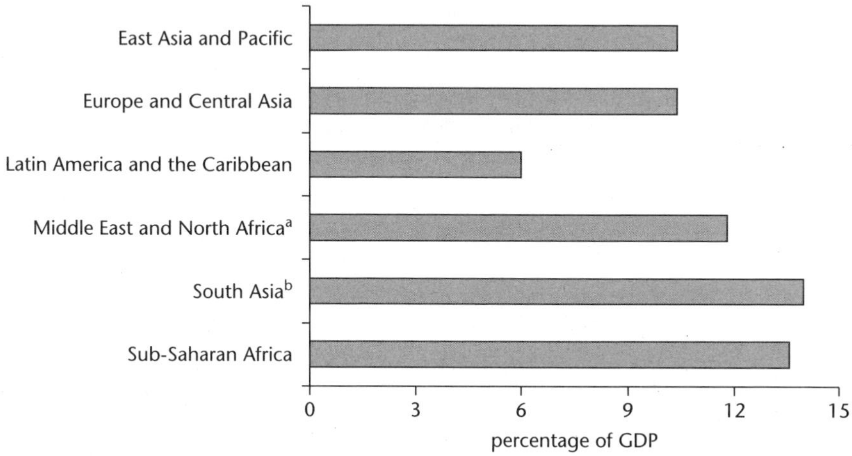


*Source:* WDI Database.
a. 2000.
b. 2006.

**Figure 1.4.** Worker Remittances Received, by Region, 2007

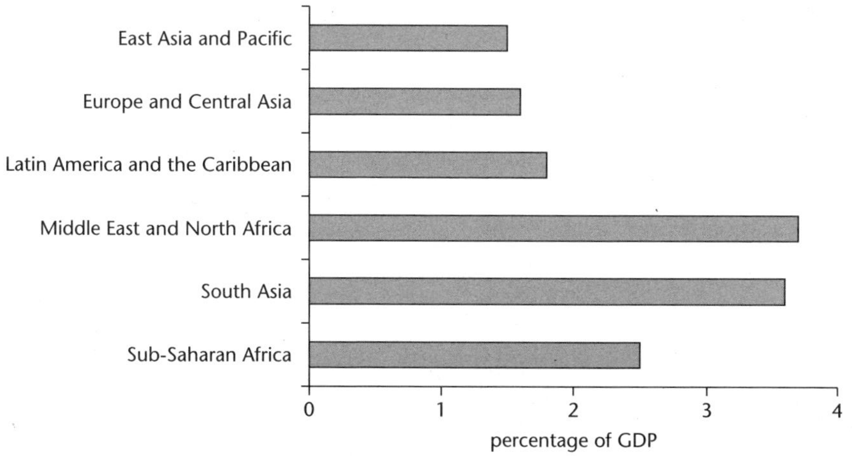


*Source:* WDI Database.
*Note:* The figure shows worker remittances received and the compensation of employees received. Some remittances are sent by temporary service providers (engaged in trade) and others by permanent migrants (not engaged in trade).

health, justice, and so on. Adding to this complexity, the international movement of natural persons to deliver services requires the involvement of immigration authorities. Governmental coordination is therefore a special challenge for policy making on trade in the field of services.

## Why These Sectors?

The choice of the sectors for the case studies compiled in this volume has been primarily driven by the desire to look afresh at the potential of the old and hint at the untapped potential of the new, while avoiding backbone service sectors that have already been studied at length. The sectors selected are all essential for the quality of the lives of individuals, the welfare of communities, and economic advancement generally. The development of an open, rule-based, predictable, nondiscriminatory trading and financial system is one of the United Nations Millennium Development Goals (goal 8, global partnership). The potential for the development of the trade in services goes beyond better access to health and education, for example, while directly contributing to the achievement of the related goals 2 (universal education), 4 (child health), and 5 (maternal health). The construction, engineering, and environmental service sectors are particularly pertinent in people's daily lives as providers of safe physical infrastructure for personal shelter, sanitation, water, energy, schooling, health services, transportation, and private sector activities. Environmental services contribute to sustainable development by helping alleviate the negative impact of economic activity on the environment (goal 7, environmental sustainability). The role of the health sector is to ensure access to quality and affordable health care, which is essential for the accumulation of the stock of human capital.

Retail and wholesale services are a vital link between producers and consumers and influence the efficiency with which resources are allocated to meet consumer needs. Inadequate distribution services can, for example, impede the consumer choice of safe and affordable food products. The accounting and legal service sectors are important in private sector development and in reducing transaction costs, the high level of which is considered one of the most significant impediments to economic growth in regions such as Africa. These services play key roles in protecting individuals and entrepreneurs, as well as in upholding the rules underpinning the financial system. They also help entrepreneurs break into new markets at home and abroad. Finally, the IT service sector is paramount to sharing information, developing knowledge, and providing the software infrastructure necessary for the electronic supply of other services.

While the chapters in this volume include discussion and analysis of the benefits of service liberalization, many of these benefits derive not from seeking better market access abroad, but from the increased competitiveness and efficiency of the domestic market. Thus, international trade not only opens up economic opportunities for developing-country exporters, but it also provides access to foreign capital and technology that, through enhanced competition and innovation, can offer consumers more choice in terms of quality and price at home. The chapters therefore devote commensurate attention to the illustration of these benefits and the related policy measures that promote them.

Many imported services provide vital inputs to manufacturing companies that substantially influence the international competitiveness of these companies. It is especially noteworthy that simulation models have predicted considerably higher gains from the liberalization of service sectors than from the liberalization of goods sectors. This is the case even in countries with high tariff barriers such as Tunisia, as Konan and Maskus (2006) have concluded. Moreover, if endogenous productivity effects are taken into account, the long-run benefits from service liberalization may be significantly greater than the static benefits.

One development that has fueled the growth of service exports is the growing trend among companies in high-income countries to outsource back-office and other service functions to take advantage of the advanced skills and lower labor costs of specialized service providers. Many developing countries have substantial untapped potential to satisfy this demand for business functions in, for example, the accounting, engineering, IT, and legal service sectors. However, as emphasized in some chapters, taking advantage of these trade opportunities often requires policy reforms that create an enabling environment for private sector service providers.

## Overview: The Trade in Services

The scope of activities that are defined as services in the framework of the General Agreement on Trade in Services (GATS) of the World Trade Organization is illustrated in table 1.1. The backbone services include, primarily, communications, financial intermediation, and transport, while the nonbackbone services that are the focus of this book comprise most of the remaining categories. In contrast to merchandise trade, services are often intangible, invisible, and perishable and usually require simultaneous production and consumption. The need in many cases

**Table 1.1.** The Scope of Services Covered in the GATS

| | |
|---|---|
| 1. Business services | 7. Financial services |
| 2. Communication services | 8. Health-related and social services |
| 3. Construction services | 9. Tourism and travel-related services |
| 4. Distribution services | 10. Recreational, cultural, and sporting services |
| 5. Educational services | 11. Transport services |
| 6. Environmental services | 12. Other services not elsewhere included |

*Source:* Authors' compilation based on Services Database.

for proximity between the consumer and the producer implies that the consumer or the producer must move to make an international transaction possible. Because the conventional definition of trade, which involves products crossing frontiers, would miss out on a whole range of international transactions, the GATS takes a wide view of trade, which is defined to include four modes of supply.

Table 1.2 presents and defines these modes of supply and indicates the modes that are particularly relevant for the eight service sectors studied in the various chapters. It does not, however, take into consideration the many policy-induced restrictions that sometimes prohibit or impede trade in these modes. The table illustrates the horizontal importance that commercial presence (Mode 3) has as a potential mode of service delivery in all the sectors.

The movement of natural persons (Mode 4) is also an important source of supply in the great majority of the sectors. Intracorporate transfers of professionals linked to foreign direct investment are crucial for all sectors. The restrictions that

**Table 1.2.** Modes of Supply and the GATS

| Presence of supplier | Other criteria | Mode | Examples of sector relevance |
|---|---|---|---|
| Service supplier *is not present* in the territory of member | Service supplied *in* the territory of one member from the territory of any other member | Crossborder supply [Mode 1] | Accounting, engineering, health, IT, and legal services |
| | Service supplied to a consumer of a member *outside* his or her territory, in the territory of any other member | Consumption abroad [Mode 2] | Health and legal services |
| Service supplier *is present* in the territory of member | Service supplied *in* the territory of one member through the commercial presence of the supplier in another member | Commercial presence [Mode 3] | Accounting, construction, distribution, engineering, environmental, health, IT, and legal services |
| | Service supplied *in* the territory of member and supplier from other member is present in the form of a *natural* person | Movement of natural persons [Mode 4] | Accounting, construction, engineering, environmental, health, IT, and legal services |

*Sources:* WTO (2001), authors' assessment.

are difficult to overcome generally target low-skilled workers, semiskilled workers, and junior professionals, while the movement of executives and managers is less restricted. However, the temporary movement of independent service providers (not linked to foreign direct investment) is generally subject to considerable restriction. The chapters indicate that labor transfers may be more indispensable for trade in nonbackbone services than they are in backbone services, particularly for independent service providers. Consumption abroad (Mode 2) is mostly relevant in the health service and legal service sectors, while crossborder supply (Mode 1) is an increasingly common mode of delivery in professional services.[1]

International exchange often takes place in both directions. For example, India is a large exporter of IT services through Modes 1 and 4, while it imports IT services through Mode 3. In addition, there are often strong complementary links across various nonbackbone sectors, including among construction, engineering, and environmental services; between accounting and legal services; and between IT and distribution services. Thus, the provision of engineering services often represents a natural expansion in construction companies that are moving up the value chain. The health and distribution service sectors may also draw heavily on the development of the tourism sector in many developing countries. The list could continue.

There are also important links between several of the nonbackbone and backbone sectors. For example, the new export opportunities associated with the fragmentation of the value chain in professional services that many developing countries seek to exploit depend to a large extent on the access, capacity, reliability, and price of information and communications network services. Similarly, accounting and legal services feed into the financial service sector and into opportunities linked to the supply of Mode 2 and Mode 4 and may involve the crossborder movement of either consumer or service suppliers, depending on the development of the transport sector. Policy makers who seek to open up markets at home and abroad ought to consider these links to appreciate the potential of new trade opportunities adequately.

### *An increasing number of developing countries are hosting successful service exporters*

The chapters reveal that many developing countries are hosting a growing number of companies that successfully export nonbackbone services within their own regions and to high-income countries. In the construction service sector, several developing (or transition) countries such as China, the Arab Republic of Egypt, India, Israel, Malaysia, the Russian Federation, Thailand, and Turkey host large international contractors. Likewise, the number of developing-country exporters among the top 225 international contractors is on the rise. In the distribution service sector, Chilean, Mexican, and South African companies are big players in their respective regions. For example, South African retailer Shoprite operates 129 outlets and employs over 9,000 people in 16 African countries.

India's IT service exports are valued at tens of billions of dollars, and there are many IT service companies in China, Egypt, and Israel that are growing rapidly based on international demand. Other export success stories include Tunisia, in the engineering service sector; Brazil, Kenya, and Malawi, in the legal service sector; and Cyprus, the Czech Republic, and Hungary, in the accounting service sector. In the health sector, Brazil, India, Malaysia, and Thailand are some of the countries that treat large numbers of foreign patients, and the Caribbean countries, Ghana, and the Philippines are some of the countries that send large numbers of health professionals to serve abroad.

### *Regulation: Necessary to address information asymmetries and the risk of market failures*

The service sector is associated with serious information asymmetries because of the character of service supply and the difficulty of assessing service quality. It can be nearly impossible for a consumer to assess ex ante the quality of a legal counseling service, of a medical checkup, or of the earthquake resistance of a new residential building. It may take considerable time before the quality of the service is demonstrated through the closing of a court case, the longevity of a patient after coronary bypass surgery, or a sudden earthquake. Similarly, it can be challenging for the service provider to assess ex post a client's intentions. A client who purchases a software product may, for example, produce illegal copies for sale on the informal market, and a client who purchases sensitive goods from a retailer may later use them for illegal purposes.

Many regulations are in place partly to counteract negative externalities or market failures that are associated with the supply of services and that affect third parties and society in general. Hence, there is a well-founded argument for some form of regulation to protect consumers in particular, but, sometimes, also the service providers. Previous research has concluded that liberalization does not always produce the expected benefits because complementary regulatory measures have not been implemented (Mattoo and Payton 2007). There may be a number of alternative strategies available to tackle information asymmetries and the associated risks of adverse selection and moral hazard. The approach that is taken to uphold, for example, minimum safety and quality standards and the appropriate conduct of service professionals ultimately decides how well markets operate.

### *Regulation: Designed and implemented in the least trade restrictive manner possible*

Ensuring that markets are competitive is a key objective for regulators in most service sectors. Consumers have much to gain if regulators seek to achieve this objective by paying close attention to the effect of rules and regulations on domestic and international supply. Regulatory audit or impact assessment with an international dimension is the most effective way to achieve this goal. In addition, the aim of regulatory reform is not to remove regulations, but, rather, to make regulations achieve their objectives with as small a footprint as possible and to ensure that regulations are as trade-friendly as possible.

### *Service sector modernization and trade liberalization may entail adjustment costs*

Trade liberalization often entails adjustment costs as resources are being reallocated to places where they may be employed more productively.[2] Modernization in the service sector—whether as a result of endogenous innovation and national upgrading or the entry of foreign competitors that bring new service offerings and new service delivery options—often requires the upgrading of skills. Thus, labor adjustment costs can be an important consideration. Most services need to be provided at the place of consumption, and the liberalization process may involve either a positive or a negative change in the absolute level of employment in the sector.

In the eight sectors studied in this book, it is only in the distribution service sector that large-scale unemployment often results from modernization. The productivity enhancements linked to the shift in urban areas from a retailing system based on mom-and-pop stores to large formats can impair the livelihoods of small store holders. There may also be a gap in the provision of retail services between city centers and suburban and rural populations. Moreover, the smallest food producers may lose their retail clients and thus their livelihoods. The ownership of the new supermarkets can raise ethnic and other social stability issues, as experienced in East Africa and Southeast Asia.

Consequently, policy makers may consider opening up markets in phases to allow local suppliers to adjust to higher standards. The process can be greatly facilitated if social safety nets and resources to assist in training and technical upgrading are in place to enable farmers and small suppliers to fulfill the minimum safety and quality standards required to integrate in the supply chains of more demanding retailers.

Employment in professional services such as accounting, legal, engineering, and IT services may also be positively affected in developing countries as a result of domestic market liberalization. The reasons many of these services are sparsely traded are often of the natural kind, involving differences in language, culture, taste, and preferences. If high-income countries suddenly open their markets to foreign professionals, as has happened, for example, in the case of nurses in English-speaking economies of the Organisation for Economic Co-operation and Development, public health may suffer; policy makers need to explore the options in safeguarding health provision.

In certain sectors, trade liberalization may affect other policy objectives. Thus, the effects of trade in health services vary considerably from one mode of delivery to another. For instance, in Modes 1 and 2, the main risk is the diversion of scarce human and financial resources to health care services entirely dedicated to the treatment of foreign patients. The risks associated with exports under Mode 4 primarily depend on the intentions of the service provider. While the movement of highly skilled workers should be especially encouraged (Mode 4, as a regulated scheme for the temporary movement of personnel, is a factor in such movements), it is nonetheless possible that the drain on human resources could have detrimental effects on public health. Thus, opportunities for individuals can translate into losses for societies. A well-regulated trade strategy under Mode 4 should therefore contribute to limiting drains on human resources—agreements on Mode 4 can include a return scheme—because nothing can prevent people from leaving a country.

In assessing the liberalization of the trade in services, policy makers should take into account not only the direct gains to consumers and clients, but also the impact that liberalization may have on the development of other sectors in the economy, including, for instance, gains in terms of competitiveness and of exports in agriculture, natural resources, and manufactured goods.

## Trade Policy Issues

International service transactions are impeded by a variety of regulatory barriers, especially barriers to foreign direct investment and the movement of the individuals who provide services. These barriers may be designed to restrict the entry of service providers, whether domestic or foreign, in an economy. As a consequence, countries may benefit from the liberalization of their own domestic barriers and the liberalization of the trade barriers of their trading partners.

Indeed, because service barriers are often sizable, the income and welfare gains accruing from a reduction in these barriers may greatly exceed the gains accruing from trade liberalization in goods. Nonetheless, the benefits of service liberalization are by no means realized automatically. Significant challenges exist in introducing genuine competition, building the regulatory institutions that are needed to remedy market failures, appropriately sequencing service sector reforms, and establishing mechanisms that promote the availability of essential services, especially among the poor.

While governments can initiate service reforms unilaterally, international engagement can play an important catalytic role. Thus, in recognition of the rising importance of the trade in services and the regulatory barriers in place, services have been included in the multilateral trade architecture of the World Trade Organization in the form of the GATS. Services have also featured prominently in the process of World Trade Organization accession and in the large and growing network of regional and bilateral trade agreements that have been concluded in the past two decades or that are still under negotiation.

### *Common restrictions on service supply through commercial presence*

Restrictions on the establishment and operation of commercial presence (Mode 3 trade) by foreign companies are common in several of the sectors analyzed in this volume. The limitations on market access revolve around ownership rules for foreign companies, the type of legal entity that a foreign company is allowed to operate, the number of suppliers allowed in a specific market, and the value of transactions or assets. Trade restrictions revolving around national treatment include registration, authorization, performance, and technology-transfer requirements; licensing, standards, and qualifications; and nationality and residency requirements. Restrictions on commercial presence assume particular significance if the services cannot be delivered through crossborder supply. For example, in the health service sector, rules may pertain to the form of establishment, foreign ownership, and nationality and residency requirements.

Other sectors such as accounting are partially protected because of domestic regulations on liability insofar as a local accountant is liable for the delivery of certain services. In the case of legal services, rules reflect legal traditions and the legal heritage and may be designed to achieve a broad set of public policy objectives. To overcome these limitations, companies frequently use a combination of affiliations and alliances to leverage the specialized expertise of professionals so that the professionals can serve the international needs of clients. In construction and distribution services, foreign companies may be required to deposit capital in a local bank and may face discrimination in government procurement. Barriers to commercial presence condition the degree to which the sector modernizes, and they delay the emergence of the sector from the informal sector, with the result that tax income is forgone.

### *Common restrictions on service supply through the presence of natural persons*

The temporary movement of natural persons (Mode 4) in service delivery enables the realization of gains from trade, while averting prospective social and political costs in host countries and the drain on human resources in sending countries. Temporary access to foreign providers of services may generate gains in income and welfare that are greater than the gains from the complete liberalization of all the barriers to trade in goods; both developed and developing countries would share in these gains (see Winters et al. 2003). Workers who are based abroad tend to remit part of their income, and many families in developing countries rely on these financial flows.

The individual chapters emphasize that Mode 4 trade is significant in many nonbackbone service sectors. For example, millions of construction workers from developing countries serve abroad in regions where large investments are dedicated to infrastructure and building projects. Indian IT companies send tens of thousands of project managers and IT professionals on assignments to foreign clients in the economies of the Organisation for Economic Co-operation and Development every year. The health service sector in some English-speaking countries relies on nurses and even medical doctors from developing countries. The accounting service market is dominated by collaboration through global networks, and the temporary movement of accountants is often the only solution to relieve short-term shortages of expertise, given the cyclical nature of the market.

There are several common limitations on the temporary movement of natural persons. These restrictions can be divided into (1) quantitative limitations, nationality requirements, and residency requirements; (2) the rules and limitations associated with obtaining work permits and business visas, as well as regulations affecting the holders of work permits or business visas while they are in host countries; and (3) inefficiencies linked to the processing of work permits or business visas, which are typically associated with time, cost, and risk.

Thus, the United States imposes a quota on H-1B work permits for the temporary employment of foreign workers in specialty occupations (which include many of the professional services under study). Indian exports of IT services to the United States are, to a large extent, reliant on H-1B work permits, and, whenever demand exceeds supply, providers and clients are disadvantaged. In some countries, foreign citizens are not allowed to practice law under any circumstances (the zero quota).

Most professional service providers, such as medical doctors, nurses, lawyers, and accountants, have to be certified to practice their professions. Certification requirements are generally imposed for quality assurance, but there is occasional discrimination in the application of the requirements to foreign providers of services. The chapter on construction, for example, argues that the sponsorship (*khafeel*) policy of several members of the Gulf Cooperation Council is prone to abuse by employers and acts as a tax on many low-skilled and medium-skilled workers.

The process of applying for work permits in foreign markets can be a major impediment. Slow, burdensome, and opaque consular services give rise to higher transaction costs and greater business risk. In many countries, legal services are subject to a broad combination of regulations and restrictions. Qualification and licensing requirements are designed to protect consumers from substandard legal advice, but the same rules also have an influence on market access and national treatment and, hence, determine a country's ability to participate in the trade in legal services.

Because of the political sensitivities associated with labor mobility, the liberalization of Mode 4 remains modest. Moreover, from the analysis of the multilateral commitments negotiated within the framework of the World Trade Organization, including the rather insignificant progress made in the Doha Round, it follows that the process of multilateral liberalization will be slow. In addition, while some progress has been achieved at the regional level, it seems that many countries prefer a cautious approach. It appears that the political concerns that have emerged are restricting the possibilities for liberalization regardless of the negotiating forum.

The chapter on labor mobility suggests a way to move forward on negotiating bilateral labor agreements. Indeed, some developed countries appear willing to explore such agreements, and these mechanisms may provide the desired flexibility from a legal and economic point of view. On the one hand, they are less legally binding than trade agreements; on the other hand, they allow for the regulation of migration flows based on the internal economic conditions of a country. In addition, they can be targeted to specific sectors and may even be based at the firm level if necessary.

A key aspect of the successful operation of bilateral labor agreements is monitoring. This can be carried out by home and destination countries as a joint responsibility, rather than putting the burden entirely on the destination country to determine the legality of workers. In addition, ensuring the temporary nature of the movement of workers is crucial. This can be achieved through guarantees that are designed and included in the agreements in the form of bonds or fines for noncompliance to encourage respect for the provisions by private parties. Finally, incentives can be designed to ensure that workers return to their home countries. For instance, the prospect of returning to the labor-receiving country might be attractive to workers, and they will be more willing to respect their contracts and return home if there is an opportunity (based on performance and need) to return to the host country for employment in the future.

## Domestic Regulation Issues

Barriers to trade in services also arise through regulations that tend to serve the purpose of addressing domestic market failures. These regulations aim at fulfilling legitimate policy objectives such as protecting health and upholding competition. Some governments delegate the regulatory authority to the private sector within the professional service sector. There are, consequently, issues revolving around the need to balance legitimate concerns and the restrictions on the provision of these services.

The regulation of distribution services is often nondiscriminatory, but may, de facto, have an adverse impact on foreign market participation. For example, distribution services restrictions may cover registration and personal requirements; licenses and permits with regard to location and surface and geographical area limits; the protection of local monopolies; limits on establishing large outlets, subsidies, and the protection of small shops; rules on product safety, labeling, and quality standards; price controls; and restrictions on loss-leading.

The chapters do not identify many of the issues that are common in backbone services (although there are exceptions). State or natural monopolies are identified in the distribution service sector (for example, in the sale of alcoholic beverages, medications, arms and military equipment, and hydrocarbon resources), the health service sector, and the environmental service sector (for example, wastewater treatment). Owing to its public policy interest, health services may also be affected by universal access requirements and public subsidies. Environmental services may be affected by public subsidies, in addition to network-duplication constraints. Moreover, regulations and proper enforcement may sometimes help attract foreign direct investment, as in the case, for example, of intellectual property, data privacy and security, the voluntary use of international standards, and certification.

In the health service sector, rules that may adversely affect foreign companies often pertain to the types of activities and practices allowed and to advertising, marketing, solicitation, and fee setting. The accounting profession is a highly regulated profession, and domestic regulations may impede market access in a number of ways, including through quantitative limitations on the number of accountants or auditors and the types of services, limits on the value of the service transactions or assets allowed, and constraints on the types of legal entity. There may also be regulations that distort competition and deny national treatment.

### *Policy makers can identify constraints by conducting regulatory audits*

The sector studies reveal some serious constraints resulting from the design and implementation of rules and regulations. Unilateral initiatives to improve a domestic business environment often seem to offer the biggest benefits to a sector. Assessing the effectiveness of regulations and the efficiency of the implementation of regulations highlights reform needs. Top-level political commitment is often a prerequisite in addressing these binding constraints. If the reformist zeal is high, governments can achieve great improvements with limited resources.

For example, the chapter on construction services highlights the fact that the issuance of building permits is an administrative labyrinth in many countries. The transaction costs and business risks associated with slow and opaque procedures have a negative impact on trade and investment flows and may result in less investment in new infrastructure and buildings. However, administrative reforms have often had positive results by focusing on streamlining project clearances, introducing time limits, and moving the processes online. The most frequent type of reform has involved streamlining project clearances. One-stop shops connect several government agencies and public utilities and provide a single point of contact between the entrepreneur and the building authority. Another common reform has involved introducing statutory time limits or silence-is-consent rules.

Regulatory audits encompassing all relevant government agencies and consultations with stakeholders such as service industry associations, consumer groups, and labor representatives can identify issues and priorities. Some of these priorities ought to include the removal of rules and regulations that are more trade restrictive than necessary so as to allow companies to take advantage of the economic benefits stemming from international exchange. Movement toward more open access to domestic markets will stimulate competition, save resources, and improve the choice available for local investors. Seeking improved market access for Mode 3 and Mode 4 transactions with major trading partners could also help increase exports to countries with protected markets. A review of these options, taking into consideration local conditions, would allow developing countries to harness trade opportunities and improve the workings of the domestic construction service sector (World Bank 2009).

One of the key contributions that policy makers can offer is to seek to ensure that competition is not impeded by the rules and regulatory framework or by the behavior of incumbent market actors. Several of the chapters identify countries in which competition has been impaired by regulation, cartels and monopolies, or simply inadequate domestic supply capacity. The establishment of retail stores can be impeded, for example, by stringent zoning restrictions or by the dominant positions of retailers that already occupy attractive locations. Regulatory capture is particularly frequent in the accounting service sector. In some North African countries, for example, the agency in charge of issuing new licenses to accountants is controlled by incumbents, who have more or less ceased to issue permits to new market entrants.

### *Cooperation and the development of opportunities*

In some developing countries, certain service sectors are hampered by insufficient domestic supply capacity, and foreign suppliers may dictate market terms to the detriment of consumers. For example, the construction service sector in many developing countries is highly fragmented and is made up of small companies unable to take on large or even medium-size projects. While these companies tend to supply international contractors through outsourcing, they may not be able to acquire the expertise or size they need to compete for large contracts on their own. Introducing incentives for cooperation and technology transfers between foreign contractors and domestic contractors may be an option for strengthening the domestic sector. Similarly, fostering an environment in which local companies can form consortia and bid for larger projects allows the homegrown sector to build capacity in markets associated with cutthroat competition among many small players.

This is common practice in professional services such as accounting, engineering, and legal services. For example, four accounting alliances dominate the global market and influence the structure of accounting service provision in many developing countries. These leaders derive approximately 65 percent of their income from work outside their home countries and are present in up to 150 countries. They maintain a partnership model that relies on local members and professionals to understand the language, rules, and operating procedures of the respective market. This arrangement helps the local members build on the multinational's reputation and take advantage of its training, expertise, IT solutions, and staff support. Trade is also frequently undertaken through various forms of cooperation between legal service companies, whereby the companies leverage networked practices to broaden and deepen their areas of expertise. This type of partnership can be particularly useful for small and medium-size enterprises that are competing for business with large companies.

### *Adoption of international standards, licenses, certificates, and degree recognition facilitates trade*

There are various best practices and international (sometimes regional) standards available throughout the service life cycle that seek to ensure or, at least, signal the quality level that a consumer may expect. They cover (1) the requirements for obtaining a professional qualification, (2) the process employed during delivery, and (3) the standards of the finished product. Professional service sectors often seek to maintain minimum standards by issuing quality certifications to individual service providers. For example, to serve as a registered nurse, a nursing graduate may be required to pass a licensure examination. An accountant may serve in certain specified roles only after having passed an examination and gained relevant work experience to become a chartered accountant.

IT service companies can seek to obtain process-oriented quality certificates that signal the maturity of internal service production methods. Carnegie Mellon Software Engineering Institute–Capability Maturity Model Integration certification is particularly common among leading developing-country exporters. Companies that deal with sensitive information in the accounting and health sectors and deliver services through electronic supply often seek to follow procedures that qualify them for data privacy and security certificates. Construction companies in advanced economies must comply with national building codes. Finally, different sectors adopt different guarantees of the services they sell. For example, a retailer may offer international guarantees of product quality, allow for goods to be returned within a number of days, offer support services, and so on.

These quality-signaling devices are often useful for small and large players alike. Many of the standards and certificates are voluntary and provided by and for the private sector. Because of these tools, though they are voluntary, there is little policy makers in developing countries can do but comply and provide the information and any technical assistance required. To attract foreign providers of services, policy makers may, however, also seek to ensure that these tools are not used unnecessarily to restrict competition. For example, the implementation of the applicable international or regional standards on construction materials and the best practices in building codes lower transaction costs and facilitate integration in international supply chains. A similar situation holds in accounting, engineering, IT, and health services. For professional degrees, policy makers can evaluate whether there is interest among trading partners and, if it makes sense from a cost-benefit perspective, negotiate mutual recognition agreements on professional degrees.

Dual standards may be of great interest to developing countries because of human capital constraints. For example, in the legal profession, paralegals may be less costly to train and can carry out some of the functions normally provided by lawyers. There are similar middle-level professionals in the accounting and health sectors, but, in general, while these professionals serve an important purpose, there is little evidence in the chapters that they have a significant role in international trade. This does not mean, however, that they do not or cannot take part in export-oriented activities.

In addition, the protection of intellectual property rights may help developing countries attract foreign direct investment in some sectors. For example, in the IT service sector, software piracy can be a serious threat. Countries that seek to attract companies with sensitive information systems or with businesses that develop intellectual property, such as many software product companies, may be more likely to succeed if they maintain and enforce proper legislation on intellectual property rights. In addition, because reputation is the strongest asset of many companies, protecting trademarks, company names, and so on may be equally important.

### *A fair and transparent government procurement process saves public resources*

Several of the sectors under study are heavily involved in public works, and the public sector may represent the single largest client of the construction, environmental, and engineering service sectors. Particularly in the case of the construction service sector, public procurement may make up half the formal market. Hence, policy makers should seek to ensure that the procurement process is transparent and designed so that smaller service providers and foreign companies are not unnecessarily shut out. Policy initiatives may address internal procedures, including the implementation of the World Bank guidelines on notification and advertisement, as well as the corruption that is so prevalent in construction projects.

Policy makers have to be particularly delicate in designing tendering criteria during government procurement. The design of tendering specifications can effectively regulate market access. Government procurement authorities are often accused of favoring either domestic or foreign contractors by explicitly providing preferential treatment for local companies or by setting minimum requirements of financial support that may be beyond the reach of domestic companies.

## Addressing Supply-Side Constraints and Promoting Trade

The chapters illustrate how information and communication technology networks have become a crucial means of delivering services electronically independent of the location of the service supplier. The chapter on health services highlights the export potential in many developing countries, but argues that policy makers have an important role in ensuring that health policies do not fuel exports at the expense of the well-being of local residents. There is also a large scope for improving the capacity of the domestic service sector to raise standards at home and its profile abroad so as to tap into foreign markets.

### *Most sectors are knowledge intensive and may require rethinking of education policies*

A majority of the nonbackbone service sectors examined in this volume rely entirely on the supply of skilled labor. While a well-trained workforce benefits all sectors of an economy, education policy is particularly relevant in the accounting, engineering, health, and legal service sectors. The same holds for the IT service sector, which consists almost entirely of computer engineers, and environmental services, which depend, for example, on the supply of engineers and biologists. The construction sector requires well-trained civil engineers and project managers, and the distribution sector is highly information intensive.

The important role of education in producing, for example, medical doctors, nurses, midwives, software programmers, lawyers, accountants, civil engineers, mechanical engineers, and biologists is evident. In trade, the domestic supply of well-trained workers is often as relevant from an import perspective as it is from an export perspective. Unfortunately, the institutions of higher education in too many countries fail to equip their graduates with the skills required to compete in international markets, as argued in the chapter on IT services. Because of inadequately trained teachers, irrelevant curricula and student literature, and insufficient investment in education, policy makers must address these issues head on. Countries such as India and Pakistan are training most of their engineers in private institutions of higher education, and there may be scope for other countries to determine if private investment can address bottlenecks. Openness to the establishment of foreign schools can also help raise standards and increase the stock of human capital; for example, the private Indian company NIIT is offering a range of training courses in the computer field in countries around the world.

### *Prospective entrepreneurs are held back by poor information and communication technology infrastructure*

The chapter on IT services also illustrates another frequent binding constraint affecting prospective exporters of services through electronic supply, including accounting, engineering, health, IT, and legal services. Countries in which the cost of a monthly subscription with an Internet broadband provider is several times the average annual GDP per capita is not likely to host many successful exporters of information-intensive services. The constraint is particularly severe in those countries in which broadband capacity is not accessible at any price or in which reliability is low. While Internet broadband access is improving in most developing countries, several countries appear to have some way to go before Mode 1 becomes a viable delivery option. Those countries that do have the necessary information and communication technology infrastructure and a well-trained, language-proficient labor force face a large prospective market that they can contest with relatively few policy-induced restrictions. Special high-technology parks have been successfully used in some countries in this connection, including China, Egypt, India, and the Philippines, to overcome infrastructure shortcomings at the national level.

### *Professional bodies can help raise standards, but policy makers must avoid regulatory capture*

The chapters on the accounting and legal service sectors, and other chapters as well, point out the valuable role that professional bodies can play, but caution against giving these bodies too much power. There is a fine balance. Strong professional bodies can play a key role in building competence at home and in linking with foreign professional bodies. They may offer market intelligence and share knowledge of national and international best practice. Engineering companies, for example, can gain benefits from the supply of commercial information, the analysis of regional market trends, and the professional exchange opportunities provided through active professional bodies. Professional bodies can also help enhance a sector's reputation at home and abroad. Ensuring appropriate quality standards among new professionals and existing companies and promoting the sector abroad are other important functions.

However, regulatory capture is a serious problem associated with professional bodies in some countries. Thus, the government is not the only regulator that intervenes in the accounting profession. Professional bodies and oversight entities also have a key role. From country to country, the organization of powers among the different regulators varies, as does the level of independence of professional bodies. Oversight may affect the certification of professionals, licensing requirements among firms, and standards in accounting processes, as well as standards on financial reports and income statements. Policy makers must therefore ensure that professional bodies do not engage in anticompetitive activities.

### *A private industry association can be an asset in the promotion of the sector abroad*

An industry association can be significant in nurturing a service sector, including through the provision of essential services such as the collection and distribution of information about the sector; organizing workshops and international trade fairs; promoting the use of international quality standards and professional certificates; initiating public-private partnerships to promote improvements in training; and facilitating information exchanges between the government and the private sector.

### *The health service sector is a public good and must be treated as such*

International trade can be part of the solution, but also part of the problem in the provision of certain services such as health services. Health services are a public good. For example, trade in health services can directly contribute to reaching or failing to achieve health-related Millennium Development Goals. A number of developing countries are competing to become key exporters of health services, in particular through health tourism. The motives for the crossborder movement of patients vary considerably, however, and different countries compete in different market segments. There is, accordingly, considerable scope to excel in certain niche markets. Mode 2 service exports may retain the competence at home and generate much needed capital and revenue for the domestic health sector, and domestic patients can benefit from this. Policy makers must therefore ensure that expansion does not come at the expense of the local supply of health services.

## Designing a Reform Strategy Conducive to Trade in Services

The reform of service regulation may be a complex undertaking. Some of the fundamental policy issues that policy makers have to define at the domestic level include the following:

- The extent of public versus private participation in the service sector
- The extent of foreign participation in the service sector
- The regulatory framework that best serves the objectives of reform and, if relevant, the sequence and pacing of reform initiatives

International experience shows that there is no one-size-fits-all approach. Certain issues, however, concern all policy makers, including (1) the corporate governance of state-owned enterprises, (2) ensuring a level playing field for all providers, (3) maintaining a regulatory framework that prevents conflicts of interest and regulatory capture, (4) achieving legitimate public policy and social policy objectives, and (5) involving all stakeholders so as to ensure sustainable policies.

### *Identifying and structuring the regulations that affect trade*

Market liberalization is generally significantly more complicated in the service sector than in the manufacturing sector.[3] Regulations may affect the market entry and ongoing operations of domestic and foreign suppliers of services. The impact will depend on how government regulation is designed and administered. Regulations can take many forms and are usually specific to the underlying service. There are numerous—and changing—restrictions on the supply of services, which makes their classification somewhat complex. There are, however, two distinctions that tend to apply across most types of services and

**Table 1.3.** Analytical Structure for the Description of Sectoral Barriers to a Service

| Discrimination | Entry, establishment | Ongoing operations |
|---|---|---|
| Nondiscriminatory | Licensing requirements | Quality and safety requirements |
| Discriminatory | Special requirements for foreign operators | Mandatory requirements for foreign operators; additional requirements such as technology transfer |

*Sources:* Authors' compilation; Deardorff and Stern (2008).

service restrictions: regulations apply to either market entry and establishment or to ongoing operations, and regulations can be applied on a nondiscriminatory or discriminatory basis. Discriminatory regulations, which add to the cost of trading services, but which do not yield any direct benefits to consumers, are a common form of trade barrier. Policy makers seeking to reform the regulatory framework that affects service sectors may start by identifying the constraints with the help of input from stakeholders and then fitting them into a simple analytical structure such as the one shown in table 1.3. The distinctions appear to be simple, but the analytical structure nonetheless fulfills the purpose of classifying different types of barriers.

Regulations that restrict or impede the establishment of service providers within a market will usually reduce the number of providers and therefore the quantity of supply at a given price. Regulations of ongoing operations, however, may not reduce the number of suppliers, but will increase the costs of the suppliers, causing them to supply a given quantity only at a higher price. Likewise, the nondiscriminatory versus discriminatory distinction determines whether a regulation only reduces the number of foreign providers of services (discriminatory) or, instead, raises the costs and shifts supply in the case of both foreign and domestic suppliers (nondiscriminatory). However, a regulation that impedes the establishment of all new service providers, while nondiscriminatory, may nonetheless limit trade and competition by favoring a domestic incumbent.

There are several ways to implement rules on nondiscrimination. In a national treatment regime, governments have the flexibility to implement their own regulations subject to the requirement that the same regulations apply to domestic and foreign suppliers, that is, a national treatment regime essentially requires nondiscrimination. Such a rule does not completely eliminate discrimination, however. For example, a legal service company may be required to establish a local office before it can provide legal counseling. While domestic and foreign firms are subject to the same requirement, it may be much easier for local firms to meet the requirement: such a rule imposes a fixed cost that excludes foreign firms wishing to do only a small amount of business locally. Similarly, a requirement that engineers and doctors obtain domestic licensing and certification can impose additional costs on foreigners who have already gone through a similar certification process in their home countries.

With regard to each cell of table 1.3, an analyst may make additional distinctions that apply to the service sector under consideration. Regulations may appear to be protectionist, but may still serve legitimate purposes, such as protecting health and safety or preventing fraud. Such regulations, if they are applied in a nondiscriminatory manner, are not protectionist. They should not necessarily be viewed as a barrier to the trade in services, even though they may result in higher standards than those prevailing abroad and thus reduce imports relative to the level they might reach without the regulations. Meanwhile, the lack of discrimination is not sufficient by itself to absolve a regulation of the charge of protectionism if, for example, it enforces a standard that has no legitimate purpose, but happens to be met by domestic providers and not foreign providers. Distinguishing legitimate from illegitimate regulations may therefore require a detailed knowledge of the industry that only industry experts possess. As a consequence, vested interests may often be involved in the regulatory process.

### *The policy framework for market openness: Principles for regulatory quality and performance*

Trade policy makers at the Organisation for Economic Co-operation and Development have identified six principles that are key to market-oriented and trade- and investment-friendly regulation (OECD 2005). The principles reflect the basic precepts underpinning the multilateral trading system. They are useful guidelines in the assessment of the extent to which a country's regulatory framework contributes to market openness. The stronger the implementation capacity of the government in question, the more ambitious the government may be in seeking to live up to these principles. The efficient regulatory principles (with illustrative good regulatory practices) from a market openness perspective are shown in table 1.4.

## Conclusions

We note the importance of the service sector in high-, middle-, and low-income countries, together with the contribution of the trade in services to the GDP of these countries. We draw a distinction between backbone services such as finance, telecommunications, and transport and the nonbackbone services that are the focus of this volume. These nonbackbone services, which include accounting, construction, distribution, engineering, environmental, health, IT, and legal

**Table 1.4.** Six Efficient Regulatory Principles and Related Good Regulatory Practices

1. Transparency and openness in decision making
   a. *Systematic public availability of information*
   b. *Clear, simple procedures for making and implementing rules*
   c. *Systematic reliance on public consultation*
   d. *Clear, open, effective appeal procedures*
   e. *Efforts to ensure transparency in particular areas*
2. Nondiscrimination
   a. *Narrow exceptions in practice (avoid overt discrimination)*
   b. *Contestable markets for government procurement*
   c. *Extent of awareness and efforts to avoid (de facto) discriminatory effects in regulation*
   d. *Liberal policies toward foreign ownership and investment*
3. Avoidance of unnecessary trade restrictiveness
   a. *Use of regulatory impact assessment with due attention to trade effects*
   b. *Demonstrated efforts to favor trade-friendly regulatory approaches*
   c. *Simplification of administrative requirements*
4. Application of competition principles from an international perspective
   a. *Open, accessible complaint procedures for challenging regulatory or private actions that may impair market openness*
5. Use of internationally harmonized measures
   a. *Reference to international standards as the basis for national standards and domestic regulations*
   b. *Systematic monitoring of efforts to use international standards*
   c. *Acceptance of foreign measures as functionally equivalent*
6. Streamlining of conformity assessment procedures
   a. *Establishing market confidence through accreditation mechanisms*
   b. *Demonstrated flexibility toward the use of alternative approaches for avoiding duplicative conformity assessment procedures*

*Source:* Authors' compilation based on OECD (2005).

services, have received less attention than other sectors (such as the financial, telecommunications, and transport sectors). As shown in the following chapters, there are many opportunities for the expansion of trade in these nonbackbone services that can be realized, provided certain accompanying policy measures are undertaken. These measures are designed to increase the competitiveness and efficiency of developing-country markets; they involve both the expansion of foreign markets for exports and of domestic markets for the imports of the various services. In this respect, international labor mobility and the outsourcing of key service activities are crucial issues.

The framework for conducting and analyzing the service trade and the liberalization of regulatory barriers that impede this trade is provided by the GATS. The four modes of classifying international service transactions are useful in clarifying the different forms and interrelationships of the service categories. We point out that a number of developing countries have achieved notable success in a variety of nonbackbone services domestically and with their trading partners. Regulations are necessary to deal with information asymmetries and the possibility of market failures; it is essential that the regulations be designed to minimize any trade effects. At the same time, adjustment costs may be encountered in modernizing service sectors and promoting liberalization. This suggests that the market opening should be phased in, and, where feasible, social safety nets should be established to assist workers and firms impacted negatively by the process. The problems involved will vary depending on the different service modes subject to liberalization.

The GATS framework provides the basis for the classification of service transactions and for the regulatory measures that apply to the different modes of service delivery. Restrictions on service supply through commercial presence (Mode 3) can be especially limiting on the establishment of foreign providers and on the firms and their personnel. There are also widespread limitations on the movement of natural persons (Mode 4) that hamper many service sectors that have come to depend on foreign workers. There has, however, been comparatively little progress in dealing with Mode 4 issues in the GATS context. Bilateral labor agreements appear more promising, provided there is effective monitoring to ensure that only the temporary movement of workers is involved rather than the permanent settlement of workers.

Trade in services can also be encouraged by designing and adopting international standards, licenses, certification procedures, and the mutual recognition of degrees. These measures can be voluntary and may be provided by the private sector, although care has to be taken that private sector involvement serves the larger social purpose. Also important is the need for a transparent and effective public procurement process that promotes social objectives, while establishing less costly measures that are open to domestic and foreign providers of services.

Key to the development of the service sectors is the enhancement of the supply of highly skilled and educated workers who can fulfill the increasingly technical requirements in the individual sectors. This means greater attention and more resources must be devoted to education policies and education institutions; these resources can be supplied by domestic and foreign firms and institutions, both governmental and private. It is also essential to devote attention and resources to building up the domestic infrastructure needed in the different sectors.

Periodic regulatory audits of service regulations are desirable so that problem areas may be identified and the effectiveness of the various regulations that have been changed or are in the process of being changed may be assessed. The regulations affect both domestic and foreign providers of services and take on a variety of forms that apply to different sectors. The goal is to minimize the discriminatory effects of the regulations, while achieving the legitimate social purposes involved. Finally, an overall policy framework may be helpful in providing a guide or checklist to foster market openness and to ensure regulatory quality and performance.

## Notes

1. The GATS definition has wider application and has been replicated in regional and bilateral trade agreements. Some agreements, such as those based on the North American Free Trade Agreement, have defined crossborder trade in services as a single category that includes Modes 1, 2, and 4.

2. *Trade liberalization* and *deregulation* are terms that are often used interchangeably, but they imply different processes. Trade liberalization refers to the process of allowing the private sector provision of services, foreign ownership, and the reduction or elimination of restrictions that impede access to foreign providers of services. Deregulation refers to the creation of a new regulatory environment that ensures the provision of services in a market-oriented framework, including rules to ensure non-discrimination and an adequate level of competition.

3. For additional discussion about the issues in this subsection, see Copeland and Mattoo (2008) and Deardorff and Stern (2008).

## References


Copeland, Brian, and Aaditya Mattoo. 2008. "The Basic Economics of Services Trade." In *A Handbook of International Trade in Services*, ed. Aaditya Mattoo, Robert M. Stern, and Gianni Zanini, 84–129. Washington, DC: World Bank; New York: Oxford University Press.

Deardorff, Alan V., and Robert M. Stern. 2008. "Empirical Analysis of Barriers to International Services Transactions and the Consequences of Liberalization." In *A Handbook of International Trade in Services*, ed. Aaditya Mattoo, Robert M. Stern, and Gianni Zanini, 169–220. Washington, DC: World Bank; New York: Oxford University Press.

Konan, Denise Eby, and Keith E. Maskus. 2006. "Quantifying the Impact of Services Liberalization in a Developing Country." *Journal of Development Studies* 81 (1): 142–62.

Mattoo, Aaditya, and Lucy Payton, eds. 2007. *Services Trade and Development: The Experience of Zambia*. Washington, DC: World Bank; New York: Palgrave Macmillan.

OECD (Organisation for Economic Co-operation and Development). 2005. "Taking Stock of Regulatory Reform: A Multidisciplinary Synthesis." OECD Reviews of Regulatory Reform, OECD, Paris.

Services Database. World Trade Organization. http://tsdb.wto.org/ (accessed September 2009).

WDI (World Development Indicators) Database. World Bank. http://go.worldbank.org/U0FSM7AQ40 (accessed September 2009).

Winters, L. Alan, Terrie L. Walmsley, Zhen Kun Wang, and Roman Grynberg. 2003. "Liberalising Temporary Movement of Natural Persons: An Agenda for the Development Round." *World Economy* 26 (8): 1137–61.

World Bank. 2009. "Negotiating Trade in Services: A Practical Guide for Developing Countries." Report, International Trade Department, World Bank, Washington, DC.

———. 2001. "Guidelines for the Scheduling of Specific Commitments under the General Agreement on Trade in Services (GATS)." Document S/L/92 (March 28), Trade in Services, WTO, Geneva.

2

# INCREASING LABOR MOBILITY: OPTIONS FOR DEVELOPING COUNTRIES

*Sherry Stephenson and Gary Hufbauer*

## Introduction

The free movement of labor is one of the four fundamental economic freedoms, together with the free movement of goods, services, and capital. However, of the four, it has met with the least receptivity by countries in the international economy, whether developed or developing. Even the most spirited free traders—countries such as Chile, Singapore, and the United Kingdom—have been reticent to open their borders to accept foreign labor. Such countries and many others shy away from a significant opening for natural persons from abroad, even when these countries experience labor shortages at home.

The contrast between the desire to promote capital mobility and investment flows and the reluctance to envisage corresponding labor mobility is stark. While more than 2,800 bilateral investment treaties have been signed across the globe, nothing equivalent exists in the area of labor. The number of trade agreements covering services is growing at a rapid pace, but the willingness to incorporate meaningful provisions on labor mobility as part of a service package is limited: most agreements contain only modest market access opportunities for foreign workers.

Consequently, there is a considerable gulf between the liberalization of capital and the liberalization of the movement of labor. Many developed countries are capital abundant and benefit from the freer movement of capital, while many developing countries are labor abundant and constrained in realizing the gains from temporary labor movement. This situation has led to a significant loss in the prospective income that could be acquired through greater labor mobility. The gains from facilitated labor mobility are substantial and likely to surpass the combined gains that would accrue from the freer trade in agriculture and manufactured goods following a successful conclusion of the multilateral negotiations of the Doha Development Round. Yet, current proposals for greater market access for foreign workers are modest, and this is a central obstacle to progress in the service negotiations.

In such a challenging and uncompromising environment for labor mobility, what are the options that developing countries might have to facilitate the movement of their workers? Given the impasse in the Doha Round and the lack of any progress on services in the related multilateral negotiations for the past several years, regional trade agreements (RTAs) might offer a more promising channel for greater labor mobility, even if these agreements are among a more limited number of partners. Other options may also be available, such as the promotion of circular migration through temporary worker agreements, which are time-bound instruments that allow greater flexibility for both labor-sending and labor-receiving countries.

In this chapter, we first discuss the concept of labor mobility. We then review the various ways in which members of RTAs have treated the issue of labor mobility so that we may assess whether RTAs between developed and developing countries have effectively promoted the entry of temporary workers. The questions we attempt to answer are as follows: Which developed countries are more amenable to greater openness for natural persons? What are the possible reasons for this? Can recent RTAs be emulated? We also try to uncover what has been achieved in bilateral or plurilateral agreements in the form of temporary worker programs with developing-country partners. Could such agreements usefully supplement the RTA approach? Finally, we elaborate a set of policy suggestions that would promote labor mobility for developing countries.

## *The concept of labor mobility*

In the international trade in services, labor mobility is conceptualized as the *temporary* movement of natural persons, or Mode 4, which the World Trade Organization (WTO) General Agreement on Trade in Services (GATS) defines as the supply of a service "by a service supplier of one Member, through presence of natural persons of a Member in the territory of any other Member" (article I.2(d)). A natural person of another member is defined as "a natural person who resides in the territory of that other Member or any other Member, and who under the law of that other Member: (i) is a national of that other Member; or (ii) has the right of permanent residence in that other Member" (article XVIII(k)).

A key feature of labor mobility in the trade arena is the concept of *temporary*. For the service trade and for the purposes of this chapter, labor mobility is understood as the movement of workers to carry out employment in another country for a time-limited period. While temporary is not defined under the GATS, the notion of moving to work for a limited period of time, as opposed to moving to emigrate permanently, is nonetheless the aspect that distinguishes Mode 4. This is affirmed in the annex on the movement of natural persons supplying services under the agreement (in the GATS), which specifies that the GATS shall not apply "to measures affecting natural persons seeking access to the employment market of a Member, nor shall it apply to measures regarding citizenship, residence or employment on a permanent basis."

While all subsequent trade agreements, following the WTO approach, consider only the temporary movement of workers, governments have been unwilling to define in precise terms what period of time is meant by temporary. While the official statistical demarcation between temporary and permanent migration is set at stays of less or more than one year, a temporary stay for trade policy purposes can vary between a few weeks to a few years, depending on the commitments governments are prepared to undertake. This lack of precision has been both a strength and weakness in defining Mode 4 treatment within trade agreements (see box 2.1 for a discussion on the extent of temporary labor migration).

**Box 2.1.** Extent of Temporary Labor Migration

The data sources that are available on labor mobility are often incomplete and fail to capture the extent of the temporary movement of labor. It is nonetheless the case that the magnitude of Mode 4 trade is a small share of overall service trade. Table 2.1 presents one estimate of the extent of Mode 4 trade based on calculations by Karsenty (2000). In his paper, Karsenty calculated Mode 4 trade at no more than 1 to 2 percent of the total two-way trade in services. Applying this range to the trade data for 2008 puts the value of the service trade through Mode 4 somewhere between US$70 billion and US$150 billion annually. This range may underestimate the actual value since remittances alone amounted to over US$200 billion in 2007.[1]

**Table 2.1.** The Magnitude of Service Trade through the Temporary Movement of Labor (Mode 4)

| | Two-Way Trade |
|---|---|
| **World Trade in Goods and Services (2008)*** | US$39,740 billion |
| **World Trade in Services (2008)*** | US$7,200 billion |
| **Services Trade through Mode 4 **** | Between US$70 billion and US$150 billion (around 1% to 2% of total trade in services) |

*Sources:* *WTO time series, two-way trade, counting both imports and exports.
**Estimate: Guy Karsenty, Statistics Division, WTO.

However, the great political sensitivity surrounding international labor mobility is aggravated by the frequent confusion, in statistical analysis and political debate, between temporary and permanent migration. Immigration authorities deal with both simultaneously. At times, the character of temporary labor movement is disregarded, and all immigrants are treated as if they were seeking permanent status. Moreover, once immigrants are inside a host country, the line often becomes blurred between immigrants who are residing permanently and immigrants who are residing on a temporary basis.

### *Potential economic gains from greater labor mobility*

There are several impediments to labor mobility. Since workers are not allowed to move easily in response to wage differentials, whereas goods move freely in response to price differentials, and capital flows around the globe in response to profit differentials, the wage differentials observed in the world today are large. The benefits to be derived from the exploitation of comparative advantage is directly proportional to the size of the wage-price-profit differences prior to trade or investment liberalization, and considerable gains could be realized by allowing workers to exploit these wage differentials. The studies attempting to estimate quantitatively the potential gains from greater labor mobility have shown that the projected benefits are substantial (table 2.2).

### *Remittances: An important part of the labor mobility story*

Although the welfare of migrants increases with expanded possibilities for international labor mobility, the sending country of the migrants may actually see its gross domestic product (GDP) decline.[2] This prospect may create some discomfort among analysts of migration. Thus, it is important to consider migration from a worldwide perspective and to view migration on the basis of *nationals* working throughout the world rather than on the basis of *territory*. From this perspective, a critical part of the picture on labor mobility is remittances. Although most of the income earned by migrants working abroad is not repatriated, remittances are substantial, and the amount of remittances sent to their home countries by migrants can more than offset the GDP loss to the sending country because of their departure. Although the amount of remittances varies from country to country, remittances are tremendously important for the majority of countries in the developing world.

World Bank data on compensation (wages and other benefits) cover border, seasonal, and other nonresident workers. The data are not restricted to service providers because they cover nonresident workers employed in any economic

**Table 2.2.** Quantitative Estimates of Gains from Increased Labor Mobility

| Authors | Title | Date | Region | Assumption | Results | | Source |
|---|---|---|---|---|---|---|---|
| **World Bank** | *Global Economic Prospects 2006: Economic Implications of Remittances and Migration* | 2006 | World | Increase in migration from developing countries to high-income countries sufficient to increase the labor force in the host countries by 3% by 2025 (revision of Walmsley and Winters 2003) | Gain: +0.6% of the world GDP, i.e., 356 billion in 2025<br>+0.4% of the developed countries GDP<br>+1.8% of the developing countries GDP (including migrants themselves) | | World Bank, Washington, DC, p31 |
| **Moses, Jonathon, and Bjørn Letnes** | "The Economic Costs to International Labor Restrictions: Revisiting the Empirical Discussion" | 2004 | World | Elimination of all restrictions on labor mobility (using 1977 and 1998 data) | For 1977:<br>*Gain from a 100% elimination of the wage differential:*<br>• from 0.34 to 11.27 trillion of 1977 US$<br>• more probably 0.58 trillion of 1977 US$<br>• from 4.3% to 111.6% of the World GDP in 1977<br>• more probably 7.5% of the World GDP in 1977<br>*A 10% elimination of the wage differential:*<br>• gain: 22% of the total potential gain<br>• wages:<br>+4.1% in poorest countries<br>+3.3% in medium countries<br>−2.5% in richest countries<br>• return to capital:<br>−8.3% in poorest countries<br>−6.9% in medium countries<br>+5.7% in richest countries | For 1998:<br>*Gain from a 100% elimination of the wage differential:*<br>• from 1.97 to 55.04 trillion of 1998 US$<br>• more probably 3.4 trillion<br>• from 5.6% to 155% of the world GDP in 1998<br>• more probably 9.6% of the world GDP in 199<br>*A 10% elimination of the wage differential produces*<br>• gain: 23% of the total potential gain<br>• wages:<br>+11.4% in poorest countries<br>+2.1% in medium countries<br>−3.1% in richest countries<br>• return to capital:<br>−21.0% in poorest countries<br>−4.4% in medium countries<br>+7.2% in richest countries | *World Development* Vol. 32, No. 10, pp. 1609–26 |

(*Table continues on the following pages.*)

**Table 2.2.** Quantitative Estimates of Gains from Increased Labor Mobility *(continued)*

| Authors | Title | Date | Region | Assumption | Results | | Source |
|---|---|---|---|---|---|---|---|
| **Walmsley, Terrie and Alan Winters** | "Relaxing the Restrictions on the Temporary Movements of Natural Persons: A Simulation Analysis" | 2003 | World | Increase in migration from developing countries to high-income countries sufficient to increase the labor force in the host countries by 3% in 2002 | *Total Gain:* +0.6% of the world GDP, i.e., 156 billion in 2002 (1.5 times the expected gains from liberalization of all remaining goods)<br>*Most of the gains come from the movement of unskilled workers:* +110 billion vs. +46 billion for the movement of skilled workers<br>*Migrants welfare:*<br>+171 billion (+73 billion in the United States, +25 billion in Japan, +68 billion in EU)<br>*Resident welfare*<br>net result: −15 billion<br>developing countries: in some cases, gain if high remittances (+16 billion in India) but most of them lose (−7 billion in Brazil)<br>developed countries: small gains (+3.9 billion in EU) | *Change in real wages of unskilled workers:*<br>• increase in developing countries (+0.7% in India)<br>• decrease in developed countries (−0.6% in the United States)<br>*Change in real wages of skilled workers:*<br>• dramatic increase in developing countries (+4.5% in Mexico)<br>• decrease in developed countries (−0.8% in the United States)<br>*Change in rental price of capital:*<br>• decrease in developing countries (−0.4% in Mexico)<br>• increase in developed countries (+0.8% in the United States) | Centre for Economic Policy Research (CEPR) Discussion Paper 3719, CEPR London |
| **Iregui, Ana** | *Efficiency Gains from the Elimination of Global Restrictions on Labor Mobility: An Analysis Using a Multiregional CGE Model* | 1999 | World | Elimination of all restrictions on labor mobility (between 37% and 53% of the labor endowment of developing regions migrate) | *Nonsegmented labor market:* Gain from 15% to 67% of the world GDP<br>*Segmented labor market (skilled vs. unskilled):* Gain from 13% to 59% of the world GDP | *If only skilled labor migrates*: Gain from 3% to 11% of the world GDP | Estudios economicos, Banco de la Republica, Bogota, Colombia |

| | | | | | | | |
|---|---|---|---|---|---|---|---|
| **Borjas, George** | *"Heaven's Doors: Immigration policy and the American Economy"* | 1999 | United States | The 1980–2000 immigration wave in the United States (immigrants representing roughly 10% of the United States workforce) | *Large redistributive effect:*<br>• return to capital +2% of GDP<br>• labor wages: −1.9% of GDP[a] | *Small net gains for natives:*<br>• 10 billion a year (0.1% of U.S. GDP)<br>• roughly 5% of the average equal to economic growth over the past years | Princeton, NJ, Princeton University Press |
| **Hamilton, Bob, and John Whalley** | "Efficiency and Distributional Implications of Global Restrictions on Labour Mobility" | 1984 | World | Elimination of all restrictions on labor mobility (using 1977 data) | Gain from 60.1% to 204.6% of the world GDP in 1977[b] | | *Journal of Development Economics,* Vol. 14, pp 61–75 |

*Source*: Authors' compilation.

*Note*: EU = European Union; GDP = gross domestic product.

a. Hatton and Williamson (1998) find similar results on wages in studying the 1870–1910 migration wage in the United States. They estimate that 1910 U.S. wages would have been 11 to 14 percent higher in the absence of immigration after 1870.

b. The large differences in estimates within and across studies may be explained by differences in the modeling framework (partial versus general equilibrium), production elasticities, cost of movement, or workforce size.

sector. However, the data only cover workers staying abroad for less than one year, while the concept of temporary labor in Mode 4 can cover employment of up to five years depending on the country in question. The concept of remittances refers to transfers by migrant workers who are employed in a foreign economy in which they are residents. This measure relates to foreign workers employed in any economic sector, not specifically the service sector. Remittances represent only the portion of worker compensation that is sent back to the home country. (This proportion is estimated at around 10 to 15 percent of the earnings of migrants.) Accordingly, remittance figures lead to a large underestimation of earnings by migrant workers; however, our data cover both temporary and permanent migrants.

The world saw a sixfold increase in compensation and remittances from 1990 to 2008, rising from US$69 billion in 1990 to US$397 billion in 2008 (adjusted for inflation). From 2000 to 2008, this flow increased by no less than 16 percent a year, with a substantial upward thrust in 2007 (a 21 percent increase). In 2007, migrant compensation and remittances accounted for around 0.7 percent of world GDP. However, for developing countries, the relative importance of remittances in GDP in 2007 was much higher.

Remittances were 2.1 percent of the GDP of developing countries as a whole and:

- 1.9 percent of the GDP of middle-income countries
- 5.8 percent of the GDP of the least developed countries (United Nations category)

The world's leading country of origin for remittances is the United States (US$42 billion in 2006), followed by Saudi Arabia (US$16 billion), and Switzerland (US$14 billion). In the case of Switzerland, the large number hides the fact that most of the remittances comes from border workers originating from France, Germany, and Italy.

As far as receiving countries are concerned, an increasing share of remittances goes to developing countries, which accounted for 76 percent in 2007, up from 46 percent in 1990. It is estimated that 1 in 10 persons worldwide is touched by remittances. Some countries are particularly large beneficiaries from remittances, and the economies of other countries are dependent on them. The main receiving countries in absolute terms are India (US$27 billion), China (US$26 billion), Mexico (US$25 billion), and the Philippines (US$17 billion). For many smaller countries, remittances represent a large share of GDP. For instance, this flow accounts for more than 36 percent of the GDP of Moldova and Tajikistan and around 25 percent of the GDP of Guyana, Honduras, and Lesotho.

Thus, remittance flows to developing countries provide a major offset to the GDP loss that occurs when migrants leave their home countries. Other ways that migrants contribute to the welfare of their home countries include their contribution to foreign direct investment back home (a major factor in some countries, such as China and India); the propensity of migrants to purchase goods and services from their home countries when they live abroad, thus boosting the foreign exchange earnings of their home countries; and, lastly, the tendency of migrants to carry out works of charity in their home countries.[3]

### *Categories of labor included in trade agreements*

While the GATS does not define specific categories of labor, WTO members have accepted four widely used categories for the purpose of inscribing commitments under Mode 4. These categories are not comprehensive because they cover only skilled professionals. In a few recent trade agreements, as we will see in the next section, countries have begun to move beyond this limited range of categories to broaden their consideration of labor categories for market access. The four traditional Mode 4 categories are the following:

- *Business visitors and salespersons* (BVs). These are foreign nationals who travel abroad for the purpose of negotiating a sale of a service or exploring the possibility of making a foreign direct investment for their company in the destination country (establishing a commercial presence, in GATS terminology). Their main purpose is to facilitate future transactions rather than actually carry out the transactions.
- *Intracorporate transferees* (ICTs). These are employees of a foreign provider of services that has set up a commercial presence abroad and transfers these employees to its foreign location.
- *Independent professionals* (IPs). These are self-employed persons who are supplying a service to a company or an individual in a host country. In the large majority of trade agreements, these have been limited to professional workers, but commitments can also be extended to lower-skilled categories of workers.
- *Contractual services suppliers* (CSSs). These are employees of a foreign provider of services that does not have a local presence or commercial presence in the host country. The employees are engaged under contract to provide a service to a firm in the destination country.

For developing countries, the greatest interest in promoting greater labor mobility resides in the IP and CSS categories rather than in employees of multinational corporations. This is because most developing countries do not yet host domestic multinational corporations (although there are exceptions, notably Brazil, China, and India). Greater flexibility in the IP and CSS categories would allow most developing countries to send a larger number of professionals abroad for temporary employment. However, the BV and ICT categories are of interest to successful emerging countries, such as Brazil, China, and India.

## Labor Mobility in RTAs

Several free trade agreements (FTAs) have been entered into by developing countries in the Americas and in Asia that contain provisions to facilitate the procedures for temporary labor movement. Some agreements include, for example, guaranteed numerical quotas for certain categories of skilled labor. In this section, we compare and contrast approaches to labor mobility in RTAs between developed and developing economies. The focus is only on RTAs negotiated following the conclusion of the North American Free Trade Agreement (NAFTA), which entered into force in 1994 and which signaled an era of deeper and more comprehensive regional agreements. The discussion is divided along geographical lines, distinguishing RTAs negotiated by Canada and the United States, the European Union (EU), Japan, and Australia and New Zealand. Tables 2.3–2.7 provide summaries of the salient labor mobility provisions of select RTAs.

### *RTAs negotiated by Canada and the United States*

NAFTA was a pioneer agreement and template for many subsequent RTAs. With respect to labor mobility, it contains a chapter entitled "Temporary Movement of Business Persons," the purpose of which is to facilitate temporary entry across Canada, Mexico, and the United States for business people who are involved in goods or service trade or in investment activities. The categories defined under NAFTA are traders and investors, business visitors, ICTs, and professionals. In the case of business visitors, there is no limit on the number of visas, and work permits are not required. As argued by Martin and Lowell (2008), the novel migration component of NAFTA is the trade NAFTA visa. This visa was uncapped in 1994 for Canadians and has been uncapped for Mexicans since 2004. Upon demonstrating proof of a job offer, the trade NAFTA visa permits employment for one year with unlimited renewal.

In addition to the chapter on temporary entry, NAFTA and subsequent agreements with a similar structure contain an annex on professionals that is specifically targeted at professional service suppliers. The annex in these agreements is intended to promote the development of mutually acceptable standards and criteria for the licensing and certification of professional service suppliers based on factors such as educational background, qualifying examinations, and experience. Additionally, the annex encourages agreement members to provide recommendations for furthering the process of mutual recognition. A qualifying list of professions is set out in an appendix. In the case of NAFTA, 62 professions are specified for which the applicant must have the necessary qualification requirements. The United States originally placed a quota on the number of professionals that could be admitted from Mexico at 5,500 per year.

Besides NAFTA, the United States has negotiated several other bilateral FTAs with developing countries. The ones we have selected for examination are outlined in table 2.3 and include those with Chile, DR-CAFTA (that is, the five countries of Central America, plus the Dominican Republic), Morocco, Peru, and Singapore. Bilateral agreements with Colombia, the Republic of Korea, and Panama have been finalized, but are awaiting ratification by the U.S. Congress.

Under the agreements with Chile and Singapore, concluded in 2002, labor mobility was expanded slightly for professional workers, and the path to an H-1B1 visa was created. This visa provided for an initial stay of 18 months, but with unlimited extensions. Furthermore, an annual quota of 1,800 visas for professionals from Chile was granted, as well as an annual quota of 5,400 visas for professionals from Singapore, in addition to the fixed total of H-1B visas from all countries. The new visa category created under these FTAs is meant for temporary migrants with stays of up to 18 months initially, but with the possibility of unlimited extensions. In summary, the current provisions governing labor movement in these three U.S. trade agreements are the following:

- NAFTA: trade NAFTA visa, uncapped for Canadians and Mexicans
- Chile FTA: H-1B1 visa, capped at 1,800 professionals
- Singapore FTA: H-1B1 visa, capped at 5,400 professionals

Opposition in the U.S. Congress to these various arrangements, particularly the FTAs with Chile and Singapore, was loud and clear. Some congressmen objected that trade agreements stepped into the realm of immigration matters. As a consequence of this opposition, no FTA negotiated by the United States since 2002 has contained a chapter to facilitate the temporary movement of skilled workers.[4] Thus, the FTAs with the DR-CAFTA members, Morocco, and Peru (like those negotiated with Colombia, Korea, and Panama) contain no chapter on temporary entry. They do, however, contain an annex on professionals with objectives similar to those of the annex under NAFTA. The annexes each state that "no provision shall impose any obligation on a party regarding its immigration measures," and the annexes contain no market-access commitments. Thus, in the United States, public and official attitudes with respect to labor mobility have regressed since 2002. Until political opinion changes, it will be nearly impossible for developing countries to negotiate greater labor mobility in trade agreements with the United States.

In the case of Canada, the situation has evolved differently (table 2.4). Perhaps because of pressures from the private sector and apparent labor shortages in the

**Table 2.3.** Agreements between the United States and Developing Countries

| | United States–Morocco | United States–Singapore | United States–Chile | DR-CAFTA | United States–Peru |
|---|---|---|---|---|---|
| Entry into force | January 1, 2006 | January 1, 2004 | January 1, 2004 | March 1, 2006 | February 1, 2009 |
| **Provisions on trade in services** | | | | | |
| Chapter on trade in services | Chap 11 | Chap VIII | Chap 11 | Chap 11 | Chap 11 |
| Treatment of foreign services | | | | | |
| National treatment | Yes (Art 11.2) | Yes (Art 8.3) | Yes (Art 11.2) | Yes (Art 11.2) | Yes (Art 11.2) |
| Most favored nation | Yes (Art 11.3) | Yes (Art 8.4) | Yes (Art 11.3) | Yes (Art 11.3) | Yes (Art 11.3) |
| Local presence required | No (Art 11.5) | No (Art 8.6) | No (Art 11.4) | No (Art 11.4) | No (Art 11.4) |
| **Provisions on Mode 4** | | | | | |
| Chapter on Mode 4 | No | Chap 11 | Chap 14 | No | No |
| Committee on Mode 4 | The joint committee shall review the implementation of the annex on professionals | Yes (Art 11.7) | Yes (Art 14.5) | The commission shall review the implementation of the annex on professionals | n.a. |
| Dispute settlement on Mode 4 | n.a. | Yes (Art 11.8) | Yes (Art 14.6) | n.a. | n.a. |
| Transparency of regulation on Mode 4 | n.a. | Yes (Art 11.5) | Yes (Art 14.4) | n.a. | n.a. |
| Side letters on Mode 4 | No | Yes (Professionals must comply with certain labor and immigration laws from an employer in the United States) | Yes (Professionals will get visa through the U.S. "H-1B" program) | Yes ("No provision shall impose any obligation on a party regarding its immigration measures") | n.a. |

| | | | | | |
|---|---|---|---|---|---|
| Worker categories covered | n.a. | Investors<br>Traders<br>ICTs<br>Professionals | Investors<br>Traders<br>ICTs<br>Professionals | n.a. | n.a. |
| Specification of length of stay | n.a. | No | No | n.a. | n.a. |
| **Provisions on professionals** | | | | | |
| Annex on professionals | Annex 11.B | Appendix 11.A.2 | Annex 14.3.D | Annex 11.9 | Annex 11.B |
| Number of professional categories covered | **0** (Pledge to work on) | **2** (Disaster relief claims adjuster, management consultant) | **4** (Disaster relief claims adjuster, management consultant, agricultural manager, physiotherapist) | 0 (Pledge to work on) | 0 (Pledge to work on) |
| Specified quotas | n.a. | **Singapore**:<br>no numerical limit<br>**United States**: 5,400 | **Chile**:<br>no numerical limit<br>**United States**: 1,400 | n.a. | n.a. |
| Postsecondary degree required | n.a. | Yes: 4 years or more | Yes: 4 years or more | n.a. | n.a. |
| Specification of length of stay | n.a. | No | No | n.a. | n.a. |

*Source:* Authors' compilation.
*Note:* n.a. = not applicable.

**Table 2.4.** Agreements between Canada and Developing Countries

| | NAFTA | Canada-Chile | Canada-Colombia | Canada-Peru |
|---|---|---|---|---|
| Entry into force | January 1, 1994 | July 5, 1997 | Signed November 21, 2008 | January 1, 2009 |
| **Provisions on trade in services** | | | | |
| Chapter on trade in services | Chap 12 | Chap H | Chap 9 | Chap 9 |
| Treatment of foreign services | | | | |
| National treatment | Yes (Art 1202) | Yes (Art H-02) | Yes (Art 902) | Yes (Art 903) |
| Most favored nation | Yes (Art 1203) | Yes (Art H-03) | Yes (Art 903) | Yes (Art 904) |
| Local presence required | No (Art 1205) | No (Art H-04) | No (Art 905) | No (Art 907) |
| **Provisions on Mode 4** | | | | |
| Chapter on Mode 4 | Art 16 | Chap K | Chap 12 | Chap 12 |
| Side letters on Mode 4 | No | No | No | No |
| Committee on Mode 4 | Yes (Art 1605) | Yes (Annex K-05) | | |
| Dispute settlement on Mode 4 | Yes (Art 1606) | Yes (Art K-06) | Yes (Art 1206) | Yes (Art 1206) |
| Transparency of regulation on Mode 4 | Yes (Art 1604) | Yes (Art K-04) | Yes (Art 1204) | Yes (Art 1204) |
| Worker categories covered | Investors<br>Traders<br>ICTs<br>Professionals | Investors<br>Traders<br>ICTs<br>Professionals | Investors<br>Traders<br>ICTs<br>Professionals<br>Technicians<br>Spouses | Investors<br>Traders<br>ICTs<br>Professionals<br>Technicians |
| Specification of length of stay | No | No | No | **Peru:**<br>Investors: 1 year<br>Traders: 90 days<br>ICTs: 1 year<br>Professionals:1 year<br>Technicians: 1 year<br>**Canada:**<br>Investors: 1 year<br>Traders: 1 year<br>ICTs: 3 years<br>Professionals: 1 year<br>Technicians: 1 year |

| | | | | |
|---|---|---|---|---|
| **Provisions on professionals** | | | | |
| Annex on professionals | Appendix 1603.D.1 | Appendix K-03.IV.1 | Appendix 1203.D | Appendix 1203.D |
| Number of professional categories covered | **63** (Accountant, architect, medical professionals, scientists, teachers, . . .) | **72** (Accountant, architect, medical professionals, scientists, teachers, . . .) | **All categories of professionals** (except health, sport, art, education, legal, and management services) **50 categories of technicians** (mechanical and avionics technicians, construction inspector, supervisor in food, beverage, textiles processing, electricians, plumbers, oil and gas well drillers, chefs, . . .) | **All professionals** (except health, sport, art, education, legal, and management services) **50 technicians** (mechanical and avionics technicians, construction inspector, supervisor in food, beverage, textiles processing, electricians, plumbers, oil and gas well drillers, chefs, . . .) |
| Specified quotas | No numerical limit except for the United States: 5,500 | No numerical limit | No numerical limit | No numerical limit |
| Postsecondary degree required | Yes: 4 years or more | Yes: 4 years or more | Yes: professionals: 4 years technicians: 2 years | Yes: professionals: 4 years technicians: 1 year |
| Specification of length of stay | No | No | No | 1 year |

*Source:* Authors' compilation.

Canadian market prior to the current crisis, the government has negotiated recent FTAs that go quite far toward providing increased access not only for professionals, but also for semiskilled foreign workers. While the FTA that Canada negotiated with Chile in 1997 looks similar to NAFTA in that the only categories of workers covered are investors, traders and BVs, ICTs, and professionals, it was already notable because the FTA placed no numerical limits on 72 of these categories of professional labor.

The recent FTAs negotiated by Canada with Colombia (2008) and Peru (2009) go much further. They cover all professional categories and impose no numerical limits and no specified length of stay, meaning that visas could, in theory, be renewed indefinitely. For the first time, they also expand coverage of worker categories beyond highly trained professionals so as to include technicians. In the Colombian and Peruvian FTAs, Canada has listed 50 categories of technicians who may be admitted into the Canadian market with no specified length of stay. These technicians must have an educational degree and two years of technical training. Technician categories include mechanics, construction inspectors, food and beverage supervisors, chefs, plumbers, and oil and gas well drillers. This recent development constitutes a major step forward for the expansion of temporary entry within trade agreements.

### *RTAs negotiated by the EU*

In this section, we examine RTAs involving the EU and third countries, not arrangements among the 27 current members of the EU. Among the members, total labor mobility is guaranteed, though only after 10 years with respect to some of the newest EU members.

The form of the RTAs negotiated by the EU differs from that pioneered by the United States. Provisions for the liberalization of services and investment are set out in a section of the EU agreements titled "Trade in Services and Establishment." The European Commission does not yet have exclusive negotiating authority from the EU member states with regard to services and investment.[5] So far, the European Commission has followed a GATS-type model and a positive list approach in its trade agreements, with lists of commitments attached to the main text of the agreements. Thus, in terms of market access, Mode 4 is brought within the scope of the EU RTAs in a way similar to that followed under the GATS. Categories of workers included in Mode 4 commitments by the EU include the four that are traditional in RTAs (traders and investors, BVs, ICTs, and IPs). However, the EU has negotiated relatively few RTAs with developing countries that cover services. Although it has numerous association agreements in place with neighboring Mediterranean countries (Egypt, Jordan, Morocco, the Syran Arab Republic, Tunisia, Turkey, and others), these agreements focus on goods and have not yet incorporated service provisions.

The EU has negotiated association agreements with Chile and Mexico and, more recently, has finalized an Economic Partnership Agreement (EPA) with the countries of the Caribbean Community (CARICOM) and the Dominican Republic (the CARIFORUM grouping). A summary of the provisions in these agreements for Mode 4 is shown in table 2.5. While there are no in-depth service provisions in the earlier agreement with Mexico, which was concluded in March 2000 when the GATS negotiations were beginning, the RTA with Chile is substantial. Besides the coverage of Mode 4 in the text of the agreement, there is also a specific article on the "Movement of Natural Persons" in the EU-Chile Association Agreement, as well as an annex on professionals (annex VII). In the annex, the EU specifies 33 categories of professional service providers that it will accept from Chile without numerical limit for a period of three months, subject to the "necessary academic qualification and experience." Chile did not commit reciprocally to accept any professionals from the EU.

The more recent CARIFORUM-EU EPA follows a similar structure. However, besides the usual categories of workers defined under Mode 4, the EU, for the first time, has expanded coverage of workers to cover three additional categories at the request of the CARIFORUM members. These include CSSs, IPs, and graduate trainees. The following applies in the case of these three categories:[6]

- The *CSS* category included in the EPA with CARIFORUM is applicable to a specific list of activities. It permits temporary entry for a cumulative period of six months. There are a number of requirements that a CSS must fulfill, and the terms and conditions are set out in EU schedules for its member states.
- The provisions for the CSS category also apply to *IPs*, again with EU schedules.
- *Graduate trainees*, a new category, applies to workers from CARIFORUM states who have a university degree and are temporarily transferred to the parent company or to a commercial establishment for career development or to obtain training in business methods. They may enter for a period of up to one year.

In the annex on professionals in the CARIFORUM EPA, the European Commission committed to accept 29 categories of professional service providers without numerical limit, provided these professionals have a university degree and three years' experience. The CARIFORUM members have not committed reciprocally to accepting any professionals from the EU.

### *RTAs negotiated by Japan*

Japan has negotiated four RTAs that are of interest for the issue of labor mobility. These are summarized in table 2.6. The RTAs with Chile and Mexico are similar in form and content to the NAFTA-type approach and agreements. There is a negative

**Table 2.5.** Agreements between the EU and Developing Countries

| | EU-Chile | EU-CARIFORUM | EU-Turkey | EU-Morocco |
|---|---|---|---|---|
| Entry into force | February 1, 2003 | December 29, 2008 | December 31, 1995 | March 18, 2000 |
| **Provisions on trade in services** | | | | |
| Chapter on trade in services | Title III, Chap I | Part II, Title II, Chap 3 | None | Title III (Pledge to work on) |
| Treatment of foreign services | | | n.a. | |
| National treatment | Yes (Art 98) | Yes (Art 77) | n.a. | n.a. |
| Most favored nation | No | Yes (Art 79) | n.a. | n.a. |
| Local presence required | No (Art 97) | n.a. | n.a. | n.a. |
| **Provisions on Mode 4** | | | | |
| Chapter on Mode 4 | Art 101 | Part II, Title II, Chap 4 | None | None |
| Side letters on Mode 4 | No | No | n.a. | n.a. |
| Committee on Mode 4 | Yes (Art 100) | Yes (Art 85) | n.a. | n.a. |
| Dispute settlement on Mode 4 | No | Pledge to create one (Art 87) | n.a. | n.a. |
| Transparency of regulation on Mode 4 | Yes (Art 105) | Yes (Art 86) | n.a. | n.a. |
| Worker categories covered | Investors<br>ICTs<br>Business sellers<br>Professionals | Investors<br>ICTs<br>Business sellers<br>Professionals<br>Graduate trainees | n.a. | n.a. |
| Specification of length of stay | **EU:**<br>Professionals:<br>3 months | Investors: 90 days<br>Transferees: 3 years<br>Business sellers: 90 days<br>Professionals: 6 months | n.a.<br><br><br>n.a. | n.a.<br><br><br>n.a. |

| | | | | |
|---|---|---|---|---|
| **Provisions on professionals** | | | | |
| Annex on Professionals | Annex VII | Annex IV | None | None |
| Number of Professional categories covered | **EU: 33** (Engineer, accounting, construction, mining, computer, legal services, . . .)<br>**Chile: 0** | **EU: 29** (Architectural, legal, accounting, engineering, computer, management services)<br>**CARIFORUM: 0** | n.a. | n.a. |
| Specified quotas | No numerical limit | No numerical limit | n.a. | n.a. |
| Postsecondary degree required | "Necessary academic qualification and experience" | University Degree +3 years of experience | n.a. | n.a. |
| Specification of Length of stay | **EU:**<br>3 months | **EU:**<br>6 months | n.a. | n.a. |

*Source:* Authors' compilation.
*Note:* n.a. = not applicable.

**Table 2.6** Agreements between Japan and Developing Countries

| | Japan-Mexico | Japan-Chile | Japan-Indonesia | Japan-Philippines |
|---|---|---|---|---|
| Entry into force | April 1, 2005 | Signed March 27, 2007 | July 7, 2008 | December 11, 2008 |
| **Provisions on trade in services** | | | | |
| Chapter on trade in services | Chap 8 | Chap 9 | Chap 6 | Chap 7 |
| Treatment of foreign services | | | | |
| National treatment | Yes (Art 98) | Yes (Art 107) | Yes (Art 79) | Yes (Art 73) |
| Most favored nation | Yes (Art 99) | Yes (Art 108) | Yes (Art 82) | Yes (Art 76) |
| Local presence required | No (Art 100) | No (Art 109) | No (Art 78) | No (Art 72) |
| **Provisions on Mode 4** | | | | |
| Chapter on Mode 4 | Chap 10 | Chap11 | Chap 7 | Chap 9 |
| Side letters on Mode 4 | No | No | No | No |
| Committee on Mode 4 | Yes (Art 117) | No | Yes (Art 96) | Yes (Art 113) |
| Dispute settlement on Mode 4 | Yes (Art 118) | Yes (Art 133) | Yes (Chap 14) | Yes (Chap 15) |
| Transparency of regulation on Mode 4 | Yes (Art 116) | Yes (Art 132) | Yes (Art 95) | Yes (Art 111) |
| Worker categories covered | Investors<br>Business visitors<br>ICTs<br>Professionals | Investors<br>Business visitors<br>ICTs<br>Professionals | Investors<br>Business visitors<br>ICTs<br>Professionals<br>Professionals with "personal contract"<br>Nurses and care workers | Investors<br>Business visitors<br>ICTs<br>Professionals<br>Professionals with "personal contract"<br>Nurses and care workers |
| Specification of Length of stay | **Japan:**<br>Business visitors: 90 days<br>Other categories: 3 years<br>**Mexico:**<br>Business visitors: 30 days<br>Other categories: 1 year | **Japan:**<br>Business visitors: 90 days<br>Other categories: 3 years<br>**Chile:**<br>Business visitors: 30 days<br>Other categories: 1 year | **Japan:**<br>Business visitors: 90 days<br>Other categories: 3 years<br>**Indonesia:**<br>Business visitors: 60 days<br>Other categories: 1 year | **Japan:**<br>Business visitors: 90 days<br>Other categories: 3 years<br>**The Philippines:**<br>Business visitors: 59 days<br>Other categories: 1 year |

| | | | | |
|---|---|---|---|---|
| **Provisions on professionals** | | | | |
| Annex on professionals | Annex 10 | Annex 13 | Annex 10 | Annex 8 |
| Number of professional categories covered | **Japan: 2** (Engineer, specialist in Humanities/international services) | **Japan: 2** (Engineer, specialist in humanities/international services) | **Japan: 14** (Legal and accounting services, engineer, specialist in humanities/international services, nurses, care workers) | **Japan: 10** (Legal and accounting services, engineer, specialist in humanities/international services, Japanese University graduate nurses and care workers) |
| | **Mexico: 42** (Accountant, engineer, lawyer, scientist, Nurse . . . ) | **Chile: 41** (Accountant, engineer, lawyer scientist, Nurse . . . ) | **Indonesia: 4** (mechanical and electrical engineer, nurses, care workers) | **Philippines: 4** (Mechanical and electrical engineer, nurses, care workers) |
| Specified quotas | No numerical limit | No numerical limit | No numerical limit **except for nurses and care workers** | n.a. |
| Postsecondary degree required | 4 years or more | 4 years or more | **Professionals:** 4 years<br>**Nurses and care workers:** National health degree +2 years of work experience +6 months of language training | **Professionals:** 4 years<br>**Nurses and care workers:** National health degree +3 years of work experience +6 months of training in the host country to pass the host country certification exam |
| Specification of length of stay | **Japan:** 3 years<br>**Chile:** 1 year | **Japan:** 3 years<br>**Chile:** 1 year | **Japan:** 3 years<br>**Indonesia:** 1 year | **Japan:** 3 years<br>**Philippines:** 1 year |

*Source:* Authors' compilation.
*Note:* n.a. = not applicable.

list of nonconforming measures, and Mode 4 is treated in a chapter on the temporary movement of business persons. This chapter defines movement for the four categories usually seen in trade agreements (traders and investors, BVs, ICTs, and IPs). However, Japan has set a time limit of three years for three of these categories (all but business visitors), which is a fairly generous interpretation of length of stay.

The two more recent RTAs negotiated by Japan with countries in Southeast Asia—Indonesia and the Philippines—are notable for their innovations in covering, for the first time, specific categories of nurses and care workers. These RTAs also have expanded the categories of workers in the chapter on Mode 4 to include "professionals with personal contracts" (essentially the same as CSSs), as well as nurses and care workers. For Japan, these categories (other than business visitors) are allowed a stay of up to three years. Japan has also increased the number of professional categories covered in the annex on professionals in these two RTAs (to 14 in the case of Indonesia and 10 in the case of the Philippines). No numerical limits are placed on these professional categories, except for nurses and care workers, for whom an annual quota is in effect. For the latter professions, specific education and training requirements are also included in the agreements, namely, a national health degree, plus two years of prior work experience and six months of language training in Japanese. Professional categories are allowed a stay of up to three years. The specification of particular categories of work with annual quotas and training requirements is an innovative approach that has not yet been seen in other RTAs.

### *RTAs negotiated by Australia and New Zealand*

Four RTAs have been negotiated by Australia and New Zealand that are relevant for this study, including one joint RTA with the 10 members of the Association of Southeast Asian Nations (ASEAN). They are summarized in table 2.7. Three of these are recent agreements that have been signed or have come into force since August 2008. The oldest of the four and the one with the least ambitious provisions for labor mobility is the P4, also known as the Trans-Pacific Strategic Economic Partnership Agreement, between the four countries of Brunei Darussalam, Chile, New Zealand, and Singapore. This agreement, which entered into force in 2006, follows a NAFTA-type structure, but with less in-depth content. The only category of workers specified in the temporary entry (or labor mobility) chapter is business persons, and no length of stay is specified. There is an annex for professional services, but it primarily sets out a best endeavors clause for the development of "mutually acceptable standards and criteria for licensing and certification of professional service providers." No professional categories of service providers are listed; therefore, the annex has no market access component.

**Table 2.7.** Agreements between Australia, New Zealand, and Developing Countries

| | P4 (New Zealand, Chile, Singapore, Brunei Darussalam) | ASEAN–Australia–New Zealand | New Zealand–China | Australia-Chile |
|---|---|---|---|---|
| Entry into force | May 28, 2006 | Signed August 28, 2008 | October 1, 2008 | March 6, 2009 |
| **Administrative provisions** | | | | |
| Chapter on trade in services | Chap 12 | Chap 8 | Chap 9 | Chap 9 |
| Treatment of workers | | | | |
| National treatment | Yes (Art 12-4) | Yes (Chap 8, Art 5) | Yes (Art 106) | Yes (Art 9-3) |
| Most favored nation | Yes (Art 12-3) | Yes (Chap 8, Art 7) | Yes (Art 107) | Yes (Art 9-4) |
| Local presence required | No (Art 12-7) | No (Chap 8, Art 4) | No (Art 108) | No (Art 9-5) |
| **Provisions on Mode 4** | | | | |
| Chapter on Mode 4 | Art 12-11 | Chap 9 | Chap 10 | Chap 13 |
| Side letters on Mode 4 | No | No | No | No |
| Committee on Mode 4 | No | No | Yes (Art 133) | Yes (Art 13-6) |
| Dispute settlement on Mode 4 | No | Yes (Chap 9, Art 9) | Yes (Art 134) | Yes (Art 13-7) |
| Transparency of regulation on Mode 4 | No | Yes (Chap 9, Art 8) | Yes (Art 131) | Yes (Art 13-5) |
| Worker categories covered | Professionals | Business visitors<br>Investors<br>ICTs<br>Contractual service suppliers<br>Installers (install a purchased machinery–only New Zealand)<br>Spouses | Business visitors<br>Investors<br>ICTs<br>Contractual service suppliers<br>Installers | Business visitors<br>Investors<br>ICTs<br>Contractual service suppliers<br>Relatives |
| Specification of length of stay | No | **Indonesia:**<br>Business visitors: 60 days<br>Investors: 60 days<br>Others: 2 years | **China:**<br>Business visitors: 6 months<br>Investors: 6 months<br>Transferees: 3 years<br>Professionals: —<br>Installers: 3 months | **Australia:**<br>Business visitor: 1 year<br>Investors: 90 days<br>Transferees: 4 years<br>Professionals: 1 year |

(*Table continues on the following pages.*)

**Table 2.7.** Agreements between Australia, New Zealand, and Developing Countries (*continued*)

| | P4 (New Zealand, Chile, Singapore, Brunei Darussalam) | ASEAN–Australia–New Zealand | New Zealand–China | Australia-Chile |
|---|---|---|---|---|
| | | **Australia:**<br>Transferees: 4 years<br>Investors: 2 years<br>Business visitors: 6 months<br>Professionals: 12 months<br>**New Zealand:**<br>Business visitors: 3 months<br>Investors: 3 months<br>Transferees: 3 years<br>Installers: 3 months<br>Professionals: 12 months<br>**Philippines:**<br>Business visitors: 59 days<br>Others:1 year<br>**Vietnam:**<br>Transferees: 3 years<br>Others: 90 days | **New Zealand:**<br>Business visitors: 3 months<br>Investors: 3 months<br>Transferees: 3 years<br>Professionals: 3 years<br>Installers: 3 months | **Chile:** — |
| **Provisions on professionals** | | | | |
| Annex on professionals | Art 12-11 | Annex 4 | Annexes 10 and 11 | Annex 13-A |
| Number of professional categories covered | **Pledge to "work on" 6 categories** (Engineers, architects, geologists, geophysicists, planners, and accountants) | **Australia: 0**<br>**New Zealand: 33** (Engineering, legal, taxation, veterinary, Computer, translation services)<br>**Indonesia: 13** (Legal, tourism, restaurant, engineering, computer, R&D, maintenance services)<br>**Philippines:** All persons "who occupy a technical, advisory, or supervisory position"<br>**Vietnam: 2** (computer and engineering services)<br>**Singapore: 0** | **China: 5** (Education, medical, translation, hotel, computer)<br>**New Zealand: 6** (Traditional Chinese medicine, Chinese chefs, Mandarin teaching aides, martial arts coaches, tour guides, skilled workers "in category identified as being in shortage") | "Subject to national criteria" |

| | | | | |
|---|---|---|---|---|
| Specified quotas | n.a. | Entry subject to national rules | **China:**<br>No numerical limit<br>**New Zealand:**<br>Traditional Chinese medicine: 200<br>Chinese chefs: 200<br>Mandarin teaching aides: 150<br>Martial arts coaches: 150<br>Tour guides: 100<br>Skilled workers "in category in shortage": 1,000 | — |
| Postsecondary degree required | n.a. | **New Zealand:** 3 years or more +6 years of experience<br>**Indonesia:** "High qualification"<br>**Philippines:** "Knowledge at an advanced level"<br>**Vietnam:** A "university degree" +5 years of experience | **China:**<br>"Appropriate education level" +2 years of experience<br>**New Zealand:**<br>"Appropriate education level" +experience | — |
| Specification of length of stay | n.a. | **Vietnam:** 90 days<br>**New Zealand:** 1 year<br>**Philippines:** 1 year<br>**Indonesia:** 2 years | **China:** —<br>**New Zealand:** 3 years | **Chile:** —<br>**Australia:** 1 year |

*Source:* Authors' compilation.
*Note:* n.a. = not applicable.

In the case of the China–New Zealand RTA that entered into force in October 2008, the chapter on labor mobility specifies five categories of labor: investors, BVs, ICTs, CSSs, and a new category, installers. The CSS category includes artisans with Chinese cultural characteristics, such as Chinese theater professionals, Mandarin teachers, and Chinese medicine specialists. While China has not taken any commitment with regard to professional service providers, New Zealand allows the entry of designated professionals from China for up to three years. ICTs from China are also permitted a three-year stay. The new category of installers carries with it a three-month stay.

The Australia-Chile RTA that entered into force in March 2009 follows a NAFTA-type structure, and the chapter on temporary entry sets out the four usual categories of labor. An annex on professional services does not contain a market access component, and no numbers are attached to any category of worker. Australia allows ICTs a stay of up to four years and CSSs a stay of one year, with the possibility of renewal. This recent RTA is quite original in its treatment of spouses and accompanying family members. They are granted the right to join the workers after the workers have been in Australia for over one year. The dependents and spouses of corporate executives, ICTs, and CSSs from the other party are allowed to enter and reside in the respective host country. Moreover, the spouse is given the right to enter, stay, and work for a period of time equal to that of the relevant worker.

In the case of the ASEAN–Australia–New Zealand RTA, which was signed in August 2008, a chapter on temporary entry includes the four usual categories of labor, plus the additional category of installers (by New Zealand). The length of stay offered by the partners to the RTA is variable; Australia and New Zealand allow the longest stay for ICTs (three or four years) and one year for IPs and CSSs. It is notable that, relative to their developed-country partners, the ASEAN members committed to much less generous stay periods for all of the labor categories.

### *Overall comparison and assessment of RTAs*

An overall comparison of the RTAs negotiated with developing countries by Australia, Canada, the EU, Japan, New Zealand, and the United States can be made easily in figure 2.1. The bars indicate the categories of labor that have been included in the various agreements. The higher the bar for a particular agreement, the more access the agreement provides for workers from the developing-country partner. The number of categories of workers encompassed within the chapter on the temporary entry and movement of natural persons is indicated, as well as the number of professionals allowed through the annex on professionals either under specified quotas or without numerical limitation. The size of the bar sections indicates the types and numbers of workers (traders and investors, BVs, ICTs, IPs,

**Figure 2.1.** Provisions on Mode 4 in FTAs between Developed and Developing Countries

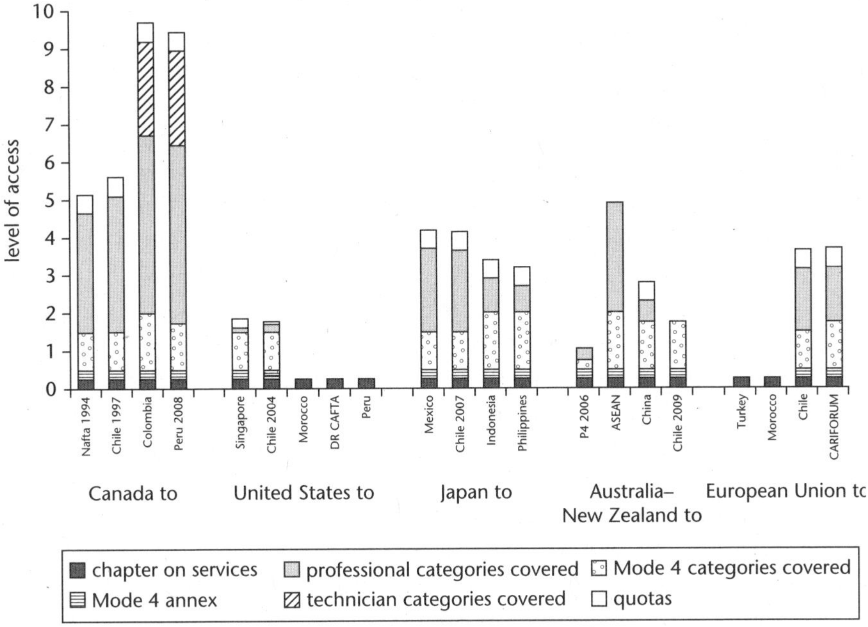


*Source:* Authors' compilation.

CSSs, and other skilled workers) that have been guaranteed access under the respective agreement. This format allows for a visual representation and comparison of the provisions on labor mobility, as well as on the extent of market access represented by each of the RTAs examined.

In general, trade agreements concluded by developed countries with developing countries focus almost exclusively on professional service providers. However, many go beyond the GATS by offering access for a greater number of categories of professional services either through expanded numbers of covered categories or through unlimited access. They also often offer long-term visa renewals once professionals are settled in the country. Therefore, distinct progress has been made with respect to professional services.

A few developed countries have been willing recently to go beyond the expansion of access only for professional service providers. This includes, notably, Canada in the two recent FTAs negotiated with Colombia and Peru. The FTAs extend access to the Canadian market to 50 categories of technicians. The innovative category also includes the EU EPA with CARIFORUM, which has extended market access to contractual service suppliers and independent professionals (for six months) and to graduate trainees (for one year). Japan has moved to liberalize the access to its labor market for nurses and care workers in its recent EPAs with Indonesia and the Philippines. Finally, Australia and New Zealand have expanded the categories of labor in their RTAs to include contractual service suppliers and installers (for New Zealand) in their recent agreement with ASEAN members and in the New Zealand RTA with China. The New Zealand RTA with China also has novel provisions for artisans that are proficient in Chinese cultural occupations, such as Chinese theater, language, and medicine. Australia has been innovative in its recent RTA with Chile in covering the spouses and dependents of ICTs and CSSs residing in the country longer than one year. Thus, over the past two years, trade agreements have moved beyond the purely professional categories of labor to cover CSSs, semiprofessionals and technicians, nurses and care workers, and even spouses and dependents.

The trading partners most willing to open their markets wider for foreign workers from developing RTA partners have been the countries that face considerable labor shortages. Canada has been the most generous in this respect, while Japan has been selective and sector specific in responding to its labor market needs. Australia has been willing to consider family dependents as part of the labor categories defined under its most recent RTA. The EU and the United States, which face heavy inward migration flows—both documented and undocumented—from Latin America (in the U.S. case) and from North Africa and Eastern Europe (in the EU case), are less willing to bind greater market openness contractually for foreign workers in their RTAs.[7] Nonetheless, the EU did expand its coverage of labor categories in the recent EPA with CARIFORUM members, albeit for a group of more sparsely populated countries. However, in the United States, official and public attitudes have soured, and no agreements have been negotiated with Mode 4 coverage since 2002 (see elsewhere above).

The story of labor mobility in trade agreements is still being written. The situation continues to evolve. Currently, several RTAs are under negotiation between developed and developing economies. The EU is negotiating with ASEAN, five countries in Central America, the four members of the Southern Cone Common Market, and Colombia, Ecuador, India, Korea, and Peru. Canada is negotiating with CARICOM, four countries in Central America, the Dominican Republic, Jordan, Korea, Panama, and Singapore. Japan is negotiating with India and Peru. Australia is negotiating with China, the Gulf Cooperation Council, Korea, and Malaysia. Only the United States is currently abstaining from further involvement in negotiations on RTAs. Thus, the sample for evaluating the treatment of labor mobility in RTAs will continue to expand in coming years. Developing countries that are able to define and push their interests proactively with developed-country trading partners should find opportunities that did not exist in the past.

## Bilateral Labor Agreements

The treatment of labor mobility in formal RTAs has focused overwhelmingly on categories of skilled labor, with only a few recent agreements moving to cover certain types of semiskilled workers (see elsewhere above). Against this background, are there other vehicles that can be used to promote labor mobility? Bilateral labor agreements (BLAs) are alternative instruments to the more legalistic and rigid RTAs; these agreements can serve to promote and regulate the flow of unskilled or semiskilled workers.

### *Background*

BLAs have provided a means by which seasonal and low-skilled foreign labor may be employed on a temporary basis. They are instruments that serve to promote and regulate the flow of unskilled or semiskilled workers by allowing mostly industrialized countries requiring foreign labor to design labor exchange programs that steer inward flows to specific areas of labor demand. For destination countries, the primary aim is to address shortages in the local labor market, whether this concerns seasonal workers (often in the agricultural sector) or low-skilled labor. Occasionally, BLAs also involve higher-skilled workers in areas experiencing labor shortages such as health or information technology.

While BLAs were quite common in Europe and the United States in the 1960s, they fell out of favor in the 1970s and 1980s because of the adverse combination of inflation and high unemployment. Between 1942 and 1964, the United States operated a program (the Bracero Program) to admit temporary agricultural workers from Mexico. Admissions under this program peaked at over 450,000 workers per year, but began to shrink as a consequence of the stricter enforcement of labor market regulations, combined with technological changes. Nonetheless, the program continued to admit over 200,000 Mexican temporary workers a year until it was ended. European temporary worker programs differed from the Mexico–United States program in several respects, including in the locus of employment, which was nonfarm manufacturing, construction, and mining, as well as in the policies toward settlement. Unlike Mexicans who filled seasonal jobs in the United States and were expected to return to Mexico every year, migrants in Europe filled year-round jobs and eventually earned the right to unify their families and settle through the acquisition of work and residence permits.

Since around 2000, several developed countries have entered into second-generation BLAs. Many of these are in the form of memorandums of understanding rather than more formal contractual arrangements. The BLAs take no set form. In fact, there is such a variety of agreements that the "Compendium of Good Practice Policy Elements in Bilateral Temporary Labour Arrangements" was developed by the International Labour Organization, the International Organization for Migration, and the Organization for Security and Co-operation in Europe as a follow-up activity after the first Global Forum on Migration and Development, which was held in 2007 (ILO, IOM, and OSCE 2008).

Even though the number of BLAs has been increasing in recent years, there is no single institution responsible for collecting and maintaining the relevant information. Neither the International Labour Organization nor the International Organization for Migration has information on BLAs at the country level. The following subsection examines several pertinent BLAs.[8] While many countries have entered into BLAs, others prefer to channel their temporary labor needs through more formal immigration pathways. The vast majority of U.S. temporary admission programs are open to citizens of all countries. The range of temporary visa programs covers both skilled professionals (for example, H-1B visas) and other kinds of temporary labor (such as H-2A temporary agricultural workers).

Our examination of the panorama of BLAs that have been identified for this study and that are presented in table 2.8 reveals that such agreements have been signed by countries in all regions of the world. In the Americas, Canada has been particularly active in entering into BLAs, including those with Barbados, Colombia,

**Table 2.8.** BLAs with Developing-Country Partners: Government Programs for Temporary Workers

| Region | Country | Developing Country Partners |
|---|---|---|
| **Americas** | Canada | Barbados, Colombia, Guatemala, Jamaica, Mexico, Organization of Eastern Caribbean States, Trinidad and Tobago |
| **Europe** | France | Mauritius |
| | Germany | Bulgaria, Croatia, Czech Republic, Poland, Romania, Slovak Republic, Slovenia, Ukraine |
| | Greece | Albania, Bulgaria |
| | Italy | Albania, Moldova, Sri Lanka, Tunisia |
| | Spain | Bulgaria, Colombia, Dominican Republic, Ecuador, Mauritania, Morocco, Philippines, Romania, Senegal |
| | United Kingdom | India, Philippines, Spain |
| **Asia** | China | Australia, Japan, Jordan, the Republic of Korea, Mauritius, South Africa, Spain, United Arab Emirates |
| **Africa** | South Africa | Botswana, Cuba, the Islamic Republic of Iran, Lesotho, Malawi, Mozambique, Swaziland, Tunisia |

*Source:* ILO, IOM, and OSCE (2008).

Jamaica, Mexico, Trinidad and Tobago, and the countries of the eastern Caribbean. In Europe, the governments of Germany, Italy, Spain, and the United Kingdom have negotiated BLAs with developing countries around the world. In Africa, the government of South Africa has pursued such arrangements, mainly with neighboring countries. In Asia, China has concluded BLAs with several developed- and developing-country partners.[9]

### *Terms of coverage*

The coverage of labor mobility in BLAs varies widely from agreement to agreement. The agreements entered into by Canada cover exclusively the agricultural sector. Based on bilateral memorandums of understanding, the Seasonal Agricultural Worker Program is managed by Human Resources and Skills Development Canada. Canadian employers submit requests for foreign agricultural workers for approval by Human Resources and Skills Development Canada. The approved requests are then communicated via Canadian network contacts in Mexico and to private recruitment agencies in the participating Caribbean countries. Finding the workers to fill the required demand is then the responsibility of the countries of origin. In 2000, some 7,300 Mexicans were among the 16,900 foreign farm workers admitted to Canada through the country's Seasonal Agricultural Worker Program; the other workers were from Barbados, Jamaica, Trinidad and Tobago, six other eastern Caribbean islands, and Colombia. The BLA with Colombia is the result of the demand by Canadian companies in Alberta and Manitoba for Colombian workers in the food packing industry.

The BLAs concluded by Spain provide for a committee that is composed of representatives of the participating governments and that is responsible for selecting the most highly qualified workers for existing job offers and for conducting training courses that may be needed. In these agreements regulating labor migration flows, the Spanish authorities, through Spanish embassies in origin countries, notify the authorities in the origin countries of the number and type of workers required. There is no set quota. Origin countries, in turn, notify the Spanish authorities of the possibility of meeting the demand through their nationals willing to go to Spain.

The bilateral agreement between Colombia and Spain, for example, covers agricultural workers who are selected to work temporarily in fruit harvesting in the Catalonia region. Within the framework of the temporary and circular labor migration mode implemented through this agreement, the National Training Institute in Colombia designs training programs for the labor migrants so that they can transfer the skills and expertise acquired in Catalonia upon their return to their communities of origin. Under this BLA, less than 10 percent of the selected Colombian workers fail to return home. In Ecuador, a migration and control unit was created within the Ministry of Foreign Affairs in 2002 to receive job vacancy notices from Spanish enterprises and match the job offers with the most appropriate candidates through a large database. Spain also has similar BLA programs with Bulgaria, the Dominican Republic, Mauritania, Morocco, Romania, and Senegal. Under the Spain-Philippines BLA, nurses and other Philippine workers are allowed into Spain and are afforded the same protections as Spanish workers.

The BLAs signed by the United Kingdom with India, the Philippines, and Spain enable the United Kingdom to recruit registered nurses and other health care professionals (physiotherapists, radiographers, occupational therapists, biomedical scientists, and other health care workers who are regulated by appropriate professional bodies in both countries) for work on a temporary basis. The Spain–United Kingdom agreement provides for the recognition of Spanish nursing skills in the United Kingdom.

The BLAs signed by Greece are in the area of agriculture and fisheries. With Albania and Bulgaria, the Greek authorities assess the annual need for seasonal agricultural workers and grant residence and permits to workers from these countries according to the demand by Greek employers. Under the BLA with Egypt, which covers the fisheries sector, temporary labor migrants are subject to specific regulations regarding the possibility to change employers and the extension of their stays in the country and are eligible for the transfer of social security rights and pensions on a reciprocal basis.

South Africa has negotiated several bilateral agreements with neighboring countries in response to the growing labor crisis there. Under the Joint Initiative on Priority Skills Acquisition Act of 2004, it was acknowledged that particular sectors require skills from outside the country. South African mining companies fought hard to keep their right to hire foreign contract workers, and the 2002 Immigration Act was modified to accommodate this pressure. Bilateral agreements are focused on recruiting workers from Botswana, Lesotho, Malawi, Mozambique, and Swaziland to work in the mines and farms of South Africa. The share of foreigners in the workforce of the mines rose from 47 percent in 1990 to 60 percent in 2000, but this share has declined recently in response to efforts to hire locally.

In Asia, the Chinese government has negotiated several BLAs with willing partners experiencing labor shortages, including Australia, Japan, Jordan, Korea, Mauritius, South Africa, Spain, and the United Arab Emirates. These agreements are diverse and cover a wide range of topics in labor cooperation, as well as specific numbers of recruited workers. In general, China has seen a substantial increase in the number of Chinese citizens working as temporary laborers abroad, increasing from 63,200 in 1987 to more than 500,000 in 2004.[10]

The BLAs in which China is a partner cover diverse labor sectors. With the United Arab Emirates, labor cooperation takes place in the areas of construction, factories, medical care centers, and the provision of sailors. With Australia, the BLA centers on nursing and other sectors and, by using government offices, attempts to curb the excessive fees involved in the reliance on recruitment agencies to hire migrants. In a BLA with Mauritius, Chinese workers may be recruited only from companies that are on an established, government-approved list. A BLA with Jordan concerns the textile and construction sectors. An agreement with South Africa was originated in 2002 and extended in 2006 and focuses on human resource development and job-creation strategies, as well as worker recruitment. The BLA between China and Japan represents a successful model; under this BLA, more than 30,000 Chinese trainees are now being sent to Japan every year through temporary labor (trainee) cooperation programs.[11]

There are numerous advantages of BLAs or temporary worker programs, particularly for lower-skilled categories of workers. The foremost advantage is that these agreements and programs can allow considerable flexibility in the management of the labor market by the countries involved. The agreements can be negotiated in response to the economic cycles of the market (see the discussion in Persin 2008). They can be targeted to specific sectors and be firm based if necessary (see above). The monitoring of the agreements can be carried out on both sides as a joint responsibility, thus relieving the destination country from bearing all the burden of determining whether workers have the proper authorizations. Guarantees can be designed and written into the agreements in the form of bonds or fines for noncompliance to encourage respect for the provisions of the agreements by private parties. Incentives are important in this context as well. The incentive to be able to return once again to the labor-receiving country has a high value for the workers; they will be more willing to respect labor contracts and return home if there is an opportunity (based on performance and need) to return to the host country for employment in the future. For those BLAs that have functioned well to date, most participants have found that they have satisfied the expectations of both sides of the agreements.

The disadvantage of BLAs is that, unlike RTAs, they are single-issue instruments. This limitation means that, within a BLA, developing-country partners do not have the opportunity to satisfy their need for labor mobility by meeting another type of need elsewhere in the economies of their developed-country trading partners.

## Recommendations for Promoting Labor Mobility

Our chapter examines how RTAs concluded since 1994 between developed- and developing-country trading partners have dealt with labor mobility. It shows that some of the most recent RTAs have involved innovative solutions for the promotion of labor mobility either by expanding the number of service suppliers accepted under particular categories (for example, without numerical quotas) or by creating new space for specifically defined categories of labor (such as technicians, nurses and care workers, and Chinese cultural occupations). However, nearly all RTAs that cover services focus on professional service suppliers. A new generation of BLAs is focusing more attention on the needs of unskilled and semi-skilled migrants. While the latest steps are encouraging for developing countries, they leave much work for future negotiators.

In our view, patience should be the watchword of negotiators based in developing countries. They should take heart and guidance from the long experience of developed and developing countries in crafting the liberalization of trade in textiles and clothing. This was a highly sensitive industry as early as the 1950s, when U.S. President Eisenhower's administration negotiated the first restraint agreement with Japan. Textiles and clothing remained sensitive for the next 50 years. Thus, Eisenhower's accord with Japan was followed by the Short-Term Cotton Agreement and the Long-Term Cotton Agreement in the Kennedy and Johnson administrations and then three generations of the Multifiber Arrangement under the auspices of the General Agreement on Tariffs and Trade.

The bilateral textile and clothing quotas under these agreements were complex and economically distortive. But, within this framework, over the span of five decades, textile and clothing trade grew substantially after trade liberalization. The breakthrough came when negotiators of good will representing both developed and developing countries discovered niches in the trade in textiles and clothing and identified suitable safeguard mechanisms so that the political costs of liberalization were not insurmountable. At every stage of this long process, the economic gains from liberalization were significant, and the negotiators succeeded because they targeted products and mechanisms that did not encounter overwhelming resistance in the developed countries. We think the same approach commends itself to labor mobility negotiations: a long, persistent, and patient search for niches in the labor markets of developed countries where the greater entry of migrants is not only tolerated, but also welcomed. Given this overview, we offer recommendations in the following four areas.

### *Professional workers*

If developing countries are able to define their interests well and are willing and able to pursue bilateral trade agreements with the major developed-country trading partners reviewed in this study (other than the United States at present), they should be able to obtain expanded market access. Labor markets are worth exploring to identify opportunities for independent professionals and for firms and individuals that can bring unique cultural talents or specialized skills. It is also important to uncover niches in which industrialized developed economies face labor shortages in particular geographical locations or occupations. If developing countries wish to promote exports of health service providers, this area certainly offers a large potential for expansion. For this market, it might be advisable to develop local training programs for the specific skills required in the target market in the way that the Philippines has done and Indonesia is currently doing.

### *Semiskilled and lower-skilled workers*

In the case of workers with lower skill levels and less formal educational training, the best vehicle for promoting greater labor mobility is not formal RTAs, but rather the more flexible BLA instrument. The latter programs can be designed to promote circular migration in a way that benefits the labor-sending and labor-receiving countries, as well as the workers themselves. BLAs are extremely flexible in design and execution and allow the parties involved to formulate clauses covering length of stay, the nature and place of employment, and appropriate guarantees. They also allow governments the possibility to be responsive to the cycles in domestic labor markets. Such agreements must elicit the positive involvement of parties on both sides, making this a framework with a buy-in, whereby all parties to the agreement have an interest in seeing the agreement succeed. While these agreements have been successfully promoted by only a handful of countries, primarily China and the Philippines, there is tremendous scope for their wider application in the world economy.

### *Developing-country governments and negotiators*

Developing-country governments and negotiators should bear six precepts in mind in line with our commentary about patience and niches:

- Developing-country negotiators should approach discussions on labor mobility with a positive attitude and emphasize the gains to the destination countries. The economic gains are invariably large, and the political costs are often exaggerated, but it is helpful if negotiators from developing countries can research particular labor markets and lay the facts on the table.
- To serve their negotiators more effectively, developing-country governments should conduct in-depth research on the labor markets of potential destination countries. The goal is to discover promising niches. This will require the participation of specialized officers or contractors working in the destination countries.
- Likewise, developing-country specialists should work with educational authorities and certification agencies in the developed countries to lay the groundwork for

mutual recognition agreements for the benefit of their independent professionals and other highly skilled workers.

- If multinational corporations are seeking to expand their operations abroad whether in a developed or developing country, government negotiators should team up with the multinational corporations to ensure agreement on the requisite number of visas for ICTs and CSSs to support the new operation. This needs to be done whether or not an RTA is in place.
- Developing-country negotiators should seek agreement on the status of Mode 4 workers, including their rights to visas, good working conditions, social security contributions, unemployment compensation, and the ability to remit funds. To some extent, these matters are covered in temporary worker programs, but important elements are often not addressed.
- Above all, senior officials in developing countries must be alert to the image of their migrants abroad and do whatever is possible to ensure that their migrants convey an impression of hardworking, law-abiding, respectful people. If there is adversity, as will happen, the government of the developing country should cooperate as appropriate, including by revoking visas and adopting other measures.

### *Developed-country governments and negotiators*

Like developing countries, the developed countries should proactively search for niches in labor markets in which additional temporary workers can become valued members of the workforce and the community. Developed-country officials must not surrender to the anti-immigrant voices of a vocal minority or to arguments that the labor market is an undifferentiated mass akin to the treasury bond market. They should hammer home the distinction between permanent immigration, which remains under sovereign control, and temporary workers who are subject to negotiated agreements. They should seek to build flexible responses not only through BLAs, but also through the quota and length-of-stay clauses in RTAs. Most importantly, they should seek out and convey positive messages about the contributions and accomplishments of temporary workers.

## Notes

1. However, remittances are sent by both permanent residents and temporary workers living abroad, and, at present, it is impossible to distinguish between the two. They are also sent by workers in all sectors of the economy, not only services.

2. The data in this subsection can be found in Hufbauer and Stephenson (2009).

3. See Orozco (2007, 2008) for a more extensive discussion.

4. The only exception is the FTA with Australia, in which no market access provisions for labor mobility were included in the text, but, after the conclusion of the negotiations, a side letter was added

that allowed for an annual quota of 10,500 professionals from Australia to be granted access to the U.S. market. This was done in 2002, and it proved to be the final straw in this area for some members of the U.S. Congress.

5. Sáez (2009) argues that, within the EU, issues in the trade in services do not fall exclusively under the competence of EU-wide entities because the issues go beyond articles of the treaty that accords supranational treaty-making powers to these entities on behalf of all the member states. Thus, in implementing the service provisions and obligations of a trade agreement, these elements must be approved by each EU member state in accordance with domestic laws.

6. However, several EU member states have attached economic needs testing requirements in their commitments on Mode 4 entry. The actual access provided, even under the expanded commitments, depends on how the tests are interpreted and applied.

7. A recent RTA between the members of the European Free Trade Association and Colombia, signed on November 25, 2008, does not even include an annex on professional service suppliers and contains no mention of the movement of natural persons other than their definition as Mode 4 in the body of the agreement.

8. The International Labour Organization has developed a multilateral framework on labor migration that constitutes a comprehensive collection of principles, guidelines, and good practices on labor migration programs, including BLAs. See ILO (2006).

9. A few recent memorandums of understanding on migratory and labor cooperation have been signed between developing countries, for example, between Peru and Chile (2006), Peru and Ecuador (2006), and Peru and Mexico (2002). These aim at exchanging information and protecting the rights of migrant workers, but do not include provisions to promote labor mobility. The Philippines has signed bilateral memorandums of understanding with several countries to cover the flows, rights, and obligations of its nationals who become temporary workers. A reciprocal temporary worker program has also been signed between Argentina and Bolivia that includes many of these protections.

10. Data taken from "Report on China's Export Interests in Services in Australia" (2008), a paper by Henry Gao provided to the authors.

11. Information provided by Dr. Shubin of China during a workshop in Beijing under World Bank auspices, May 21–22, 2009. The information has been confirmed by the Japan International Training Cooperation Organization.

## References

Hamilton, Bob, and John Whalley. 1984. "Efficiency and Distributional Implications of Global Restrictions on Labour Mobility: Calculations and Policy Implications." *Journal of Development Economics* 14 (1): 61–75.

Hatton, Timothy J., and Jeffrey G. Williamson. 1998. *The Age of Mass Migration: Causes and Economic Impact.* New York: Oxford University Press.

Hufbauer, G., and S. Stephenson. 2009. "Increasing Labor Mobility: Options for Developing Countries." Unpublished working paper, June 9, World Bank, Washington, DC.

ILO (International Labour Organization). 2006. *ILO Multilateral Framework on Labour Migration: Non-binding Principles and Guidelines for a Rights-Based Approach to Labour Migration.* Geneva: International Labour Office.

ILO (International Labour Organization), IOM (International Organization for Migration), and OSCE (Organization for Security and Co-operation in Europe). 2008. "Compendium of Good Practice Policy Elements in Bilateral Temporary Labour Arrangements." Revised version, December 2, Geneva, IOM.

Iregui, Ana. 1999. "Efficiency Gains from the Elimination of Global Restrictions on Labor Mobility: An Analysis Using a Multiregional CGE Model." Estudios economicos, Banco de la Republica, Bogota.

Karsenty, Guy. 2000. "Assessing Trade in Services by Mode of Supply." In *GATS 2000: New Directions in Services Trade Liberalization*, ed. Pierre Sauvé and Robert M. Stern, 33–56. Washington, DC: Brookings Institution.

Martin, Susan, and B. Lindsay Lowell. 2008. "Examining Labor Mobility Provisions for the United States." Paper presented at the Pacific Economic Cooperation Council–Asia-Pacific Economic Cooperation Business Advisory Council Conference "Demographic Change and International Labor Mobility in the Asia Pacific Region: Implications for Business and Cooperation," Seoul, March 25–26.

Orozco, Manuel. 2007. "Sending Money Home: Worldwide Remittance Flows to Developing Countries." International Fund for Agricultural Development, Rome; Inter-American Dialogue, Washington, DC. http://www.thedialogue.org/PublicationFiles/FINAL_-Sending%20Money%20Home.pdf.

———. 2008. "Remittances in Latin America and the Caribbean: Their Impact on Local Economies and the Response of Local Governments." In *Decentralization and the Challenges to Democratic Governance*, 25–43. Washington, DC: Department of State Modernization and Good Governance, Secretariat for Political Affairs, General Secretariat, Organization of American States. http://www.thedialogue.org/PublicationFiles/English%20Decentraliztion.pdf.

Persin, Daniela. 2008. "Free Movement of Labor: UK Responses to the Eastern Enlargement and GATS Mode 4." *Journal of World Trade* 42 (5): 837–64.

Sáez, Sebastián. 2009. "The EU EPA Negotiations." Presentation at the World Bank training course on services, Washington, DC, March 21.

*Region: Dynamics, Issues and a New APEC Agenda,* ed. Graeme Hugo and Soogil Young, 171–200. Singapore: Institute of Southeast Asian Studies.

Walmsley, Terrie L., and L. Alan Winters. 2003. "Relaxing the Restrictions on the Temporary Movements of Natural Persons: A Simulation Analysis." CEPR Discussion Paper 3719, Centre for Economic Policy Research, London.

World Bank. 2006. *Global Economic Prospects 2006: Economic Implications of Remittances and Migration*. Global Economic Prospects and the Developing Countries Series. Washington, DC: World Bank.

3

# LEGAL SERVICES: DOES MORE TRADE RHYME WITH BETTER JUSTICE?

*Olivier Cattaneo and Peter Walkenhorst*

## Introduction: Why Is Trade in Legal Services of Interest for Developing Countries?

An effective law and justice system is one of the key structural pillars of sustainable development and poverty reduction. The World Bank has been instrumental in promoting a number of legal reforms in developing and transition economies that have led to the establishment of fair and efficient courts and the conceptualization, drafting, enactment, publication, and enforcement of clear and coherent rules (Messick 1999, World Bank 2003). However, the trade component of law and justice reforms has received little attention. While international integration might be of minor relevance for judges, court staff, or bailiffs, trade in legal services could prove important for alleviating resource and skill bottlenecks for other legal professionals, notably lawyers, and thereby help ensure the availability and quality of legal services in developing countries.

For a long time, services—in contrast to goods—have been treated as nontradable. In particular, legal services were considered country specific and thought to be embodied in a country's legal heritage, tradition, and culture. But this view has proved obsolete. Developments in public international law have led to the adoption of a large body of common rules in areas such as investment law, trade law, and transportation law. Also, trade in legal services has surged over the past decade as a result of globalization and the ensuing movement of individuals, merchandise, and capital. Legal advisers are increasingly requested to provide their services in overseas locations as clients expand abroad. Indeed, for many transactions, international rules and regulations have become the core of the legal corpus, requiring legal expertise that goes well beyond the scope of domestic law. In this context, more open markets and greater international integration in legal services can bring new expertise and best practice knowledge to a country and help professional bodies and educational institutions adjust to the new challenges and opportunities that they and their clients face in global markets.

Opening the market for legal services can also help overcome the resistance of vested interests to changes involving new practices. Interest groups in some countries may have pushed their governments to impose regulations on the legal profession that are more restrictive than necessary to meet the legitimate objectives of quality assurance and user protection. The outcome has often been a shortage of quality services and the concentration of the profession's output in the hands of a few. This regulatory environment may therefore generate economic rents for vested interests, while not necessarily contributing to the common good. In this context, trade can help introduce greater competition, induce domestic service providers to adopt new work methods and practices, and raise the efficiency of the provision of legal services.

The employment impact of easing restrictions on market access and national treatment depends on the importance of two factors. Serving multinational firms requires a different skill set than providing services to domestic clients. Given the scarcity of sufficiently qualified staff for international legal work in host countries, newly implanted multinational firms will rely on their legal advisers at headquarters, and the result will be limited job and knowledge spillover to the host country. Alternatively, economic integration offers opportunities for domestic law firms to expand their practice areas and client base. For example, firms in developing and developed countries might engage in cooperative arrangements to handle host country, home country, third-country, and international law in parallel. Ultimately, developing-country law firms might be able to go beyond serving domestically implanted multinational firms and move into the export of legal services within the region and beyond, thereby creating high value added jobs.

In what follows, we synthesize background information on the legal profession and discuss policy initiatives that decision makers interested in developing the legal profession can undertake so as to improve regulatory conditions domestically and promote potential export markets. The next section provides an overview of the legal profession and illustrates the extent and benefits of the trade in legal services. Thereafter, we discuss initiatives to pursue a policy dialogue at the national and regional levels designed to identify trade-related issues and constraints and potential policy initiatives to build professional value and improve market access abroad. Finally, a concluding section contains a list of questions that stakeholders should bear in mind as they advance reforms.

## What Is the Current Situation and What Are the Prospects for Trade in Legal Services?

A viable legal sector is of significant economic and social importance. Access to high-quality legal services enhances the predictability of the business environment, facilitates engagement in contracts, and mitigates investment risk. Firms throughout the economy use legal services to assess commercial interests, activities, and investments. Hence, a robust and disciplined legal service profession facilitates commerce, trade, and investment by lowering the costs of commercial transactions.

In 2006, the legal service sector employed an estimated 2.3 million professionals and generated worldwide revenue of about US$434 billion. These turnover figures exceeded the revenues generated by the textile industry, for example. The legal profession is an increasingly globalized industry that has been experiencing robust growth (box 3.1). It has become, to some extent, based on international trade and investment flows.

The world's largest law firm, Baker & McKenzie, employs 3,900 lawyers in 38 countries. Such large-scale firms are the exception, though, and the market

**Box 3.1:** Some Key Facts about Legal Services

*Revenue*

- The global revenue of the profession was estimated at US$434 billion in 2006 and, at an average 6.7 percent annual increase thereafter, should reach US$600 billion by 2011.
- The top 10 firms in terms of earnings generated US$16 billion in gross revenues in 2007, a rise of 13 percent over the year.

*Employment*

- The number of legal professionals worldwide was estimated at 2.3 million in 2006, an increase of 3 percent over the year.
- The top 10 firms employ more than 23,000 lawyers; the top 100 firms employ about 100,000 lawyers.

*Corporate headquarters*

- Among the top 100 firms, 69 are U.S. firms; 17 are British; 6 are Australian; 4 are Canadian; 2 are Spanish; 1 is Dutch; and 1 is French.

*Foreign presence*

- The top 10 firms all have offices in more than 10 countries. The average top 10 firm has offices in 21 countries, and 52 percent of its lawyers are employed outside the home country. The average top 100 firm has offices in 7 countries, and 17 percent of its lawyers are employed outside the home country.
- Of the top 100 firms, 21 have offices in more than 10 countries.

*Sources:* Lloyd (2008), Datamonitor (2007).

for legal services remains mostly segmented. The majority of legal services are provided by small law firms that primarily deal with domestic law. The world's top 10 law firms represent some 4 percent and 1 percent, respectively, of the profession's output and employment. This contrasts with the accounting sector, for example, in which there is significant horizontal integration and in which the big four (Deloitte Touche Tomatsu, Ernst & Young, KPMG, and PricewaterhouseCoopers) represent more than three-quarters of the profession's revenues in many countries.

A closer analysis of employment in major law firms reveals that the ratio of staff (including lawyers) to partners is about 10 to 1, and the majority of the staff is located in offices abroad. While the majority of offices are in the countries of the Organisation for Economic Co-operation and Development, a number of locations in transition and developing countries emerge as regional hubs for global service providers. Establishment is essentially driven by investment and trade flows: law firms will only establish an office where the local client base is sufficiently developed or where major economic reforms, such as large-scale privatization programs, are under way (box 3.2).

**Box 3.2:** Growth and Investment Have Created a Viable Market for Legal Services in Developing Countries

Legal practices in developing countries have grown as a result of market reforms. In South Asia, practicing attorneys have found professional opportunities as in-house counsel in restructured banks that have undergone privatization. The expansion in the banking sector has provided many new career opportunities for lawyers (Bokhari 2008). Similarly, in Saudi Arabia, the expansion of the private sector in infrastructure projects and other sectors of the economy has increased the opportunities for law firms (Haberbeck 2007). Moreover, corporate activity in South Africa has attracted lawyers to the practice of mergers and acquisitions, and the expansion of the private sector and economic growth present commercial opportunities for law firms in the region.

Foreign direct investment has also widened the opportunities for practitioners. Recent investment by Chinese, European, and Indian firms in Africa has increased the legal service market in the area of project finance. North Africa and Sub-Saharan Africa have experienced growth in power plants and infrastructure development, as well as in oil and gas works, thereby attracting law practitioners in these fields. As a consequence, the international law firm of Denton Wilde Sapte, for example, collaborates with firms in Botswana, Ghana, Mauritius, Tanzania, Uganda, and Zambia to deliver advisory services in project financing.

Firms from developing countries can specialize to preserve or gain market share. For example, with economic expansion in Islamic states, law firms have responded to consumer demand for financial products compliant with Sharia law. They have deepened their knowledge of Sharia law requirements and now advise financial institutions on Sharia-compliant insurance products, investment banking operations, and publicly issued convertible bonds, or *Sukuk* (Tait 2006). Hence, economic growth has helped expand and develop a broader scope for legal advisory services.

The global market for legal services is evolving rapidly with the growth of manufacturing and services among multinational firms and the correspondingly changing client needs. Size matters. The bigger the client, the more diversified its needs, and the broader the legal expertise to be provided. This trend is at the origin of the concept of the global law firm that is capable of servicing its clients across countries, time zones, cultures, and the spectrum of legal needs, from mergers and acquisitions to labor, environmental, tax, and real estate law.

## Trade in Legal Services Occurs through Several Channels

Trade in legal services is generally closely tied to trade in goods and the movement of persons and capital. A company will rarely seek advice from a law firm based abroad unless the company is well established or does significant business with the home country of the law firm. Similarly, most law firms will establish abroad only to accompany a major client involved in an export business.

Trade generally accounts only for a small part of the legal profession's overall output, but can nonetheless play a major role in shaping the development of the profession. For example, when U.S. law firms established offices in Europe, they brought a fundamentally different business model with them. In particular, their practice of billing services by the hour increased the transparency of service provision relative to the established practice of giving clients broad estimates. The larger scale of the U.S. firms made it possible to offer shorter turnaround times on individual cases. These practices were subsequently taken up by European law firms to the benefit of clients.

Trade takes place when a service, a service provider, or a service consumer crosses a border. Trade can take place through courier, telecommunications (phone, fax, videoconference), or electronic means (e-mail), establishment (offices abroad), and the movement of the service provider or service consumer (box 3.3).

Not all legal activities are equally tradable across all modes. Some branches of law, such as administrative or penal law, are domestic in nature and generally require a permanent presence. Others, such as commercial, taxation, and dispute settlement law, are more easily amenable to temporary provision and crossborder transactions.

The intangible nature of legal services makes it difficult to measure the volume and value of the service trade in general and the legal service trade in particular. One problem is that a substantial share of legal service trade occurs among affiliates of multinational companies and might not be recorded properly. Moreover, balance of

**Box 3.3:** The Four Modes of Supply for Legal Services

The General Agreement on Trade in Services (GATS) of the World Trade Organization defines four modes of supply in the trade in services. The modes of supply have been identified to help trade negotiators determine trade commitments in trade agreements. Essentially, the modes are a construct for trade negotiations and are meant to reflect how businesses operate. Most firms use a combination of some or all the modes of supply to conduct business. The modes focus on the location of the service provider and the location of the service consumer. They are defined in the GATS as follows:

Mode 1: Crossborder supply, whereby nonresident service suppliers supply services across the border in a client's territory; for example, a Tunisian firm e-mails a memo to a client operating in Algeria.

Mode 1 trade may be inhibited, for instance, by restrictions on Internet use and weak telecommunications infrastructure.

Mode 2: Consumption abroad, whereby a country's residents purchase services in the territory of another country; for example, a Tunisian firm represents an Algerian client in a Tunisian court.

Mode 2 trade may be inhibited, for instance, by excessively restrictive capital controls.

Mode 3: Commercial presence, whereby foreign service suppliers establish, operate, or expand a commercial presence in a client's territory, such as a branch, agency, or wholly owned subsidiary; for example, a Tunisian law firm establishes a front office in Algeria.

Mode 3 trade may be inhibited, for instance, by arduous qualification requirements and licensing procedures and by equity limitations.

Mode 4: Movement of natural persons, whereby foreign individuals enter and temporarily stay in a client's territory to supply a service; for example, a Tunisian lawyer visits a client in Algeria to prepare an acquisition.

Mode 4 trade may be inhibited, for instance, by excessively restrictive visa fees or unpredictable and time-consuming work permit procedures.

Analysts and policy makers can use the modes of supply to identify constraints on the growth in trade. This can then inform policy decisions designed to expand the legal service trade and promote exports.

payments statistics do not always contain detailed data that disaggregate beyond broader categories such as professional services or business services or explicitly list legal services. The available data on the trade in legal services are therefore often based on estimates, which should be treated with care.

Despite the frequent paucity of detailed data on trade in legal services, the available information suggests that trade takes place and accounts for substantial flows in several developing countries, such as Brazil or India (table 3.1). Moreover, there is quantitative information for some countries on the relative importance of

**Table 3.1.** Trade in Legal Services, 2007
*US$, millions*

| Economy | Exports | Imports | Economy | Exports | Imports |
|---|---|---|---|---|---|
| Albania | 0.2 | 0.0 | India[c] | 758.3 | −126.0 |
| Anguilla | 4.9 | — | Italy | 378.5 | −412.9 |
| Argentina | 749.5 | −223.3 | Jamaica | 0.1 | −9.2 |
| Armenia | 2.8 | −3.8 | Kazakhstan | 49.2 | −21.1 |
| Australia[a] | 134.5 | −64.2 | Korea, Rep. | 572.3 | −696.7 |
| Austria | 229.2 | −260.4 | Latvia | 10.2 | −10.7 |
| Azerbaijan | 1.6 | −6.2 | Lithuania | 3.2 | −5.7 |
| Bangladesh | 3.3 | −1.1 | Madagascar[b] | 0.1 | 0.0 |
| Belarus[b] | 2.0 | −3.5 | Montserrat | 0.5 | — |
| Belize | — | −0.8 | Mozambique | — | −1.6 |
| Brazil | 1,868.2 | −421.3 | Netherlands Antilles | 53.5 | −13.5 |
| Bulgaria | 49.7 | −18.3 | Norway | 177.2 | −112.1 |
| Côte d'Ivoire[c] | — | −51.6 | Pakistan | 8.0 | −39.0 |
| Cyprus | 418.6 | −60.4 | Panama | 127.3 | −16.2 |
| Czech Republic | 54.7 | −26.4 | Paraguay[f] | 0.1 | −0.8 |
| Dominica | 0.1 | n.a. | Portugal | 203.3 | −42.3 |
| Estonia | 23.6 | −5.7 | Romania | 127.0 | −44.0 |
| Ethiopia | 16.8 | −2.6 | Russian Federation | 296.6 | −345.1 |
| Fiji[c] | 5.7 | −14.1 | Slovak Republic | 74.1 | −69.3 |
| Finland | 62.4 | −137.7 | St. Kitts and Nevis | 7.3 | 0.0 |
| Georgia | 0.1 | −0.9 | St. Vincent and the Grenadines | 11.9 | — |
| Grenada[d] | 0.0 | 0.0 | | | |
| Guatemala[e] | 2.9 | −0.3 | Sweden | 449.1 | −406.7 |
| Guinea | 0.7 | −3.6 | Tonga | 0.1 | −0.1 |
| Hungary | 116.0 | −41.6 | Turkey | — | −52.0 |

*Source:* International Monetary Fund balance of payments statistics, http://www.imf.org/external/np/sta/bop/bop.htm.
*Note:* — = not available.
a. 1997.
b. 2005.
c. 2006.
d. 2004.
e. 2003.
f. 2002.

the different modes of legal service trade (table 3.2). However, even if quantitative evidence is lacking, qualitative information on legal trade flows, such as the number of offices established abroad by major law firms (GATS Mode 3), the number of business visas attributed to lawyers (GATS Mode 4), and the list of

**Table 3.2.** Importance of Trade under the Different Modes of Legal Service Supply

| Mode of supply | United Kingdom | United States |
|---|---|---|
| Mode 1: Crossborder supply | US$3.2 billion (2003) | US$3.4 billion (2003) |
| Mode 2: Consumption abroad | — | — |
| Mode 3: Commercial presence | 484 branches of solicitors firms established abroad (2003) | US$958 million (2002); top 71 law firms with 343 offices abroad (2000) |
| Mode 4: Movement of natural persons | 881 work permit requests to U.S. lawyers alone (2000) | 775 work permits issued to lawyers (2000) |

*Source:* Hook (2007).
*Note:* — = not available.

foreign clients or operations abroad posted on the Web sites of law firms (all modes), can often be found. Table 3.3 provides an example of such evidence collected for Morocco; it reveals the importance of foreign presence, the significant workload associated with the provision of services to foreign companies, the diversity of partnerships and trade models, and the wide array of specialization among firms.

While most developing-country trade in legal services occurs with partners in developed countries, there are also examples of South-South transactions. In the Middle East and North Africa Region, a number of mutual recognition agreements among national or regional bar associations facilitate trade in legal services between, for example, the Algiers and the Tunis bars. Other examples of South-South trade in legal services include the opening of offices by the Pakistani firm Zafar & Mandviwalla Law Associates in Afghanistan and by the Pakistani firm Rizvi Isa Afridi & Angell in China and the United Arab Emirates. Pakistani firms also visit clients in the Middle East and the United Kingdom to provide legal advice (Saeed, Qureshi, and Hussain 2005).

Another avenue of South-South trade operates through the work of paralegals. These assistants undertake a large part of the background analysis for criminal and commercial law cases, and trainers of paralegal advisers have crossed borders to provide their services. In Malawi, for example, the Paralegal Advisory Service offers paralegal aid in criminal law matters. Four nongovernmental organizations work in partnership with the Malawi Prison Service, the Malawi Police Service, and the courts to offer legal education on the front lines of criminal justice. This area agreement has been in force since May 2000 and involves 38 trained paralegals. The Paralegal Advisory Service is in the process of being transformed into

**Table 3.3.** Trade in Legal Services: The Example of Morocco

| | Main site | Staff | Main fields of practice | Illustrative list of clients |
|---|---|---|---|---|
| **Foreign law firms established in Morocco and local law firms with a significant international presence** | | | | |
| **Bennani & Associés LLP** | Morocco | 10 | Corporate and M&A, dispute resolution and litigation, arbitration | Microsoft, Wafasalaf, CNIA, Axa, BMCI |
| **CMS Bureau Francis Lefebvre** | France | 10 | Corporate and M&A, projects and public law, tourism | Bouygues, Akzo Nobel, Lacoste |
| **El Andaloussi** | Morocco | | Dispute resolution and litigation, arbitration | – |
| **Ernst & Young–Associated Advisers** | Morocco (Global) | | corporate and M&A, projects and public law | – |
| **Gide Loyrette Nouel–Naciri et Associés** | France-Morocco | 25 | Corporate and M&A, banking finance and capital markets, dispute resolution and litigation, arbitration, projects and public law, tourism | SAHAM, Akwa Group, Meditelcom |
| **Guarrigues Maroc Sarl** | Spain-Morocco | | Corporate and M&A | – |
| **Hajji et Associés** | Morocco | 9 | Corporate and M&A, banking finance and capital markets, dispute resolution and litigation, arbitration, projects and public law | Lenovo, JP Morgan, Hutchinson Port |
| **Kettani Law Firm** | Morocco | 20 | Corporate and M&A, banking finance and capital markets, dispute resolution and litigation, arbitration, projects and public law | BNP Paribas, Merrill Lynch, Roche SA |

(*Table continues on the following page.*)

**Table 3.3.** Trade in Legal Services: The Example of Morocco (*continued*)

| | Main site | Staff | Main fields of practice | Illustrative list of clients |
|---|---|---|---|---|
| **Foreign law firms established in Morocco and local law firms with a significant international presence** | | | | |
| **Laraqui Fassi Fihri & Kettani** | Morocco | 20 | Dispute resolution and litigation, arbitration | — |
| **Mehdi Salmouni-Zerhouni** | Morocco | 10 | Intellectual property | Bic, Moulinex |
| **Mernissi–FIGES** | Morocco | 3 | Corporate and M&A, dispute resolution and litigation, arbitration, projects and public law | CMS, ONEP, Veolia |
| **PricewaterhouseCoopers** | Morocco (Global) | | Corporate and M&A | — |
| **SFM** | Morocco | | Corporate and M&A | Royale Marocaine d'Assurance, BMCI |
| **UGGC et Associés** | France | 7 | Corporate and M&A, dispute resolution and litigation, arbitration, projects and public law, tourism | Afric Invest, BEI/Club Med |
| **Foreign law firms not established in Morocco, but doing significant business in the country** | | | | |
| **Clifford Chance** | Global | 191 | Projects and finance | Maroc Telecom, IFC/Meditel, |
| **Freshfields Bruckhaus Deringer** | Global | 243 | Projects and finance | Tangier Mediterranean Special Agency, Holmarcom |
| **Norton Rose** | Global | 75 | Corporate and M&A | ONA |
| **Orrick, Herrington & Sutcliffe** | Global | 90 | Corporate and M&A | Vivendi Universal, Altadis |

*Source:* Legal 500 "Morocco" (2006), http://www.legal500.com/c/morocco.
*Note:* Main fields of practice are the fields in which the firm appears among the recommended law firms in the Legal 500 directory. M&A = mergers and acquisitions.
— = not available.

the Paralegal Advisory Service Institute and is expected to continue to implement the program in Malawi and offer services in countries as far afield as Bangladesh.

## Cooperative Arrangements Are Prevalent Vehicles for Integration

If small local law firms are to benefit from legal service exports, they will often have to specialize in a particular area of law and work closely with domestic or international partners to provide the scope of services that large-scale clients demand. Also, cooperation with foreign partners can be seen as a second-best solution in circumventing barriers to establishment, mobility, and practice in a partner country.

Indeed, trade in legal services is frequently undertaken through various forms of cooperation between law firms of different national origins. Because of the greater access to new information and communication technologies, who in the legal partnership network actually delivers legal services will depend on the practice area, the law firm, the client, the jurisdictions involved, and the respective regulatory frameworks. Depending on the particular regulatory environment and the client needs, cooperation arrangements among global and local law firms may take the form of the following:

- integrated international partnerships
- associations of independent local practices
- local firms hiring foreign practitioners
- international firms hiring local lawyers
- international firms establishing partnerships with local lawyers
- contractual outsourcing arrangements
- practitioners serving as foreign legal consultants (box 3.4)

Reductions in costs and improvements in the performance of information and communications technology have facilitated collaboration between law firms and business relations between law firms and clients in different countries. Law firms are leveraging networked practices to broaden and deepen their area of expertise. This type of partnership can be particularly useful for small and medium law firms in competing for business with large, multinational clients. For example, practitioners from more than 60 countries, including Algeria, Ecuador, Morocco, Nigeria, Pakistan, Papua New Guinea, Thailand, Ukraine, and Vietnam, participate in the online International Lawyers Network (http://www.iln.com/) to engage clients electronically on matters of commercial law, litigation, and contracting. Also, the Lex Africa law community provides a network of law firms in 27 African countries that specialize in corporate and commercial law. Networked

**Box 3.4:** Using Foreign Legal Consultants to Facilitate Trade

The category of foreign legal consultants represents a common means of allowing foreign lawyers to operate in a market as advisers on a restricted basis. Frequently, these consultants are prohibited from practicing host country law, but may practice home country, third-country, or international law with the appropriate qualifications and licensure (WTO 1998). Foreign legal consultants may also work on providing legal documentation and certification services and other advisory and information services.

Jordan, Oman, and Saudi Arabia offer examples. Jordan allows foreign practitioners to advise on third-country law even though only Jordanian nationals can represent clients in Jordanian courts (WTO 2000a). Similarly, Saudi Arabia allows foreign practitioners to advise on third-country law and international law, but reserves host country law to nationals. Only Saudi nationals may appear in court to plead cases (WTO 2005). Oman allows foreign practitioners to advise only on home country law, third-country law, and international law (WTO 2000b). Representation is reserved to Omani nationals. Thus, foreign law professionals interested in working in Jordan, Oman, or Saudi Arabia would be allowed to provide advisory services in select areas. However, they would not be allowed to appear in court in any of the countries. In addition, they would have to adhere to each country's licensing requirements and national rules.

Countries may use the category of foreign legal consultant to facilitate the practice of home country, third-country, and international law. Practitioners who are in good standing, have adequate qualifications, and are expert in home country, third-country, or international law are frequently allowed to practice under this limited designation. For example, Morocco permits the activity of foreign legal consultants, while limiting representation in court and specialized legal services to nationals (World Bank 2007). In Tunisia, in contrast, while the use of the foreign legal consultant title is tolerated, the absence of a legal framework exposes established foreign law firms to uncertainty.

practices provide education to members, assist in the management of law practices, and facilitate crossborder referrals (ABA 2002).

## Legal Process Outsourcing Offers New Export Opportunities

Establishing an online presence and partnering with other law firms can be effective ways of reaching foreign clients. However, the Internet is helping law firms to partner, market, and deliver their services, and it has become a prominent tool among clients seeking to procure legal services. Online case matching is being used, for example, to post legal needs and request bid proposals from law firms.

Moreover, business process innovation enables the unbundling of legal services and the consequent outsourcing and offshoring of discrete legal service activities. Law firms are increasingly specializing and offering distinct products such as electronic discovery, document preparation, and negotiation. Legal process outsourcing, that is, the crossborder supply of fragments of the legal service value chain, is currently still a relatively small business. The outsourcing and offshoring of legal services started with standardized administrative tasks, such as document editing and proofreading. Over time, they have moved toward more skill-intensive work, such as litigation research and intellectual property cases involving patent research and analysis and the drafting of patent applications. Analysts expect this trend to continue and legal process outsourcing to become a significant export industry in coming years. Low-income countries that can offer a combination of reliable information and communication technology infrastructure and language-proficient human capital with the required legal expertise will have the occasion to tap into these business opportunities.

Forrester Research forecasts that the market for outsourced legal services in India will expand from US$80 million in 2005 to US$4 billion in 2015 (Jaksic 2007). However, the export growth of legal services is not limited to the outsourcing powerhouse, India. Countries as diverse as Argentina, Brazil, Panama, and the Russian Federation have seen dynamic growth in legal service exports in the recent past (figure 3.1). Moreover, U.K. law firms are, for example, outsourcing patent prosecution work to lawyers in South Africa, where the legal education is rigorous, but wage costs are comparatively low (Wesemann 2007).

**Figure 3.1.** Exports of Legal Services from Selected Countries, 2001–07

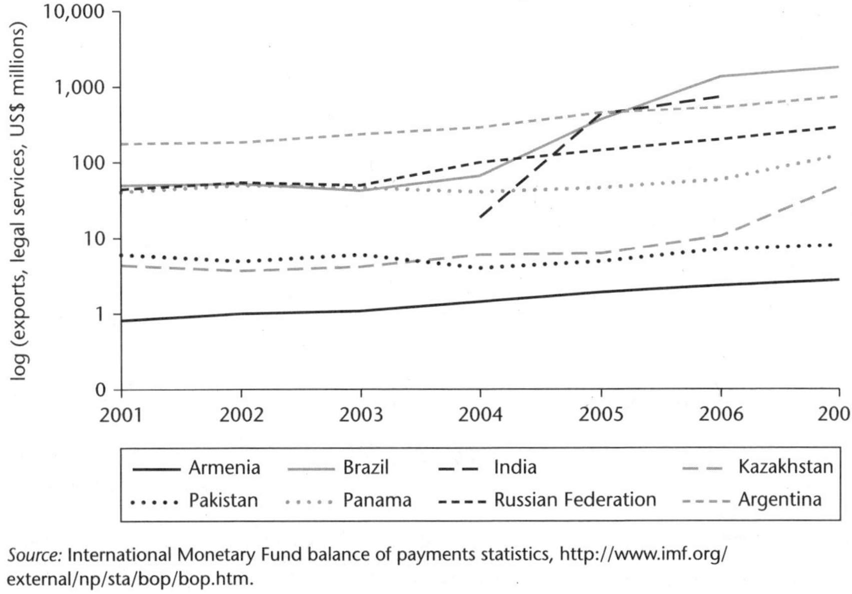


*Source:* International Monetary Fund balance of payments statistics, http://www.imf.org/external/np/sta/bop/bop.htm.

**Table 3.4.** Examples of Offshorable Legal Services

| Litigation support | Contract support | Patent support | Investment support | Business development |
|---|---|---|---|---|
| Document review<br>Writing of briefs<br>Writing of motions<br>Collecting and processing of digital evidence | Drafting of contracts<br>Administration<br>Monitoring<br>Auditing | Research<br>Analysis<br>Prosecution support | Market research<br>Regulatory research<br>Environmental compliance<br>Tax research and compliance | Research on current and potential clients |

*Source:* Perla (2006).

While *back-office* functions have been outsourced in the past to domestic and international suppliers, large law firms are increasingly seeking to realize the cost savings associated with handling *front-office* functions in low-cost environments. Table 3.4 presents examples of front-office functions that have the potential to be successfully offshored and that might therefore provide future export opportunities for service providers in developing countries.

## What Can Be Done to Harness Trade Opportunities?

Countries have much to gain from opening their domestic legal markets to foreign service providers and from seeking reciprocal access to the markets of their trading partners. While regulation of the legal profession to ensure consumer protection against deceitful practices is desirable, regulation should not be more restrictive than necessary and should avoid discriminating among domestic and foreign service providers. Unfortunately, the regulatory process, which often involves self-regulation through the legal profession itself, may be hijacked by special interest groups favoring protectionism at the expense of consumer welfare and access to justice generally (box 3.5). In this context, a periodic review of the regulatory framework designed to establish pro-competitive practices is often desirable.

### Reviewing Domestic Regulations to Highlight Reform Needs

The regulation of legal services has developed as an integral part of national judicial systems. Rules reflect distinct legal tradition and heritage and may be designed

**Box 3.5:** Self-Regulation Often Results in Cartelization of the Legal Profession

It is particularly challenging for policy makers to engage professional bodies effectively in reform. Professional associations often resist increased competition. Indeed, a weak or excessively protectionist professional body may delay the evolution of the legal profession.

There is evidence that the self-regulation of legal services does not work well and that deregulation can have substantial benefits. For example, after the 180-year monopoly of the legal profession in the United Kingdom ended in 1983 in the provision of the services required to buy or sell real estate, the average price for conveying services dropped by 10 percent over the following three years, despite an increase in the value of the underlying housing transactions (World Bank 2004). Moreover, consumers buying or selling real estate after demonopolization have reported the same or greater satisfaction with the services.

Cartelization of legal services with the associated adverse impacts on pricing and service quality is an even bigger problem in developing countries, in which press and public oversight is generally weaker than it is in the countries of the Organisation for Economic Co-operation and Development. In this context, policy makers can try to facilitate discussions between professional bodies and legal service users to help identify commercial needs that domestic law firms can strive to meet. Exposing professional bodies to successful counterparts is another practical means of helping such entities adopt international best practices. The efficiency and credibility of these approaches to bring down prices and ensure access to high-quality legal services will be enhanced if the initiatives are complemented by an opening up of parts of the domestic legal market to international competition and by anchoring reforms in international agreements with partner countries.

to achieve a broad set of public policy objectives. For example, qualification and licensing requirements are designed to protect consumers from substandard legal advice. But the same rules also have an influence on market access and national treatment and, hence, determine a country's ability to participate in the trade in legal services.

In many countries, legal services are subject to a combination of regulations and restrictions. Prevalent measures concern nationality and residency requirements; restrictions on incorporation, partnerships, and multidisciplinary practices; qualification requirements; the reservation of certain activities for local firms or lawyers only; and restrictions on fee setting and advertising. Indeed, in a survey of restrictions on trade in professional services, Nguyen-Hong (2000) has found that legal services (together with accounting) were the most highly regulated sectors in terms of measures related to establishing a presence and measures pertaining to continuing operations. Similarly, analysis by Paterson, Fink, and Ogus (2003) on regulation of the legal profession in European Union countries suggests a more rigid environment than, for example, in the technical professions, at least with respect to conduct regulations. Concerning market entry and educational requirements, these authors have found that the situation differed substantially across the European Union.

It is good practice for governments to review the domestic regulatory framework on a periodic basis to ensure that it corresponds to the evolving needs of service providers, clients, and the economy generally. For best results, the review should not only include government entities involved in regulating the legal profession, but also service users, professional bodies, law firms, and academic experts. Such a national services dialogue can help determine if changes in the regulation of legal services are needed to accommodate international developments, to strengthen the profession, and to promote exports.

A regulatory structure that ensures high standards for the legal profession can contribute to the growth and development of the profession. In some cases, improving the regulatory framework may require closing a regulatory gap in the sense that some countries may only have a nascent regulatory structure for the legal profession and face the challenge of designing appropriate regulatory environments. For example, qualification requirements may not be ambitious enough to ensure that legal practitioners have the required expertise to function effectively in an international setting (World Bank 2008). In this case, the government and professional bodies should upgrade their education and training efforts, possibly in cooperation with neighboring countries (box 3.6).

To prepare for or enhance international integration, regulatory entities should regularly review domestic regulations to ensure they are crafted to achieve their objectives effectively (for example, consumer protection, availability of adequate legal services) in a least trade restrictive manner. There are many ways in which regulations can impede the trade in legal services and discriminate against foreign service providers (see table 3.5 for examples), and trade facilitating measures, such as limited licensing systems for foreign legal consultants and mutual recognition agreements, are worth exploring.

**Box 3.6:** Professional Bodies Play a Prominent Role in Legal Skill Development

Professional bodies can serve an important role as supporters of professional preparation and development. They frequently set the standards for qualification and licensing requirements, interact with law schools to ensure that curricula reflect the current demand of the legal profession, offer access to continuing education, and facilitate the exchange of ideas on issues of importance to the profession. They also set and enforce standards of professional practice and ethics. In addition, professional bodies often represent the interests of the profession in dealings with the government. They manage relationships with foreign and international counterparts and are involved in the negotiation of mutual recognition agreements.

**Table 3.5.** Frequently Encountered Restrictions on Legal Practice by Foreigners

| Type of measure | Generic examples of restrictions | Case example of Tunisia |
|---|---|---|
| Form of establishment | • Prohibition of incorporation<br>• Only some forms of incorporation permitted | Société d'avocats or individual practice |
| Foreign partnership, association, or joint venture | • Prohibition on partnership with foreign professionals<br>• Partnership or joint venture with local professionals required | Prohibited, except for legal counsel |
| Investment and ownership by foreign professionals | • Firms to be owned or controlled by local professionals<br>• Maximum foreign equity participation permitted | Prohibited, except for legal counsel |
| Investment and ownership by nonprofessional investors | • Firms to be owned or controlled by professionals<br>• Maximum equity participation permitted | Prohibited, except for legal counsel |
| Nationality/ citizenship requirements | • Nationality required to qualify or to practice<br>• Nationality required for use of professional title | Practitioner to be Tunisian for at least five years |
| Residency and local presence | • Permanent or prior residency required<br>• Prior residency required for local training<br>• Domicile or representative office only | Practitioner to be a resident |
| Quotas/economic needs tests on the number of professionals and firms | • Quotas or economic needs tests apply | Quotas/economic needs tests for some professions, for example, notaries |
| Licensing and accreditation of foreign professionals | • Local retraining required for full practice<br>• Local examination required in all cases<br>• Case-by-case assessment of foreign license and aptitude tests | Recognition of foreign diplomas possible |
| Movement of people | • No entry of executives, senior managers, or specialists<br>• Burdensome and slow visa procedures | General conditions for visas, some bilateral reciprocity agreements |
| Activities reserved by law to nationals | • Core activities such as pleading in courts permitted only for national professionals | Some activities reserved, for example, notary acts, pleading in courts |
| Multidisciplinary practices | • Prohibition on partnership or association with other professions<br>• Majority partnership required | Multidisciplinary practices prohibited, some exceptions |
| Advertising, marketing, and solicitation | • Prohibition of advertising, marketing, and solicitation<br>• Restrictions apply to some groups or activities | Advertising, marketing, and solicitation prohibited |

(*Table continues on the following page.*)

**Table 3.5.** Frequently Encountered Restrictions on Legal Practice by Foreigners (*continued*)

| Type of measure | Generic examples of restrictions | Case example of Tunisia |
|---|---|---|
| Fee setting | • Minimum and maximum fees for all or some groups and activities in the profession | Fee setting for some activities, for example, notaries |
| Other restrictions | • Restrictions on the use of firm's international names<br>• Restrictions on repatriation of benefits (exchange and capital control)<br>• Double taxation | None |

*Source:* Author compilation.
*Note:* The table is not exhaustive. It gives an idea of the potential regulatory obstacles to trade. The table also does not address the adequacy of domestic regulations. Some are fully justified to ensure the quality of the service, and some might be more restrictive than necessary to achieve this end.

The review can help determine the usefulness and impact of the regulatory framework and identify the following:

- the objectives of specific rules
- when the rule was enacted
- when the rule was last invoked
- when the rule was last reviewed
- if the rule is consistent with current government policy
- if the objectives of the rules are being achieved

If the review suggests that some regulations should be reviewed, two characteristics of legal services make it likely that a liberalization and market opening will be smoother than is the case in many other sectors (Geloso Grosso 2004). First, most trade in legal services occurs among firms and not between firms and consumers; thus, there are few specific risks of adverse impacts on consumers. Second, the impact of the liberalization of domestic service suppliers is also likely to be less pronounced because they retain a competitive advantage in the practice of domestic law.

The character of legal services continues to evolve, and, even in sophisticated economies, policy makers regularly have to review, adapt, and improve rules. For example, in the United Kingdom, the 2007 Legal Services Act introduced major regulatory changes that are intended to bring greater competition and oversight into the practice of law. Notably, it is enabling multidisciplinary practices, allowing foreign investors to hold equity positions in partnerships, creating an external independent regulatory body with nonlawyer representation, and establishing an office for consumer complaints and review (Peel 2007).

Similarly, in 2005, Japan undertook reforms of its legal service market to increase productivity in the economy. It lifted a number of restrictions to enhance the functioning of the legal system, increase the availability of legal services, and improve the handling of business matters. The business community acted as a catalyst for this change, arguing that enhanced cooperation between Japanese and foreign lawyers would provide better legal services (Goodwin 2005). In particular, business representatives urged the government to lift market-access restrictions, raise standards of due diligence for commercial transactions, increase confidence in commercial contracts to attract investment, and increase the availability of cross-jurisdictional advice. As a result of the reforms, foreign firms can establish joint offices with Japanese attorneys to offer legal services. Foreign firms can also employ Japanese lawyers and offer a broader range of expertise. Japanese practitioners have therefore gained greater exposure to new business and new practice areas.

## Enhancing the Skill Base to Strengthen Domestic Law Firms

Labor costs represent as much as 75 percent of the expenditures of law firms, reflecting a concentration of value in the expertise of professional staff (table 3.6). Hence, recruiting, nurturing, and retaining highly qualified staff are key to the competitiveness of law firms. At the same time, lawyers in firms have to be mindful of their service delivery costs because clients are becoming more and more sophisticated in comparing and evaluating the cost-effectiveness of the legal services they receive (box 3.7).

**Table 3.6.** Typical Cost Structure of a Law Firm

| Labor and benefits | Technology | Other services | Overhead |
|---|---|---|---|
| 70% to 75% | 25% to 30% | | |
| Partners<br>Associates<br>Financial, operating, and information officers<br>Support staff | Computer infrastructure<br>Phone, fax, personal digital assistants<br>Copiers, printers, scanners | Communications<br>Utilities<br>IT support<br>Business and financial services | Office space<br>Travel<br>Marketing and client entertainment<br>Cost of capital |

*Source:* Cotterman (2003).
*Note:* IT = information technology.

**Box 3.7:** Cost Pressures Force Clients to Rethink Their Approach to Legal Services

In a more global competitive market, law firms are encountering greater cost pressure from their clients. Consumers of legal services such as governments, corporations, and individuals are increasingly scrutinizing how law firms price their services and deliver results. Some clients are using competitive procurement processes to secure economically priced legal services. Others use software to audit their legal services bills or establish in-house counsels familiar with the business to control legal expenses (Tucker 2008).

Law firms are responding to this client demand for more cost-effective offers by making internal changes to lower their costs. Some may adjust their billing structures to include fixed fee rates for routine services, capped fees to prevent cost overruns, and discounted rates for large volumes of work (Murphy 2008). Others employ technology to work more efficiently and unbundle services to offer specialized products. But an increasing number of firms also move work overseas, including to developing countries, to improve their cost position relative to competitors.

The prominent share of expenses for labor compensation gives developing countries, with their lower wage levels, a major advantage over competitors in developed countries as long as the qualifications of domestic lawyers match international standards. There are several avenues for law firms to strengthen their skill base: (1) improving professional education over the long run, (2) providing supplemental education to practitioners in the medium term, or (3) quickly hiring missing talent from competitors in the domestic or overseas markets.

Raising educational standards will help build value in the profession over time. Policy makers and professional associations can work with colleges of law to raise standards to an internationally competitive level. Jordan, for example, is undertaking a process of assessing educational outcomes in the profession, benchmarking them against standards designed by international accreditation bodies, and reworking curricula to ensure that degrees are internationally recognized. More generally, consultations with the local colleges of law can determine the status of accreditation of these colleges, as well as benchmarking indicators related to curriculum and teaching practices (for example, professor-to-student ratios), which can then be compared with those of other colleges of law in the region and farther afield. If standards are found to be comparable with those in export markets of interest, policy makers might want to try to negotiate a mutual recognition agreement in order to facilitate market access (box 3.8). On the other hand, if marked knowledge gaps exist in particular areas, student exchanges between local and foreign law schools or distance learning partnerships can be a cost-effective means to expand the educational offerings to local students.

**Box 3.8:** Negotiating Mutual Recognition Agreements Can Facilitate Trade in Legal Services

Achieving mutual recognition of qualification requirements can be a practical means of facilitating the trade in legal services. Neighboring and regional markets may not recognize the qualifications of legal professionals from a domestic market. On a bilateral and regional basis, professional bodies and government entities regulating the law profession can be brought together to promote the mutual recognition of credentials.

Qualification requirements vary substantially from market to market; they may include the following (WTO 2001):

- University degrees from accredited institutions
- Postgraduate education from accredited institutions
- Periods of practice
- Professional examination

Policy makers can work with the professional body and associated government entities to assess and present domestic qualification requirements and licensing procedures to their counterparts in export markets of interest. It should be noted, though, that the negotiation, implementation, and management of mutual recognition agreements can absorb substantial administrative resources. Hence, such undertakings seem most desirable if the commercial interests involved are indeed sizable.

Adult education initiatives that target practicing professionals can be used to present the latest knowledge and complement past tertiary training. In the shorter run, online training, professional internships, exchange programs, and continuing law school education can expand the knowledge of legal practice areas and multiple jurisdictions. Moreover, joint partnerships or on-the-job training with different law firms can help legal professionals widen their scope of expertise.

The most immediate route to enhancing legal capacity is the recruitment of missing talent (if available) by domestic law firms from domestic competitors, hiring foreign practitioners who have the sought-after expertise, or partnering with foreign law firms. Recruits can bring with them new practice areas, technological skills, and ways of conducting business. But law firms should be concerned with not only the skills of their legal professionals, but also the ability of managerial staff to handle the administrative side of the business. In any case, restrictions that inhibit law firms from employing the best professionals, including foreign nationals, will put domestic firms at a competitive disadvantage with respect to firms in other countries that do not face such limitations. At the same time, being part of a global network can be a significant plus in developing a strong professional reputation and a firm-specific brand, which are significant in an industry characterized by low switching costs (table 3.7).

**Table 3.7.** Law Firm Investments to Create Intangible Assets

| Intangible assets | Investment |
|---|---|
| Brand | Firms focus on professional expertise and every aspect of service delivery |
| Professional expertise | Rigorous recruitment, continuing education, exposure to new practice areas |
| Management acumen | Recruitment of suitable financial, operating, and information officers |
| Technology deployment | Acquisition of technology infrastructure and services |
| Global network | Relationship building |

*Sources:* Collins (2006), Pinnington and Bilinsky (2003).

## Designing a Proactive Trade Agenda to Improve Foreign Market Access

Arguably, imports of legal services are as important as exports from a development perspective. In a situation of skill shortages, imports can facilitate the access of local consumers to high-quality, affordable services, increase knowledge transfer, and enhance the security and predictability of transactions for prospective foreign investors and traders. Moreover, imports and strategic partnerships with foreign law firms are often a necessary step to reaching a critical size for export.

Once this critical mass has been achieved, policy makers have an active role to play in advancing the agenda for exports of legal services. They can contribute by identifying the strengths and weaknesses of domestic service providers, designing a comprehensive sector strategy, and helping law firms improve access to clients abroad.

A service trade dialogue with stakeholders can create a snapshot of the domestic market and identify specific export interests. Government representatives, domestic law firms, legal clients, and academic analysts can, together, identify constraints in the domestic market, pinpoint institutional weaknesses, and collect information on barriers in export markets of interest. Stakeholders can then initiate changes that seem desirable in the domestic market and engage in bilateral, regional, or multilateral trade negotiations to lift restrictions that hinder domestic law firms from expanding abroad. These restrictions can take a number of different forms. They pertain to the following:

- recognition of foreign credentials
- licensure of nationals or residents
- practice of host country, home country, third-country, or international law

- practice area
- form of establishment
- conditions for the name of the firm (a key form of branding)
- ability to hire or partner with local lawyers
- ability to work for a local law firm or work as a foreign legal consultant
- marketing and advertising
- capital controls
- tax policy (for example, double taxation)
- access to visas and transit requirements

On the bilateral level, export promotion activities can help domestic law firms build relationships with potential partners and clients. Such efforts can be used to introduce and match law firms with foreign partners, include law firms in industry exhibitions abroad and at home, train firm representatives in export market research, or take other measures to facilitate trade. Box 3.9 provides an example of a particular type of trade facilitating arrangement pertaining to the crossborder movement of professionals.

**Box 3.9:** Negotiating Fast-Track Visa Procedures to Facilitate Crossborder Movement

Often, lawyers must cross borders to visit and represent clients abroad. Cumbersome, unpredictable, and slow visa procedures are serious obstacles to trade in legal services. Concessions under Mode 4 of the GATS are a major request of developing countries in the Doha Round of multilateral trade negotiations. However, no compromise has so far been found. Yet, pragmatic solutions can sometimes be discovered at the bilateral or regional level to facilitate the movement of professionals.

The fear of a host country is that a nonresident entering its territory overstays and becomes an illegal immigrant. Temporary movement is often seen as a stepping-stone for permanent migration. Countries therefore tend to be more restrictive than necessary for the attribution of business and other temporary visas. Yet, a guarantor for the return of the traveling professional might, in this context, overcome the concerns of the host country about illegal immigration. And, in the case of the legal profession (or, similarly, for other professions), the bar of lawyers could play this guarantor role because formal registration to this professional body is often mandatory, and members are well identified, incorporated, and established.

In Tunisia, a number of professions have negotiated a fast-track visa procedure with the French Consulate. Thus, the professional body of accountants collects requests for business visas from its members, submits them to the consulate, and receives multiple-entry visas within a day or two. The engineers have negotiated a similar arrangement and have different priority lists depending on the seniority of the member and the type of business. The professional body can therefore assess the credibility and urgency of each request. As a side benefit, this system also helps keep track of professional movement and international transactions, thereby contributing to the collection of better data on the trade in legal services.

The use of international trade agreements for legal service reform remains nascent. Indeed, the coverage of legal services in bilateral or regional trade agreements, outside the European Union, has been rather spotty (Cone 2007). Similarly, relatively few countries made commitments with respect to legal services in the Uruguay Round of trade negotiations (table 3.8) or have submitted respective proposals in the ongoing GATS negotiations of the Doha Round (Geloso Grosso 2004). Yet, this unremarkable coverage might not necessarily suggest a fundamental lack of interest of the negotiating parties in legal service reform, but, rather, it might suggest that other service sectors, including large infrastructure services, offer bigger and more straightforward negotiation rewards. The complexity and country specificity of legal service regulations, as well as the multitude of stakeholders involved, notably, subnational bar associations, favor gradual, bilateral change over multilateral negotiations of ambitious, large-scale reforms.

## What Questions Should Stakeholders Bear in Mind as They Advance Reforms?

The preceding discussion touches on a number of issues that merit the attention of policy makers as they advance the trade integration agenda for legal services. We offer a checklist of questions that might help structure the reflections and ensure a comprehensive approach to reform (table 3.9).

## Conclusion

In a world in which people, goods, services, and capital increasingly move across borders, access to affordable, high-quality legal services both at home and abroad is essential to facilitating and securing international commercial transactions. Legal resources and services have become internationalized, and trade in the profession has flourished. This chapter informs analysts and developing-country officials who are engaged in law and justice reforms about experiences and options so that they may more effectively avail themselves of trade opportunities.

Trade in legal services generally accounts only for a small part of the legal profession's overall output, but can nevertheless play a major role in shaping the profession's development. Most trade is closely tied to international shipments of goods and the movement of persons and capital. It is rare that a company will seek advice from a law firm based abroad unless the company is established in or does significant business with the law firm's home country. Similarly, most law firms will establish abroad only to accompany a major client in the client's export business.

For small local law firms in developing countries to participate in and benefit from legal service exports, they will often have to specialize in a particular area of

**Table 3.8.** Uruguay Round Commitments on Legal Services

| Country | Host country law | | International law | | Home country law | | Modes |
|---|---|---|---|---|---|---|---|
| | Advisory | Representation | Advisory | Representation | Advisory | Representation | |
| Antigua and Barbuda | | | X | | X | | All[a] |
| Argentina | X | X | X | X | X | X | All[a] |
| Aruba | | | X | | X | | All, NT 4: unbound |
| Australia | | | X | X | X | X | All[a] |
| Austria | | | X | | X | | 1,2,4[a] |
| Barbados | | | | | | | 3, 4 |
| Bulgaria | | | X | | X | | All[a] |
| Canada | | | X | | XF | | All[a] |
| Chile | | | X | | | | 3, 4[a] |
| Colombia | | | X | | XF | | 1, 2 |
| Cuba | X | X | X | X | X | X | 2, 3, 4[a] |
| Czech Republic | X | X | X | X | X | X | All[a] |
| Dominican Republic | | | | | | | MA: 1, 2, 3; NT: 3 |
| Ecuador | | | X | | X | | All[a] |
| El Salvador | | | | | | | All[a] |
| European Communities | FRA and LUX | FRA and LUX | X | | X | | All[a] |
| Finland | | | X | | X | | All[a] |
| Gambia, The | X | X | X | X | X | X | All[a] |
| Guyana | X | X | X | X | X | X | All[a] |
| Hungary | | | | | X | | All[a] |
| Iceland | | | X | | XF | | All[a] |
| Israel | X | X | X | X | X | X | All[a] |
| Jamaica | | | X | | X | | All[a] |
| Japan | X | X | X | X | X | X | All[a] |
| Lesotho | X | X | X | | XF | | 3, 4[a] |

(*Table continues on the following page.*)

**Table 3.8.** Uruguay Round Commitments on Legal Services (*continued*)

| | Host country law | | International law | | Home country law | | |
|---|---|---|---|---|---|---|---|
| Country | Advisory | Representation | Advisory | Representation | Advisory | Representation | Modes |
| Liechtenstein | | | X | | X | | 1, 2,4[a] |
| Malaysia | (Domestic laws) | | X | | X | | 1, 2, 4[a]; 3 limited to Labuan |
| Netherlands Antilles | | | X | | X | | All |
| New Zealand | X | X | X | X | X | X | All[a] |
| Norway | | | | | X | | All[a] |
| Panama | | | X | | X | | All[a] |
| Papua New Guinea | X | X | X | X | X | X | All[a] |
| Poland | X | X | X | X | X | X | 1, 2 |
| Romania | X | X | X | X | X | X | 1, 2 |
| Rwanda | X | X | X | X | X | X | All |
| Sierra Leone | X | X | X | X | X | X | All[a] |
| Slovak Republic | X | X | X | X | X | X | All[a] |
| Slovenia | X | X | X | X | X | X | All[a] |
| Solomon Islands | | | X | X | X | X | All[a] |
| South Africa | X | X | X | X | X | X | 3, 4[a] |
| Sweden | | | X | | X | | All[a] |
| Switzerland | | | X | | X | | All[a] |
| Thailand | X | X | X | X | X | X | 2, 3 |
| Trinidad and Tobago | | | X | | | | All |
| Turkey | | | X | | XF | | All |
| United States | X | X | X | X | X | X | All[a] |
| Venezuela, R.B. de | X | | X | | X | | 2, 4[a] |

*Sources:* WTO (1998), Geloso Grosso (2004).

*Note:* X = partial or full market access and national treatment commitment. XF = partial or full commitment in home and third-country law. MA = market access. NT = national treatment.

a. Mode 4 unbound, except as indicated in the horizontal section.

**Table 3.9.** A Checklist of Questions on Trade-Related Aspects of Legal Services Reform

**Building professional value**

1. Are programs to pursue online education, professional internships, professional exchanges, and continuing adult education encouraged?
2. Are there any obstacles to on-the-job training with different law firms?
3. Do independent third-party audits of curricula and educational standards take place?
4. What is the student-to-professor ratio in colleges of law, and, if it is high, are there any efforts to reduce it?
5. Do domestic colleges of law have online partnerships with law schools abroad?

**Facilitating crossborder supply**

1. Can nonresident suppliers of legal services serve the market on a crossborder basis?
2. Which fields of law are allowed or restricted as regards crossborder supply?
3. Are there any restrictions on the electronic transmission of legal services by nonestablished foreign legal service providers?
4. Where and how clearly are the restrictions spelled out?
5. What are the policy reasons for the restrictions (for example, ensuring knowledge of local rules or accountability)?
6. Can the policy rationale be addressed through other, less trade restrictive means (for example, insurance liability)?

**Encouraging commercial presence and the movement of persons**

1. Are there any nationality requirements? If so, do they apply only to the practice of host country law? Are foreign firms and practitioners interested in practicing home country, third-country (for which they have qualifications), or international law allowed to do so in spite of the nationality requirements?
2. What is the definition of home country law and is this definition unduly restrictive?
3. Are foreign suppliers required to establish locally through particular legal forms? If so, which ones?
4. Are there any prior residency requirements for foreign firms and practitioners? What about permanent residency requirements for foreign practitioners?
5. Can foreign firms enter into partnerships with local professionals? What about hiring locally licensed professionals?
6. Are there staffing requirements for the establishment of branch offices, for example, number of partners or lawyers per office, or ratio of domestic to foreign lawyers?
7. Are there restrictions on the use of international foreign firm names?
8. Where and how clearly are the restrictions spelled out?
9. What are the policy reasons for the restrictions (for example, ensuring knowledge of local rules, competence, proximity, and accountability)?
10. Can the policy rationale be addressed through other, less trade restrictive means (for example, objective competency-based testing and local practice requirements, appointment of a representative agent, or insurance liability)?
11. Are there any foreign equity restrictions?
12. Are there any restrictions on the movement of professional, managerial, and technical personnel? What about intracorporate transferees? And contractual service suppliers? Do these restrictions apply to natural persons seeking long-term establishment or to individuals travelling for business purposes for short periods of time?

(*Table continues on the following pages.*)

**Table 3.9.** A Checklist of Questions on Trade-Related Aspects of Legal Services Reform (*continued*)

13. For contractual service suppliers, do the same restrictions apply to employees of law firms and to independent lawyers?
14. Are there prior experience requirements or postqualification experience requirements attached to the granting of visas?

**Reviewing licensing and qualification requirements**

1. What laws and regulations discipline the licensing of legal services?
2. By whom are licenses issued and monitored?
3. Are licenses required of domestic or foreign companies (or both)?
4. Are foreign service suppliers subject to different licensing conditions than domestic suppliers?
5. Is multidisciplinary practice allowed?
6. What are the qualification requirements to practice host country law? How long is the period of local practice required under supervision before qualification?
7. Is recognition of foreign qualifications provided for?
8. By whom are applications treated? How frequent are exams for qualification carried out? Is it a transparent process?
9. Are there differential restrictions on domestic lawyers practicing abroad?
10. Are there any qualification requirements concerning the practice of foreign country law or international law? If yes, is there a different or limited licensing scheme for foreign practitioners interested in practicing only home country law, third-country law (for which they possess a qualification), or international law?
11. Are these practitioners required to observe the host country rules of professional conduct? Are these practitioners considered lawyers?
12. Are these practitioners allowed to provide advisory services on host country law if such advice is based on the advice of a fully qualified local lawyer?
13. Can these practitioners present themselves as members of the local profession or do they have to use a different title? If so, in which language?
14. Do these practitioners need to register with the local bar or pass a professional examination? Is such an examination different from a full local professional examination? In which language is the examination carried out?
15. Do these practitioners need to have practiced for a certain number of years in their home country to be licensed to practice in the host country? If so, how many years?

**Pursuing preferential integration**

1. Are there any preferential agreements affecting the supply of legal services and the movement of natural persons? Which measures are subject to preferential treatment?
2. What conditions must foreign suppliers fulfill to meet the requirements of existing mutual recognition agreements to which host country providers are parties to? Do foreign service providers need to be locally established to be eligible for participation in a mutual recognition agreement?
3. Does the importing country maintain preferential access arrangements for developing-country service providers?

4. Are there any links between professional bodies, government regulatory agencies, and colleges of law with their counterparts in neighboring and regional markets?
5. Do activities such as exchanges of specialists, regional forums on professional trends, or regional negotiating consultations take place?

**Ensuring a level playing field**

1. Are there sectoral exemptions to competition law in the importing country that affect the conditions of competition in legal services markets?
2. How does the competition law deal with instances of cartels?
3. Do domestic law firms have adequate access to Internet resources so they can establish an online presence and engage in online relationships with other law firms?
4. Are law firms allowed to participate in trade exhibitions at home and abroad to introduce themselves to potential partners and clients?

*Sources:* Geloso Grosso (2004), author compilation.

law and work closely with domestic or international partners to provide the scope of services that large-scale clients demand. Indeed, trade in legal services is frequently undertaken through various forms of cooperation between law firms of different national origins.

Legal process outsourcing, that is, the crossborder supply of fragments of the legal services value chain, is currently still relatively limited in magnitude. But analysts expect that activities, such as document editing and proofreading, litigation research, and intellectual property work, will expand, so that legal outsourcing could become a significant export industry in coming years. Low-income countries that can offer a combination of reliable information and communication technology infrastructure and the required legal expertise will have occasion to tap into these business opportunities.

Arguably, for development, imports of legal services are as important as exports. Countries have much to gain from opening their domestic legal markets to foreign service providers. While regulation of the legal profession to ensure consumer protection against deceitful practices is necessary, regulation should not be more restrictive than needed. It should also avoid discriminating among domestic and foreign service providers. Unfortunately, however, the regulatory process, which often involves self-regulation through the legal profession itself, may lend itself to being hijacked for protectionist purposes. In this context, periodic assessment of the regulatory framework with a view to establishing procompetitive practices is often desirable.

Moreover, policy makers have an active role to play in the area of education and training. They can, notably, work to raise educational standards in colleges of law. They can also contribute to the development of the legal sector by designing a comprehensive sector strategy and helping law firms improve access to clients abroad. And they can work toward closing the skills gap in particular areas and exposing the domestic legal sector to international best practices by creating and promoting the status of foreign legal consultants, that is, a category of foreign professionals who are licensed to practice in specific branches of law.

To date, international trade agreements for legal service reform have been only of minor importance. The complexity and country specificity of legal service regulations and the multitude of national and subnational stakeholders involved have generally favored gradual, bilateral change over multilateral negotiations of ambitious, large-scale reform programs.

## References

ABA (American Bar Association). 2002. "Innovations in the Delivery of Legal Services: Alternative and Emerging Models for the Practicing Lawyer." Standing Committee on the Delivery of Legal Services, ABA, Chicago. http://www.abanet.org/legalservices/downloads/delivery/innovations.pdf.

Australian Permanent Mission to the WTO. 2006. "Collective Request: Legal Services." Australian Department of Foreign Affairs and Trade, Canberra.

Bokhari, Farhan. 2008. "Law in Pakistan Is Shield against Hard Times." *Financial Times*, April 24.

Collins, M. Thomas. 2006. "The Business of Legal Services." *Law Practice Today*, August.

Cone, Sydney M. 2007. "Legal Services and the Doha Round Dilemma." *Journal of World Trade* 41 (2): 245–72.

Cotterman, James D. 2003. "Getting the Capital Structure Right." *Law Practice Today*, November.

Datamonitor. 2007. "Legal Services." November 15, Datamonitor Industry Market Research, London.

Geloso Grosso, M. 2004. "Managing Request-Offer Negotiations under the GATS: The Case of Legal Services." OECD Trade Policy Working Paper 2, Organisation for Economic Co-operation and Development, Paris.

Goodwin, Tom. 2005. "Japan Widens Access to Legal Services." *International Financial Law Review* 24 (1): 9–10.

Haberbeck, Andreas. 2007. "Bridging the Gulf." *The Lawyer*, May 28: 29.

Hoare, Steve, and Ben Moshinsky. 2007. "DWS Project Finance Team Sets Its Sights on African and Middle East." *The Lawyer*, August 20.

Hook, Alison. 2007. "OECD Sectoral Study on the Impact of Domestic Regulation on Trade in Legal Services." Paper presented at the Organisation for Economic Co-operation and Development–World Bank Sixth Services Experts Meeting, "Domestic Regulation and Trade in Professional Services," Paris, February 5–16. http://www.oecd.org/secure/pdfDocument/0,2834,en_21571361_40531731_40778878_1_1_1_1,00.pdf.

Jaksic, Vesna. 2007. "Three Bar Groups Offer Ethical Guidelines on Outsourcing." *Legal Intelligencer*, May 2.

Lloyd, Richard. 2008. "The 2008 Global 100: The English Advantage." *American Lawyer*, October 2. http://www.law.com/jsp/article.jsp?id=1202424974363.

Messick, Richard. 1999. "Judicial Reform and Economic Development: A Survey of the Issues." *World Bank Research Observer* 14 (1): 117–36.

Murphy, Megan. 2008. "Time to Stop the Lawyers' Clock from Ticking." *Financial Times*, May 19. http://us.ft.com/ftgateway/superpage.ft?news_id=fto051920081427540471&page=2.

Nguyen-Hong, Duc. 2000. "Restrictions on Trade in Professional Services." Productivity Commission Staff Research Paper 1638, AusInfo, Canberra. http://papers.ssrn.com/sol3/papers.cfm?abstract_id=270787.

Paterson, I., M. Fink, and A. Ogus. 2003. *Economic Impact of Regulation in the Field of Liberal Professions in Different Member States*. Final Report prepared for the European Commission. Vienna: Institute for Advanced Studies.

Peel, Michael. 2007. "National News: Lawyers Step up Lobbying on Legal Services Reform." *Financial Times*, June 22.

Perla, David. 2006. "Next, Outsource All the Lawyers." *Chief Executive* 219 (July–August): 40–41.

Pinnington, Dan, and Dave Bilinsky. 2003. "How Am I Doing? Cash Flow Planning/Statements." *Law Practice Today*, June.

Saeed, Faisal, Ammar Ali Qureshi, and Yusuf Hussain. 2005. "EC Trade Related Technical Assistance Programme for Pakistan: Services Capacity Report." Project PAK/75/17E, September, International Trade Centre, Geneva. http://www.wto-pakistan.org/documents/publications/P_S_C_R.pdf.

Tait, Nikki. 2006. "Legal Expertise: Originality to the Fore." *Financial Times*, June 29: 8.

Tucker, Katheryn H. 2008. "Blunt Advice from Five In-House Counsel." *Fulton County Daily Report*, May 14.

Wesemann, Ed. 2007. "New Life for Commodity Legal Services." *Of Counsel* 3 (January): 10.

World Bank. 2003. *The World Bank Legal Review: Law and Justice for Development*. Washington, DC: World Bank; The Hague: Kluwer Law International.

———. 2004. *World Development Report 2005: A Better Investment Climate for Everyone*. Washington, DC: World Bank; New York: Oxford University Press.

———. 2007. "Morocco's Backbone Services Sectors: Harnessing the Export Potential in New Services, Volume II." World Bank, Washington, DC.

———. 2008. *Tunisia's Global Integration: A Second Generation of Reforms to Boost Growth and Employment*. Washington, DC: World Bank.

WTO (World Trade Organization). 1998. "Legal Services: Background Note by the Secretariat." Document S/C/W/43 (July 6), Council for Trade in Services, WTO, Geneva.

———. 2000a. "The Hashemite Kingdom of Jordan: Schedule of Specific Commitments." Document GATS/SC/128 (December 15), Trade in Services, WTO, Geneva.

———. 2000b. "Oman: Schedule of Specific Commitments." Document GATS/SC/132 (December 22), Trade in Services, WTO, Geneva.

———. 2001. *Guide to the GATS: An Overview of Issues for Further Liberalization of Trade in Services*. WTO Guide Series. London: Kluwer Law International.

———. 2005. "Schedule of Specific Commitments in Services: List of Article II MFN Exemptions." Addendum, Part II of "Report of the Working Party on the Accession of the Kingdom of Saudi Arabia." Document WT/ACC/SAU/61/Add.2 (November 1), Working Party on the Accession of the Kingdom of Saudi Arabia, WTO, Geneva.

———. 2007. *International Trade Statistics 2007*. Geneva: WTO.

4

# HEALTH WITHOUT BORDERS: INTERNATIONAL TRADE FOR BETTER HEALTH SYSTEMS AND SERVICES

*Olivier Cattaneo*

## Introduction

### *Trade in health services in a nutshell*

A number of countries are competing to become key exporters of health services. In particular, the growing phenomenon of health tourism appeals to many developing countries in which clinics servicing foreign clientele are flourishing. An increasing number of countries offer attractive surgery, recuperation, and rejuvenation holiday packages, from Costa Rica or South Africa to India or Thailand. On the demand side, the United States remains the largest consumer of health services worldwide. Deloitte Consulting has estimated that 750,000 Americans went abroad for health care in 2007, and, with a projected growth rate of 100 percent from 2007 to 2010, the number is expected to reach 6 million outpatients in 2010 (Deloitte 2008). On the supply side, developed and developing countries are competing: over 35 countries serve more than a million medical tourists annually. In 2008, more than 400,000 nonresidents sought care in the United States and spent almost US$5 billion for health services; there were 450,000 in India, 300,000 in Malaysia, 410,000 in Singapore, and 1.2 million in Thailand (Deloitte 2008). The motives behind the crossborder movement of patients vary considerably, however, and not all countries compete in the same market segments. There is, accordingly, a case for specialization in market niches on the basis of each country's resources and trade opportunities.

Medical tourism has received significant media attention. However, the trade in health services is not limited to the crossborder movement of patients, which represents Mode 2, only one of the four possible modes of service delivery identified by the General Agreement on Trade in Services (GATS). Other key components include the temporary movement of health professionals to deliver services across borders (Mode 4, for example, the crossborder movement of doctors and nurses), foreign establishment (Mode 3, for example, the opening abroad of a branch of a clinic), and the crossborder provision of health services through technological means (Mode 1, for example, telemedicine). In addition, a number of other services and goods are traded at the margin of health services; it is a common characteristic of many services that they enable trade in other sectors. Some examples of the different modes are indicated in table 4.1.

The trade in health services has potentially significant effects on the availability of these services, the quality of the health system, and the population's health generally in both the exporting country and the importing country. The effects of trade in health services also vary considerably from one mode of delivery to another, and imports often appear more important than exports in improving a country's domestic health system. An excessive enthusiasm for medical tourism that is not backed by serious business plans or coherent government policies could result in a low return on investment, lead to frustrated expectations, and prejudice the local supply of health services. Not all countries have a comparative advantage in the health service trade. While a carefully designed trade strategy in the health sector could have significant positive spillover effects on the domestic supply of and access to health services (in addition to the positive global impacts of trade), a poorly designed strategy could divert already scarce resources from people in need in developing countries.

Health is not a typical commodity or service; it is a public good. Trade in health services could directly contribute to reaching—or missing, if negative effects prevail—health-related Millennium Development Goals.[1] Trade objectives in the health sector should be compatible with other legitimate social objectives (for example, universal access). Health is also a highly regulated profession, for legitimate purposes: even more than other professional services, medicine is characterized by the asymmetry of information between the service provider (a doctor trained in the practice of medicine) and the patient (seeking treatment). Regulation of the health sector is necessary to protect patients against malpractice. Trade promotion in the health sector therefore revolves not around deregulation, but around more effective regulation and, sometimes, even more regulation, for example, adopting better quality standards for hospitals and clinics. Similarly,

**Table 4.1.** What Are the Modes of Trade in the Health Sector?

| Mode | Trade in health services | Trade in ancillary services | Trade in goods associated with health services |
|---|---|---|---|
| **Mode 1** **Crossborder supply** | – Telemedicine, including diagnostics, radiology | – Distance medical education and training<br>– Medical transcription, back office<br>– Medical research tools and databases<br>– Medical insurance | – Health care equipment<br>– Drugs<br>– Medical waste<br>– Prostheses |
| **Mode 2** **Consumption abroad** | – Medical tourism, that is, voluntary trip to receive medical treatment abroad<br>– Medically assisted residence for retirees<br>– Expatriates seeking care in country of residence<br>– Emergency cases (for example, accident when abroad) | – All activities associated with health tourism (for example, transport, hotel, restaurant, paramedical, local purchases)<br>– Local medical education and training of foreign nationals | |
| **Mode 3** **Commercial presence** | – Foreign participation or ownership of hospital/ clinic or medical facilities (for example, capital investments, technology tie-ups, collaborative ventures) | – Foreign-sponsored education or training centers<br>– Foreign-sponsored medical research facilities | |
| **Mode 4** **Presence of natural persons** | – Movement of doctors and health personnel for the purpose of commercial medical practice | – Movement of doctors and health personnel for other purposes (for example, education or training) | |

*Source:* World Bank staff.

trade promotion revolves not around challenging the public health sector, which often plays a crucial role in the supply of health (and medical education) services, but around designing efficient services in a more competitive environment. Experience shows that public involvement is often necessary for the success of export promotion strategies in the health sector (see, for example, Cuba, the Philippines, or Thailand). Nonetheless, private investment (including foreign investment) remains a crucial factor in success, particularly where public resources are too scarce to maintain an efficient health care system.

The difficulties in sustaining public health insurance schemes, the aging of the population, and related supply bottlenecks in the health system are among the drivers of frustrations and outbound medical tourism in the North. Most developing countries face far more critical health issues, including critically low medical density and the poor quality of the infrastructure and services, which, combined with other factors, result in poor public health and higher mortality rates. In all these countries, trade in health services should be seen not only as a source of income in the balance of payments, but also as a primary means to remedy shortages and improve domestic health systems. Therefore, the main challenge will be to find adequate accompanying policies that maximize the positive domestic spillovers and minimize the negative domestic spillovers of trade in health services.

The media and many expert studies have focused mainly on North-South trade (in the case, for example, of the movement of patients) or South-North trade (in the case, for example, of the movement of doctors and nurses). The potential of South-South trade has often been ignored or neglected, in sharp contrast with the reality of trade. In Tunisia, for example, Libyans represent more than 80 percent of the foreign medical patients; similarly, more than 80 percent of the Omani patients treated abroad go to India. There is a case for more cooperation in the South. This may involve the creation of regional health centers of excellence (for medical education or treatment) that would help in spreading out the cost of medical education and infrastructure and in reaching a critical mass for writing off investments in technologies.

### *Objectives and outline of the chapter*

A number of studies and volumes have been published that cover the trade in health services extensively (see, for example, Blouin, Drager, and Smith 2006). The scope of this chapter is more modest. It is an effort to summarize existing knowledge and to select the most relevant information to help individuals or organizations involved in the design of health or trade reforms and policies so that they may understand the potential benefits and risks of trade in the health sector, as well as ways to maximize the former and minimize the latter. It is designed to assist nontrade (health) experts in understanding how trade can help improve health systems and the access to health services and to assist trade specialists in understanding the specific characteristics of the health sector.

The second section explores what a country could expect from increased imports or exports of health services and suggests accompanying policies aimed at maximizing the benefits and minimizing the costs of liberalization. Thereafter, strategies are outlined that may foster trade in the health sector and combine domestic reforms and offensive trade negotiations.

### *What may one expect from increased trade in health services?*

The impact of trade on the health systems of countries may vary considerably depending on the mode of service delivery, the structure of the domestic market for the provision of health services, and the adequacy of the accompanying regulations and policies. At the same time, trade in health services may create opportunities and have a number of benefits not only for the business partners involved in trade, but for the population as a whole. However, there could also potentially be cost and other negative effects. Hereafter is a review of these effects and suggested solutions—on the basis of country case studies—to maximize the positive and minimize the negative spillover effects of trade. It is stressed that there is a common tendency to protect the domestic market against imports that could prove particularly damaging in the health sector. The point is that imports are as important as exports, if not more important. Given that the four modes of service delivery are intertwined, the attempt at protection could prove vain. For example, a country that does not allow foreign investment in the health sector or does not allow foreign doctors to practice locally might be able to limit its imports under Modes 3 and 4. But this policy is likely to result in higher imports under Mode 2 because a number of nationals will seek treatment abroad to access a certain quality of care (technologies and internationally known doctors). This scenario would create further inequalities in access to health care, and money spent on health care abroad would never benefit the domestic system, unlike, potentially, foreign investment or a domestic practice by a foreign doctor.

The discussion analyzes the impact of trade from the perspective of the importing and exporting parties, underlining potential threats and opportunities as well as ways to minimize the former and maximize the latter. Table 4.2 distinguishes exporters and importers of health services by mode of provision.

## The Import Side: Using Trade to Improve Domestic Access to Quality Health Services

Most countries, particularly, but not exclusively those in the South, suffer from shortages in the health sector (human or capital). Increasing imports through foreign direct investment (FDI) or other channels could contribute to remedying these shortages, although it could present some challenges for countries in which private participation in the provision of health services has been deliberately limited. In this context, the regulatory environment and the respective roles of the public and private sectors, especially, are key determinants of trade policy choices, trade opening effects, and the accompanying measures to be taken.

**Table 4.2.** Who Is the Exporter? Who Is the Importer?

Under **Mode 1**, the exporter and the importer do not move across borders; only the service crosses the border:
- A patient in country A (importer) receives treatment from a doctor located in country B (exporter).
- A hospital in country A (importer) outsources transcription services in country B (exporter).

Under **Mode 2**, the importer moves across the border toward the exporter:
- Country A (importer) sends patients for treatment in country B (exporter).
- A tourist from country A (importer) receives treatment while traveling to country B (exporter).

Under **Mode 3**, the exporter moves across the border toward the importer:
- Country A (importer) authorizes the establishment on its territory of a medical facility partially owned and eventually operated by a healthcare provider from country B (exporter).

Under **Mode 4**, the exporter moves across the border toward the importer:
- Country A (importer) authorizes a health professional from country B (exporter) to practice medicine on its territory and on a temporary basis.

*Source:* Author compilation.

### *Benefits (realized and expected) from imports*

The benefits of imports will vary according to the mode of service supply and according to whether the service is provided or consumed locally (for example, imports under Mode 3) or abroad (for example, imports under Mode 2): in other words, whether the money spent benefits the domestic (minus leakages) or the foreign health system.

#### Mode 1

Telemedicine remains underdeveloped. One could imagine that the benefits would be the same in Mode 1 as in Mode 2, without the inconvenience associated with travel (that is, the same benefits available to more people). These would include the alleviation of some human and infrastructure resource constraints, particularly in remote and underserviced areas, and broader access to higher quality personnel, diagnosis, and treatment. One could imagine that trade under Mode 1 would promote expertise and technology transfer, similar to Modes 3 and 4.

With regard to services such as medical transcription, trade reduces the cost of operating medical practices and therefore may make access to medicine more affordable.

## Mode 2

The treatment of patients abroad helps alleviate some of the domestic human and infrastructure resource constraints. The case of Oman is typical of a developing country with low medical density that needs to send patients abroad, at least in the short term, until adequate treatment can be provided locally (box 4.1). In Oman and in a number of other countries, the traveling patient can seek reimbursement if the treatment is not available locally. This sponsoring is costly, however, and not all countries can afford such schemes. In addition, in many developing countries, medical travel remains driven by a lack of confidence in

**Box 4.1:** Case Study: Remedying Health Shortages through Trade under Modes 4 and 2, Oman

Oman is an upper-middle-income, resource-rich, labor-importing country. In 2003, the Ministry of Health employed 18,558 professionals, of whom almost 40 percent were foreigners, including up to 76 percent of the physicians (figure 4.1). Most health administrators are Omani nationals. In 2003, there were also 2,838 health professionals employed in the private sector, and 95 percent of these were foreigners. Most of the foreign professionals came from the Arab Republic of Egypt, India, Iraq, Pakistan, the Philippines, and Sudan.

**Figure 4.1.** Foreign Professionals Working in the Public Health Sector, Oman, 2003

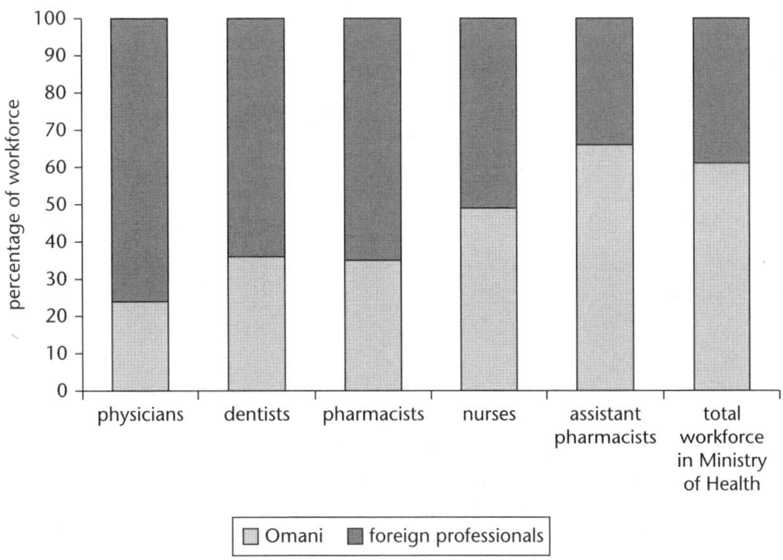


(*Box continues on the following page.*)

**Box 4.1:** Case Study: Remedying Health Shortages through Trade under Modes 4 and 2, Oman (*continued*)

Despite these significant imports, the Omani health sector still falls below international benchmarks, with a density per 10,000 inhabitants of 12.6 doctors, 31.6 nurses, 0.7 pharmacists, and 0.7 dentists. Therefore, Oman has to supplement these imports under Mode 4 with imports under Mode 2, that is, it sends some of its patients for treatment abroad. Accordingly, there is an official policy to sponsor Omanis for treatment abroad if treatment is not available locally. The average annual cost was US$3 million in 2001–03. The number of patients treated abroad dropped from 418 in 1990 to 237 in 2006 because of public investments in the sector (figure 4.2). In 2006, 44 Omani patients were treated for neoplasm abroad (compared with 180 in 2000), 58 for orthopedic ailments, 39 for cardiac ailments, and 31 for ophthalmologic ailments. Targeted public investment could help reduce significantly the cost of these health care imports. For example, government-funded medical travel for oncology fell by 92 percent from 2004 to 2005 after an oncology center opened.

At the margin of health care services, Oman also imports medical education services under Mode 2. In 2003/04, 1,341 medical students received foreign training; 52 percent were government sponsored, and 48 percent were self-sponsored.

**Figure 4.2.** Omani Patients Treated Abroad, 2006

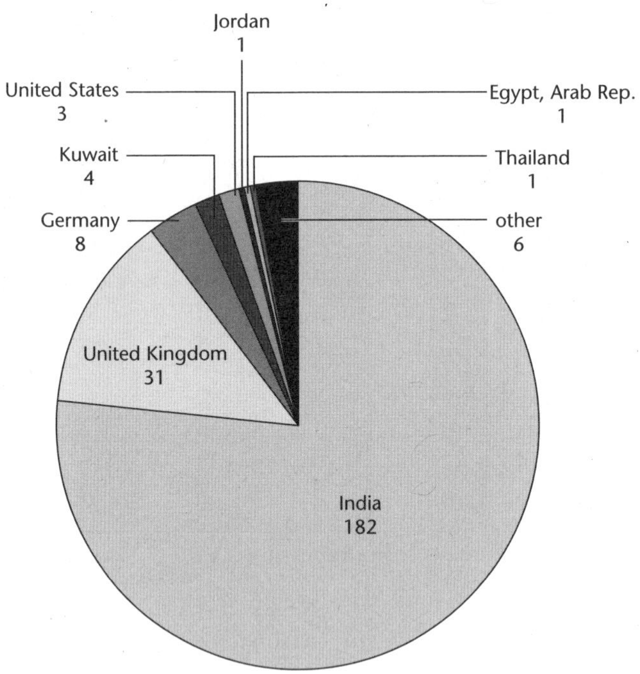


*Sources:* Suleiman (2005), http://www.who.int/en/, http://www.moh.gov.om/.

local health care providers and continues to be perceived as a luxury rather than a necessity.

In countries, mainly in the North, where treatment is more expensive than in the countries of competing health service providers, imports under Mode 2 could ease some tensions on health insurance systems and make them sustainable. According to Mattoo and Rathindran (2006), the health care system of the United States, for example, would save US$1.4 billion annually if only 1 in 10 patients were to go abroad for a limited set of 15 highly tradable low-risk treatments.

### Mode 3

Foreign investment plays a crucial role in many parts of an economy in developed and developing countries. However, because of the structure of many health systems, the role of the public sector in health, and the difficulty of articulating public and private interests in the provision of health services, FDI in the health sector has remained underdeveloped in many countries. Potential gains are nonetheless important and should not be overlooked.

FDI could bring new resources to the health system, foster competition among health service providers (raising standards and quality and lowering prices), and encourage technology and knowledge upgrades and transfers (for example, the training of medical and management personnel or economies of scale on medical supplies). FDI could also reduce the burden on public spending by diminishing the need for sponsoring expensive treatments abroad and creating more jobs. The case of India (box 4.2) illustrates these effects (and their limits).

It should be noted that, depending on the basic regulatory environment, the provision of health insurance services (primarily through Modes 3 and 1) by foreign companies also could have a significant impact on the sustainability of domestic health systems and facilitate access to health services.

In India, for example, HLL Lifecare Limited and the Acumen Fund (United States) have created a joint venture to develop a small chain of high-quality and affordable (30–50 percent of the usual prices) maternity hospitals designed to serve low-income populations in underserviced Indian regions. The supporters of this initiative hope that it could serve as a global model for increasing access to high-quality and affordable health care by the world's poor.[2]

### Mode 4

A number of developed and developing countries resort to Mode 4 imports to remedy shortages in key health personnel. From the importer's perspective, this reduces the cost of medical education and training, allows greater flexibility in the management of health personnel, and provides access to top-quality personnel

**Box 4.2:** Case Study: Remedying Health Shortages through Trade under Mode 3, India

The Indian health care delivery market is one of the largest service sectors in the economy (an estimated output of US$18.7 billion and 4 million jobs). It has grown at about 13 percent annually in recent years. Nonetheless, the performance of India's health sector still falls well below international benchmarks, including in comparable developing countries, and needs to scale up considerably in terms of the availability and quality of physical infrastructure and human resources. Given the growing demand, the significant and growing role of the private sector in health care delivery and expenditure (75 percent of total health care expenditure, with public health expenditure accounting for less than 1 percent of gross domestic product, compared with an average 3 percent in developing countries and 5 percent in developed countries), and the huge investment needs, there has been increasing interest among foreign providers and nonresident Indians in the advantages of entering the Indian health care market.

Indian foreign investment policy is liberal for hospitals, and foreign investors do not face major regulatory hurdles on entering the Indian market. Some 90 FDI projects in hospitals and diagnostic centers were approved in 2000–06, for a total of US$53 million and covering developed countries (Australia, Canada, the United Kingdom, the United States) and developing countries (Malaysia, Mauritius, Saudi Arabia, Singapore, the United Arab Emirates). This list, however, does not include the well-known corporate hospitals in the country (the identified projects involved small or midsize hospitals, within the US$1 million to US$2 million investment range), and FDI is sometimes received only for routing purposes (for example, a promoter company based in Mauritius invests in India for the tax benefits only). Overall, it appears that foreign investment in Indian hospitals remains limited, notwithstanding the liberal regulatory framework. According to one estimate, foreign investors have tapped only 10 percent of the Indian health care market.

It is perceived that there will be an increased inflow of foreign funds into India's hospital sector in the near future and major expansion plans by existing and prospective corporate providers. These plans include huge medical "cities" with large super-specialized or multispecialty hospitals and integrated health care services, as well as the scaling-up of existing operations and the establishment of new hospitals around the country. While there are several prospective providers in the Indian hospital market (for example, Dubai, the United Arab Emirates; Singapore; the World Bank), the main source countries for FDI are anticipated to remain Australia, Singapore, the United Kingdom, and the United States. It is also recognized that large investments (US$100 million or more) can be implemented only through investments in corporate hospitals (chains) and that it would be some time before India can replicate the developed-country model of large corporate chain hospitals given that the average size of hospitals in the developed countries is several times that of some of the largest hospitals in India (10,000 versus 2,000 beds, for example). Reputation and brand value are key to accessing funds through private equity, foreign institutional investors, or external commercial borrowing. Hence, new hospital projects would have to rely primarily on domestic debt and would not see much foreign capital inflows except through individual nonresident Indian investors or through groups of small investors.

Additional analysis of the reasons for the limited presence of foreign investment in Indian hospitals reveals a number of external and domestic constraints. They include limits to the number of foreign providers, the many competing investment destinations, and the fact that there are difficulties for foreign providers in entering independently and in maintaining joint ventures. In addition, the gestation period in hospital projects is long, and investors may not be willing to make such a long-term commitment. More important, various domestic factors adversely affect the returns to investment in hospitals in India: high initial establishment costs (for example, the prohibitive cost of procuring land), low health insurance penetration in the country (that is, the smaller consumer base for corporate hospitals), restrictions on medical training and providers (that is, supply bottlenecks and adverse effects on the quality of the personnel), the high cost of importing medical devices (and a limited domestic manufacturing capacity in this area), other regulatory deficiencies (for example, lack of standardization, proper governance, and quality assurance), and lack of policy clarity and priority with regard to the health care sector. Thus, the Indian experience shows that a liberal foreign investment policy is not sufficient to secure strong foreign participation in the hospital sector.

An examination of the impact of foreign investment in hospitals in India reveals the following:

- Hospitals receiving foreign funds are likely to focus on more advanced procedures and specialty areas.
- They are more likely to focus on curative and intervention-oriented treatment than on preventive and long-term treatment.
- They are likely to employ a higher ratio of technology to personnel in health care delivery and thus involve a substitution of human resources with technology and equipment.
- They are likely to invest much more in medical equipment and devices and also in specialized and experienced medical personnel, thus involving a focus on high-end human resources and high-end technology.
- They tend to have better systems and processes and to use information technology, which creates a more efficient and professional work environment.
- They pay staff more at all levels and particularly to senior medical personnel.
- They are more likely to attract foreign doctors and specialists than other hospitals.
- They are more likely to be accredited domestically and internationally.
- Their costs are likely to be comparable with or slightly higher than those of large hospitals that do not receive foreign funds.
- Their costs tend to be higher than the costs of small and medium nursing homes and hospitals mainly because of their greater capital intensity and their focus on quality systems and processes and on hygiene.
- There could be positive externalities in other areas, some of which could also drive foreign investment in hospitals.
- The hospitals could draw away medical personnel at all levels from other hospitals and could adversely impact the quality of the medical personnel available to competing institutions.
- There is likely to be closings of substandard institutions, some consolidation of the hospital sector, and the appearance of new arrangements between larger and smaller players as the health care sector evolves.
- There could be greater segmentation between the public and private sectors, with more resource flows toward the latter and greater wage disparity, unless innovative arrangements emerge between the two sectors and reforms are undertaken in public sector hospitals.

While there are clearly concerns about the implications for equity, affordability, and market segmentation associated with the growing presence of foreign investors in India's hospital sector, it is evident that the root cause lies in structural problems that already exist in the health care sector, such as lack of affordable health insurance schemes or inappropriate regulations governing medical education providers. The benefits of foreign investment in hospitals are therefore likely to outweigh these adverse effects, and the solution lies not in restricting foreign investment, but in strengthening the public health care system, in amending certain regulations that affect all providers, and in introducing schemes that provide affordable access to health care for all.

*Source:* Chanda (2007).

trained in specialties that are sometimes not available locally. In turn, this contributes to facilitating technology and knowledge transfers.

The flexibility of Mode 4 also allows some countries to remedy shortages among the health care providers in remote or underserviced areas (see, for example, Canada). In many countries, the attribution of visas to health personnel is subject to economic needs tests.

### *Risks associated with increased trade or aversion to opening*

Domestic health markets are significantly regulated and are often characterized by a high level of protection against imports. The motives underlying some regulation and protection may be legitimate, although a number of measures help mitigate the risks and maximize the benefits of opening. A distinction should be made according to the mode of service supply and according to whether the service is provided or consumed domestically or abroad.

#### Mode 1

So far, trade in health services under Mode 1 has remained limited mostly for technological reasons. At the current level of technological development, Mode 1 does not appear to be cost efficient. For other services ancillary to health, such as back-office or transcription services, the argument may not prevail; however, these activities could be a challenge for regulators, for example with regard to securing the confidentiality of medical information.

In general, Mode 1 imports could fall through the cracks of domestic regulation. How does one ensure that a doctor operating abroad meets all the qualification criteria or respects applicable medical ethics rules? Mode 1 trade in health services could increase the risks of malpractice unless an adequate regulatory framework is put in place.

#### Mode 2

Mode 2 and trade in general should not become a substitute for domestic reforms. In the case of Oman, government-sponsored medical travel is supplemented by domestic reforms aimed at limiting imports under Mode 2 (see box 4.1). Between 1990 and 2006, the number of Omani seeking treatment abroad was cut in half; investment in an oncology center meant that the number of patients seeking such treatment abroad dropped by 92 percent. In Abu Dhabi in the United Arab Emirates, government-funded medical travel for cardiology decreased by 55 percent from 2004 to 2006 after a surgery team specialized in cardiology and with significant international experience was set up in the city (Ehrbeck, Guevara, and Mango 2008). Mode 2 imports are only second best and should remain a temporary solution awaiting domestic capacity building.[3]

Mode 2 and Mode 1 present similar regulatory challenges. How is one to control the quality of the services provided abroad? Who should bear the costs of follow-up operations in case of medical complications? (Many insurance companies refuse to reimburse for such operations.) On what basis should there be reimbursement? The answers to these questions have important ramifications. At stake are the equity of access—absent an adequate sponsoring or insurance scheme, only the rich can afford to seek treatment abroad—and the quality of health care. For patients, travel abroad remains suboptimal because of the inconvenience of travel and the desire to undergo medical procedures in a familiar environment.

It should also be noted that resources spent abroad are diverted from the domestic health system, while the dynamic effects are enjoyed abroad. In addition, the unit cost of hospital care depends on the volume and overall capacity utilization of a facility; thus, increased imports under Mode 2 may result in higher treatment costs at home (and, in the worst case scenario, among those who cannot afford to travel).

### Mode 3

The impact of imports under Mode 3 will vary considerably according to the nature and the objective of the investment. It is often feared that foreign establishments will only target a traveling foreign clientele or a rich domestic clientele, which would raise concerns regarding the equality of access to health care. Moreover, foreign establishments (supposedly paying higher salaries than the public sector or the domestic private sector) could divert scarce human resources to treat a more wealthy clientele, to the detriment of the poor and of the objective of universal access to health care. For the government, this internal human resource drain could be a drag on public investment in education. It could also add to the initial cost of attracting foreign investors (fiscal incentives, building infrastructure, and so on).

There are, however, a number of measures that a government can take to mitigate these risks. Leakages are greater if markets are segmented. For example, in Tunisia, offshore clinics benefit from a more significant degree of openness to trade (such as investment incentives for foreigners, authorization for foreign doctors to practice), but they can treat local patients only within a certain legal limit (20 percent of the clientele). As a result, there is more leakage, while the spillover effects on the local population are minimal. In contrast, in Indonesia, foreign investment is directed at private wings in teaching and tertiary care hospitals in cities other than Jakarta so that positive spillover effects are maximized. Similarly, in the case of Thailand, the government has introduced compulsory public service and requires the private sector to contribute to investments in education to help avoid and also offset the effects of the internal drain on human resources (see box 4.7).[4]

### Mode 4

Imports under Mode 4, if not properly managed, could raise a number of issues. First, Mode 4 movements of personnel are often confused with permanent migration. The media has related a number of stories about nurses and, sometimes, doctors from developing countries who have been exploited while working on assignments abroad. Foreign temporary employees could be perceived as a threat by national employees if different labor conditions apply (including salary). This is, unfortunately, a frequent scenario, and, while it is not a disincentive for Mode 4 trade, importing countries should make a special effort to avoid such abuses and more closely regulate the temporary movement of health personnel.

## The Export Side: Trade in Health Services as an Engine of Export Growth and Diversification

Exports are the focal point of a large segment of the literature on trade. The gains promised to participants in the global race for medical tourism have caused countries to enter the race. Long neglected, trade in health services now appears as a credible engine of export growth and diversification in selected developing countries. While the benefits could be important, it should be noted that not all countries have a comparative advantage in the sector, and some forms of export could have negative effects domestically unless adequate accompanying measures are adopted.

### *Global trade and prospects at a glance*

Statistics on trade in services are generally scarce and imprecise, in part because services are intangible and, hence, long considered nontradable. Health is no exception, and it remains difficult to assess the real size of the global market in the trade in health services. Estimates vary significantly. For example, a 2004 McKinsey study reported that 150,000 foreigners had visited India for treatment that year, while a more recent 2008 study by the same consulting firm suggested that the market is not as large as reported and placed the current market at 60,000 to 85,000 medical tourists a year (Ehrbeck, Guevara, and Mango 2008). Another consulting firm, Deloitte (2008), estimated the value of the world medical tourism market at around US$60 billion in 2008 (expected to grow to US$100 billion by 2010), with more than 1 million medical tourists annually and 750,000 outbound from the United States alone (the latter expected to reach 6 million by 2010).

Despite these variations, it is widely recognized that trade in the health sector has strong growth potential. It is also recognized that developing countries are likely to be the main beneficiaries of these new trade opportunities. Factors in the growth of the market in developing countries include the aging of the population and growing demand in the North (shortages of health care providers) and rising incomes (and, hence, demand) and the emergence of a middle class in the South. These factors, combined with a greater control on health care spending in the North, are creating new trade opportunities particularly for developing countries. Deloitte (2008) anticipates a 100 percent annual growth in outbound medical tourism in the United States over the next few years. However, obstacles need to be removed before trade will really flourish; the nonportability of health insurance is an example of the barriers.

Not all trade modes are equally developed or have similar prospects. Herman (2009) suggests that there is a great deal of variation in the different segments of the international trade in health services. For the most part, trade in the European Union involves the movement of foreign health professionals among countries (Mode 4), as well as the presence of foreign health care firms in local markets (Mode 3). Trade based on the travel of health care consumers to foreign markets remained limited (Mode 2), but still significantly more active than the international crossborder trade in health services (Mode 1).

It should be noted also that a number of ancillary services and products are traded at the margin of the global health services trade. These include medical education and training, offshore business services, paramedical and wellness services, health insurance, pharmaceuticals, medical equipment and supplies, and so on. Sometimes, health services are also commingled with other services, such as tourism and travel or real estate, for example retirement homes with medical facilities (box 4.3). The global health market is therefore much larger than the rough estimates on services suggest.

### Mode 1

Evidence on trade in health services under Mode 1 remains largely anecdotal at this stage, at least if one adopts a narrow definition of health services (Nielson 2006). If one includes the offshoring of other business or financial services, such as medical transcription or health insurance and claims processing, then the market is larger and largely untapped. According to the McKinsey Global Institute (MGI 2005), up to 55 percent of the jobs in such services in the health sectors of high-income countries could be outsourced (figure 4.3). Most outsourcing would be done domestically, but some developing countries could capture part of the market. In the case of the Philippines, exports of medical

**Box 4.3:** Case Study: Travel and Health Industries Commingling, Thai Airways

A number of travel and leisure companies have invested in the health sector or offer their clients packages that include some health care. For example, Thai Airways offers health packages through its Royal Orchid Holidays Program. These include the following:

### Package in Bangkok

- Superior physical checkup at Bangkok Hospital (3 hours)
- Medical checkup: health care program at Bangkok Hospital (3–4 hours)
- Premier health examination at Bumrungrad International (3–4 hours)
- Physical checkup at Ramkhamhaeng Hospital (3–4 hours)
- Dental examination and cleaning at Bumrungrad International (30 minutes)

### Package in Chiang Mai

- Physical checkup at Chiang Mai Ram Hospital (3–4 hours)
- Checkup at Rajavej Chiang Mai Hospital (3–4 hours)

### Package in Phuket

- Medical checkup at Bangkok Phuket Hospital (3–4 hours)

*Source:* http://www.thaiair.com/holiday-packages/royal-orchid-holidays/en/discover-thailand.htm.

**Figure 4.3.** Health: A Sector with Strong Potential for Outsourcing

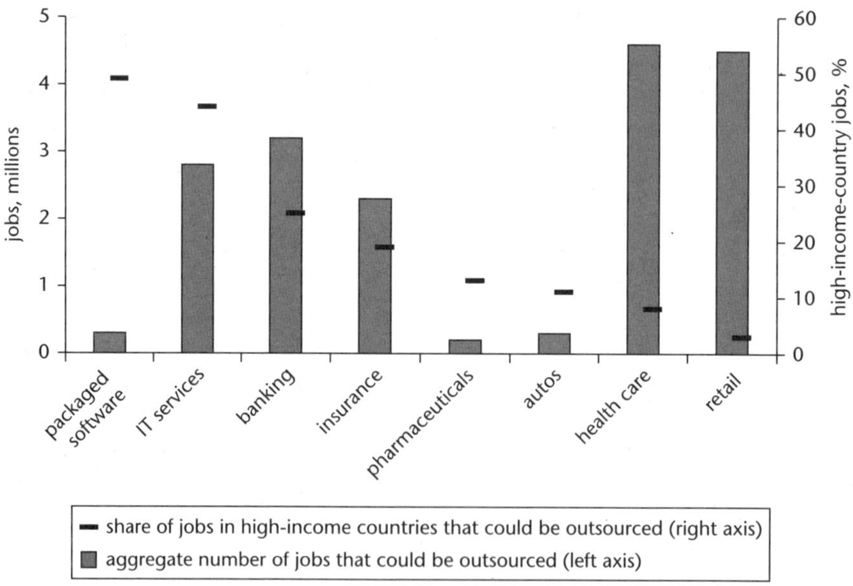


*Source:* MGI (2005).
*Note:* IT services = information technology services.

**Box 4.4:** Case Study: Exports of Offshore Medical Transcription Services, the Philippines

The Philippines has benefited from the first wave of offshoring of medical transcription services (that is, the process of interpreting and electronically encoding the oral dictation of health professionals regarding patient assessment, therapeutic procedures, diagnosis, and so on). Outsource Transcription Philippines Inc., the first large medical transcription company, was started in the late 1990s and has benefited from a rapid expansion of medical transcription needs in the United States because of changes in the accountancy requirements for health insurance (the 1996 Health Insurance Portability and Accountability Act). The demand for outsourced medical transcription services in the United States is growing at 20 percent per year and is coupled with an annual 10 percent decline in the number of transcriptionists in the United States. The United States therefore remains the main driver of the trade in this field.

The comparative advantage of the Philippines is mainly explained by its pool of English-speaking workers. (The Philippines is the third largest English-speaking nation in the world and has a 94 percent literacy rate.) Transcriptionists are usually graduates of medical schools who are working part time while preparing for medical board exams. The country also has a strategic location; there is a 12-hour time difference with the United States. In addition, the government provides strong incentives for foreign investment in the sector and has supported the industry by implementing key regulations (for example, on e-commerce and data protection) and developing information technology infrastructure.

As a result, the market for outsourced medical transcription services grew at a 130 percent rate between 2001 and 2004, by far the most rapidly growing outsourcing sector in the country. The majority of the 25 companies exporting these services in 2004 were owned by U.S. investors and should benefit from an acceleration of the outsourcing phenomenon. In 2004, US$13 billion was spent on medical transcription in the United States and only US$2.3 billion on outsourcing. In absolute value, Philippine exports still represent less than 1 percent of the market, and the growth potential remains substantial. Recent projections suggest that the Philippines will continue to be among the largest markets for medical transcription outsourcing over the next five to seven years and could contribute to filling the 47 percent supply gap in the U.S. transcription market.

*Sources:* Blouin, Drager, and Smith (2007), Arunanondchai and Fink (2007).

transcription services have grown at a rate of over 100 percent annually in recent years (box 4.4).

### Mode 2

Estimates of the number of patients traveling to seek care abroad vary significantly from one source to another. According to an official of the World Health Organization, the number could reach 4 million patients a year, with over 1 million in Thailand alone (India, Malaysia, and Singapore are expected to reach this level by 2012) and an estimated global market of US$20 billion to US$40 billion (reaching over US$100 billion by 2012) (Drager and Smith 2009).

But is it all trade? In figure 4.4, Ehrbeck, Guevara, and Mango (2008) adopt a narrow definition of medical travel that excludes expatriates seeking care in their

**Figure 4.4.** A Definition of Medical Travel

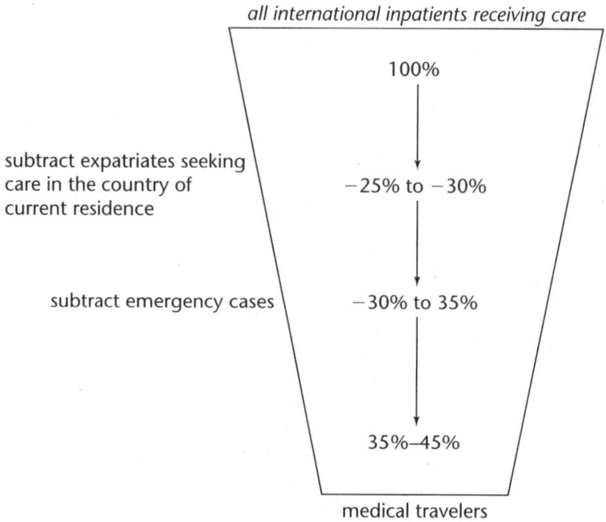


*Source:* Ehrbeck, Guevara, and Mango (2008).
*Note:* Outpatients are excluded from analysis because providers do not collect detailed outpatient data; a few providers, however, have substantial numbers of international outpatients.

country of residence (25 to 30 percent of all patients treated abroad) and travelers seeking emergency care (30 to 35 percent); in total, medical travelers would represent only 35 to 45 percent of all patients treated abroad.

A main question, beyond statistics, is the rationale of medical tourism. Why do patients seek treatment abroad? According to the study by Ehrbeck, Guevara, and Mango, the main drivers of medical travel are as follows:

- More advanced technology
- Higher-quality care for medically necessary procedures
- More rapid access for medically necessary procedures
- Care at lower cost for medically necessary procedures
- Care at lower cost for discretionary procedures

Figure 4.5 shows a breakdown of the main components involving medical travel.

The main driver of trade in health services is quality, not price. This suggests that high-income countries will remain popular destinations for medical tourists (and, therefore, exporters of health services), and low- and middle-income countries with less-sophisticated health systems will remain importers of health services under Mode 2. It also suggests that there is significant room for South-South trade and a potentially high return on qualitative investments made in the

**Figure 4.5.** Relative Size of Medical Traveler Segments

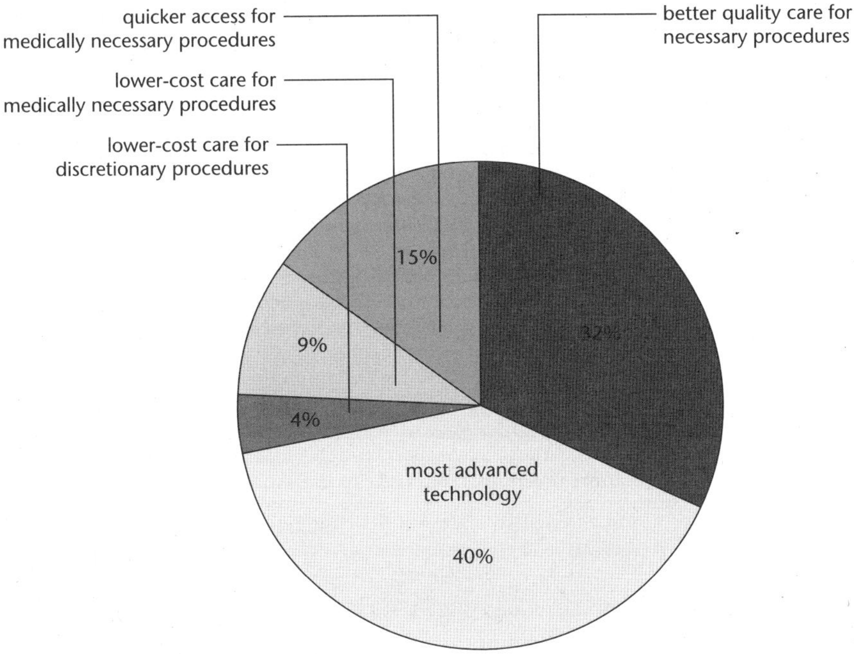


*Source:* Ehrbeck, Guevara, and Mango (2008).
*Note:* 100% = 49,980 patients. The number of patients is supplied by providers who participated in the research. The total market size assumes that participating providers represent 60%–80% of the market.

health sector in the South. Finally, it shows that North-South trade is confined to a small portion of the market (more rapid access and lower cost account for less than 30 percent of the trade) and probably does not deserve the excessive attention it has received, at least under current conditions (particularly with regard to the portability of health insurance, keeping in mind that the United States is by far the largest consumer of health services in the world, followed by the European Union).

These statistics and conclusions seem to be confirmed by empirical observations. In the case of the Association of Southeast Asian Nations (ASEAN), which hosts the top medical tourism destinations in the world, about 70 percent of exports are regional, that is, South-South (with the exception of Thailand, which seems to attract Japanese clients); this is probably driven by access to higher quality care and more advanced technologies (box 4.5).

Some developing countries might want to target niche markets and continue to tap into the North-South trade potential. For these countries, the two main drivers of trade will be more rapid access and lower costs. Malta, for instance, specializes in the provision of health care treatments (such as hip or knee

**Box 4.5:** Case Study: Exports under Mode 2, ASEAN

Three of the top six medical tourism destinations in the world are in the ASEAN region. As illustrated in table 4.3, Thailand, Malaysia, and Singapore have become major exporters of health care, servicing developing countries in the ASEAN region and developed countries such as Japan.

The competitiveness of these three countries primarily stems from two factors. First, because of lower labor costs, they can offer medical services at a significantly lower price than their industrial country competitors (see table 4.4). Ancillary services are also much cheaper: a hospital bed is almost 25 times more expensive in the United States than in Thailand. Second, hospitals in these countries have established a reputation for high-quality services. In Thailand, service quality has been explicitly promoted by an accreditation system administered by a dedicated government agency, the Institute of Hospital Quality Improvement and Accreditation. The top-rated establishments of the country usually treat foreign patients; they also happen to offer specialized services not available in other ASEAN countries, especially the poorer ones.

**Table 4.3.** Export Revenues and Patient Profile, Three ASEAN Countries

| Country | Export revenues | Number of patients | Origin of patients |
|---|---|---|---|
| Malaysia (2003) | RM 150 million (US$40 million) | More than 100,000 | 60% from Indonesia, 10% from other ASEAN countries |
| Singapore (2002) | US$420 million | 210,000 | 45% from Indonesia, 20% from Malaysia, 3% from other ASEAN countries |
| Thailand (2003) | B 20 million (US$482 million) | 470,000 in 2001, 630,000 in 2002, 974,000 in 2003 | 42% from East Asia (mostly Japan), 7% from ASEAN countries |

*Source:* Arunanondchai and Fink (2007).

replacements) for which the waiting list is longest in the United Kingdom. The cost-driven market is limited by the lack of portability in health insurance that confines the market to discretionary procedures, such as plastic surgery, or that creates an important threshold. (The comparative price is not the price of the intervention, but the cost to the patient after reimbursement.) A number of countries have therefore packaged their medical services with other services, such as tourism, so that the cost becomes only part of the equation. It should be noted that this niche market strategy could pay in the medium and long run given the forecasted increase of the needs in the North and the necessity for high-income countries to contain their health expenses and make their health insurance schemes sustainable.

**Table 4.4.** Comparative Costs of Surgical Procedures

| | Costs, US$ | | | | Costs compared to the United States, % | | |
|---|---|---|---|---|---|---|---|
| **Procedure** | **United States** | **Singapore** | **Thailand** | **India** | **Singapore** | **Thailand** | **India** |
| Heart bypass | 130,000 | 18,500 | 11,000 | 10,000 | 14.2 | 8.5 | 7.7 |
| Heart valve replacement | 160,000 | 12,500 | 10,000 | 9,000 | 7.8 | 6.3 | 5.6 |
| Angioplasty | 57,000 | 13,000 | 13,000 | 11,000 | 22.8 | 22.8 | 19.3 |
| Hip replacement | 43,000 | 12,000 | 12,000 | 9,000 | 27.9 | 27.9 | 20.9 |
| Hysterectomy | 20,000 | 6,000 | 4,500 | 3,000 | 30.0 | 22.5 | 15.0 |
| Knee replacement | 40,000 | 13,000 | 10,000 | 8,500 | 32.5 | 25.0 | 21.3 |
| Spinal fusion | 62,000 | 9,000 | 7,000 | 5,500 | 14.5 | 11.3 | 8.9 |

*Sources:* Herman (2009), based on Einhorn (2008) and authors' calculation.

### Mode 3

Commercial presence constitutes an important mode of international trade in health services, commonly taking the form of joint ventures between domestic and foreign partners either in equity investments (for example, hospitals) or non-equity investments (for example, management) (Drager and Smith 2009). India is a good example of trade under Mode 3, with close to 100 FDI projects in hospitals and diagnostic centers approved during 2000–06 for a total of US$53 million and covering developed countries (Australia, Canada, the United Kingdom, the United States) and developing countries (Malaysia, Mauritius, Saudi Arabia, Singapore, the United Arab Emirates) (see box 4.2).

According to the United Nations Conference on Trade and Development, the number of mergers and acquisitions in the health and social services sector has boomed in recent years, reaching sales of about US$14 billion in 2006 (figure 4.6). However, the available data are insufficient to allow one to determine the share of developing countries in Mode 3 exports. Nonetheless, the largest health service companies have headquarters and operate in high-income countries (mainly Canada, the United Kingdom, and the United States), and a vast majority of developing countries do not export health services under Mode 3.

### Mode 4

Remittances and the compensation of employees are the two items in the balance of payments that are commonly used as an estimate of exports under Mode 4. Developing countries largely dominate the list of top remittance-receiving

**Figure 4.6.** Mergers and Acquisitions in the Health and Social Services Sector

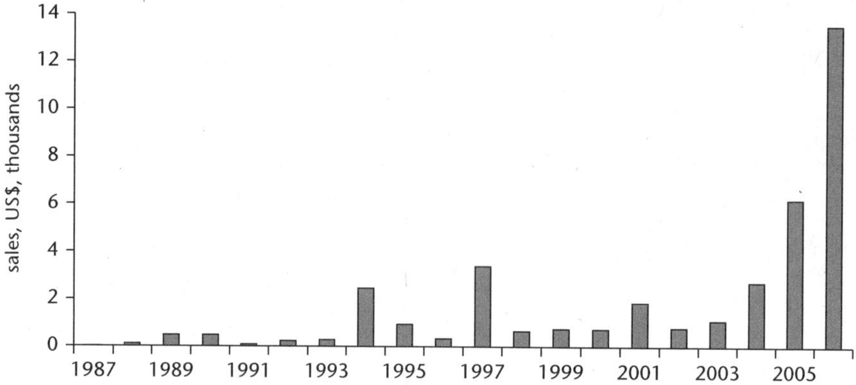


*Source:* Foreign Direct Investment Database.

countries, with close to US$26 billion a year for China, US$27 billion for India, US$25 billion for Mexico, and US$17 billion for the Philippines; in total, yearly remittances in the world represent close to US$300 billion (Ratha and Xu 2008). Remittances have become a major source of income for many developing countries, including those exporting labor in health care. This income reflects only Mode 4 trade, however, since one cannot distinguish between the remittances of permanent migrants versus temporary migrants or between the remittances of workers in the service sector versus workers in other sectors. As a result, measuring exports under Mode 4 in one specific sector, such as health care, is not possible, and no satisfactory proxy exists.

Despite this lack of reliable data, one could assume that Mode 4, along with rapidly growing Mode 2, is a main channel of developing-country exports in the health sector. Some countries, like the Philippines, have specialized in the training of nurses as export labor. The increasingly severe shortages in health personnel in high-income countries also guarantee that this segment of the market will continue to grow at a rapid pace. In 2004, the United Kingdom reported that close to 10 percent of its health care labor force (and 18 percent of its doctors) was accounted for by foreign nationals—a number that must have increased since then. Meanwhile, the Netherlands reported that close to 14 percent of its health care workforce consisted of foreign nationals (Herman 2009). Table 4.5 suggests that, on average, 10 percent of all physicians trained in Africa now reside in Canada or the United States; this includes up to 30 percent of the physicians trained in Ghana and 43 percent of those trained in Liberia. In the case of Tunisia, nurses

**Table 4.5.** African Physicians Practicing in Canada and the United States

| Country of origin | Number of African-trained physicians, United States | Number of African-trained physicians, Canada | Number of physicians remaining in the home country | % of total African-trained physicians, Canada and United States |
|---|---|---|---|---|
| Nigeria | 2,158 | 123 | 22,894 | 9 |
| South Africa | 1,943 | 1,845 | 23,844 | 14 |
| Ghana | 478 | 37 | 1,210 | 30 |
| Ethiopia | 257 | 9 | 1,564 | 15 |
| Uganda | 133 | 42 | 722 | 20 |
| Kenya | 93 | 19 | 4,001 | 3 |
| Zimbabwe | 75 | 26 | 1,694 | 6 |
| Zambia | 67 | 7 | 676 | 10 |
| Liberia | 47 | 8 | 72 | 43 |
| 12 other countries | 83 | 35 | 12,912 | 1 |
| **Total, average** | **5,334** | **2,151** | **69,589** | **10** |

*Source:* Authors compilation based on journals at http://www.human-resources-health.com/.

represent the bulk of the expatriate health care workforce, and the percentages for physicians are much lower (box 4.6). This suggests that the movement of health care personnel is driven primarily by financial incentives and the absence of opportunities at home (the lower the domestic income and the fewer the opportunities at home, such as in Sub-Saharan Africa, the more movement). It also suggests that, given wealth differentials among developing countries, there is a considerable potential for South-South trade under Mode 4. In the case of Tunisia, Saudi Arabia is by far the main destination in the movement of the health care workforce, and the Persian Gulf countries capture more than 80 percent of the total flows.

### *The expected benefits of health service exports*

For all four modes of delivery, exports generate income that benefits the domestic economy and contributes to improving the balance of payments. The dynamic effects of this income will vary depending on the mode of service delivery.

Exports under Mode 1 increase the revenues of domestic health service providers, allow additional investment, and potentially improve profitability and competitiveness (for example, through economies of scale). They also create opportunities for health care providers at home (for example, work on new technologies) and help curtail the flight of human resources.

**Box 4.6:** Case Study: Exports under Mode 4, Tunisia

One should interpret the numbers in table 4.6 with caution because Mode 4 covers only the temporary movement of persons, and, in many cases, the intent (with or without success) of the migrant is to stay permanently in the host country.

**Table 4.6.** Tunisian Exports under Mode 4, 2004

| Indicator | Physicians | Technicians | Nurses | Total | Percent |
|---|---|---|---|---|---|
| Saudi Arabia | 65 | 336 | 827 | 1,228 | 53 |
| Qatar | 6 | 229 | 130 | 365 | 16 |
| United Arab Emirates | 9 | 107 | 163 | 279 | 12 |
| Kuwait | 0 | 1 | 55 | 56 | 2 |
| Europe | 1 | 2 | 278 | 281 | 12 |
| Others | 21 | 18 | 81 | 120 | 4 |
| Total | 102 | 693 | 1,534 | 2,329 | 100 |
| Number remaining at home | 13,330 | 10,799 | 28,537 | 52,666 | n.a. |

*Source:* Achouri and Achour (2005), based on data of the Tunisian Agency for Technical Cooperation.
*Note:* n.a. = not applicable.

Exports under Mode 2 have similar effects. The spillover effects will depend on the legal and regulatory framework and business model adopted by the exporting country (see the potential risks of imports under Mode 3 noted earlier). These effects will be maximized if the local population can benefit from the infrastructure and treatments developed for foreign patients or if some of the returns to local health service providers are injected back into the domestic health system. The example of Morocco illustrates the different channels that the dynamic effects of Mode 2 exports can take. The high concentration of tourists resulted in an increase in the supply of health services (available to both foreigners and locals), and the opening of residences for retirees (that provide medical services) somewhat changed local attitudes toward elders. The necessity to conform to international standards in exportation also creates a local demonstration effect. Doctors, nurses, and other health care personnel are offered greater opportunities at home, and Mode 2 exports create a disincentive to expatriation. In sum, a properly designed strategy to export health services under Mode 2 has the potential of improving the access to higher-quality health care services for the local population.

Exports under Mode 3 are returns on investment that are more or less similar to those in any other sector.

Exports under Mode 4 could be an important source of income (for example, the remittances of Philippine nurses). This income would directly benefit the local population (recipients of the remittances) and, hence, public health. The benefits for the exporting country's health system are indirect only. Temporary movement abroad provides local health care providers with a number of opportunities, including access to training, new technologies, acquisition of additional skills and specialization, and so on. Upon their return to their origin countries, these service providers will help the local population (and their local colleagues) benefit from the skills acquired abroad. Given the rapid evolution in medicine, these movements across borders are particularly important to the sector.

### *The potential risks associated with health service exports and the measures to mitigate them*

The risks associated with exports in health services largely mirror those described above for imports. They can therefore be quickly reviewed.

For Modes 1 and 2, the main risk is the diversion of scarce human and financial resources to health care services entirely dedicated to the treatment of foreign patients. The case of Thailand reveals that an additional 100,000 foreign patients seeking medical treatment in the country could lead to an internal human resource drain of 240–700 doctors (box 4.7). Exports of health services therefore represent a challenge to the objectives of universal access and equity of access to quality health services. The internal human resource drain also represents a loss of public investment in medical education and training. Potentially, the richest local clientele are also diverted to these high-end health care service providers to the detriment of the profitability and sustainability of the public health sector. As suggested in the case of Thailand, however, a number of accompanying policies could help minimize these diversion risks, including through the cross-fertilization of public and private health initiatives.

The risks associated with exports under Mode 4 primarily depend on the intentions of the migrants. While the flow of expertise should be encouraged (Mode 4, as a regulated scheme for the temporary movement of personnel, is a factor in the flow of expertise), the human resource drain could have dramatic effects on local public health. Opportunities for individuals can translate into losses for a society. This is particularly true in the health sector, where medical density dramatically varies across countries and across regions within countries. Well-regulated trade under Mode 4 should contribute to preventing the human resource drain because nothing can prevent people from leaving a country. (Agreements on Mode 4 can include a scheme to foster the return of migrant workers.) Some countries, such as the Philippines, have introduced special curricula and created private schools to train nurses desiring to move abroad. The benefit of such schemes is to limit the losses (in terms of education) and avoid diverting the local supply of health care

**Box 4.7:** Case Study: Mitigating the Distributive and Other Adverse Effects of Trade in Health Services, Thailand

The combination of rapidly rising domestic demand for health care, a rapid increase in medical tourism, and a publicly subsidized medical education system that supplies health professionals to both the public and private sectors presents a formidable policy challenge for policy makers. Thailand's experience with policies aimed at mitigating negative distribution effects and other adverse impacts of Mode 2 trade in health services provides an important set of possible options for policy makers in countries looking to promote medical tourism.

## The problems

In Thailand, private hospitals that treat foreign patients do not participate in social health insurance schemes. Foreigners and upper-income Thai pay out of pocket or are covered by private health insurance. This diverts medical personnel away from public hospitals that serve Thai patients only, many of which participate in the social health insurance schemes. By one estimate, an extra 100,000 patients seeking medical treatment in Thailand leads to an internal human resource drain of 240–700 doctors (Arunanondchai and Fink 2007, Pannarunothai and Suknak 2004). A related concern is that tertiary medical education is provided almost exclusively by the public sector. Thus, private exporting hospitals hire from the same resource pool as public hospitals, but do not share in the costs of medical education.

## The solutions

Thailand has long enforced a three-year program of compulsory public service for medical graduates. Two-thirds of these graduates work in rural areas. The financial incentives for rural doctors include a hardship allowance, a no-private-practice allowance, paid overtime, and special service allowances. Universal coverage was implemented in 2001, and the financial incentives were announced in 2004–05. Because of the incentives, a new medical graduate in the most remote rural district can earn a salary equal to that of a senior doctor in the central department with 25 years of experience. In 2004, the government approved the One District, One Doctor Project, whereby new medical students are recruited from high schools in rural districts, educated in a local university and local hospital, and retained to work in their own districts. These measures are aimed at curbing the urban concentration of medical professionals, an important concern in Thailand. In mid-2004, the government also approved a project to increase the acceptance of medical graduates rapidly during 2005–14. The first batch of these graduates is expected in 2011. This highlights the need for a long-term, proactive approach to human resource planning in the health sector, in which the duration of education is long. Finally, awards and high-level career classifications encourage rural service and help counter the internal human resource drain.

These measures on the supply side are supplemented by measures on the demand side, for example, health promotion campaigns that are expected to encourage preventive care and curb the population's need for curative care.

*Source:* Blouin, Drager, and Smith (2007).

providers (since the training curricula for the nurses is kept separate). Some foreign governments have also offered to sponsor some of these dedicated schools in developing countries, which would contribute to reducing the risks of public resource leakages even further. In the case of South Africa, some private health service providers have concluded agreements with foreign health care networks to provide short-term opportunities for their staff abroad, while controlling returns (personnel are prohibited from working in the U.K. system for two years after the completion of their temporary assignment within the U.K. branch of the South African group) (see box 4.10).

## What Should Be Done to Foster Trade in Health Services?

Increasing trade in health services could be beneficial to both importing and exporting countries and in the high-income developing countries, as well as in the poorest ones. A number of conditions are attached to success, however. The market is competitive, and not all countries have a comparative advantage in health services; countries interested in entering and contesting the market need to assess carefully their resources and design trade promotion strategies that have domestic and international dimensions.

The section above reviews the potential benefits and risks of trade opening from a public health perspective, suggesting accompanying measures to make the most of trade. This section consists of a checklist of questions to be raised and measures to be adopted by governments in designing effective trade strategies in the health sector.

Trade does not take place in a vacuum. In the same way that trade alone is not sufficient to fix a country's health system, a country cannot presume to compete on the international health services market if its domestic health system is dysfunctional. A country cannot suddenly decide to export health services the same way it could decide to export other basic goods, such as asparagus or freshly cut flowers, if only because of the high level of human expertise and technology required. There are prerequisites for trade in health services, and a number of elements have been identified that make a country attractive, for example, for medical tourists or foreign investors.

### *Country endowments: Strengths (how to exploit them) and weaknesses (how to remedy them)*

In determining whether a country could enter and compete on the world health services market, a typical first step is the assessment of the country's strengths and weaknesses and, eventually, the design of policies to exploit most effectively the strengths and remedy the weaknesses. The SWOT analysis—the analysis of strengths, weaknesses, opportunities, and threats—is a diagnostic and planning tool commonly used in the private sector that could also be used as a logical framework for our purposes.

The example of a SWOT analysis for Morocco (box 4.8) reveals the country's current competitive advantages and shortages in the health sector. The analysis covers strengths and weaknesses, which include the price competitiveness, availability, quality, and reputation of health personnel (doctors and nurses), geographical and cultural factors (such as language), respect for international management standards and standards of hygiene (for example, clinics certified by the International Organization for Standardization), a tradition of exports, the organization of the sector (public versus private, the critical mass of clinics), and so on.

In a second step in determining whether a country could enter and compete on the world health services market, the SWOT analysis focuses on opportunities and threats, that is, external factors affecting the future of the market. From a trade perspective, this analysis is important because countries want to diversify in sectors where international demand is growing and not declining. Also, the parallel reading of strengths and opportunities helps in identifying the trade niches on which countries could concentrate their efforts. Among the opportunities identified in the Maghreb are the aging of the European population (and the parallel increase in the demand for care, retirement facilities, accompaniment personnel); the health supply shortages in Europe and in neighboring developing countries (waiting lists for certain operations, skill shortages in Africa); the boom in cosmetic surgery, thalassotherapy, and health tourism generally; and the gaps in European health insurance schemes (and the deterioration in the levels of reimbursement, particularly in dentistry). The trade niches identified include the dental and prosthesis market, the French-speaking comfort surgery and wellness market, retirement residential programs, and so on.

Not all strengths and weaknesses have the same weight in triggering trade. Quality remains the main driver of trade in the health sector. The entry costs in the health services market are therefore high in terms of education, training, and equipment. Some countries, such as Morocco, benefit from traditionally well-trained medical personnel. One cannot acquire a qualified labor force and, even less, a reputation overnight. Some countries therefore resort to foreign labor in the short run to supplement their domestic resources. In Malaysia, for example, the government has increased the allowed stay under a medical visa from 30 days to 6 months. It is not sufficient to have good doctors if clinics and hospitals are not properly managed or if nurses and other medical personnel are

**Box 4.8:** Case Study: SWOT Analysis, Health Services Trade, Morocco

The SWOT analysis is shown in table 4.7.

**Table 4.7.** Health Services Trade, Morocco

| *Strengths* | *Weaknesses* |
|---|---|
| – Lower cost of services relative to Europe<br>– Cultural heritage, diversity of the landscape, tourist attractions, climate<br>– Geographical and cultural, including language, proximity with Europe<br>– Facility of access to residential property and resulting strong foreign presence in residential areas (retirees and temporary residents)<br>– Qualification and reputation of the doctors or hospitals gained through training or exchanges with foreign universities and medical institutions and participation in networks with hospitals and research centers abroad (particularly in France) | – No statistics and sectoral strategy at the government level<br>– Only individual initiatives; difficulty in financing large-scale projects<br>– Skill shortages: insufficient number of doctors and key health personnel (absolute terms); lower relative density of health personnel than Algeria, Egypt, Libya, and Tunisia<br>– Qualification of nurses and other medical staff<br>– Late in the race with Tunisia and other competitors<br>– Lack of application of international standards and certifications (for example, the International Organization for Standardization)<br>– Absence of a clear legal framework for medical tourism, which could result in malpractice and represents an important risk for the reputation of the country<br>– Strict nationality requirements that prevent foreigners from opening practices (and investing) |
| *Opportunities* | *Threats* |
| – Booming market focused on seniors and retirees (aging of the population): residential programs, medical accompaniment in Morocco and abroad, paramedical services<br>– Booming market for cosmetic surgery, thalassotherapy and other forms of health tourism<br>– Booming market for dental surgery and prosthesis<br>– Specialization in some advanced surgical procedures, including cardiology, cancer treatment, epidemiology, to treat patients in the region<br>– Expected shortages of certain medical personnel in Europe<br>– Offshoring of certain medical services; the use of the existing infrastructure<br>– Deterioration in the level of reimbursement of treatments in Europe and the development of portability in health insurance<br>– Increasing need for medical training in the region: Mali, Mauritania, and other countries | – Protectionist reaction of European countries and bans on medical tourism<br>– Competition of emerging countries in Asia, Eastern and Central Europe, and the Middle East and North Africa<br>– Loss of human resources through the permanent establishment abroad of key health personnel |

*Source:* World Bank staff.

not properly trained or qualified. Required investments in infrastructure and technology are also important. In Taiwan, China, for example, the government has announced a US$318 million project to help develop health services. Also, the lack of a global database on the safety and quality of care has increased the importance of international voluntary standards. The Joint Commission International, a specialized body, has accredited over 120 hospitals worldwide, and several other organizations, such as the International Society for Quality in Health Care, the National Committee for Quality Assurance, the International Organization for Standardization, and the European Society for Quality in Healthcare, have taken steps to ensure that medical travelers receive the highest quality care (Deloitte 2008).

### *Improving the domestic regulatory framework and removing unnecessary obstacles to trade*

Strict regulation of the health sector is needed, for example, to prevent malpractice or encourage the choice of the most efficient providers. At the same time, most obstacles to trade in health services, and services more generally, are found in domestic regulations (obstacles behind the border). A necessary step for countries aiming to enter and compete on the world health services market is therefore a regulatory audit to ensure that the measures in place contribute to achieving legitimate policy objectives and are the least trade restrictive in efficiently achieving these objectives.

The World Bank, the Organisation for Economic Co-operation and Development, and the Australian Productivity Commission, among others, have developed trade restrictiveness indexes that aim to identify common barriers to trade in services, including in the health sector. While they do not address the question of the adequacy of national rules (and their suitability in relation to the legitimate objectives to be achieved), they help identify problem areas for foreign investors and in terms of best practices. In the case of Tunisia, for instance, all the types of restrictions usually tested are present in the domestic regulatory framework (box 4.9). This suggests that the government will need to reassess these rules in light of its domestic public health and foreign trade objectives. These include rules pertaining to the form of establishment, foreign investment, nationality and residency requirements, the movement of health personnel, and so on.

It often appears that easing trade does not revolve around deregulation, but rather more effective regulation and, sometimes, even filling regulatory gaps. For example, the ethics of medical tourism is often a grey area in domestic regulations. This includes issues such as advertising for medical services, the role of tour

**Box 4.9:** Case Study: Regulatory Audit for Health Services, Tunisia

A portion of the restrictions are listed in table 4.8.

**Table 4.8.** Regulatory Audit, Tunisia

| Type of restriction | Medical |
|---|---|
| **Form of establishment** | Clinic, hospital, individual practice |
| **Foreign partnership, association, joint venture** | Authorized, restrictions apply |
| **Investment and ownership by foreign professionals** | Authorized, restrictions apply |
| **Investment and ownership by nonprofessional investors** | Authorized, restrictions apply |
| **Nationality, citizenship requirements** | Must be Tunisian |
| **Residency and local presence** | No |
| **Quotas, economic needs tests on the number of professionals and firms** | Numerus clausus (for example, pharmacies per inhabitants) |
| **Licensing and accreditation of foreign professionals** | Possible recognition of foreign diplomas |
| **Licensing and accreditation of domestic professionals** | Inscription on the Tableau de l'ordre des médecins |
| **Movement of people** | Usual visa conditions, exceptional authorizations to practice (for example, training) |
| **Activities reserved by law to the profession** | Yes, practice of medicine |
| **Multidisciplinary practices** | Authorized, restrictions apply |
| **Advertising, marketing, and solicitation** | Prohibited for doctors, authorized for clinics with restrictions |
| **Fee setting** | Yes, distinction between public and private sectors |

*Sources:* World Bank staff compilation of laws and regulations; restriction index based on Nguyen-Hong (2000).

*Note:* The list is not exhaustive. It gives an idea of potential regulatory obstacles to trade. It does not address the issue of the adequacy of the domestic regulations, some of which are fully justified to ensure the quality of services, while others might be more restrictive than is necessary to achieve the objective.

operators and other intermediaries between the patient and the doctor that might affect the quality of the advice given on decisions to have surgery, the privacy of medical files, and so on. Without creating unnecessary obstacles to trade, an ethics code or a set of rules might be necessary to prevent fraud and deceptive practices not only for the sake of patients, but also for the domestic health service sector as a whole, given that the risks to a system's reputation are particularly high in the health sector.

The difficulty of the regulatory review and reform exercise should not be underestimated. First, some regulations that apply to the health sector are not sector specific (for example, some rules on foreign investment or visa approvals). Second, not all rules are set by the government. In many professions, including the medical profession, the professional orders or associations may enjoy important delegated public authority to regulate the profession (for example, in the recognition of qualifications or the certification to practice). For these reasons, a health sector strategy requires cooperation among the government, ministries, the private sector, and professional associations.

### *Promoting exports*

In a highly competitive global market, it is not enough to fix the fundamentals, including the regulatory framework, to become an exporter of health services. As in any other sector, a trade promotion strategy is necessary to gain market shares abroad. The elaboration of this strategy is mainly the responsibility of the private sector (or health service providers generally), but the government also has a major role.

### *Business strategies: Niches and prospective markets*

The description of the drivers of trade in health services under Mode 2 suggests that not all markets may be contested and not all business strategies can be successful. For example, targeting the French market for medical treatments that are fully covered by health insurance cannot succeed; in contrast, targeting the U.K. market for medical procedures that are not readily accessible in the United Kingdom may be rewarding. The knowledge of foreign markets, including health care needs (such as the age structure of the population), medical care supply factors (such as the density and shortages in medical personnel, particularly in specialty areas), and gaps in health insurance coverage, is essential in the design of efficient export promotion strategies. The United States is and will remain the world's largest consumer of health services and therefore a main target of health service exports. The increasing demand for health services in high-income countries and, in parallel, the increasing shortages in health care supply could have major effects on trade opportunities. Not only might net exporting countries become major importers of health services, but they could experience shortages in the resources they need to supply those developing countries that now import their services. Thus, there would be room for the most advanced developing countries to compete for market share in the North and in the South.

A good knowledge of global supply, that is, competition, is also required. Innovation, as in the trade in goods, is important for success. This could take the form

**Box 4.10:** Seizing Opportunities in the United Kingdom: The Case of South Africa

South African hospital companies have been successful in winning health care contracts abroad, particularly with the U.K. National Health Service. Netcare, an investment holding company based in South Africa, began operations in the United Kingdom in 2001. An early project of the group involved taking part in helping reduce waiting lists in selected areas. Surgical centers in Greater Manchester and Stracathro in Angus, Scotland, performed 8,000 procedures in one year; cataract centers have performed 20,000 procedures to date; and walk-in centers have so far treated 30,000 patients. In 2006, Netcare led a consortium that acquired General Healthcare Group, the owner of the largest independent hospital operator, BMI Healthcare. This has increased the business by 89 percent, transformed Netcare into one of the world's largest health care groups (119 hospitals and almost 11,000 beds), and given Netcare an outstanding platform for enhancing its relationship with the U.K. National Health Service. As part of this contract, Netcare will send teams of medical personnel from South Africa for fixed, short-term periods in the United Kingdom. These personnel are prohibited from employment with the U.K. National Health Service for a period of two years. Netcare has also piloted a project that allows nursing employees to work in foreign countries for four to six weeks at a time. The objective is to expose South African doctors and nurses to opportunities in U.K. hospitals and enable them to supplement their incomes through fixed-term contracts abroad. Staff turnover has been significantly reduced as a result, and the group could retain skilled staff in South Africa.

South African health care groups are also targeting patients in Africa. Netcare has set up a network of referral agents in a number of African countries to attract patients to the group's hospitals and doctors in South Africa. They also arrange transport, accommodation, and recuperative care for these patients. Competitors have established centers in Johannesburg to assist foreign patients and their families with transport, visas, accommodation, and medical treatment. They employ English-, French-, and Portuguese-speaking interpreters and clearly target African patients.

*Source:* http://www.netcare.co.za/live/netcare_index.php.

of the development of new technologies and medical procedures or packaging health services differently (for example, health tourism packages, airport pickup services, translation services, and facilitated billing, etc.).

There are a number of success stories that should be examined carefully by new entrants. The cases of Cuba and South Africa illustrate successful export promotion strategies under Mode 3 (establishment abroad) and Mode 2 (health tourism) (boxes 4.10 and 4.11).

### *Reforming the institutional framework to promote trade*

The example of Cuba shows that a successful export promotion strategy in the health sector is fully compatible with significant state involvement and the preservation of a predominantly public health sector. Indeed, experience shows that

**Box 4.11:** Case Study: A Successful Government-Led Strategy to Develop Medical Tourism, Cuba

The Cuban government views health export promotion as an important part of its overall economic development strategy. Cuba has long been a popular destination for medical tourism, attracting patients mostly from Europe and elsewhere in Latin America and the Caribbean and North America.

A number of specialized clinics in the country provide high-quality care at competitive prices and also function as training centers for medical schools for domestic and foreign students. Early in the process, Cuba's strategy focused on health spas and mineral springs, medical support and emergency care for travelers, and the supply of specialized medical care not readily available elsewhere in Latin America and the Caribbean. It also aimed at specialized services, focusing on the treatment of certain kinds of skin disease that are not treated in other countries and on the development of new procedures and medicines. This trade promotion strategy had several underlying objectives, including the employment of qualified health service providers, the use of excess capacity for the manufacture of medical and pharmaceutical products, and the use of trade resources to invest in health care infrastructure and the public health system.

Cuba's success in the health service trade may be attributed to the foresight and long-term planning of the Ministry of Health, in collaboration with other institutions, in the areas of tourism, migration, commerce, and industry. An important factor in this success has been the establishment of Grupo Cubanacan (formerly Servimed), a state-run trading company hosted by the Ministry of Health, which supports the marketing and promotion of Cuban health services overseas. Cubanacan, together with tour operators and travel agents in target markets, prepares health packages that include air travel (on Cubana de Aviación, Cuba's national airlines) for patients and accompanying persons, companion personnel to accompany patients after arrival at the airport, 24-hour assistance, treatment, repatriation, and postoperative checkups. Cubanacan relies on a network of 35 clinics and 42 resorts in Cuba, private clinics overseas, and commercial representation in target markets such as Argentina, Brazil, Chile, Mexico, and República Bolivariana de Venezuela.

Cuba offers free or subsidized care to patients from some countries, essentially countries in Africa and Latin America. Cuba has also concluded bilateral agreements with social security institutions in several countries in Latin America and the Caribbean to facilitate trade. In addition, the government has provided for easy payment facilities for credit cards in any convertible currency. Two smaller agencies have also been established in health tourism to provide rehabilitative and convalescent health services through resorts and spas following the Cubanacan model.

*Source:* Blouin, Drager, and Smith (2007).

governments have played an important role in the success of the countries that are leading health service exporters. Public sector involvement could be crucial at all stages from the design to the implementation of export promotion strategies.

A common problem is the lack of statistics on trade in health services that could translate into a lack of coherent sectoral development strategies by governments. For example, in elaborating an export strategy for medical tourism, one would need to know the number of medical tourists, the type of procedures offered, the type and level of expenses for care, and so on. Only rough approximations are available in most countries. Some countries have undertaken efforts to remedy this situation and improve national statistics on the trade in health services. For instance, Morocco has introduced a count of foreign patients treated in local hospitals. The *Manual on Statistics of International Trade in Services* provides useful guidelines for governments willing to tackle this problem (United Nations 2002).[5]

A related common problem is the absence of cooperation among ministries (for example, health, trade, and tourism) and of dialogue among actors. Too many actors are involved in the trade in health services that do not necessarily communicate with each other. They include tour operators, private practitioners, clinics, hospitals, research institutes, ministries, professional bodies or associations, real estate developers, and foreign and local investors. Experience shows that the countries performing most effectively in the international trade in health services, such as Thailand, have created horizontal administrative structures to coordinate the domestic stance and the strategies on health tourism. (These are sometimes known as medical tourism observatories.) In contrast, the dispersion of actors remains a technical challenge for lagging countries, for example, in the Maghreb, where success stories in exports appear to result from individual and uncoordinated initiatives rather than real strategies.

A number of countries have set up trade promotion agencies, primarily to encourage and facilitate exports of domestic goods and services. However, these agencies often focus on exports of traditional goods rather than services and, hence, neglect the health service sector. In the case of Cuba (box 4.11), the creation of an agency charged with promoting and marketing health tourism in Cuba has proved successful. Depending on the country context, such a function could be carried out by an existing trade promotion agency or as part of the mandate of the administrative coordination structure. In any case, marketing and promotion are essential to boosting trade in health services, particularly because of the lack of transparent data worldwide on the quality of health care and because of the important role reputation plays in the choice of destination among consumers.

Finally, it should be noted that public (often university) hospitals have been important in the development of the reputations of many countries in the health sector and often showcase expertise and attract foreign patients or health professionals.

### *Using international cooperation (public and private) to promote trade*

A number of obstacles to trade in health services are found in domestic regulation and can be addressed through unilateral domestic reforms. However, partners are needed to trade, and market access can be hindered by policies in other countries. Hence, unilateral reforms can be undertaken in exchange for concessions (market access) by major trading partners. Using the SWOT analysis terminology, a country's opportunities and threats may reflect the country's offense and defense (and, therefore, negotiating positions) in trade negotiations.

For example, the lack of portability in health insurance is the main obstacle to the development of the health tourism market. The prohibition preventing tour operators from selling health care packages (for example, in France) and the limited recognition of medical qualifications are two other examples of the external obstacles to health trade. The removal of these obstacles can be negotiated in a number of trade forums and implemented through trade agreements, including bilateral and multilateral trade arrangements. It is the government's responsibility to design an aggressive trade agenda and use all available instruments to promote its trade interests in the health sector. The private sector also has a major role in this process indirectly, by informing the government's negotiation positions, or directly, by, for example, encouraging exchanges of personnel or the mutual recognition of qualifications. Experience shows that pragmatic solutions could be found at all levels of international cooperation.

### Bilateral and regional initiatives and agreements

Bilateral and regional agreements are the most common instruments of trade promotion in the health sector. They can be used to remove obstacles to trade and harmonize domestic rules across a region (and eventually adopt regional rules). They can have different shapes, content, and legal value (binding and nonbinding) and may involve developed or developing countries, or both. In part, this flexibility is the reason for their success in the health sector in cases in which governments must deal with a number of sensitive issues and fine-tune the opening of trade to realize public health objectives. Examples of state-to-state agreements (in a broad sense and not limited to trade agreements) include the following:

- Social security conventions and other agreements pertaining to the insurance coverage of traveling patients: Some social security institutions in Latin America have concluded bilateral agreements with Cuba that contain mutually agreed rates for medical treatments in Cuba. Algeria and Libya, respectively, have signed protocols with Jordan and Tunisia on sponsorship for the treatment of patients abroad (which explains the success of Tunisia in the Libyan market, primarily under Mode 2).
- Bilateral labor agreements: for example, between Germany and Croatia or Slovenia; between the United Kingdom, India, the Philippines, and Spain; and between Norway and the Philippines for the recruitment of nurses.

- Conventions on the education and training of medical personnel that encourage the temporary crossborder movement of health personnel.
- Bilateral and regional free trade agreements: An increasing number of free trade agreements cover health services, such as the most recent Economic Partnership Agreement between the European Commission and the Caribbean region.[6]
- Bilateral investment treaties: This mushrooming category of agreements could also be directly relevant to the trade in health services under Mode 3.

The conclusion of a bilateral or regional trade agreement is not a guarantee of liberalization or deeper market access in partner countries. The flexibility that has led to the success of these agreements also constitutes their weakness because a number of exceptions could be carved out in each sector that potentially nullify or impair the general commitments of the partners. The level of implementation of the agreements also varies significantly from case to case. The example of the Morocco–United States free trade agreement in table 4.9 illustrates how health services could be subject to many more exceptions than other service sectors. It is often the case that health is excluded from bilateral or regional negotiations, such as in the context of the Union for the Mediterranean (the Euro-Mediterranean Partnership).

In addition to these state-to-state agreements, a number of arrangements that also facilitate trade could be concluded between public and private institutions or among private institutions. Typically, hospitals or universities conclude twinning agreements with counterparts abroad that include provisions on the exchange of health personnel for training or education purposes. Depending on the public authority delegated to them, professional associations in the medical profession can also agree on the mutual recognition of diplomas and qualifications with foreign counterparts. The involvement of private insurance networks in health insurance conventions could help remove the ultimate obstacle to trade in health services: the absence of health insurance portability.

Finally, regional cooperation is a potential solution to some health care shortages and can mitigate some of the risks associated with increased trade. For instance, the development of health centers of excellence in Africa could help neighboring countries share the cost of medical education and infrastructure investment.

### Multilateral initiatives and agreements

A vast literature exists on health services, the GATS, and multilateral trade negotiations. It is not the purpose of this chapter to analyze the GATS provisions pertaining to health or the World Health Organization (see Blouin, Drager, and

**Table 4.9.** Restrictions on Health Services Trade Listed by Morocco in the United States–Morocco Free Trade Agreement

Annex I-Morocco: Existing measures that are not subject to some or all relevant provisions of chapters 10 and 11

*Physicians*: A foreign physician may engage in the private practice of medicine only if he or she fulfills certain conditions, including the following conditions, which are inconsistent with the obligations listed above:
(a) have permanent residency in Morocco;
(b) have status as the spouse of a Moroccan national or as a national of a State that has entered into an agreement with Morocco authorizing a national of either State to practice medicine in the territory of the other State; and
(c) have government authorization.

Notwithstanding paragraphs (a) and (b), the Ministry of Health may authorize foreign physicians to practice in Morocco for periods not exceeding one month with respect to specialties that do not exist in Morocco.

*Establishing clinics or comparable medical facilities*: Only physicians who have fulfilled the requirements for practicing medicine in Morocco may establish private clinics and comparable medical facilities, such as birthing centers, water therapy (*thalassotherapie*) centers, medical care centers and other centers providing in-patient care for periods of at least twenty-four hours, kidney dialysis centers, radiotherapy centers, and chemotherapy centers.

*Pharmacists*: In deciding whether to authorize a foreign national to practice the profession of pharmacist, Morocco may take into account the needs of the sector.

*Pharmaceutical firms*: The establishment in Morocco of a firm engaged in the manufacture or wholesale distribution of pharmaceutical products is contingent on the requirement that 51 percent of the capital stock be held by pharmacists. A majority of that 51 percent of capital stock (*i.e.*, at least 26 percent of the total capital stock) must be held by persons authorized to practice as pharmacists in Morocco. In an enterprise established in Morocco and engaged in the manufacture or wholesale distribution of pharmaceutical products, the following persons must be pharmacists:
(a) in sole proprietorships, the sole proprietor;
(b) in corporations, the president and one-half plus one of the members of the board of directors;
(c) in limited-liability companies and limited partnerships, all managerial personnel; and
(d) in other types of enterprises, all the principals.

*Dental surgeons, midwives, nurses, and opticians*: In deciding whether to authorize a foreign national to practice the profession of dental surgeon, midwife, nurse, or optician, Morocco may take into account the needs of the sector.

*Private biomedical analysis laboratories*: A foreign pharmacist, physician, or veterinarian may establish, operate, and manage a private biomedical analysis laboratory only if he or she fulfills certain conditions, including the following conditions, which are inconsistent with the obligations listed above:
(a) have permanent residency in Morocco; and
(b) have status as the spouse of a Moroccan national or as a national of a State that has entered into an agreement with Morocco authorizing a national of either State to establish, operate, or manage private biomedical analysis laboratories in the territory of the other State.

*Source:* The full text of the agreement, http://www.moroccousafta.com/ftafulltext.htm.

Smith 2006; Fidler, Correa, and Aginam 2005). A few remarks are nonetheless useful to debunk myths surrounding the GATS.

The GATS allows sufficient flexibility for countries to maintain regulations that are essential to the pursuit of important policy objectives, such as the protection of public health.[7] The main advantage of GATS commitments is to anchor domestic reforms into the international system and to preserve the government from the eventual pressures exerted by interest groups. The commitments also send a strong signal to the investor community about the government's will to engage in and secure a trade opening and reform with regard to the health service sector. Multilateral negotiations also adequately supplement regional ones. Apart from the economies of scale in negotiations, topics that are set aside in regional negotiations can be more easily addressed within the World Trade Organization (in which the balance of power is different because of the larger number of members). Still, agreements are more difficult to reach. The Doha Round was initiated in 2001, and little progress has been made on services. The level of commitments in the health sector remains particularly low, with only 39 percent of members with commitments, which is the lowest percentage in all sectors (up to 95 percent of the members have commitments in the tourism sector). Similarly, health is dragging in the GATS negotiation proposals, with only five developing countries offering additional liberalization of the sector (Sauvé 2008).

For each country engaged in the GATS negotiations, the following steps are suggested. A first step would be to make a clear assessment of all rules regulating the national health service sector and bind no less than the status quo. At no cost, this binding of already engaged reforms (the status quo) could represent a bargaining chip for a government and help the government negotiate more market access with its major partners. A second step would be to clarify existing rules to measure the eventual cost of a trade opening and elaborate a strategy to harness most effectively the benefits of the trade opening and multilateral concessions. Where no clear rules exist, a country can keep the right to legislate at a later stage, without slowing the liberalization process. A third step would be to define the country's interests clearly in the negotiations and bargain for key commitments by major partners. This could pertain to sectoral negotiations and negotiations on rules.

Finally, the GATS is not the only multilateral agreement relevant to trade in health services. In the World Trade Organization, other agreements, such as the Agreement on Trade-Related Aspects of Intellectual Property Rights for rules relating to patenting or the General Agreement on Tariffs and Trade for commitments on nonagricultural market access (for instance, on medical equipment and supplies), are also relevant (WHO and WTO 2002). Other international organizations, such as the International Organization for Standardization, also play a fundamental role in setting standards in the health sector that are main drivers of the trade in health services. It is therefore important for all countries involved in the international trade in health services to participate actively in international rule making, implementation, and enforcement.

## Conclusion

This chapter aims to help policy makers increase their understanding of the trade in the health service phenomenon by providing guidelines on ways to foster the trade in health services and, most important, the benefits of this trade. Some of the key steps that are described in this chapter and that should be taken before making decisions pertaining to a country's participation in the global trade in health services are indicated below. The chapter provides guidance to countries in addressing key issues and making optimal choices with regard to trade and public health.

- What is the balance between the potential benefits and the costs of increased trade in health services? For each of the four modes of service delivery identified in the GATS (crossborder, consumption abroad, foreign establishment, and the movement of persons), what are the expected benefits and costs of increased imports and what are the expected benefits and costs of increased exports?
- What are the accompanying measures that will help maximize the benefits and minimize the costs of increased trade? These measures include avoiding an internal and external human resource drain, preserving universal access and other legitimate public health objectives, avoiding a two-tier health system, improving quality and widening the access to health services, promoting transfers of technology and expertise, and increasing the human and financial resources in health care. The measures involved should cover each of the delivery modes, as well as imports and exports.

There is a need to identify the strengths, weaknesses, opportunities, and risks of the country in the health service sector. When considering how to remedy weaknesses, it is necessary to fix the fundamentals (education, training, infrastructure, and technology) and to adapt the domestic regulatory framework (regulatory audit and the reform of the rules that are more trade restrictive than necessary to achieve legitimate public health objectives). Maintaining the strengths involves designing an export promotion strategy (finding the right niches, tapping the right markets) and improving coordination in the public sector and with the private sector (improving statistics and creating a horizontal structure for cooperation, marketing, and promotion). To address the risks and create new opportunities abroad will involve negotiating bilateral and regional agreements (trade and non-trade agreements, such as social security conventions or labor agreements) and negotiating multilateral agreements (the GATS and other World Trade Organization agreements, plus international standards).

## Notes

1. Millennium Development Goals pertaining to health include goal 4 (reduce by two-thirds the mortality rate among children under 5), goal 5 (reduce by three-quarters the maternal mortality ratio; achieve, by 2015, universal access to reproductive health), and goal 6 (halt and begin to reverse the spread of HIV/AIDS; achieve, by 2010, universal access treatment for HIV/AIDS for all those who need it; halt and begin to reverse the incidence of malaria and other major diseases).
2. See http://www.lifespring.in/index.html.
3. It remains necessary for governments to prioritize their expenses in the health sector; in some countries, the cost of certain technologies might justify continuing to send patients abroad instead of diverting resources from other, more vital investments.
4. These measures could also have negative effects, such as increasing absenteeism in the public sector, and should be designed with great care.
5. The manual has been developed and published jointly by six organizations—the United Nations, the European Commission, the International Monetary Fund, the Organisation for Economic Co-operation and Development, the United Nations Conference on Trade and Development, and the World Trade Organization—and managed through the mechanism of an interagency task force. It sets out an internationally agreed framework for the compilation and reporting of statistics on international trade in services in a broad sense. See United Nations (2002), which is available on the Web sites of each of the six organizations.
6. For examples of health coverage in free trade agreements, see Mikic (2007).
7. GATS article VI covers domestic regulation.

## References


Achouri, Hédi, and Noureddine Achour. 2005. "Health Services in Tunisia in the Light of WTO Agreements." Regional Office for the Eastern Mediterranean, World Health Organization, Cairo.

Arunanondchai, Jutamas, and Carsten Fink. 2007. "Trade in Health Services in the ASEAN Region." Policy Research Working Paper 4147, World Bank, Washington, DC.

Blouin, Chantal, Nick Drager, and Richard Smith, eds. 2006. *International Trade in Health Services and the GATS: Current Issues and Debates*. Washington, DC: World Bank.

———, eds. 2007. "Trade and Health Workbook." Preliminary draft, University of Ottawa, Ottawa.

Chanda, Rupa. 2007. "Foreign Investment in Hospitals in India: Status and Implications." Report for Ministry of Health and Family Welfare and World Health Organization, New Delhi, India Country Office, World Health Organization.

Deloitte. 2008. "Medical Tourism: Consumers in Search of Value." Deloitte Center for Health Solutions, Washington, DC.

Drager, N., and R. Smith. 2009. "Trade in Health Services." Trade in services course, 2009 session, World Bank Institute, Washington, DC.

Ehrbeck, Tilman, Ceani Guevara, and Paul D. Mango. 2008. "Mapping the Market for Medical Travel." *McKinsey Quarterly*, May.

Einhorn, Bruce. 2008. "Top Medical Tourism Destinations." BusinessWeek Online. http://images.businessweek.com/ss/08/03/0317_hospitals/index_01.htm?technology+slideshows.

Fidler, David P., Carlos Correa, and Obijiofor Aginam. 2005. *Draft Legal Review of the General Agreement on Trade in Services (GATS) from a Health Policy Perspective*. Project leader, Nick Drager. Globalization, Trade, and Health Working Papers Series. Geneva: World Health Organization.

Foreign Direct Investment Database. United Nations Conference on Trade and Development. http://www.unctad.org/Templates/Page.asp?intItemID=1923&lang=1 (accessed August 4, 2009).

Herman, Lior. 2009. "Assessing International Trade in Healthcare Services." ECIPE Working Paper 03/2009, European Centre for International Political Economy, Brussels.

Mattoo, Aaditya, and Randeep Rathindran. 2006. "How Health Insurance Inhibits Trade in Health Care." *Health Affairs* 25 (2): 358–68.

MGI (McKinsey Global Institute). 2005. *How Supply and Demand for Offshore Talent Meet*. Part III of *The Emerging Global Labor Market*. San Francisco: McKinsey & Company.

Mikic, Mia. 2007. "Health-Related Services in Multilateral and Preferential Trade Arrangements in Asia and the Pacific." Working Paper 30 (January), Asia-Pacific Research and Training Network on Trade, Bangkok.

Nguyen-Hong, Duc. 2000. "Restrictions on Trade in Professional Services." Productivity Commission Staff Research Paper 1638, AusInfo, Canberra. http://papers.ssrn.com/sol3/papers. cfm?abstract_id=270787.

Nielson, Julia. 2006. "Ten Steps to Consider before Making Commitments in Health Services." In *International Trade in Health Services and the GATS: Current Issues and Debates*, ed. Chantal Blouin, Nick Drager, and Richard Smith, 133–37. Washington, DC: World Bank.

Pannarunothai, Supasit, and Khanchit Suknak. 2004. "The Impact of Health Services Liberalization on Thailand." Paper presented at the 27th Annual Symposium of Thammasart University, Bangkok.

Ratha, Dilip, and Zhimei Xu. 2008. *Migration and Remittances Factbook 2008*. Washington, DC: Development Prospects Group, World Bank.

Sauvé, Pierre. 2008. "Trade in Health-Related Services: Key Trends and Policy Challenges." Presentation at the Prince Mahidol Award Conference, "Three Decades of Primary Health Care: Reviewing the Past and Defining the Future," Bangkok, January 30-February 1.

Suleiman, B. J. 2005. "Trade in Health Services and GATS in the Sultanate of Oman." Regional Office for the Eastern Mediterranean, World Health Organization, Cairo.

United Nations. 2002. *Manual on Statistics of International Trade in Services*. UN document ST/ESA/STAT/SER.M/86, Statistical Papers, Series M 86. New York: Statistics Division, Department of Economic and Social Affairs, United Nations.

WHO (World Health Organization) and WTO (World Trade Organization). 2002. *WTO Agreements and Public Health: A Joint Study by the WHO and the WTO Secretariat*. Geneva: WTO and WHO.

5

# MARKET STRUCTURE, LIBERALIZATION, AND TRADE: THE CASE OF DISTRIBUTION SERVICES

*Julian Arkell*

## Introduction: Why Is Trade in Distribution Services of Interest to Developing Countries?

The distribution sector represents one of the largest activities in an economy (see the description of distribution services in box 5.1). It comprises 10–20 percent of gross domestic product (GDP), 15–30 percent of employment, and up to 40 percent of the total number of enterprises in most countries.[1] The distribution sector's share in a country's GDP tends to increase in parallel with GDP per capita until a level is reached at which economies of scale and scope are exhausted, after which the proportion declines slowly. Retail sales of food are the largest element in total retail sales, but, as income per capita rises, this proportion of household expenditure declines.

The economic importance of the distribution sector arises from its role in providing an essential channel between producers and consumers. The productivity of the distribution sector greatly affects the prices of a wide range of goods and services: 10 to 50 percent of final consumer prices are often accounted for by the distributors. The functioning of the distribution market should be a priority for policy makers because it largely determines the price, quality, and choice of the goods and products that are available to consumers. Government policies that restrict competition in the distribution sector are one of the main

The editors have based this chapter on a fuller draft by the author.

**Box 5.1:** Principal Activities in the Distribution Sector

*Wholesale distribution services* include warehousing, bonded sites, cold storage, and associated trucking and other transport facilities.

*Retail distribution* is predominantly comprised of family businesses and small outlets. The common types of retail stores include the following:

- Grocery stores: selling mainly fruits and vegetables, but also various other food and nonfood items.
- Convenience stores: in effect, small grocers stocking a limited line of high-convenience snack foods and drinks. Some are sited at gasoline stations and also sell car-related items.
- Supermarkets: self-service stores larger than grocers with various departments offering a variety of food and household goods.
- Superstores and hypermarkets: extensive retail facilities that carry a wide range of products, including full lines of grocery and general nonfood items.
- Independents: retailers with a limited number of branches.
- Multiple or chain stores: retailers with more than 10 branches that may be specialty shops, including shops that sell furniture, clothing, books, and periodicals.

Other descriptions of retail activities cover public markets, cash and carry stores, discount stores, drugstores, specialty stores, super-centers, DIY (do-it-yourself) outlets, home improvement outlets, food services, e-commerce, virtual stores, informal hawkers, and small stands. Nonstore retailers include catalogue, telephone, and Internet sales; market stalls; door-to-door direct sales, and vending machines. Services related to wholesale and retail include maintaining inventories, breaking down bulk for redistribution in smaller lots, assembling selected goods, home delivery services, and sales promotions.

*Commission agents* trade as wholesalers on behalf of others (including commodity brokers) by supplying products, usually owned by the producers, to retailers and wholesalers or to large customers.

*Franchising service suppliers* purchase the right to use a business format designed by a franchisor or to sell certain of a franchisor's trademarked products or services in return for a fee or royalty paid to the franchisor. The contract between the franchisor and franchisee covers the product, the service, and the trademark, as well as the entire business format.

*Source:* Authors' compilation based on data of the Organisation for Economic Co-operation and Development.

reasons consumers in many developing countries lack access to safe and affordable products.

For most developing countries, the prospective gains from trade in distribution services are predominantly linked to the inflows of capital, technology, and efficient supply chain practices stemming from a more open domestic market. Greater competition in the distribution sector is likely to raise standards and help modernize distribution practices because market participants are required to improve their offerings to customers. This, in combination with properly

**Box 5.2:** Estimates of the Economic Scope of the Distribution Sector

In 2007, global retail sales equaled roughly US$12 trillion, having grown, on average, by 8 percent annually in 2001–07 (Joseph et al. 2008). Grocery sales made up 40 percent of total retail sales, and 60 percent in poorer African countries. At the firm level, in 2006, total retail sales of the top 250 multinationals amounted to US$3.5 trillion. With average retail sales of US$13 billion, all these companies had retail sales exceeding US$2.7 billion, and companies from the United States accounted for 45 percent of sales, Germany for 11 percent, France for 9 percent, the United Kingdom for 8 percent, and Japan for 7 percent (Deloitte 2008). In 2002, the top 30 retailers were active in 88 countries, or nearly three-quarters more countries than in 1997 (UNCTAD 2005). Foreign direct investment (FDI) in distribution services was among the vanguard in FDI until 1990, when it accounted for a quarter of the total inward stock in services. It subsequently dropped to 18 percent by 2002 (UNCTAD 2004).

In the International Monetary Fund balance of payments statistics, the value of distribution services is embedded in the value of goods sold through international channels either in the value of the exports and imports of goods or in the value of the sales of goods through affiliates.[2] For example, in 2002, about 3 percent of the sales of U.S. wholesalers were exports, valued at about US$153 billion. Given that the wholesalers provided an average of some 22 cents worth of distribution services for each dollar in sales, these exports included US$34 billion in services in the value of the goods exported. Exports accounted for a much lower proportion of the total sales of retailers, and under US$1 billion of retailer services were embedded in the value of the goods retailers exported (Borga 2006).

enforced regulation, may allow consumers not only to benefit from more choice and lower prices, but also higher-quality products and better safety standards. In most developing countries, a significant proportion of retail activities is part of the informal economy, which official statistics fail to capture. (Box 5.2 presents estimates of the economic scope of the distribution sector.) However, facilitated market access in the distribution sector may bring foreign participation that increases the share of the sector anchored in the formal economy and, hence, provide a broader base for taxation.

From an export perspective, several developing countries are dependent on tourism, and a more developed retail sector generates more income from purchases by foreign visitors. The integration of domestic producers in international supply chains also provides new business opportunities for the producers. Distribution companies in developing countries such as Mexico and South Africa are active in expanding their operations in neighboring countries, which demonstrates the potential for increased levels of South-South trade in distribution services.

In addition, modernization in the distribution sector will increase the use of information technology and just-in-time logistics systems, which can greatly reduce inventory levels. The improved quality standards set by large retailers can contribute even within developing economies to help bring local produce to the consumer more quickly, in better condition, and at lower prices. Supply chain control is the key to reducing waste, which is estimated in the range of 25–40 percent in farm produce. Product compliance monitoring and testing against private and regulated standards are information intensive; they involve large numbers of suppliers and increase in complexity whenever the regulatory regimes governing consumer goods necessitate closer relations with suppliers (Nordås, Geloso Grosso, and Pinali 2007).

An increased market presence by foreign distribution companies not only offers prospective gains, but also prospective costs, particularly if the sector is subject to strong pressures to restructure. Retailing forms the major part of the value added and is largely based on single outlets under sole proprietorships (mom-and-pop stores). If large, efficient supermarkets and hypermarkets are built by domestic or foreign investors, many of these small shops are likely to close down in major population centers. The poorest people in rural areas and some city suburbs may be inadequately served if overall consumer demand increases because major retail companies tend to build their large stores to cater mainly to urban areas. Policy makers in developing countries who undertake to open their markets in the distribution sector will thus be at an advantage if they proceed with caution and implement measures in parallel that soften the adjustment process for small entrepreneurs (discussed below).

The market structure of the distribution sector varies widely in terms of market concentration, joint purchasing, vertical wholesale and retail with one's own brands, and internationalization. The economies of scale and scope are significant, and the largest companies tend to innovate more often than do the smaller companies. In developed markets, concentration is more marked in food retailing, but the pattern varies because of differences in national regulations on market entry and ongoing business. Small independent retailers tend to form joint purchasing groups to counter the power of large food producers and retailers. Vertical integration has spurred growth in own-brand products, while restrictive regulations often impede the development of large national retail groups.

Cultural and historical differences account for regulatory differences on shop opening hours and weekend openings. In general, the liberalization of opening hours leads to a rise in the supply of new services and greater levels of employment. Regulations on product safety, hygiene, labeling, quality standards, and loss-leading can have a significant effect on ongoing business. Three factors account for most of the variances across countries: general restrictions on access (start-up formalities, the need for authorization to sell certain products, and restrictions on the size of larger stores), regulations on operation (opening hours, involvement in sectoral bodies, local monopolies), and price regulation (Boylaud 2000).

Global sales through modern retail formats are estimated to have grown more rapidly than total retail sales; they accounted for 52 percent of total retail sales in 2006. The share differs widely across countries: 1 percent in Pakistan, 4 percent in India, 20 percent in China and Indonesia, 22 percent in Vietnam, 35 percent in the Philippines, 36 percent in Brazil, 40 percent in Thailand, 55 percent in Malaysia, and 80 percent in economies of the Organisation for Economic Co-operation and Development (OECD) (Joseph et al. 2008). In the least developed countries and in most developing countries, retail sales are primarily dominated by small family-run neighborhood shops and open markets that are frequently large covered clusters of outlets. Box 5.3 presents selected developing-country experiences in the distribution sector.

In developing countries, modern retailing occurred in three broad waves. It started in the early 1990s in South America (Argentina, Brazil, and Chile), East Asia (Maldives; the Republic of Korea; the Philippines; Taiwan, China; and Thailand) and South Africa. It then took off in Central America, Indonesia, and Mexico in the late 1990s, before reaching some Central and South American countries, China, India, Kenya, the Russian Federation, and Vietnam in the early 2000s. China, India, and Russia lagged because of severe restrictions on inward FDI in the retailing sector (Joseph et al. 2008). For large emerging markets, it is likely that the pattern of development will follow that of the distribution sector in developed countries, and that the pace of development will depend to a large extent on the level of market access for foreign participation. There will be increasing concentration through mergers and acquisitions and some vertical integration in which retailers control both the traditional wholesale function and, in some cases, food processing and production. This vertical integration may extend to the road transport fleets owned by the largest retail chains, whose trucks often form part of the storage capacity in lean supply chains.

Other impacts may affect social exclusion, raising the need for the provision of social spending and safety nets within overall budgetary limits. This might cover training in management, logistics, and information technology skills and training for alternative employment among those people displaced from small traditional outlets. Other factors that should be borne in mind are the propensity of people to migrate, the eradication of extreme poverty and hunger, the promotion of gender equality and the empowerment of women, and ensuring environmental sustainability (Arkell and Johnson 2005).

**Box 5.3:** Selected Developing-Country Experiences in the Distribution Service Sector

In Africa, supermarkets, hypermarkets, and large discount stores started to expand abroad in the mid-1990s. South African retailers were the first to establish themselves in foreign markets; they were soon followed by Kenyan retailers. African foreign direct investment (FDI) has targeted the retailing sectors in Botswana, Namibia, Swaziland, Zambia, and Zimbabwe, and, more recently, Angola, Ghana, Madagascar, Mauritius, Mozambique, Tanzania, and Uganda (Weatherspoon and Reardon 2003). In 2003, South Africa's formal retail sector was made up of 70,000 stores. Of these, 2 percent were supermarkets and hypermarkets that controlled 55 percent of the country's food retailing market.

In the Arab Republic of Egypt, the distribution services sector is relatively unorganized and fragmented. A significant proportion of the retail sector consists of small stores that supply a wide range of goods without a particular customer target group. Publicly owned retailers account for 42 percent of all establishments and dominate sales of fuel, gas, food, beverages, and tobacco. Many of the stores have low returns and survive because of their access to inexpensive, low-skilled labor. Retailing is concentrated in Greater Cairo and Alexandria, where most foreign retailers are active. In 2003, there were 3,900 commercial agents representing 105,200 foreign companies because commercial agents and importers have to be Egyptian nationals. Wholesale and retail services accounted for 11 percent of GDP in 2005/06 and employed nearly 13 percent of the labor force, of which 89 percent were men (Dihel and El Shinnawy 2006).

Retailing in China has, in a relatively short time, been transformed from state-owned operations and traditional small shops to modern hypermarkets. Domestic companies dominate the supermarket segment, and foreign companies dominate the hypermarket segment in big cities. Sales by foreign department stores account for less than 5 percent of total consumer goods sales and about 10 percent in major cities. In 2006, wholesale and retail trade accounted for over 7 percent of GDP, employing 51 million people and representing an accumulated net FDI of US$129 billion (17 percent of total FDI) (WTO 2008a).

In Latin America, the share of supermarkets in retail sales rose from 20 percent in 1990 to over 50 percent in 2002. For groceries, the supermarket share ranges from as high as 63 percent in the Philippines and 33 percent in Indonesia, Malaysia, and Thailand to 5 percent in India and Nigeria (UNCTAD 2005). In 2007, Guyana's wholesale sector comprised a mix of domestic and foreign companies, while the retail sector consisted of small domestic operations. Anecdotal evidence indicates that the foreign sources for the wholesale and retail trade emanated mainly from the Caribbean (Carana Corporation 2008).

In Thailand, following the 1997 financial crisis, divestments by Thai investors enabled European and U.S. companies to enter the local market for distribution services. The new competitors built a few hypermarkets and supermarkets offering a wider range of products, as well as cash and carry outlets for good value. These establishments displaced many mom-and-pop stores, which led to a tense political situation (WTO 2002).

## What Is the Situation of and What Are the Prospects for Trade in Distribution Services?

### *The import perspective for developing countries*

International trade in distribution services is conducted mainly through outward direct investment in foreign affiliates or joint ventures. The foreign investment decisions of large retail companies depend, for example, on the level of saturation and competition in their home markets, the desire for greater efficiency in economies of scale and scope, and shareholder pressure for greater dividends, which become possible especially though increased turnover. The aim to gain first-mover advantages in previously protected markets and to preempt the expansion plans of competitors can be a major consideration. Foreign retail groups usually target the upper and middle classes in city centers. Inward investment in distribution can be hampered if prime sites are occupied and local brand names are well established. Local cooperative wholesale and retail groups often exclude foreign participation.

In countries in which foreign retail outlets are prohibited, franchising may be a significant mode of access for international retailers because it enables expansion at lower risk and allows companies to work around restrictions on capital investment. Local entrepreneurs can build shopping malls with a range of outlets for well-known franchise consumer brands and restaurants and can thus closely match shopping malls that would otherwise consist of foreign-owned retail outlets. Foreign retailers may also enter the market through wholesale cash and carry, test marketing, local manufacturing, single-brand retailing, and shops within the shops of their joint venture partners.

Foreign penetration can increase rapidly, and, in some developing countries, foreign companies already form a major part of the retail sector (box 5.4). The modern retailing practices that are imported may not only provide higher-quality products, more choice, and lower prices, but also improve the shopping experience and create better jobs and higher wages. They can create jobs in ancillary food processing, logistics, supply chain management, and information technology–based back-office outsourcing, including modern purchase tracking and accounting practices. They may even spur a rise in real estate prices. However, to achieve the full potential of a modern distribution sector, parallel improvements are often required in the transport networks (especially road transport), electricity supply, and telecommunications on which distribution services depend. Thus, coordination among the various ministries and agencies involved in such improvements is essential.

In most countries, there is no tradition of the state provision of a universal public distribution service such as in the utilities, telecommunications, and transport sectors. For some product categories, however, there may be state

**Box 5.4:** Examples of Multinational Retailers with Foreign Affiliates

For wholesale and retail services, investment in the commercial presence of foreign affiliates is the most significant mode of supply. In the retail sector, the principal global actors are European and U.S. companies. The greater proportion of sales by U.S. foreign affiliates in the distribution sector arises from wholesale services, with only a few large retail groups active internationally, mostly in specialist lines and franchising. Large European retailers operate in a number of developing countries, as illustrated in table 5.1. In January 2009, European Retail Roundtable members had 6,117 stores outside Europe. Dominated by multinationals such as Aldi, Auchan, Carrefour, Metro, Rewe-Zentral, and Tesco, these companies had numerous stores in developing countries (counting only countries with 10 or more such stores).

Globally, there is a relatively limited number of multinational retailers, and they are mostly present in large emerging markets that permit foreign participation. Given that the distribution markets in OECD economies are mostly saturated, these multinationals generally seek to expand their presence in rapidly growing markets that are currently protected if income levels are seen as adequate and inward investment regimes are predictable. For example, following India's decision in 2006 to allow foreign ownership of 51 percent in single-brand retail companies, a survey of 300 companies revealed that over a quarter had already opened a store in 2007 or planned to do so. Since Vietnam's accession to the World Trade Organization (WTO) in 2007, the country has become the most attractive new emerging market for retail investors (World Bank 2007). Table 5.2 illustrates the international footprint of five large retail groups in 2008.

**Table 5.1.** Stores Owned by European Retail Roundtable Members, Developing Countries

| | | | | | | | |
|---|---|---|---|---|---|---|---|
| Argentina | 570 | India | 19 | Malaysia | 48 | Saudi Arabia | 104 |
| Bahrain | 13 | Indonesia | 111 | Morocco | 17 | Thailand | 522 |
| Brazil | 520 | Jordan | 11 | Philippines | 19 | United Arab Emirates | 45 |
| China | 608 | Kuwait | 28 | Qatar | 14 | Venezuela, R. B. de | 24 |
| Colombia | 81 | | | | | | |

**Table 5.2.** International Footprint of Five European Retail Groups, 2008

| Name of group | Auchan (France) | Carrefour (France) | Metro (Germany) | Rewe (Germany) | Tesco (United Kingdom) |
|---|---|---|---|---|---|
| Employees | 209,000 | 479,000 | 241,000 | 290,000 | 364,000 |
| Presence in number of foreign countries | 12 | 17 | 44 | 15 | 12 |
| Total number of stores | 1,483 | 8,006 | 2,003 | 12,719 | 4,332 |
| Total sales/turnover (billion) | €40 | €98 | €67 | €45 | £59 |
| Sales abroad (billion) | — | €49 | €14 | — | £18 |

*Source:* Company Web sites.

*Note:* — = not available.

monopolies in the sale of goods such as gasoline, pharmaceuticals, tobacco, and alcohol. Privatization in the distribution sector has therefore not produced the large opportunities for the foreign direct investment (FDI) that have arisen in many other sectors. There has been little cross-subsidization and price control by governments apart from price setting for a few basic foodstuffs and the types of products mentioned above.

In assessing the impact of trade liberalization on consumer experience, the governments of developing countries could consider whether they wish largely to follow a typical pattern of retail market development by permitting the top global grocery firms (that is, mainly the major European retailers) to expand into the local market. Such global chain supermarkets would likely act as gatekeepers for food production that puts profit before quality, the environment, or public health because they make more money by selling bland processed food. Such products would be sourced from a few large and captive suppliers, and the terms and prices imposed on farmers would encourage intensive farming rather than more quality-conscious producers. This approach rewards volume and standardization, not flavor or biodiversity. These supermarket chains would eventually also place convenience outlets on main streets, typically stocking prepared foods with a rapid turnaround and a low proportion of fresh unprocessed food. This would make shopping in city centers an anonymous experience without attraction. Although many fruits and vegetables do not naturally stay fresh for more than a few days, they are offered because supermarket advertising teaches suppliers to harvest green and backward produce that looks acceptable on shelves and does not rot quickly even if it is tasteless. Few supermarkets stock the raw materials for traditional home food preparation, instead offering restaurant-like instant meals so as to improve profitability, with the added value to the basic raw ingredients provided solely through food processing and packaging.

### *Market liberalization in the distribution sector often entails significant adjustment costs*

The positive effects of increased foreign participation will be greater if there is adequate regulation and if trade liberalization is carefully sequenced. If regulatory policies are not in place or are poorly coordinated with trade policy, the potential gains and sustainable development are likely to be compromised. The social risks arise from the crowding out of the mom-and-pop stores operated by families in urban areas. This can have a severe social impact through the unemployment generated following the establishment of more productive supermarkets, and it can also create a gap in the provision of retail services between city centers and outer urban and rural populations. The smallest food producers may lose their retail clients and thus their livelihoods.

The ownership of the new supermarkets can raise ethnic tensions and social stability issues, as has occurred in Kenya, where the smallest retail shops are owned by indigenous Africans and the largest wholesale and retail businesses are owned mainly by Africans of Asian descent. The employment issues include both the ethnic balance—as in Malaysia in relation to the indigenous Bumiputra people—and gender balance in supermarkets and regulations on the employment of women and maternity leave. The purchasing power of the multinational retailers can depress the income of small food producers. If price controls are aimed at protecting the purchases of certain products by the poorest people, the impact of any changes must be considered.

Agricultural trade is dependent on efficient distribution channels, in addition to transport facilities and logistics systems. The major distribution chains increasingly dominate the market for fresh fruits and vegetables, which affects production patterns in the producer territories and accentuates the economic, social, and environmental impacts flowing from agricultural development, including the beneficial and damaging effects. The indirect impact on biodiversity include the effects on crop varieties, crop rotation, the protection of ecosystems and species, soil erosion, and the use of pesticides and other chemicals that build up in the soil, in aquifers, and in the body tissues of wild animals. Increased foreign competition can stimulate intensive animal farming methods and create more pressure for the genetic engineering of crops and also the greater involvement of multinationals in the production process. Policy makers in developing countries need to be aware of the prospective long-term implications for product standards, biodiversity, and animal welfare.

Direct impacts on the environment arise from the construction of wholesale facilities and large supermarket stores and their associated car parks and from the consequent increases in road traffic, noise, and pollution. The effect of liberalization on environmental sustainability can be gauged by the impact on biodiversity and on natural resource stocks. Environmental impacts will tend to increase as consumption rises and, with this, the volume of products produced both for domestic consumption and for export. The associated issues include the disposal of waste and the need for regulations to encourage the recycling of household goods and packaging. However, it is a challenge to isolate the impacts of distribution from those caused by wider economic development and social factors.

For the smallest suppliers, liberalization presents huge challenges because of the large scale of procurement and the demanding quality and safety standards; some suppliers become, in effect, excluded from international supply chains. Where there are only smaller farmers who cannot meet the standards set by supermarkets, these retailers have to rely on imports, and this may only change through capacity building projects that help small farmers meet quality, safety, and consistency standards and the higher cost levels. In addition, retailers can help create new business opportunities by branding certain products for their social equity as a marketing tool, such as pineapple chunks, certain fruit juices, wines, and coffee (Weatherspoon and Reardon 2003).

In meeting the demands of retail multinationals, only the farmers in developing countries who are more well endowed with land, finance, management skills, and education may succeed. They may be required to invest in cool sheds, refrigerated trucks, irrigation equipment, greenhouses, and packing machines. Retailers may not offer loans and may delay payments for up to 90 days after harvest. The equipment of the farmers has to meet health and safety standards. This puts pressure on governments to regulate supermarket development and implement policies for assistance with training and capital to enable farmers to sell to the big retail chains.

### *The impact of internalization on demand and supply*

Nordås (2008) identifies three current trends in the retail sector that have a direct effect on imports, that is, internalization, market concentration, and private labels. Empirical results indicate that internationalization has stimulated the international sourcing of consumer goods, including through developing countries and particularly food products, but that this process has been reversed in the case of private labels. High retailer concentration tends to be associated with more diversified food imports, whereas, even though less concentrated markets import more, the related food sourcing is based on fewer countries. It may be that the largest retailers can absorb the cost of diversification in sourcing and in relying on high-margin suppliers in the face of lower average margins because of lower tariffs. These trends depend on how retailers are regulated; following trade liberalization, lightly regulated countries, on average, increase their reliance on nonfood imports by about twice as much relative to heavily regulated countries.

A limited number of multinationals are responsible for the major trends in internationalization. The development pattern reveals that retailers that have operations in more countries expand more quickly than those operating in only a few countries. Retailers with operations in more than 10 countries show an average profit margin of 5 percent; this is higher than the corresponding profit margin of retailers operating in fewer countries (Deloitte 2008). This may arise because of the expansion of operations in more rapidly growing and less saturated emerging markets. The companies that have higher stock market capitalization in proportion to the value of tangible assets reflect the success of their branding; specialty apparel performs the best, followed by drug stores, cash and carry, and supermarket retailers.

Demand stemming from new shopping habits in urban centers is the key determinant of retail growth among multinationals. Food products are sourced from low-cost suppliers. If the harvesting, grading, and dispatching work is labor intensive, powerful retail buyers exercise great purchasing power that depresses the prices producers can charge and thus producer income levels. This may occur even in developed countries, where growers may have to sell their produce to individual retailers (Lawrence 2004). Retailers can promote food exports from developing countries by integrating their producers into international supply chains. Partnerships among retailers, logistics companies, wholesalers, and processing companies can establish efficient supply chains. Some retailers enter into partnerships with nongovernmental organizations, donors, or governments, which then finance investment in public infrastructure, training, and other essential inputs (Nordås, Geloso Grosso, and Pinali 2007).

Internationalization may allow consumers to purchase fruits and vegetables all year round that are consistent in appearance and taste and have a longer shelf life. The range of food varieties on offer may also be expanded (Lawrence 2004). Food constitutes a significant proportion of the retail price index, and, so, price competition, which stabilizes or reduces food prices, can reduce general inflation. However, any improvement in availability and choice may not extend to the rural population or, possibly, to some peripheral and poor urban areas. In general, modern retailing stores improve employment opportunities for women and provide better working conditions.

### *Prospects for exports by developing countries*

The liberalization of trade in services is sometimes perceived in terms of a North-South relationship; this perception focuses, on the one hand, on the interests of capital-abundant multinationals based in developed countries and, on the other hand, on the concerns in developing countries about foreign domination of local economies. Some retailers based in developing countries have already expanded into neighboring markets in Africa, Asia, and Latin America. They will increasingly do so as part of the worldwide trend toward concentration and larger outlets in distribution. In view of the rapid growth rates in many developing countries, South-South trade is gaining ground in the distribution sector.

Export growth can only be achieved by companies with sufficient capital, managerial expertise, and capacity in information and communication technology to invest abroad once they have gained strong positions in domestic markets. The major multinationals in developed countries will only consider markets that offer sufficient commercial potential and thus do not enter poorer developing countries. This offers opportunities for South-South investment in retail outlets.

Government export promotion programs could support potential exporters. Wholesale and retail companies in developing countries always face the possibility of competition from OECD-based companies that may have easier access to capital markets, operate sophisticated information and communication technology systems, possess expertise in entering overseas markets, and enjoy significant economies of scale. However, companies that originate in developing countries may have lower overhead costs and a better understanding of local tastes and preferences and may enjoy close relationships with local suppliers.

South-South trade can be a useful testing ground for entrepreneurs in developing countries in their effort to build export capacity. For example, South African companies have invested heavily in Kenya and Uganda, including in a number of distribution companies. Chilean distribution companies are active in the Argentine market. Through the World Trade Organization (WTO) negotiations on the General Agreement on Trade in Services (GATS), Brazil has made requests to Argentina, China, India, Korea, Mexico, Paraguay, and Uruguay for market access in their distribution sectors (UNCTAD 2004). Least developed countries will not be significantly affected because they are unlikely, over the foreseeable future, to attract large-scale international investments in distribution given their limited market size. Trade liberalization alone is therefore unlikely to have a significant impact on the volume of FDI flows into such countries. Moreover, they are unlikely to host national companies that are capable of setting up subsidiaries abroad.

Countries that have experienced advanced retail expansion have benefited from competition policies that restrict concentration and collusion, as well as from fewer limitations on town planning, zoning, and opening hours. Some have also prohibited pricing below cost, ensured prompt payments to suppliers, strengthened supply-side capacity (technology and business organization), and improved access to finance. All countries have had to find a balance between enhancing modern retailing and the interests of traditional retailers and small suppliers (Joseph et al. 2008).

## What Can Be Done to Harness Trade in Distribution Services?

The distribution service sector that is part of the formal economy is generally subject to a thick layer of regulations. It is regulated directly in relation to physical facilities (location, size, juxtaposition with other buildings, activities, and effects on traffic) and indirectly to protect against market failure (such as anticompetitive practices) and to ensure noneconomic values and societal objectives in employment and working conditions, health, the safety of facilities and products, and the impact on farmers, horticulturalists, and the environment. The regulations can significantly affect how the suppliers of distribution services operate and trade. For example, an econometric model simulating the impact of regulations on distribution in eight OECD countries has revealed that the consequent sector inefficiencies might impose substantial welfare costs, rivaling even those associated with trade barriers (Bradford 1995). This finding is likely to be relevant also in the case of the effect of regulations in developing countries.

The dimensions that governments should consider in regulating the distribution sector are the range of services available to consumers and the welfare of consumers in the various market segments; the efficiency, productivity, and technical innovation of retail stores and their supply chains; the degree of competition (by type of concentration, whether horizontal cooperation or vertical) and specialization; pricing issues; internationalization; health and safety; urban planning and zoning; and social and labor conditions. In trade terms, these characteristics of the sector can affect the extent and nature of the market access of foreign companies and the degree of national treatment once such companies are established in markets, that is, the extent to which the regulations apply equally to local companies and workers, as well as to foreign affiliates and temporary foreign employees or consultants.

The economic development of the distribution sector is shaped by consumer demand factors and societal aims. Political and legal decisions that are taken in the context of liberalization could serve to speed up this process. The choices facing governments revolve around the way to phase in far-reaching changes and to mitigate the inevitable costs of structural adjustment that adversely affect the poorest people, whether these are shop owners, agricultural producers, or consumers. These costs arise if family-owned shops are put out of business, leading to the need for unemployment benefits, early retirement on state pensions, or retraining for alternative employment. Various regulatory and administrative tools must be deployed to mitigate the negative effects, but the required human, institutional, and financial resources may not always be available.

The impacts of liberalization on which governments should focus are conditioned by the level of social and economic development; the quality of legal governance; the availability of information and communication technology infrastructure, equipment, and skills; and the effect on the environment. There is no panacea to propose to governments. It may be important to phase in liberalization measures if there are sensitive social issues at stake (such as racial and gender balancing), if the resources to address the adverse consequences of structural adjustment are lacking, or if aid for capacity building is necessary. The most singular issues revolve around ethnic history, social networks, the prevailing legally recognized structure of enterprises, the privileges accorded to certain categories of citizens, land ownership, real estate prices, the state control of outlets, and product prices.

The impact of trade liberalization on the overall number of distribution enterprises could lead to significant changes in the shares of GDP and employment in the wholesale and retail sectors. The trend toward vertical integration within larger enterprises will have consequences on the distribution of inputs to other sectors of the economy and, hence, on overall economic development and competitiveness. It will also have an impact on informal retailers and street markets. The extent of the liberalization of market access in developing countries ultimately depends on the balance achieved between the expansionist aims of the multinationals and prevailing societal objectives, expressed through land use zoning and limits on the number and size of supermarkets, hypermarkets, and medium outlets and, in some cases, employment and equity aims in income distribution.

If there are labor market rigidities, the limitations on layoffs may discourage foreign suppliers of services from establishing local subsidiaries that could otherwise create employment. The establishment of an adequate social safety net and of effective retraining programs is thus needed to enhance labor market flexibility. The temporary entry of foreign service personnel may be required to provide the training in necessary skills for national workers. Regulations on work-related issues include those on worker rights (the observance of International Labour Organization standards, including on freedom to unionize), conditions of employment (working hours, holiday entitlements, minimum wages, job security, gender equality, opportunities for the handicapped), and insurance benefits. Liberalization may result in different, usually opposite, effects among workers at large companies relative to workers in family-owned shops (microenterprises), in which employment conditions may be much inferior.

Governments also need to take into account the macroeconomic effects of liberalization and the flows of inward FDI associated with the arrival in the market of large foreign-owned companies that could have consequences for national finances, including tax collection, and an impact on consumer prices. There could be wide-ranging effects on supply chains, both national and international, and on land use and prices in the urban areas where the new, large-scale supermarkets are located.

Ambiguous tax laws and cumbersome regulations are regarded by investors as serious impediments. Deregulation should focus on enhancing transparent enforcement and on reducing the trade restrictiveness of regulations that fulfill objectives not directly related to trade in distribution services. Laws have to be taken into account that prohibit the sale of certain products such as tobacco; alcoholic beverages; pharmaceutical, medical, and orthopedic goods; weapons, munitions, and other arms and military equipment; chemical products; precious metals and precious stones; art; and petroleum and petroleum products. The protection of intellectual property rights in consumer products is easier to carry out among large retail chains, which can be monitored and prosecuted for infringements, whereas small companies and market stalls can usually avoid preventive measures undertaken by the authorities.

The preparations for the trade liberalization of distribution services will entail a review of the existing regulations that govern market access for foreign investors and their ongoing operations once they have been established, whether the regulations are specifically imposed on the investors or result from domestic regulations that are applied in a nondiscriminatory fashion on national and foreign suppliers, but that may nonetheless affect trade. This review will need to cover many issues (for example, see box 5.5). A wide range of government policies will need to be covered because of the central importance of distribution services to the domestic economy and to trade.

An assessment needs to be carried out to identify government policies that significantly affect the distribution sector either directly or indirectly, particularly any regulations that are unnecessarily trade restrictive and that therefore should be modified. The direct impacts on the ownership of distribution enterprises and the capitalization and development of these enterprises must be considered first, including initial market access conditions, while the operations of foreign companies that have been permitted to establish a commercial presence should be considered next. More generally, the effect on employment levels, the pace of liberalization, and the need to take account of ethnic makeup and the ethnic sensibilities

**Box 5.5:** Regulatory Reform in the Retail Sector

A study by Boylaud and Nicoletti (2001) of regulatory reforms in the retail sector in OECD countries offers useful guidance that is also relevant for developing-country policy makers. The restrictions on market access prevailing in the distribution sector, many of which apply more widely to businesses, relate to the following:

- Initial registration (trade registers that can involve the imposition of delays of up to a year)
- Fit and proper person requirements for directors and managers
- Licenses or permits for location, siting, and limits on surface area and geographical area
- The location and surface area of commercial premises, town planning and zoning, parking areas, road access
- Regulations on specific operations and products and the range of goods permitted
- Local monopolies for the sale of some products, including pharmaceuticals, tobacco, alcohol
- Legal restrictions on the establishment of large outlets (quantitative limits), including the protection of small shops to provide local proximity services and endorsement by established retailers and local lobbies that resist foreign entrants through their membership in local authority planning committees

Boylaud and Nicoletti find that these restrictions can slow consolidation and modernization and, by extension, deter efficiency gains from economies of scale and scope and limit specialization. They also help impede prospective positive spillovers from the establishment of large malls because of the support these restrictions offer for fringe stores in a locality. The restrictions are not all of equal weight, and their application varies from market to market. In general, however, it is likely that the most serious types of barriers are the legal impediments to commercial establishment rather than the regulations affecting existing operations.

The regulations that affect ongoing operations cover opening hours (including Sunday opening); the protection of employees; labor laws on religious, cultural, and historical grounds; the regulation of product safety and hygiene; labeling; and quality standards. Regulations affecting the freedom to set prices can arise through price controls on pharmaceuticals, tobacco, and gasoline or on promotional activities and the restriction or prohibition of loss-leading. Boylaud and Nicoletti find that variations in the data on distribution services in individual countries can largely be explained by general market access restrictions (formalities, authorizations, licensing), the regulation of business operations (opening hours, labor, monopolies), and price regulations. Boylaud and Nicoletti do not take into account the effect of any anticompetitive activities of private companies.

Kalirajan (2000) has assessed the effect on price-cost margins of various restrictions on companies that enter and operate in the food retail markets of 38 countries. The most stringent market access restrictions are those imposed by governments for the acquisition of commercial land, on inward FDI, and on large-scale stores. Restrictions on ongoing operations include nationality requirements for managers and requirements on local employment. Kalirajan concludes that such restrictions are primarily cost creating and that the largest impacts arise from the restrictions on initial establishment. Because food retailing has to be carried out through the establishment of a shop store, restrictions on land zoning, licensing requirements, limits on store size, and restrictions on opening hours must be added to the adverse effects of investment hurdles and the other requirements on foreigners seeking to enter a domestic market. Kalirajan lists countries by restrictions as follows:

### Restrictiveness on foreign entry

- High: India, Indonesia, Malaysia, Korea, Thailand
- Medium: Brazil, Colombia, República Bolivariana de Venezuela
- Low: Chile, South Africa, Uruguay

### Domestic restrictiveness on operations

- High: Korea
- Medium: Colombia, India, República Bolivariana de Venezuela
- Low: Argentina, Brazil, Chile, Indonesia, Malaysia, the Philippines, South Africa, Thailand, Uruguay

The principal restrictions on ongoing operations include restrictions on wholesale licenses and import licenses for certain products. There are limits on promoting and advertising retail products. Some markets are affected by the existence of statutory government monopolies and the inadequate protection of intellectual property rights. A significant limitation is also represented by the requirements that a majority of directors and managers be nationals or residents.

in society should also be assessed. Finally, the issue of whether the regulations, including competition law, are properly enforced should be examined. National systems of regulation can be designed to mitigate the adverse economic, social, and environmental effects of liberalization in the distribution sector. Government action can also be taken to improve the efficiency of the domestic market and to promote trade in distribution services.

The establishment of wholesale and retail chains in foreign markets requires large investments. Foreign investors have an aversion to caps on equity participation and to any general needs tests or labor market tests applied by local authorities through the authorization criteria establishing distribution outlets. Depending on the criteria applied, such tests can be restrictive, and foreign applicants may already be at a disadvantage if these applicants are not present or are not represented in the market. Other government regulations not specifically related to the distribution sector can affect the ongoing supply of distribution services. Examples include regulations on urban planning that are necessary to achieve a desired geographical distribution and coverage of businesses, the protection of historical sites, restrictions on the acquisition of real estate, and specific rules concerning the distribution of certain products.

In developing countries, the enactment and enforcement of balanced and transparent regulations governing corporate behavior, labor, social standards, environmental protection, and so on will also become essential. If this cannot be achieved without outside assistance, governments should seek technical support from donor agencies in the preparation and implementation of appropriate regulations.

## Market Access Terms, Limitations, and Conditions

In this section, we discuss the policies likely to affect the trade in distribution services so that the impact of these policies on productivity, efficiency, and innovation can be taken into account. In the subsequent section, we also examine possible government flanking measures that may help domestic companies improve their performance and meet competition at home and abroad. In the following section, we consider ways in which trade agreements can enhance export potential.

### *Administration of business registration, licensing, and local permits for wholesale units and retail stores*

#### Regulations, licenses, and permits

Foreign companies will be required to apply initially to state authorities for licenses to register the establishment of subsidiaries and for screening clearances for the initial investments to conduct specific types of supply operations. The requirements may include the deposit of a certain amount of capital with a local bank, an audit report on the deed of incorporation, and a financial plan to demonstrate viability. There may also be a requirement to register with the chamber of commerce or trade association. Additional conditions may involve social security charges, compulsory health care, and mandatory employer liability insurance. A one-stop shop for all such applications would greatly ease market access formalities.

Local authorities and municipalities will issue permits for the construction of wholesale facilities and retail outlets. These building permits typically place conditions on location, size, and geographical coverage, including franchise outlets. Health, safety, and fire regulations will apply during construction and, thereafter, also to ongoing business in the new facilities.

### Commercial conditions for access to the market

The regulations that affect the market access of foreign suppliers the most directly include regulations on any prohibitions on the entry of certain types of distribution suppliers, as well as regulations on capital participation, geographical and product coverage, legal form, name, and the number of foreign employees of foreign suppliers. The key commercial restrictions are the restrictions on the use of commercial land (ownership is not permitted or the size is limited) and limits on equity participation through direct investment. Other aspects include any prohibitions on large-scale stores; other size limitations; restrictions on takeovers, certain operations, or product imports; performance requirements; and economic needs tests or labor tests.

Initial restrictions on establishment are probably the most significant limitation on the price-cost margins of distributors because of cost creation. Once a supplier is in the market, the restrictions on ongoing operations have a smaller effect. This is probably because both foreign suppliers and local companies can pass on the added costs to consumers. In each case, it should be clarified whether these restrictions apply only to foreign suppliers so as to discriminate against them, or, equally, to both domestic and foreign companies.

### Temporary presence of foreign persons supplying services

Entry visas will be required both for foreign persons supplying advisory services under contract to distribution companies and for the foreign employees who work in foreign affiliates where they help ensure the training of local workers. Whether visas have to be obtained before departure from the origin country or are issued upon arrival in the host country can be significant. Certain occupations may be subject to requirements on fit and proper persons. Work permits may also be required and typically will be time limited. Employment limitations such as bans on the entry of foreign staff in certain occupations or restrictions on the duration of the stay of staff in a host country can also be significant.

### *Regulations affecting ongoing operations: Commercial presence conditions, qualifications, and national treatment*

The aim of the review of nondiscriminatory domestic regulations and the implementation of these regulations is to eliminate inappropriate regulations that reduce the efficiency and productivity of the distribution system.

#### Town planning and zoning

Town planning, zoning, and land ownership and use restrictions can condition ongoing business operations. They cover such aspects as the permitted ratio of new stores to traditional small outlets; the siting of wholesale facilities and major retail outlets; and traffic volumes and ease of circulation, including the construction of new roads for access to motorways, railway goods yards, seaports, and parking areas that affect consumer access, which are among the chief issues. Overall urban density will be a consideration. These issues may be highly regulated and contentious because of actual or perceived local environmental impacts. Regulation can be subject to political pressures exerted by local retailers who, often through membership on relevant committees, influence the local authorities and municipalities that control licensing.

For example, in China, new regulations on stores of more than 10,000 square meters require public hearings on the impact of the stores on communities. Assessment panels comprise regulators, competing retailers, and representatives of local residents. The government gives grants for the establishment of small convenience stores in rural areas. Door-to-door direct selling has been permitted since December 2005. Sales representatives must be remunerated according to overall revenue up to a limit of 30 percent. They are not permitted to receive additional compensation based on sales by sellers they have engaged because this might lead to illegal pyramid schemes. Both domestic and foreign suppliers must establish a commercial presence, with a minimum capital of Y 80 million and an initial security deposit of Y 20 million. By the end of 2005, products permitted for direct sale included cosmetics, health food, cleaning products, health care equipment, and small kitchen utensils and appliances (WTO 2008a).

#### Opening hours

Consumers, notably working women, benefit from longer shop opening hours and weekend openings. Restrictions can be aimed at preventing employers from forcing employees to work excessive hours and at protecting smaller stores that cannot afford to hire the extra employees needed to stay open longer. Crossborder shopping may also be a factor if opening hours are different on either side of a border.

### Health and safety regulations

The health and safety of workers in retailing depend on in-store practices in handling certain products and on the existence of procedures to minimize work-related accidents, especially during the movement of goods. The health and safety of consumers in relation to the quality and safety of the products purchased are also key concerns. This may involve restrictions on advertising that targets children and that promotes unhealthy foods.

### Environmental considerations

The environmental aspects to be considered will revolve around air and water quality, increased effluents and other emissions, and greater fertilizer use in the cultivation of food products. If petroleum-based packaging materials are used rather than forest-based packaging, this can lead to an unsustainable drain on natural resources.

### Competition law enforcement

The competition policy tool should be used by governments to prevent the abuse of power by major wholesalers and retailers, as well as manufacturers and food processors. Typical abuses are predatory pricing to drive out smaller outlets, passing the risks of demand fluctuation along to small producers, and the imposition of low farmgate prices because of the significantly inequitable distribution of economic bargaining power. Other issues include resale price maintenance, exclusive dealing, territorial restraints, limits on the services provided, and product assortment (such as full-line forcing). A prime objective would be to ensure the provision of high-quality services and products at competitive prices.

Poor enforcement is frequently a problem, putting foreign companies at a disadvantage because reduced competition in the distribution sector acts, in effect, as an import barrier to goods the foreign retailers would otherwise sell. Ongoing operations are directly affected by any government retail monopolies of products such as gasoline, alcohol, and pharmaceutical drugs. Government monopolies are often exempt from competition laws.

### Coverage of standards

There is general support in OECD countries for an international system to set product standards at the level of governments that would be coordinated through international bodies such as the International Organization for Standardization, but for implementation on a voluntary basis. This presents a challenge for many developing countries, in which systems for setting and implementing the assessment and testing of standards may be inadequate or barely exist. The enforcement of detailed standards by government agencies could lead to excessive day-to-day intervention in company affairs, bureaucratic delays, increased costs, and obstacles to innovation. Private sector distributors are grouping together regionally and even globally to set standards for the products they purchase at the beginning of their own supply chains. Such standards may cover product quality, production processes (including farming methods, which are an increasingly sensitive matter, particularly for consumers in developed countries wishing to support fair trade), and the labor conditions at suppliers.

The governments of developing countries can encourage distribution companies voluntarily to observe clear and agreed standards on operations and on social and environmental impacts, especially if the laws and regulations on companies are less rigorous or, in some areas, nonexistent. The imposition of high product and contamination standards on local microproducer enterprises may, in effect, exclude them from access to international supply chains. Varied, overlapping, and possibly conflicting requirements on standards, whether official or private, can be a severe problem in developing countries and in the least developed countries for smaller suppliers who do not have the financial, technical, and educational resources to comply. Furthermore, it is not possible for the myriad small and medium enterprises and microproducers in different countries to join together to counteract the global power of the multinationals.

Standards that are required in developed countries, whether set centrally by accredited national standards bodies or observed voluntarily by companies, could increasingly dominate. The governments of developing countries should consider whether this process could have advantages because of the global trend in standard setting and implementation leading toward greater coordination and consistency, because the standards in developed countries are frequently more stringent than those in developing countries and because the introduction and application of these standards can assist in technology transfer, training, and improvements in quality. If developing countries are to raise their exports to developed countries, it is essential for the suppliers in developing countries to be able to comply with the standards in the markets of the developed countries. This could provide an impetus for support for the process of building up independent standard-setting procedures and accreditation bodies in developing countries.

### Corporate social responsibility initiatives

Most major international retailers now operate corporate social responsibility programs, which are usually described in published annual reports. Such programs cover foreign subsidiaries, franchisees, and suppliers and include rules on the condition of goods entering distribution chains and transport operations. The labor conditions covered in these programs may include working hours, minimum wage levels, physical working conditions, and bans on child labor. Such programs gradually achieve greater coordination and consistency. They will usually be more inclusive than similar programs in the poorer developing countries and can form the basis for technology transfers, staff training, and product quality improvements. By complying with corporate social responsibility standards, suppliers in developing countries are more likely to boost exports.

However, there is an absence of regulations governing the ways independent auditors assess social and environmental issues in the context of company reporting, and there is little opportunity for workers to contribute to the process other than through internal corporate structures. The governments of developing countries could urge multinationals, whether foreign or locally owned, to institute and implement corporate social responsibility policies, though, ultimately, these are voluntary even if they include regional or international standards.

## Government Flanking Measures to Mitigate the Adverse Effects of Liberalization

### *Enhance the competitiveness of domestic companies in the distribution sector*

While the liberalization of the distribution sector may produce positive economic effects arising from improved structural efficiency, the governments of developing countries will need to take various measures to mitigate adverse effects. The main focus should be on direct social and environmental impacts and also on the indirect effects arising from changes in patterns of supply inevitably driven by consumer demand. This will no doubt involve the phasing-in of liberalization, taking into account social and economic priorities and the quality of governance and regulatory capacity to the extent feasible in the national context. This would include the following:

- Requirements for joint ventures between foreign and domestic companies
- Controls on the outward transfer of funds by foreign distribution companies
- Requirements for foreign companies to train national employees
- Government equity stakes in large companies that might crowd out small companies
- Reductions in the dominance of state-owned enterprises
- Removal of monopoly rights over certain products whether exercised by public or private companies

- Fiscal measures such as subsidies and tax incentives
- Price controls on basic goods so as to protect the poor
- Relaxing state control over advertising media
- Improving bankruptcy laws
- Enforcement of patent and copyright laws
- Publication of new regulations before these enter into force and allowing for prior comment
- Protection of historical heritage sites, sites of natural beauty, and sites important for wildlife

To the extent that government resources permit mitigation of the adverse effects of domestic liberalization, such programs, given their practical relevance and likely effectiveness, could include the following:

- Training for workers in distribution sector skills
- Retraining for employment in other sectors
- Provision of credit to small and medium enterprises
- Assistance in the creation of cooperative wholesale and retail groups of locally owned companies
- Technical assistance in business methods and information and communication technology (bar coding, product tracking)
- Unemployment benefits for employees put out of work

The establishment of wholesale and retail cooperatives would be aimed at increasing local sectoral competitiveness by raising the ability of consumers to purchase local products. These cooperatives would not be open to participation by foreign suppliers, although they might need, initially, to rely on the advice of foreign experts. Other positive policy responses might include, for example, concessionary interest rates to enable smaller enterprises to borrow so as to modernize, as well as support for consolidation among companies to reach economies of scale in terms of store size, information technology equipment, and purchasing power. Governments could encourage consumers to buy local, seasonal, and organic produce from street markets or directly from farms.

### *Promotion of tourism and retail services*

Foreign tourists can be an important source of demand for retailers in popular tourist areas, and governments could consider supporting the quality of the products of these retailers, taking into account the proportions of tourists arriving by land or by air, who account for the majority of tourists. Worldwide, the number of international tourists was estimated at 806 million in 2005, and growth has recently been particularly strong in Asia and the Pacific and in the Middle East. The promotion of tourism can include support for heritage trails and local culinary traditions, in addition to the menus of hotels. The accent could be on retail food outlets. Clearly, retailers also have an interest in airport shopping centers, the promotion of ecotourism, and the tourism associated with health and wellness centers, as well as cultural and sporting events. The national trade promotion strategy should include export activities in the distribution sector. A survey and consultation process would be necessary to identify and cater to the needs of companies that are already investing abroad or are planning to do so. Usually, such companies will ask the government to negotiate proactively with foreign governments to permit entry or expansion in chosen markets.

### *International cooperation to promote trade*

International cooperation to promote trade in services can be pursued at the bilateral, regional, and multilateral levels. Preferential trade agreements can achieve greater liberalization and economic integration among trading neighbors at roughly the same level of development, but may discriminate against other countries and distort trading patterns. For this reason, the multilateral level is considered the first-best option (unless it creates delays in the liberalization achievable in a region). Agreements reached at this level also provide benefits to developing countries and the least developed countries that lack negotiating leverage because these countries are accorded the same market access achieved by others in a round of negotiations and may even be accorded special, differential treatment.

#### Bilateral and regional trade agreements

A review of the preferential trade agreements of 35 WTO members (counting the then European Union–15 as one) found that a large majority of the members had gone beyond the GATS scope of liberalization in at least one distribution subsector either by binding commitments where they had none at the multilateral level or by improving upon these (Roy 2008).[3] This was notable in the case of the developing countries that had no commitments or only limited commitments at the WTO. The countries that have bound significant GATS commitments in preferential trade agreements have accomplished this with the United States (apart from China, which had already bound them on accession to the WTO). However, India and a number of economies in the Association of Southeast Asian Nations have little or no commitments in preferential trade agreements beyond the offers submitted in the current WTO service negotiations. Some African countries, including the Arab Republic of Egypt, are not involved in preferential trade agreements or do not have GATS commitments on distribution.

Several South-South trade agreements are based on a staged approach to trade liberalization. For example, the framework agreement would initially include only a partial liberalization, perhaps accompanied by an early harvest program, together with a commitment to undertake negotiations in the future (Fiorentino, Verdeja, and Toqueboeuf 2006). Trade agreements can support reform plans or, at least, consolidate past efforts at liberalization. The value added of preferential trade agreements for the temporary movement of workers consists mainly in minor expansions in the number of categories of individual service providers; few achieve increased quotas or the elimination of economic needs tests. It has been suggested that no preferential trade agreement has bound a full commitment for the equivalent of GATS Mode 4 in any subsector (Fink and Molinuevo 2007).

### The WTO Doha Development Agenda

The liberalization of trade in retail services has, so far, primarily occurred as a result of the GATS multilateral negotiations and recent WTO accessions. The distribution service sector has elicited fewer multilateral commitments than most service sectors, highlighting a large gap between the sector's access conditions in the GATS context and its economic importance. Since 1995, 22 developing countries have offered commitments as part of their accession negotiations, compared with only 19 developing countries, out of 103, that were bound by them in January 1995 as a result of the Uruguay Round. For distribution services, the outcome of the Doha Round will mainly be assessed in terms of the extent to which key markets targeted by the plurilateral request by a group of WTO members will bind recent or ongoing reforms, which are typically undertaken on a gradual basis (Roy 2008). In the current Doha Round of negotiations, there have been several requests relating to retail services, including requests to remove barriers to FDI and improve the transparency of licensing procedures (USITC 2008). By 2005, 21 offers had been made on distribution services: 8 of them by developed countries and 13 by developing country WTO members, of which there were then a total of 58 (UNCTAD 2005).

While the concentration of ownership in the retail sector is already high, the gains achieved through binding liberalization in market access may be much smaller than expected, and governments may therefore need to complement trade liberalization with competition policy to ensure that consumers reap the potential benefits, particularly in terms of food. For nonfood consumer goods, product market regulation can be the most important policy (Nordås 2008). The retail services trade can be affected by nondiscriminatory regulations that constitute unnecessary barriers to trade, such as licensing requirements that are determined to be more burdensome than necessary to ensure the quality of the service and thus in violation of GATS article VI.4 on domestic regulation, the rules for which are being discussed in the multilateral Doha Round (USITC 2008).

#### Trade facilitation

The regulations and practices affecting goods imports can have a major impact on international supply chains, which could be strongly influenced in a positive way by the WTO negotiations on trade facilitation. Inadequate port management and customs practices in many developing countries result in long delays and give rise to unnecessary trade transaction costs. The demands of border and port officials for informal payments may impede trade. The Doha negotiations address ways to help exporters of goods who need information on import and export regulations and customs procedures in other countries. Cutting the red tape associated with imports of goods into a country and providing easier access to accurate information on import requirements are two ways of facilitating trade. The aim is to clarify and improve the relevant articles of the General Agreement on Tariffs and Trade of the WTO with a view to expediting the movement, release, and clearance of goods, including goods in transit. However, developing countries and the least developed countries will not be obliged to undertake investments in infrastructure projects beyond their means.

The negotiations also aim at enhancing technical assistance and support for capacity building in developing countries and at improving the provisions for effective cooperation among customs authorities and other appropriate authorities on trade facilitation and customs compliance issues. This is considered vital to enabling these authorities to participate fully in the negotiations and to benefit from them. There will be a collaborative effort in this area by the WTO, the International Monetary Fund, the OECD, the United Nations Conference on Trade and Development, the World Customs Organization, and the World Bank.

## Questions Governments Should Assess as They Advance the Reform of the Trade-Related Aspects of Distribution Services

A number of issues merit the attention of policy makers as they advance the trade integration agenda for distribution services. A checklist of questions that might help structure the assessment and guide a comprehensive approach to regulatory reform and the formulation of trade policy follows.

***Licenses, permits, and other official clearances and their trade-distorting effects on market access and national treatment***

1. Which laws and regulations discipline the licensing of distribution services?
2. Which authorities issue licenses and permits and monitor compliance?
3. Are licenses required for domestic or foreign companies?
4. Are foreign service suppliers subject to different registration and licensing conditions relative to domestic suppliers?
5. How does the national application process for licenses, permits, and clearances compare with the corresponding process in other countries in terms of the number of administrative steps involved, the average processing time for applications, and the associated fees and costs? Do the steps involve different ministries, departments, provinces, local authorities, and municipalities?
6. Are there significant differences in administrative performance across national regions or across different types of distribution suppliers? If so, why?
7. Are there unnecessary steps in the process that could be shortened or eliminated? Are there any particular bottlenecks in the process that can be addressed? Can the number of required documents and signatures be reduced by centralizing the application process, for example by providing a one-stop shop facility so as to reduce compliance costs? Can the process be made less expensive, while still safeguarding important policies?
8. Is the official decision-making process transparent and does it involve consultation with other interested parties? If not, what can be done to increase transparency and predictability in the process?
9. Are there disproportionately high fees or other charges levied through the application process?
10. Is there any government or independent body to which a decision can be appealed?
11. What types of grants or subsidies are provided to distribution service suppliers operating in the local market? Are such subsidies allocated in an equitable way or are they tied to specific criteria and, if so, what are the criteria?
12. What are the regulations for land and real estate ownership for foreign distribution companies, including on size limitations, road access, parking areas, and residential areas? Are these regulations different from the regulations covering local investors? What effect do potential differences in these regulations have on distribution activities?
13. Which authorities establish and monitor building codes and product standards in the distribution sector?
14. Which practices are followed by local authorities in carrying out ongoing inspections of distribution facilities? Is this a regular process or a random process?

15. Do such inspections tend to involve informal payments to officials? Are foreign companies especially targeted?
16. Would it make economic sense and does the government have the necessary capacity to adopt any regional or international product standards or wholesale and retail outlet building codes that would facilitate the integration of the local market and international markets (in addition to maintaining or improving quality, health, safety, or other relevant standards)?

*Commercial presence of foreign affiliates (GATS Mode 3)*

1. Are there legal restrictions on market entry by foreign distribution companies through commercial activities?
2. If so, what are the types of restrictions and what is the impact of the restrictions on inward FDI? What is the motivation for imposing any such screening? Do the restrictions include limitations on takeovers and mergers?
3. Are foreign suppliers required to establish locally through a particular legal form or use a specific legal name? If so, what are these requirements?
4. Is there a requirement for foreign distribution companies to form joint ventures with local companies? If so, have these joint ventures been successful and fulfilled the prospective aims? Have they helped build local expertise in the distribution sector by transferring technology and management knowledge?
5. Are there staffing requirements for the establishment of each wholesale unit or retail outlet? Do these involve regulations on shop opening hours and Sunday openings? Are there requirements for foreign suppliers to hire local executives?
6. Are the restrictions on commercial presence compliant with the country's prospective offer for binding commitments under the GATS in the Doha Round of WTO negotiations?
7. Could the policy rationale behind restrictions be addressed through other, less trade-restrictive means?
8. Are there sectoral exemptions to competition law that affect the conditions of competition in the domestic distribution service market? Do these include any government product retailing monopolies?
9. How does competition law deal with instances of anticompetitive practices such as cartels, collusion, and predatory pricing? Is competition law enforced effectively in the distribution sector?
10. Which products are prohibited from sale by foreign retailers or restricted in some way by import licensing?
11. Are there any significant government monopolies or state-owned enterprises that restrict private sector activities (directly or indirectly) and product retailing, and does this affect the competitiveness of private companies?

12. Are there restrictions on product promotions and advertising that affect retailers?

***Temporary presence of foreign suppliers (GATS Mode 4) and foreign employees in foreign-owned wholesale units and retail outlets***

1. What types of restrictions exist on individual foreign service suppliers under contract or as employees of foreign affiliates? Are there any bans, quotas, economic needs tests, labor market tests, or other impediments imposed on the temporary entry of foreign employees? Are any occupations subject to a fit and proper test of the individual?
2. Is there a quota system in place for intracorporate transferees and contractual service suppliers and is it changed frequently?
3. Are the rules different for each category or occupation?
4. Is there implicit or explicit discrimination against the nationality of certain foreign service suppliers?
5. Are the business visa and work permit application processes administered in a reasonably expeditious and cost-effective way? Or are they opaque, slow, cumbersome, and valid for different periods? Could they be combined? What can be done to improve the administrative efficiency of the application process?
6. Are there any restrictions or issues related to the nonrecognition of qualifications for high-skilled workers?
7. Are there domestic regulations that have an adverse impact on foreign service suppliers and that affect their welfare or the local labor market (for example, discriminatory remuneration and benefit structures)?
8. What are the policy objectives of the restrictions? Could the policy rationale be addressed through other, less trade-restrictive means?
9. Are there any nationality requirements for workers in distribution services, and do the requirements vary according to the different types of distribution services? Are there any exceptions for workers from specific countries?
10. Are there any prior residency requirements for foreign employees?
11. What are the nationality and residency requirements for board members, directors, and managers?

***Distribution services in crossborder trade (GATS Mode 1)***

1. Are there restrictions on the crossborder supply of any distribution services, including solicitation and marketing?

2. Are there restrictions on imports of the goods to be supplied by wholesalers, retailers, or franchisees?
3. Are there differential import duties on the foreign goods to be sold by wholesalers, retailers, and franchisees?
4. Could there be improvements in trade facilitation at the border by the customs authority?

### *Government policies that can affect distribution services*

In view of the positive effect that large modern retail outlets can have in shopping malls and multiplexes and the creation of jobs in modern wholesaling units and logistics, food processing, and cold storage companies through higher wage levels, the quality of new jobs, and opportunities for improved gender balance in employment, do government policies take into account the following related issues to ensure that the optimum benefits are obtained?

#### Direct assistance

- Encouragement for the creation of cooperatives among local retailers so as to increase bulk purchasing at lower supplier prices
- Investment in the supply chain to link farmers and horticulturists to retailers
- Assistance or subsidies for small and medium enterprises in packaging, labeling, and bar code technology and the use of information technology so as to increase local sourcing by foreign retailers
- Government training for employees in the use of information technology, customer relations, and customer services
- Assistance for owners and employees made redundant because of the modernization process, such as for retraining, unemployment benefits, and early retirement

#### Land utilization

- Availability of land designated for modern retail outlets, such as shopping malls, shopping centers, supermarkets, hypermarkets, and street markets

#### Fiscal means

- Tax formats for corporations, value added tax, raw material import duties for retail products, stamp duties

#### Infrastructure services

- Infrastructure availability to support modern retail outlets, including transport, electricity, water supply, sewage treatment, and telecommunications
- Improved retail facilities and the appearance of such facilities in popular tourist areas

**Other regulations**

- Need for coordination among the ministries and agencies responsible for business registration, FDI approvals, land use, building regulations, food quality, hygienic food handling, food processing, agriculture, and transport at the federal, provincial, and local or municipal levels
- Regulations on online trading, direct marketing, and consumer protection against fraud, including with respect to the use of credit cards
- Protection of intellectual property rights
- Bankruptcy laws

### *Preferential trade agreements and bilateral investment agreements*

1. Are there any preferential trade agreements affecting the inward supply of distribution services and the movement of natural persons within the sector?
2. If so, are these bilateral and regional trade agreements compliant with GATS obligations, particularly most favored nation treatment (article II) and economic integration (article V)?
3. Which specific measures are given preferential treatment in the distribution service sector and for which activities and products?

## Conclusion

The distribution sector accounts for 10–20 percent of GDP, 15–30 percent of employment, and up to 40 percent of the total number of enterprises in most countries. The economic importance of the sector arises from its role in providing the essential channel between producers and consumers. The productivity of the distribution sector greatly affects the prices of a wide range of goods and services; depending on the product, 10 to 50 percent of final consumer prices are often attributed to the distributor. The functioning of the distribution market should be a priority for policy makers because the market largely determines the price, quality, and choice among goods and among many services. An open market and adequate regulatory framework are key in realizing the prospective gains from modernization.

In 2007, global retail sales were valued at an estimated US$12 trillion, having grown, on average, by 8 percent annually in 2001–07. Grocery sales made up 40 percent of retail sales worldwide and approximately 60 percent of retail sales in poorer African countries. Sales through modern retail systems have grown more quickly than total retail sales and accounted for over 52 percent of all retail sales in 2006. In the OECD countries, these sales represented up to 80 percent of total sales. In most developing countries, the retail sector is largely unorganized and principally consists of small family-run neighborhood shops and outdoor markets. While the leading global actors are mainly European and U.S. companies, some retailers based in developing countries are successfully expanding in their respective regions, including in Africa, Asia, and Latin America. They are part of a worldwide trend toward concentration and larger outlets in distribution, and South-South trade is increasingly prominent in this development.

In the future, it is likely that the pattern in the evolution of large emerging markets will follow that of the distribution sector in developed countries. The pace of change and modernization will largely depend on the pace of liberalization in market access. Regulation and competition policy will additionally affect the degree of market concentration and vertical integration. The gains from liberalization in market access in the retail sector will be greater if adequate regulation and trade liberalization are carefully sequenced. If regulatory policies are not in place or are poorly coordinated with trade policies, the gains from distribution service liberalization are likely to be compromised. Countries that have experienced modern retail expansion have benefited from competition policies that restrict concentration and collusion and from reduced limitations on town planning, zoning, and opening hours. They have also prohibited pricing below cost, ensured prompt payments to suppliers, and strengthened supply-side capacity and access to finance.

The international trade in distribution services is mainly conducted through outward direct investment in foreign affiliates or joint ventures. Strict market entry conditions in the past delayed modernization in the distribution sector in countries such as China, India, and Russia. The opening of domestic retail markets has led to rapid increases in foreign participation in some countries. Besides prospective improvements in quality, choice, and pricing, modern retailing practices may provide a more convenient shopping experience and safer and relatively high-paying jobs. They may also create jobs in ancillary food processing, logistics, supply chain management, and information technology–based back-office functions, including modern purchase tracking and accounting practices. However, parallel improvements are often needed in the transport networks, electricity supply, and telecommunications services on which the distribution service sector depends. Thus, coordination among the various ministries and agencies involved in development in these areas is essential.

Liberalization in the distribution sector generally entails significant adjustment costs, as well as benefits. Modern retailing is likely to lead to the closure of many mom-and-pop stores, other small or less efficient retailers, and, in poorer developing countries, open markets for fruits, vegetables, meat, and fish products. It may also require better health and safety standards, in addition to frequent deliveries of large quantities of produce. Farmers with superior endowments in management skills, land, and financing are therefore likely to prosper, while smaller farmers may be pushed down the value chain. Governments need to adopt policies to assist in training and the provision of capital to enable farmers to sell to big retail chains. For the smallest suppliers, market liberalization often represents significant challenges.

The sector is regulated directly in relation to physical facilities (for example, location, size, juxtaposition with other buildings, effects on traffic). It is also regulated indirectly to ensure against market failure (for example, anticompetitive practices) and to protect noneconomic values, including societal objectives relating to employment, working conditions, health, the safety of facilities and products, and the impact on farmers, horticulturalists, and the environment. There is no panacea to propose to governments: it may be important to phase in liberalization measures if there are sensitive social issues at stake (such as racial and gender balancing) or if the resources to address the adverse consequences of structural adjustment are lacking and aid in capacity building is necessary.

An assessment must be carried out to identify any government policies that can significantly affect the distribution sector either directly or indirectly, especially any regulations that are unnecessarily trade restrictive and therefore should be modified. The direct impacts on the ownership, capitalization, and development of distribution enterprises must be considered first, including initial market access conditions, and the operations of foreign companies that have been permitted to establish a commercial presence should be considered second. More generally, the effect on employment levels, the pace of liberalization, and the need to take into account ethnic makeup and sensibilities in society should also be examined. Finally, it is important to determine whether regulations, including competition law, are adequately enforced.

The liberalization of trade in retail services has, so far, principally occurred as a result of the GATS multilateral negotiations and WTO accessions since 1995. The distribution service sector has been the focus of fewer multilateral commitments than most other sectors, highlighting the large gap between the economic importance of the sector and the access conditions in the sector in the context of the GATS. The regulations and practices affecting goods imports can have a major impact on distribution supply chains, which could be strongly influenced in a positive way by the WTO negotiations on trade facilitation.

## Notes

1. Disaggregated data on distribution services are not published in the National Accounts Main Aggregates Database of the United Nations. Distribution is instead grouped with hotels and restaurants, and this category accounts for 14.6 percent of GDP in developing countries (excluding China)

and 15.6 percent of GDP in developed countries. However, the numbers hide great variation because developing countries account for both the 11 lowest and 11 highest proportions, or 6–10 percent and 22–33 percent, respectively. The average for the least developed countries is 17 percent. Since 1995, the value added of distribution services has been highest in the least developed countries and in low-income and Sub-Saharan African countries (UNCTAD 2005).

2. For the balance of payments statistics of the International Monetary Fund, see http://www.imf.org/external/np/sta/bop/bop.htm.

3. The European Union-15 are the members prior to 2004: Austria, Belgium, Denmark, Finland, France, Germany, Greece, Ireland, Italy, Luxembourg, the Netherlands, Portugal, Spain, Sweden, and the United Kingdom.

## References

Arkell, J., and M. D. C. Johnson. 2005. "Sustainability Impact Assessment of Proposed WTO Negotiations: Final Report for the Distribution Services Study." Report, June, International Trade and Services Policy and Institute for Development Policy and Management, School of Environment and Development, University of Manchester, Manchester, United Kingdom.

Borga, Maria. 2006. "Improved Measures of U.S. International Services: The Cases of Insurance, Wholesale and Retail Trade, and Financial Services." Paper presented at the National Bureau of Economic Research–Conference on Research in Income and Wealth "Joint Conference on International Services Flows," Bethesda, MD, April 28–29.

Boylaud, Olivier. 2000. "Regulatory Reform in Road Freight and Retail Distribution." Economics Department Working Paper 255, Organisation for Economic Co-operation and Development, Paris.

Boylaud, Olivier, and Giuseppe Nicoletti. 2001. "Regulatory Reform in Retail Distribution." OECD Economic Studies 32 (2001/1), Organisation for Economic Co-operation and Development, Paris.

Bradford, Scott. 1995. "The Welfare Effects of Distribution Regulations in OECD Countries." *Economic Enquiry* 43 (4): 795–811.

Carana Corporation. 2008. "Guyanese Services: Opportunities for Increased Economic Growth and Trade Liberalization." Report, U.S. Agency for International Development, Washington, DC.

Cattaneo, Olivier, Peter Walkenhorst, and S. Ighiliahriz. 2007. "Harnessing the Benefits of Services Trade for Algeria." World Bank Policy Note, World Bank, Washington, DC.

Deloitte. 2008. "2008 Global Powers of Retailing: Standing Out from the Crowd." Deloitte Consumer Business, London.

Dihel, N., and A. El Shinnawy. 2006. "Assessment of Trade in Distribution Services in Egypt in Relation to the GATS." Report, June, Ministry of Trade and Industry, Cairo.

Fink, Carsten, and Martín Molinuevo. 2007. *East Asian Free Trade Agreements in Services: Roaring Tigers or Timid Pandas?* Report 40175. Washington, DC: East Asia and Pacific Region, World Bank.

Fiorentino, Roberto V., Luis Verdeja, and Christelle Toqueboeuf. 2006. "The Changing Landscape of Regional Trade Agreements: 2006 Update." Discussion Paper 12, World Trade Organization, Geneva.

Joseph, M., N. Soundararajan, M. Gupta, and S. Sahu. 2008. "Impact of Organised Retailing on the Unorganised Sector." ICRIER Working Paper 222 (September), Indian Council for Research on International Economic Relations, New Delhi.

Kalirajan, Kaleeswaran. 2000. "Restrictions on Trade in Distribution Services." Productivity Commission Staff Research Paper, August, AusInfo, Canberra.

Lawrence, Felicity. 2004. *Not on the Label: What Really Goes into the Food on Your Plate.* London: Penguin Books.

National Accounts Main Aggregates Database. Statistics Division, United Nations. http://unstats.un.org/unsd/nationalaccount/.

Nordås, Hildegunn Kyvik. 2008. "Gatekeepers to Consumer Markets: The Role of Retailers in International Trade." *International Review of Retail, Distribution and Consumer Research* 18 (5): 449–72.

Nordås, Hildegunn Kyvik, Massimo Geloso Grosso, and Enrico Pinali. 2007. "Market Structure in the Distribution Sector and Merchandise Trade." Document TAD/TC/WP(2007)16/FINAL, Working Party of the Trade Committee, Trade Committee, Trade and Agriculture Directorate, Organisation for Economic Co-operation and Development, Paris.

Roy, Martin. 2008. "Out of Stock or Just in Time? Doha and the Liberalization of Distribution Services." In *Opening Markets for Trade in Services: Countries and Sectors in Bilateral and WTO Negotiations*, ed. Juan A. Marchetti and Martin Roy, 224–63. Geneva: World Trade Organization; New York: Cambridge University Press.

UNCTAD (United Nations Conference on Trade and Development). 2004. *World Investment Report 2004: The Shift towards Services*. Geneva: UNCTAD.

———. 2005. "Distribution Services: Note by the UNCTAD Secretariat." Report TD/B/COM.1/EM.29/2 (September 7), UNCTAD, Geneva.

USITC (United States International Trade Commission). 2008. *Recent Trends in US Services Trade: 2008 Annual Report*. Investigation 332–45, Publication 4015. Washington, DC: USITC.

Weatherspoon, Dave D., and Thomas Reardon. 2003. "The Rise of Supermarkets in Africa: Implications for Agrifood Systems and the Rural Poor." *Development Policy Review* 21 (3): 333–55.

World Bank. 2007. *World Development Report 2008: Agriculture for Development*. Washington, DC: World Bank.

WTO (World Trade Organization). 2002. "Communication from Thailand: Assessment of Trade in Services." Document TN/S/W/4 (July 22), Special Session, Council for Trade in Services, WTO, Geneva.

———. 2008a. *Trade Policy Review, Report by the Secretariat: China*. Report WT/TPR/S/199 (April 16). Geneva: WTO.

———. 2008b. *Trade Policy Review, Report by the Secretariat: Republic of Korea*. Report WT/TPR/S/204 (September 3). Geneva: WTO.

6

# BUILDING EMPIRES OVERSEAS: INTERNATIONALIZATION IN THE CONSTRUCTION SERVICES SECTOR

*Michael Engman*

## Introduction: Why Is Trade in Construction Services of Interest for Developing Countries?

Trade in construction services is of interest for developing countries because of the inflows of remittances and the significant productive opportunities that may be provided to the economies of these countries. While many developing countries are large importers of construction services, often with World Bank capital as part of the financial solution, several developing countries are also becoming successful exporters of these services. (Box 6.1 illustrates the main characteristics of the sector, and box 6.2 defines the scope of the sector.) Trade data reveal that China, the Arab Republic of Egypt, India, and Turkey, in addition to some countries in Eastern Europe and East Asia, host an increasingly competitive construction service sector that is active in foreign markets, particularly in other developing countries. The companies are often of sufficient size and possess the expertise to take on large construction projects in the regions where they operate. Major centers of investment in construction projects—from the large building sites in the Persian Gulf region to Las Vegas and Moscow—also attract hundreds of thousands of guest workers from countries such as Bangladesh, Indonesia, Mexico, and the Republic of Yemen, as well as many Central American and Central Asian countries. Many poor countries gain from the financial flows that the guest workers generate.

From the perspective of imports, market access for international contractors increases the choice for domestic investors in construction services. International

**Box 6.1:** The Main Characteristics of the Construction Service Sector

The role of the construction service sector is especially pertinent in the daily lives of people because it provides the physical infrastructure for personal shelter, sanitation, water and electricity distribution, schooling, health services, transportation, and private sector activities. It is one of the major service sectors in most economies in terms of employment and value added. Global spending on construction, broadly defined, is likely to have exceeded US$4 trillion in 2005 (Tulacz 2005). This would represent roughly 9–10 percent of world gross domestic product (GDP). In a study of gross value added of GDP in construction services in 75 countries, Ruddock and Lopes (2006) find that the mean is 6 percent (figure 6.1). In large economies of the Organisation for Economic Co-operation and Development (OECD), the sector represents 6–9 percent of total employment, which illustrates its intensive use of labor (Geloso Grosso, Jankowska, and Gonzales 2008).

The sector is associated with a limited number of large international companies and a large number of local small and medium-size companies. In 2007, the top 225 international contractors generated US$827 billion in revenue, of which US$310 billion represented exports (ENR 2008). Of these 225 companies, 51 were Chinese, and 23 were Turkish. Brazil; Egypt; India; Israel; Kuwait; Lebanon; the former Yugoslav Republic of Macedonia; Mexico; Pakistan; the Russian Federation; Saudi Arabia; Serbia; Taiwan, China; and the United Arab Emirates each had one to three companies on the list. The world's largest international contractor, Hochtief AG, generated US$21.3 billion in exports, while the 225th largest international contractor, China National Electronics Import & Export Corporation, generated US$62.3 million. The ranking of

**Figure 6.1.** Construction Services: Mean Gross Value Added in GDP, 75 Countries

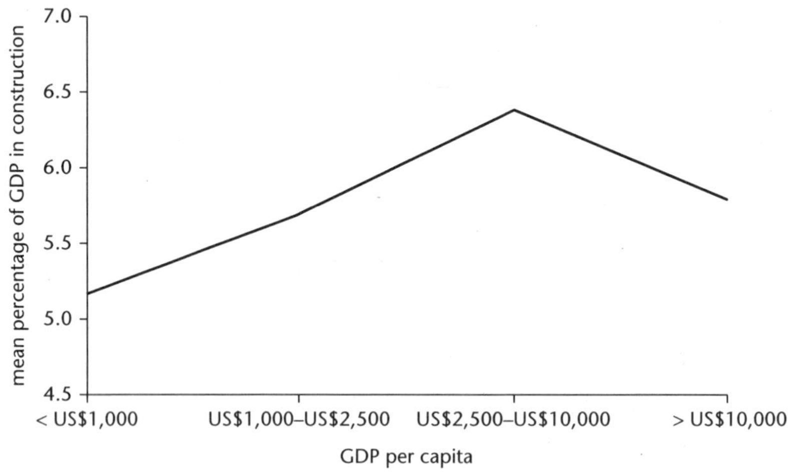


*Source:* Ruddock and Lopes (2006).

**Figure 6.2.** Construction Services: Market Share by Sector

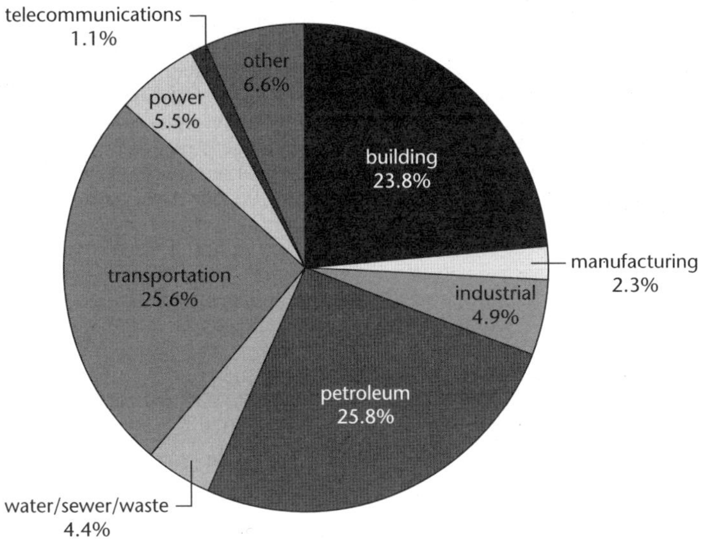


*Source:* ENR (2008).

companies changes from year to year, signaling significant market contestability (UNCTAD 2000a). Three dominant market segments—transportation, building, and petroleum extraction—make up approximately three-fourths of the overall market (figure 6.2). Input-output analysis indicates that the sector has one of the highest backward links in OECD economies, which reflects its reliance on inputs of domestic goods and services (Pietroforte and Gregori 2003).

The largest client segment for the construction sector is often the public sector. According to Mburu (2008), government procurement accounts for almost 50 percent of construction expenditures in many developing countries. These investments cover the building of roads, bridges, ports, housing complexes, and public utility infrastructure such as water, sanitation, and electricity. Demand for some of these projects is supported by official development assistance that may have strings attached in the form of rules and preferences in the procurement process. The market for projects financed by official development assistance is dominated by multinationals that possess the expertise, market intelligence, and financial wherewithal to take charge of the project process. Local companies are engaged as subcontractors. The corporate client segment invests primarily in industrial and commercial real estate, and investments are sensitive to the business cycle and the costs of capital. The household client segment covers residential building and is mainly served by local small and medium-size enterprises. Informal sector activity often makes up a large share of investment.

**Box 6.2:** What Do Construction Services Cover?

Construction services are part of a larger bundle of goods and services in the construction value chain. There are several definitions of construction services, and they are broadly comparable across classifications of international standards (Geloso Grosso, Jankowska, and Gonzales 2008). The services sectoral classification list of the World Trade Organization (WTO) divides the construction value chain into two main categories: engineering and architectural services and construction services (see WTO 1991). The former category is classified as professional services, while the latter category covers mainly general construction work for buildings and civil engineering, installation and assembly work, and building completion and finishing work. The supply of the two types of services is integrated throughout the project life cycle, and there are significant links between them. This chapter focuses exclusively on trade in construction services, while acknowledging the significant links and synergies with engineering and architectural services. An accompanying chapter in this volume focuses on engineering services.

contractors bring new technology and building techniques, offer a wider and deeper selection of financial resources, and provide project management experience in large and complex designs. Foreign competition also provides incentives for domestic contractors to adopt best practices and raise productivity. Those developing countries that have yet to nurture the full scope of domestic construction services may have no choice and must sign contracts with foreign providers. Other countries host a thriving domestic construction service sector in which the companies may lack the size or the sophistication to undertake large infrastructure and building projects. The gains from opening domestic markets to foreign competition can be substantial, particularly in developing countries confronted by demographic expansion, rapid urbanization, and strong growth in demand for new and improved infrastructure. Consequently, these countries tend to import relatively sophisticated technical and project management expertise from developed countries or major emerging market economies.

From the perspective of exports, companies that compete for projects in international markets have to ensure that they offer an attractive product to prospective clients. This requirement puts pressure on companies to innovate, raise internal productivity, and manage their supply chains of input material and adjacent services more effectively. It also helps companies focus on what they do best because they often need to specialize to obtain business.[1] Access to foreign markets brings potential economies of scale in production, exposure to international best practices, and opportunities to partner with leading foreign companies. Consequently, the efforts of policy makers to facilitate the operations of a local export sector may not only improve domestic contractors to the advantage of local clients, but also help create local employment and boost inflows of foreign exchange.

In addition, the construction service sector is one of the sectors that is most susceptible to the effects of cycles in the world economy. For example, between 1997 and 1999, during the economic crisis in Indonesia, the share of the construction sector in total workforce employment dropped from 10.2 to 6.8 percent (UNCTAD 2000b). This cyclical behavior arises because of the private sector's tendency to invest heavily in construction if interest rates are low or if the economy is expanding. Trade may help alleviate some of these fluctuations in two main ways. First, it allows domestic investors to tap into foreign supply during periods of economic boom when local companies are operating at full capacity. Second, it allows domestic construction service companies to offer some of their surplus capacity abroad in times of economic downturn at home.

## What Is the Situation of and What Are the Prospects for Trade in Construction Services?

Construction services are intensively traded through two major modes of supply. The choice of mode is closely linked to the nature of the service. For example, an online betting service can be delivered electronically to any corner of the world, whereas a haircut requires perfect proximity between customer and hairdresser if a transaction is to take place. The General Agreement on Trade in Services (GATS) of the World Trade Organization (WTO) defines four modes of supply. These are crossborder supply (Mode 1), consumption abroad (Mode 2), commercial presence (Mode 3), and temporary movement of natural persons (Mode 4). Construction services are almost exclusively provided through the latter two modes, as follows:

- *Commercial presence (Mode 3)*: such as when a construction company in country A establishes a subsidiary in country B to provide construction services locally; for example, a Turkish company with a commercial presence in Kazakhstan is awarded a government contract and builds a motor highway in that country.
- *Temporary movement of natural persons (Mode 4)*: such as in the entry and temporary stay in a client's territory of foreign individuals to supply a service; for example, a contractor based in the United Arab Emirates brings in South Asian construction workers to help build a fertilizer factory.

Because of the requirement of the physical presence of labor, capital, and various material inputs in construction projects, trade through crossborder supply and consumption abroad makes up a small component in the construction service sector. The business is based on domestic production. While the production process can be imported, the physical work in its entirety must be carried out in the client country (the construction of oil platforms is a notable exception). This helps allay concerns about labor adjustments that sometimes are associated with trade liberalization linked to foreign direct investment. However, the inflow of foreign guest workers remains a sensitive issue in most countries. The two common modes of supply—commercial presence and the movement of natural persons—are complementary in construction services, but the strength of the link may vary depending on the entry strategy of the exporter.

Over the last few decades, companies have moved increasingly toward a more permanent presence in new markets relative to the alternative of a project-specific or mobile presence. Chen (2008) finds that contractors are more likely to use a permanent entry mode than a project-specific entry mode if cultural distance or competitive intensity is significant or if colonial ties, language proximity, or entry restrictions are insignificant. Companies with permanent presence are less dependent on the circulation of project staff from abroad. Because substantial entry restrictions in client countries tend to push international contractors to depend on shorter-term establishments, they also lead companies to make use of more foreign staff than necessary.

### *Several developing countries are major importers and exporters of construction services*

The leading exporters of construction services in absolute terms are large developed countries, such as Japan, the United States, and member countries of the European Union, followed by large emerging economies such as China, India, the Russian Federation, and Turkey (table 6.1). Egyptian, Israeli, Malaysian, and Thai construction companies also have significant presence abroad. For example, Egypt exported construction services worth more than US$0.5 billion in 2005. While developed affluent countries are the biggest exporters in absolute terms, exports of construction services are more significant as a share of the national economy in some developing countries. Among the top importers, the largest Organisation for Economic Co-operation and Development (OECD) economies are comparable with hydrocarbon exporters such as Angola, Azerbaijan, Kazakhstan, and Russia. Several countries around the Persian Gulf would also feature prominently on the list if their trade data were made available.

The data on trade in construction services are limited and fragmented because the annual flows of only a few countries are recorded in the International Monetary Fund balance of payments statistics. Figure 6.3 presents export data for the non-OECD countries that report data on a regular basis. There is a clear upward trend that indicates the growing participation of developing countries in this trade. All the countries recorded an increase in construction exports between 2002 and 2007, with

**Table 6.1.** Major Exporters and Importers of Construction Services, 2005

| Rank | Exporters | Value (US$ millions) | Share in 15 economies (%) | Annual % change | Rank | Importers | Value (US$ millions) | Share in 15 economies (%) | Annual % change |
|---|---|---|---|---|---|---|---|---|---|
| 1 | European Union (25) | 26,142 | 55.3 | 13 | 1 | European Union (25) | 18,743 | 48.3 | 6 |
| | Extra–European Union (25) exports | 14,171 | 30.0 | 17 | | Extra–European Union (25) imports | 7,957 | 20.5 | 6 |
| 2 | Japan | 7,224 | 15.3 | 5 | 2 | Japan | 4,765 | 12.3 | −1 |
| 3 | United States | 4,139 | 8.8 | 15 | 3 | Russian Federation | 4,034 | 10.4 | 32 |
| 4 | China | 2,593 | 5.5 | 77 | 4 | Kazakhstan | 1,941 | 5.0 | 165 |
| 5 | Russian Federation | 2,209 | 4.7 | 40 | 5 | China | 1,619 | 4.2 | 21 |
| 6 | Turkey | 882 | 1.9 | 19 | 6 | Azerbaijan | 1,499 | 3.9 | 9 |
| 7 | India (estimated) | 828 | 1.8 | — | 7 | Angola | 1,323 | 3.4 | 53 |
| 8 | Malaysia | 811 | 1.7 | 148 | 8 | Malaysia | 1,087 | 2.8 | 133 |
| 9 | Singapore | 566 | 1.2 | 1 | 9 | United States | 1,039 | 2.7 | 7 |
| 10 | Egypt, Arab Rep. | 503 | 1.1 | 24 | 10 | India (estimated) | 774 | 2.0 | — |
| 11 | Israel | 349 | 0.7 | 7 | 11 | Indonesia | 726 | 1.9 | 2 |
| 12 | Hong Kong, China | 313 | 0.7 | −17 | 12 | Taiwan, China | 376 | 1.0 | −33 |
| 13 | Thailand | 255 | 0.5 | 8 | 13 | Thailand | 314 | 0.8 | 37 |
| 14 | Norway | 254 | 0.5 | 119 | 14 | Hong Kong, China | 273 | 0.7 | −21 |
| 15 | Romania | 195 | 0.4 | 63 | 15 | Singapore | 271 | 0.7 | 1 |
| | **Above 15** | **47,265** | **100.0** | — | | **Above 15** | **38,785** | **100.0** | — |

*Source:* WTO (2008).

*Note:* European Union (25) = member states of the European Union before January 2007: Austria, Belgium, Cyprus, the Czech Republic, Denmark, Estonia, Finland, France, Germany, Greece, Hungary, Ireland, Italy, Latvia, Lithuania, Luxembourg, Malta, the Netherlands, Poland, Portugal, the Slovak Republic, Slovenia, Spain, Sweden, and the United Kingdom. — = not available.

**Figure 6.3.** Exports of Construction Services, Selected Economies

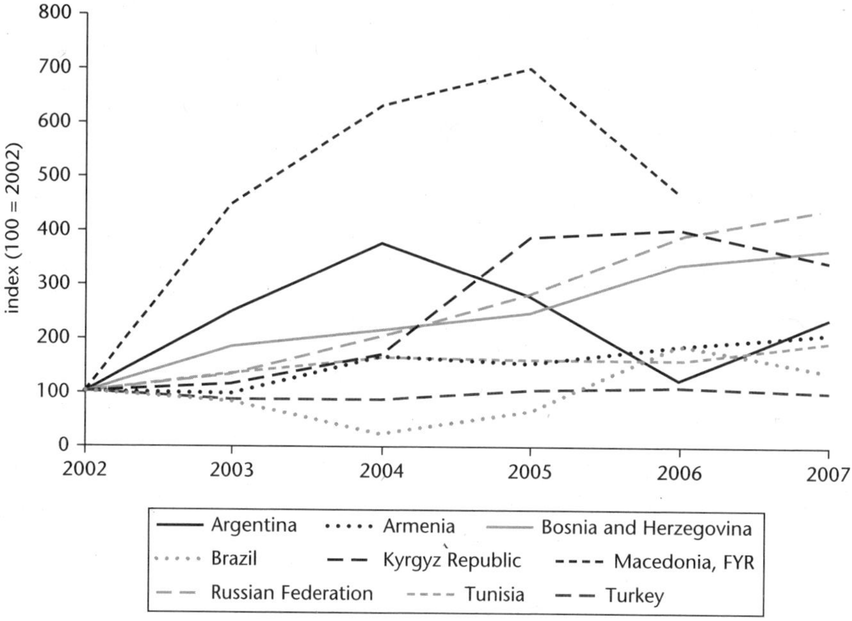


*Source:* International Monetary Fund balance of payments statistics, http://www.imf.org/external/np/sta/bop/bop.htm.

large percentage increases for Armenia, Bosnia and Herzegovina, the Kyrgyz Republic, Russia, and Tunisia. The exports of Argentina, Brazil, and the former Yugoslav Republic of Macedonia also expanded, but at greater volatility. Turkey's export performance was more or less flat. The economic and financial turmoil that started to affect markets in 2008 is likely to lead to a decrease in global construction activity in the years ahead. However, public sector investment in infrastructure projects is expected to mitigate the effects of the drop in private sector investment.

The data fail to capture the great flows of construction workers who supply their services temporarily abroad. These transfers of project-related staff are seldom recorded in official statistics. Nonetheless, large numbers of Latin American construction workers are based in the United States, while many Eastern European workers are located in Western Europe. Workers from Egypt, Yemen, and countries in South Asia and East Asia are counted in the millions in the Persian Gulf region. Chinese builders are also employed on construction sites in East Asia, while Indonesian builders dominate in Malaysia, and Myanmar builders in Thailand. In Russia alone, approximately 40 percent of the estimated 4 million to 9 million foreign guest workers are employed in the construction service sector (Human

Rights Watch 2009). These workers save parts of their salaries and transfer them to families back home. The remittances are used for consumption, family formation, and investment in homes, children's education, and the establishment of small companies (Ratha and Xu 2008). The economic impact from these resources is considerable in many poor countries, and the construction sector's contribution is noteworthy because of the sheer number of foreign workers.

### *Developing countries host a growing number of homegrown multinationals in construction services*

The number of foreign companies that operate in any given market reflects several factors, including the host market's openness to trade and investment, the sophistication of local competitors, the size and profitability of the construction market, and the availability of human capital. Recent firm-level data show that some companies in large developing countries are growing rapidly and have broken into the list of the top 225 international contractors (ENR 2008). The list is dominated by companies in OECD countries and China, but also includes companies in Brazil, Egypt, India, Kuwait, Lebanon, FYR Macedonia, Pakistan, Russia, Saudi Arabia, Turkey, and the United Arab Emirates. The top 225 companies generated US$310 billion in revenue in 2007 from projects outside their respective home countries. The Chinese construction companies have the largest market share of foreign contractors in Africa (27 percent) and the second largest share in Asia (17 percent), In 2003, China's 48,688 construction companies employed 24.1 million workers (Corkin and Burke 2006). Turkey also has a particularly successful export-oriented construction service sector, which includes a 10th of the top international contractors.

Figure 6.4 plots the number of these companies that are present in various countries. Some trends can be discerned. First, large hydrocarbon exporters, particularly countries in the Persian Gulf region, enjoy a significant presence of foreign contractors in their relatively small economies. Second, many of the members of the Association of Southeast Asian Nations also have a relatively large number of international contractors relative to the size of their economies. Third, African countries appear to be open markets because many of them host a relatively large number of foreign contractors. Fourth, almost all high-income OECD countries host a relatively lower number of large foreign contractors than the size of their economies would indicate. France, Germany, Italy, Japan, the Republic of Korea, the Nordic countries, Spain, and the United States are all in the lower, outer limit. Finally, all 144 countries and territories shown in figure 6.4 host at least one foreign contractor, which indicates that the great majority of the world's countries are open to some form of foreign commercial presence.

**Figure 6.4.** Commercial Presence of Large International Contractors in Foreign Markets

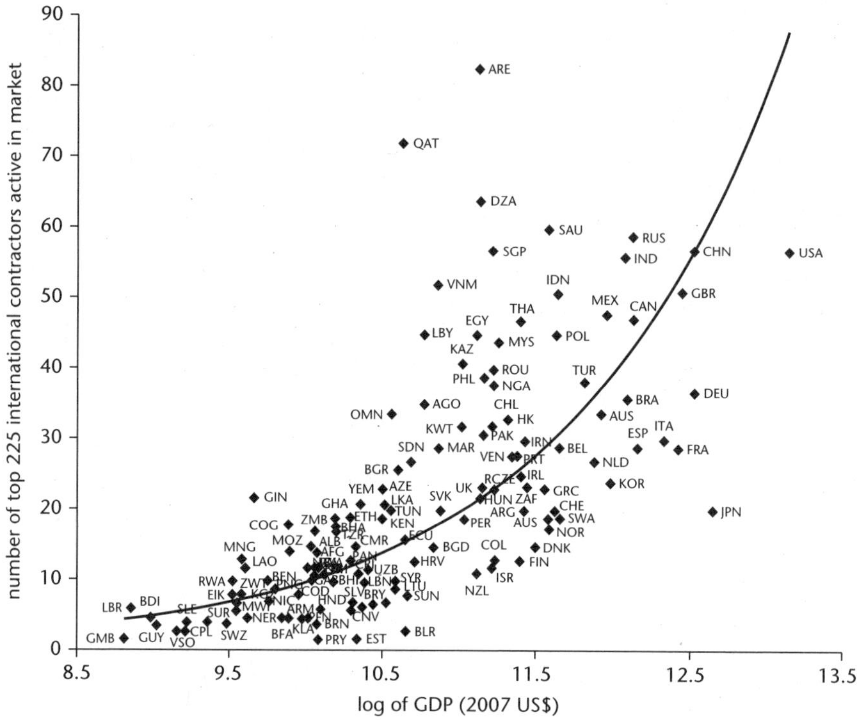


*Sources:* ENR (2008), PovcalNet, authors' calculations.

The number of large international contractors in a market is not a perfect proxy for their combined market share. Yet, it is likely to be a reasonable indicator of the openness of the domestic market, particularly if the market is sizable. Some of the more extreme outliers in figure 6.4 are Algeria, Guinea, Japan, Qatar, and the United Arab Emirates. Guinea has a large number of Chinese construction companies, and there is a strong presence of Chinese companies in several other African economies (see box 6.4). Algeria, Qatar, and the United Arab Emirates are medium-size economies with large numbers of international contractors. These countries are large-scale investors in construction projects, many of which are in the petroleum sector, while others are financed by income from the petroleum sector. Japan, the world's second largest economy, hosts comparatively few foreign contractors (see CLR News 2006 for an overview of the Japanese construction sector).

The current global economic downturn is, in the short term, likely to result in a significant setback in the expansion of trade in construction services. In the medium and long term, the prospects for growth will become more positive as the global economy starts to pick up again. Interest rates around the world have fallen to historically low levels in many countries. The reduced cost of capital should have a positive impact on private sector investment in construction projects, particularly when banks are ready to return to business as usual. Fiscal expansion programs in some of the world largest economies, such as China, Japan, the United States, and the European Union, will also result in large investments in infrastructure projects. The expansion of the Chinese construction sector into foreign markets has gained momentum in the last decade and is expected to continue. Prices for oil, gas, and many other natural resources have recently come down as a result of the economic turmoil. This has caused many projects to be put on hold and guest workers to go back to their home countries. However, if the emerging markets around the world were to return to the positive growth path they enjoyed prior to the economic turmoil, there is reason to expect that trade in construction services would recover to the relatively steady growth it once experienced.

## What Can Be Done to Harness Trade Opportunities?

Policy makers in developing countries may have significant scope to facilitate trade in construction services. The sector is hampered by poor productivity growth in a number of countries, not least within developed-country markets, and effective competition would generate gains by clients and suppliers. This section identifies three broad areas where countries may want to focus their attention. The first set of initiatives would involve reviews of domestic regulations to highlight reform needs. Improving the administration of construction permits and the management of government procurement could greatly facilitate investments in construction projects. However, while effective reforms may require limited commitments in terms of government capacity, they are likely to consume significant political capital given the sector's political influence (more on this below).

The second set of initiatives would seek to remove rules and regulations that are more trade restrictive than necessary. This would allow companies to take advantage of the economic benefits stemming from international exchange. Movement toward more open access to domestic construction markets will stimulate competition, save government resources, and improve the choice for local investors. Seeking improved market access for Mode 3 and Mode 4 transactions in major trading partners could also help increase exports to countries with protected markets. A review of these options, taking into consideration local conditions, would allow developing countries to harness trade opportunities and improve operations in the domestic construction service sector.

The third and final set of initiatives would aim to enhance the competitiveness of the domestic construction service sector. The implementation of applicable international or regional standards for construction materials and best practices for building codes would lower transaction costs and facilitate integration in international supply chains. Addressing human resource shortages and introducing incentives for cooperation and technology transfers between foreign contractors and local contractors would strengthen the domestic sector. Similarly, fostering an environment in which local companies can form consortia and bid for larger projects would also allow the homegrown sector to build capacity in markets associated with cutthroat competition among many small players.

### *Reviewing domestic regulations and their implementation to identify reform needs*

Domestic regulations and the effectiveness of their implementation can have a large impact on the functioning of the construction service sector. Many of these regulations are not discriminatory and affect domestic and foreign companies more or less equally. Other regulations are discriminatory toward foreign providers. This subsection considers both types of regulations and identifies a number of common weaknesses that can be addressed through mostly unilateral initiatives.

#### Administration of construction permits

The *Doing Business 2009* report of the World Bank (2008) presents data on indicators related to dealing with construction permits in some 181 countries. While any benchmarking exercise with a reach and simplification similar to the Doing Business Project should be interpreted with caution, the data still tell of large differences in the administrative capacity in construction permits around the world. The transaction costs and business risks associated with slow and opaque procedures have a negative impact on trade and investment flows. Yet, the size of this impact is not clear. Some of the transaction costs involved in dealing with construction permits may end up in the pockets of officials, as rents to smooth the application process. However, most of the resources are wasted, and the price of larger than necessary transaction costs is paid by the clients. Normal economics apply. Higher than necessary prices result in lower investment in new infrastructure and buildings. Less building activity equals fewer jobs in the construction sector, lower utility for prospective end users, and higher rents charged by landlords, who are often relatively affluent citizens. Figures 6.5–6.7 show the time and

**Figure 6.5.** Number of Procedures Involved in Dealing with Construction Permits

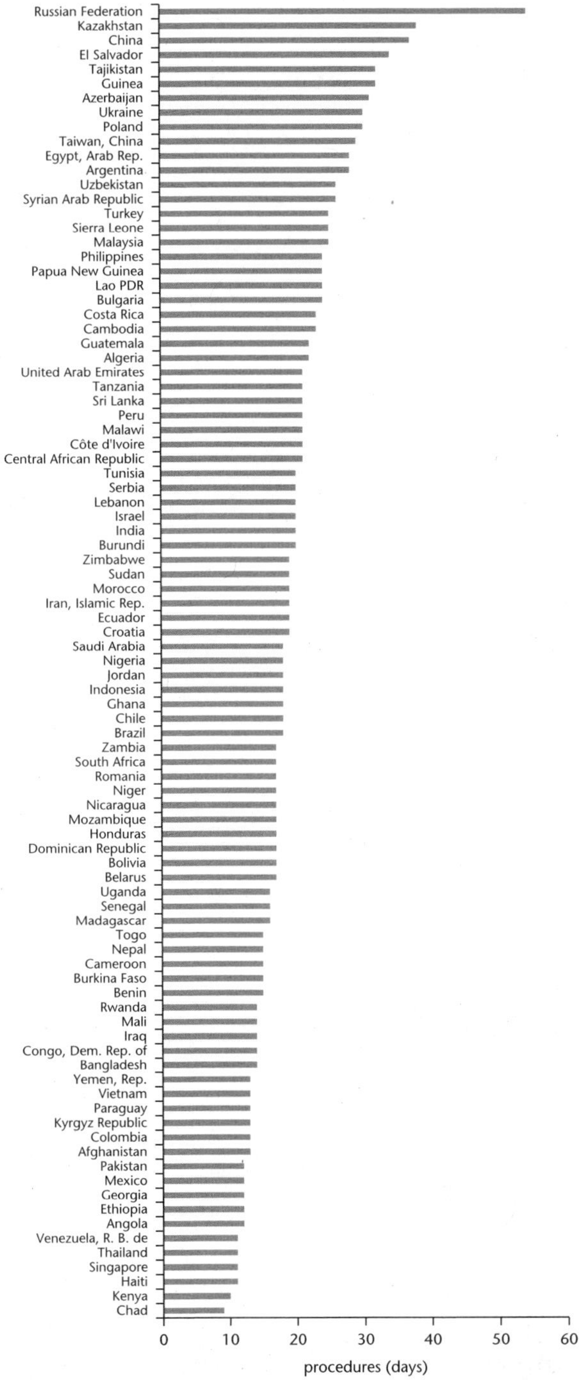


*Source:* World Bank (2008).

**Figure 6.6.** Number of Days Required to Deal with Construction Permits

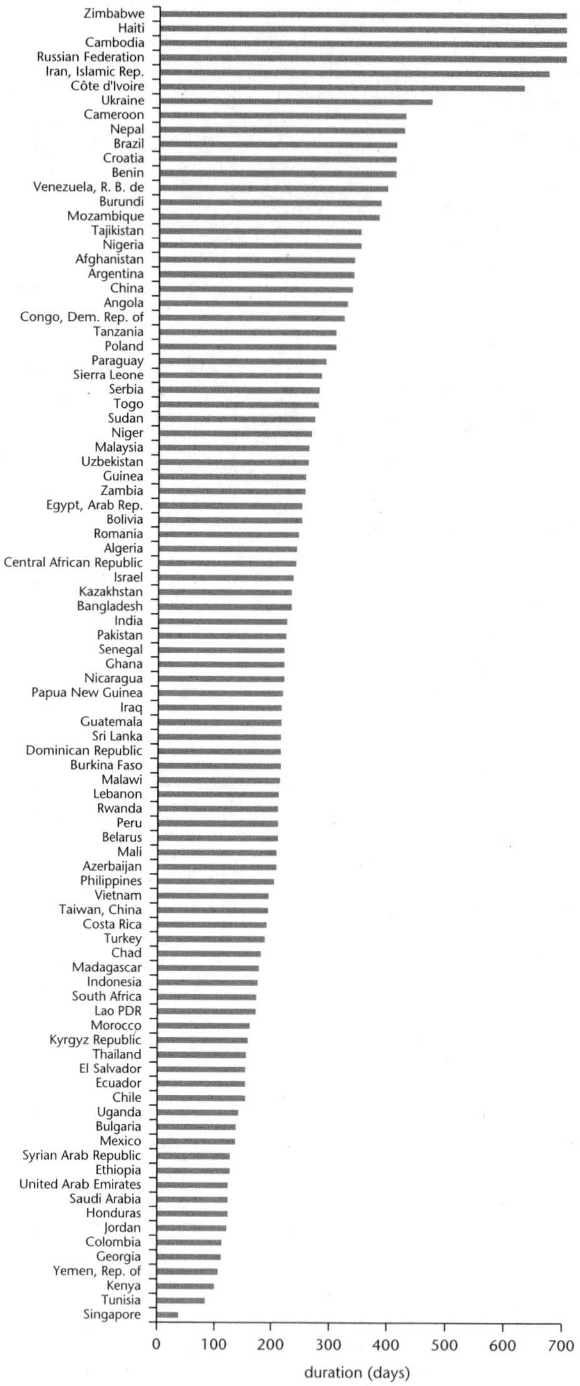


*Source:* World Bank (2008).

**Figure 6.7.** Cost of Dealing with Construction Permits

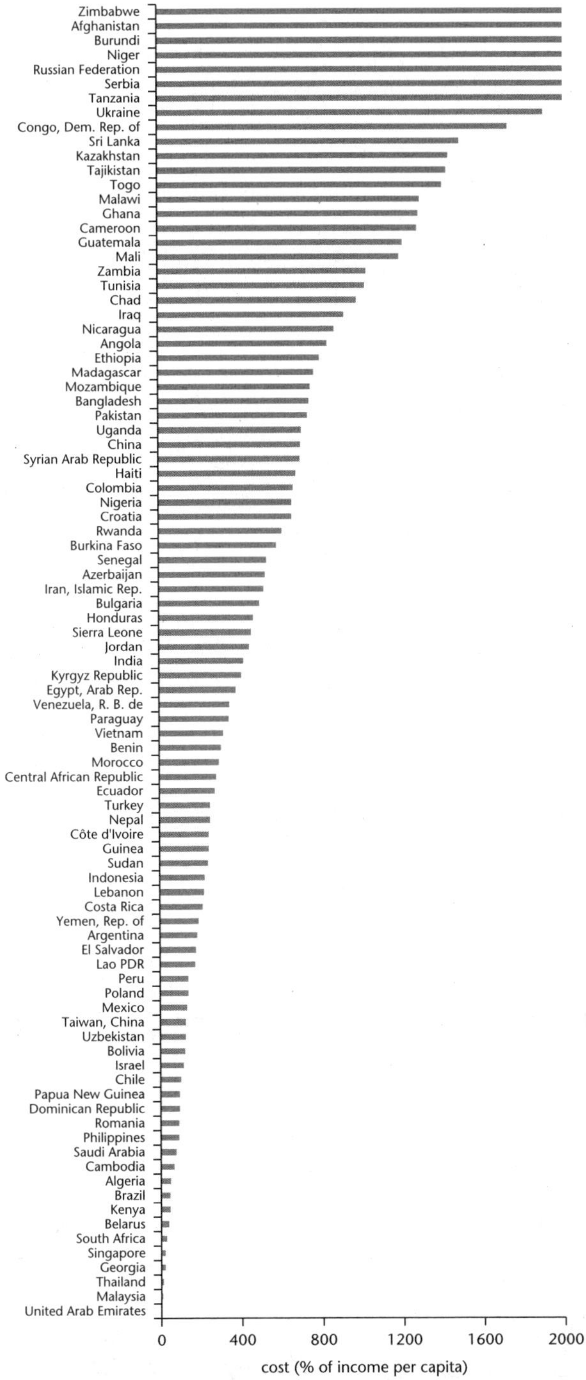


*Source:* World Bank (2008).

cost involved in dealing with construction in the business capitals of non-high-income OECD countries with populations of more than 4 million each.

The discrepancy in administrative performance is remarkable even for countries with similar levels of economic standards. For example, Kenya has a seemingly effective administration of construction permits. It takes 100 days to go through the 10 procedures at a cost of 46 percent of annual income per capita. Only Singapore is noticeably more effective, with a shorter duration (38 days) and lower cost as a share of income per capita (21 percent). In South Africa, it takes six months to carry out the 17 procedures at a cost of 28 percent of income per capita. In Kenya's neighbor, Tanzania, it takes 10 months, 21 procedures, and more than 2,000 percent of income per capita to obtain a construction permit. The countries that operate the slowest and most expensive construction permit bureaucracies are fragile states such as Afghanistan, Haiti, Niger, and Zimbabwe. However, among the largest emerging markets, China and, particularly, Russia administer relatively expensive and bureaucratic processes as well. Russians go through 54 procedures—currently the worst record—that take, on average, 23 months and cost 2,600 percent of Russian income per capita. The Chinese must wait 11 months for the completion of 37 procedures at a cost of 700 percent of income per capita. The Brazilian administration of construction permits is slower (411 days), but less expensive (47 percent), while the Indian administration is more rapid (224 days) and more expensive (400 percent).

Tables 6.2 and 6.3 present a breakdown of the various procedures required to build a warehouse in Kenya and Russia. In Kenya, the most costly and time-consuming procedure is the request for and issuance of a building permit (50 days). In Russia, particularly time-consuming procedures include (1) the request for and issuance of a conclusion on compliance form for a proposed building with appropriate city planning and territory use registrations (152 days), (2) the request for and issuance of a disposition of a prefect on the inception of a construction design (60 days), and (3) the request for and issuance of a project approval by the appropriate Moscow state expertise (60 days). In addition, the procedure for requesting and obtaining the proper technical conditions for an electricity connection with Mosenergo incurs an estimated cost of Rub 5.5 million. Overall, the most time-consuming procedures in many countries relate to the issuance of building permits and zoning clearances, as well as electricity, water, and telecommunication connections. The list of obscure documents and permits that are required and the number of government agencies involved in the registration process can take on Kafkaesque proportions (see table 6.2).

Thus, the data indicate that there are substantial differences across the world and that the administration of construction permits in some countries is prohibitively long and costly. Some of these differences occur because of legitimate

**Table 6.2.** Procedures, Time, and Costs Involved in Building a Warehouse, Russian Federation, 2008

| No. | Procedure | Time to complete (days) | Cost to complete (Rub) |
|---|---|---|---|
| 1 | Apply for act of permission for use to Department of City Planning Documentation Development at MoskomArchitektura | 1 | n.a. |
| 2 | Request and obtain situation plan of district and conclusion for a District Land Commission from Architecture Planning Department | 15 | 43,680 |
| 3 | Request and obtain a conclusion from Territorial Union of Land Use Regulation (TOP3) | 15 | 4,330 |
| 4 | Request and obtain a decision by the District Land Commission on land plot provision and city planning regulation | 30 | n.a. |
| 5 | Request and obtain clearance of draft disposition of Prefect with the Architecture Planning Department (APD) | 7 | n.a. |
| 6 | Request and obtain clearance of draft disposition of Prefect with the local government | 7 | n.a. |
| 7 | Request and obtain clearance of draft disposition with the Territorial Union of Land Use Regulation (TOP3) | 7 | n.a. |
| 8 | Request and obtain the disposition on preparation of an act of permission for use (APИ) by the Prefect | 7 | n.a. |
| 9 | Request and obtain a conclusion on compliance of proposed building with specified city planning and territory use regulations | **152** | 4,500 |
| 10[a] | Request and obtain technical conditions from water and sewage services | 45 | 17,673 |
| 11[a] | Request and obtain technical conditions for an electricity connection with MosEnergo | 30 | **5,490,520** |
| 12[a] | Request and obtain technical conditions to connect to telephone line | 30 | 3,000 |
| 13[a] | Request and obtain approval from MoskomArchitektura on engineering of the facility | 14 | 4,500 |
| 14 | Request and obtain an act of permission for use (APИ) from MoskomArchitectura | 30 | 6,700 |
| 15 | Request and obtain disposition of Prefect on the inception of construction design (decision on construction) | 60 | n.a. |
| 16 | Request and obtain approval of design conditions by the Department of Well-Being of MoskomArchitektura | 7 | 53,300 |
| 17[a] | Request and obtain approval of design conditions by Department of Preparation of Project Approvals of MoskomArchitektura | 14 | 12,100 |
| 18[a] | Request and obtain approval of design conditions by local government | 7 | n.a. |
| 19[a] | Request and obtain approval of design conditions by the Prefect's Office | 14 | n.a. |
| 20[a] | Request and obtain approval of design conditions by the Emergency Situation and Civil Defense Department | 14 | 14,728 |

(*Table continues on the following pages.*)

**Table 6.2.** Procedures, Time, and Costs Involved in Building a Warehouse, Russian Federation, 2008 (*continued*)

| No. | Procedure | Time to complete (days) | Cost to complete (Rub) |
|---|---|---|---|
| 21[a] | Request and obtain approval of design conditions by Moscow State Expertise | 14 | 7,364 |
| 22[a] | Request and obtain an act of the Moscow Geological-Geodesic Department | 15 | 36,700 |
| 23[a] | Request and obtain approval of design conditions by the Sanitary Services (Rospotrebnadzor) | 30 | 13,800 |
| 24[a] | Request and obtain approval of transport routes from the Moscow City Transport Agency | 30 | 8,837 |
| 25[a] | Request and obtain approval from the State Inspectorate of Road Safety (GIBBD) | 30 | 8,837 |
| 26[a] | Request and obtain approval from the Department of Comprehensive Well-Being of the city | 30 | 4,600 |
| 27[a] | Request and obtain approval from the Department of Nature Use under State Ecological Expertise | 21 | 29,455 |
| 28 | Request and obtain Sketch No. 2 from the Moscow Geological Institute | 30 | 10,100 |
| 29 | Request and obtain approval of Sketch No. 2 from the Moscow Architecture Committee (MoskomArchitektura) | 30 | 4,000 |
| 30 | Request and obtain the construction passport from the Moscow Geological Institute | 30 | 8,837 |
| 31[a] | Request and obtain approval of volumes of "outline of construction arrangement" and "GenPlan" from MoskomArchitektura | 30 | 6,500 |
| 32[a] | Request and obtain approval of volumes of "outline of construction arrangement" and "GenPlan" from the Prefecture | 30 | n.a. |
| 33[a] | Request and obtain approval of volumes of "outline of construction arrangement" and "GenPlan" from the GenPlan Institute | 30 | 12,200 |
| 34 | Request and obtain Regulation No. 2 and certificate of approval of Architectural City Planning Decision | 30 | 3,600 |
| 35 | Request and obtain project approval by Moscow State Expertise | 60 | 58,000 |
| 36 | Request and obtain permission for construction (building permit) | 10 | 11,460 |
| 37 | Receive inspection by State Inspectorate of Architecture and Construction Supervision during foundation construction | 1 | n.a. |
| 38 | Receive inspection by State Inspectorate of Architecture and Construction Supervision during structure construction | 1 | n.a. |
| 39 | Receive inspection by State Inspectorate of Architecture and Construction Supervision during engineering works | 1 | n.a. |
| 40 | Receive inspection by the Union of Administrative Technical Inspection (UATI) - I | 1 | n.a. |
| 41 | Receive inspection by the Union of Administrative Technical Inspection (UATI) - II | 1 | n.a. |

| | | | |
|---|---|---|---|
| 42 | Receive inspection by the Union of Administrative Technical Inspection (UATI) - III | 1 | n.a. |
| 43 | Receive inspection by the Union of Administrative Technical Inspection (UATI) - IV | 1 | n.a. |
| 44 | Receive inspection by the Union of Administrative Technical Inspection (UATI) - V | 1 | n.a. |
| 45 | Receive inspection by the Union of Administrative Technical Inspection (UATI) - VI | 1 | n.a. |
| 46 | Receive inspection by the Union of Administrative Technical Inspection (UATI) - VII | 1 | n.a. |
| 47 | Connect to water services | 30 | n.a. |
| 48[a] | Request and receive inspection by the Energy Supervision Board | 1 | n.a. |
| 49 | Connect to electricity and sign an agreement with Energosbyt | 14 | n.a. |
| 50[a] | Request and connect to telephone services | 5 | n.a. |
| 51 | Request and convene the Approval Commission | 30 | n.a. |
| 52 | Request and receive the disposition on operation of building (occupancy permit) | 10 | n.a. |
| 53 | Request and receive plans from the Bureau of Technical Inventory (BTI) | 30 | 55,000 |
| 54 | Register the building after completion | 30 | 7,500 |

*Source:* World Bank (2009a).
*Note:* n.a. = not applicable, no charge.
a. Takes place simultaneously with another procedure.

**Table 6.3.** Procedures, Time, and Costs Involved in Building a Warehouse, Kenya, 2008

| No. | Procedure | Time to complete (days) | Cost to complete (Ksh) |
|---|---|---|---|
| 1 | Request and obtain a building permit | 50 | 12,500 |
| 2[a] | Seek approval of project plans and architectural drawings from municipal authority | 25 | 100 |
| 3 | Receive an on-site inspection by the municipal authority | 5 | 100 |
| 4 | Obtain an occupancy certificate | 14 | 500 |
| 5 | Apply for water and sewerage connection | 1 | 1,100 |
| 6 | Pay water and sewerage installation costs and obtain connection | 30 | 6,000 |
| 7[a] | Request electricity connection from the local electricity provider | 1 | 2,000 |
| 8 | Receive an on-site inspection by the local electricity provider | 1 | n.a. |
| 9 | Obtain electricity connection | 21 | n.a. |
| 10 | Apply and pay for telephone connection | 5 | 2,300 |

*Source:* World Bank (2009b).
*Note:* n.a. = not applicable, no charge.
a. Takes place simultaneously with another procedure.

reasons related to special rules and an emphasis on impact assessments. However, a more streamlined and investment-friendly administration would benefit everyone in the process, except perhaps potential bureaucrats or facilitators and middlemen who enrich themselves in lethargic systems. Corruption is particularly prevalent in the construction sector (see elsewhere below), and policy makers can reduce prospective instances of public sector corruption by removing unnecessary licenses, reducing the number of registrations required at various government agencies, and providing more transparency and clear rules associated with inspections. In general, the fewer interfaces between investors and various agencies, the better. A transparent and streamlined application process will not only reduce the risk of corruption, but also speed up the start of the construction work. In addition, any governments that generate revenue from the permits may reap more by taxing the investors at a later stage when the investment is generating income.

For example, no good reason seems to exist for making the average investor in Moscow wait 19 months longer than an average investor in Tbilisi, Georgia, and pay 129 times the fee as measured in income per capita. The same comparison can be made between China and Mexico. The average investor in Mexico obtains a construction permit more than six months faster and at less than a fifth the cost. There is considerable scope for cutting red tape and costs so as to stimulate more investment in construction projects. The biggest beneficiaries would be those small and medium-size enterprises that are usually most affected by strenuous administrative hurdles. Box 6.3 examines a number of initiatives successfully implemented to facilitate the administration of building permits in countries around the world.

#### Ensuring a fair and transparent government procurement process

Policy makers have to be particularly delicate in designing tendering criteria in government procurement. On the one hand, weak minimum criteria relating to bidding companies in terms of solvency, proven expertise, and in-house capacity can delay projects because weak suppliers fail to deliver services on time or at the specified quality. On the other hand, standards that are too strict exclude many of the small and medium-size enterprises that dominate the market for construction services in developing countries. In an expert meeting on construction services organized by the United Nations Conference on Trade and Development in 2000, specialists from around the world debated the impact of minimum performance indicators (UNCTAD 2000b). Several of these specialists emphasized the experience of their countries with foreign multinationals that took the larger and more advanced contracts and left the smaller and less advanced contracts to local businesses. Local companies are eliminated already at the prequalification stage in

**Box: 6.3:** Facilitating the Administration of Building Permits

In 2005–08, the World Bank (2008) recorded 60 reforms specifically aimed at easing the process for obtaining construction permits. Of these, 35 were initiatives targeted at reforming the legal framework, and the other 25 were administrative improvements. Legal reform dealt with building codes, regulations, and bylaws that change the standards and organization of construction permitting. These reforms were generally more complex and time consuming to implement than the administrative reforms, which typically focus on streamlining project clearances, introducing time limits, and moving the processes online. The most frequent type of reform involved streamlining project clearances. One-stop shops connect several government agencies and public utilities and provide a single point of contact between the entrepreneur and the building authority. Another common reform was the introduction of statutory time limits or silence-is-consent rules.

For example, in Jamaica, the government implemented a 90-day statutory time limit and managed to cut the actual time to obtain a building permit by 80 days. In Egypt, a new building code established a single authority for building permit applications and enforces a 30-day statutory time limit. Before this reform, each utility connection required three separate letters from a municipality. In Colombia, the implementation of a silence-is-consent rule helped to reduce the processing time from three to two months. Authorities in the Kyrgyz Republic launched a new one-stop shop for issuing architectural planning terms and construction permits. They also eliminated the location permit by presidential decree that previously required the signature of the capital's mayor and took 60 days to obtain. These initiatives helped cut nine procedures and 173 days off the processing cycle. Finally, several African countries implemented a number of reforms. Liberia advertised a 30-day statutory time limit, designed a user-friendly checklist of required documents, reduced the building permit fee by half, and eliminated the requirement of some high-level signatures. Sierra Leone reformed its inspection regime, recruited professional inspectors, and cut down on random visits. Kenya overhauled all its building regulations.

many countries because they are deemed unable to fulfill the criteria established by donors. Strict criteria mean that the home sector is unable to develop and upgrade its technical expertise, which, by extension, makes it less attractive to foreign suppliers. However, other experts noted that domestic companies in some countries were not sufficiently strong to take on large donor-financed projects and that international contractors can have a positive effect on the local sector because much work is subcontracted to domestic contractors.

The design of tendering specifications in government procurement can effectively regulate market access. Government procurement agencies are often accused of favoring either domestic or foreign contractors, for example, by explicitly providing preferential treatment for local companies (through preference margins) or by setting minimum requirements for financial support that may be within reach for local companies. Market entry for foreign providers can, for instance, be impeded by rules on the temporary admission of construction equipment (Geloso Grosso, Jankowska, and Gonzales 2008). The plurilateral agreement on government procurement in the WTO is designed to make laws, regulations, procedures, and practices in government procurement more transparent and to ensure that these do not protect domestic products or suppliers or discriminate against foreign products or suppliers.[2] So far, none of the 39 WTO members that have signed the agreement—and, hence, that can pursue legal recourse in the WTO in case of international disputes—are developing countries. Consequently, developing countries can neither be challenged in the WTO nor challenge foreign governments for using discriminatory procedures. The construction service sector in advanced developing countries with interests in exporting to developed-country markets may therefore gain if their countries have signed the WTO Agreement on Government Procurement.[3] Box 6.4 describes the operations of Chinese construction firms in Africa in the context of government procurement.

**Box 6.4:** Chinese Construction Companies Dominate the Infrastructure Market in Africa

Government procurement makes up the largest share of the African construction service market. Because many investment projects are donor financed, the procurement process is often in line with the WTO Agreement on Government Procurement, whereby an international bidding process is conducted for projects above certain threshold values. Chinese companies are now dominating the market for large infrastructure projects in Africa. They generally beat international competitors on price, and they beat local competitors because of their size, financial solutions, and expertise. For example, in Tanzania, local contractors are seldom able to compete for projects worth more than US$2 million. However, local contractors still capture the contracts that are below the value thresholds, and many of them seek to partner with foreign contractors by forming joint ventures or by supplying services to the larger contractors that outsource parts of the value chain.

The majority of Chinese construction companies in Africa are state owned and enjoy a number of advantages. These include access to generous export credits for feasibility studies and for financing operational costs, government guarantees for bank loans, and lines of credit for capital goods and machinery. These benefits may not be unique to Chinese contractors, but they do put African companies at a competitive disadvantage. While restrictions on the temporary movement of project staff are prevalent, they have not stopped Chinese companies from bringing large numbers of Chinese staff to their African worksites. A majority of the professional staff are Chinese, and a majority of nonprofessional staff are African in African construction projects according to a recent study by the World Bank. In Angola, Chinese contractors import virtually all materials, technology, and staff from China partly because of the scarcity of local skilled labor and the relatively high prices of local materials. However, in Tanzania, the majority of building materials are locally produced, and domestic companies are increasingly adept at supplying Chinese multinationals with construction and other services.

*Source:* World Bank (2007).

Developing countries also have much to gain from unilateral initiatives. Operating a transparent and competitive government procurement process is paramount in the effort to limit the wasteful spending of public resources. Transparency enhances predictability, trust, and fairness in the system and, by extension, forces companies to compete by raising productivity and lowering costs. Announcements of government contracts should be adequately advertised and easily accessible. The winning bids should be announced so that competing bidders can assess their shortcomings and the fairness of the process. Governments can also establish a body for dispute resolution or at least a mechanism to address complaints if bidders suspect collusion or discrimination. It is likewise best practice to allow suppliers to challenge the due process of procurement conduct. The World Bank's guidelines on international competitive bidding provide sound principles on ways to manage government procurement, and they leave some flexibility in the bidding process (box 6.5). A standardized information technology system is an excellent tool for sharing information and informing prospective bidders about outstanding projects.

**Box 6.5:** Enhancing Transparency: World Bank Guidelines on Notification and Advertising

Timely notification of bidding opportunities is essential in competitive bidding. According to the World Bank, for projects that include procurement on the basis of international competitive bidding, the borrower is required to prepare and submit a draft general procurement notice. The World Bank will arrange for its publication in United Nations Development Business.[4] The notice shall contain information concerning the borrower (or prospective borrower), the amount and purpose of the loan, the scope of procurement under international competitive bidding, and the name and address of the borrower's agency responsible for procurement. If known, the scheduled date of issue of prequalification or bidding documents should be indicated. The borrower is to maintain a list of responses to the notice. The related prequalification or bidding documents should not be released to the public earlier than eight weeks after the date of publication of the notice. The general procurement notice is to be updated annually for all outstanding procurement.

The international community is also to be notified in a timely manner of the opportunities to bid for specific contracts. To that end, invitations to prequalify or to bid, as the case may be, are to be advertised as specific procurement notices in at least one newspaper of national circulation in the borrower's country (and in the official gazette, if any). Such invitations are also to be transmitted to those who have expressed interest in bidding in response to the general procurement notice. Publication of the invitations in United Nations Development Business is encouraged. Borrowers are also strongly encouraged to transmit such invitations to embassies and trade representatives of countries of likely suppliers and contractors. Additionally, for large, specialized, or important contracts, borrowers are to advertise the invitations in United Nations Development Business or in well-known technical magazines, newspapers, and trade publications of wide international circulation. Notification is to be given in sufficient time to enable prospective bidders to obtain prequalification or bidding documents and prepare and submit their responses.

### Tackling corruption in the construction sector

Corruption can be detrimental to development. In construction, corruption may reduce the quality of infrastructure services and limit access, particularly for the poor. For the millions of people living in earthquake-prone areas, corruption has resulted in many lost lives, including in Italy and Turkey. In the words of James Lewis, "earthquakes don't kill people; collapsing buildings do" (Transparency International 2005a, 23). Of the 156,000 deaths, 584,000 injured, and 9 million rendered homeless by 400 recorded earthquakes in the last 15 years, many have been the result of buildings that folded because of diluted concrete, excised steel bars, and other substandard building practices, some of which were fostered by corruption. Similarly, many poor roads are the result of corruption, and accidents occur and road safety suffers. Corruption in construction projects may lead not only to unviable, defective, dangerous, or environmentally or socially destructive projects, but also investments in uneconomic projects (Stansbury and Stansbury 2006).

A fertile breeding ground for corruption is found in the process of obtaining construction permits and in government procurement. According to Reyna (2007), graft in the construction sector is estimated to amount to as much as 5 percent of Africa's GDP. This is a higher share of GDP than the share some countries spend on health or education. Corruption has a negative economic effect not only on consumers, investors, and the government, but also on service providers. It damages companies by giving rise to uncertainty in the tendering process, wasted tender expenses, increased project costs, reduced business opportunities, extortion, blackmail, criminal prosecutions, fines, blacklisting, and reputational risk. The sector is prone to corruption because of the sheer size of projects, their uniqueness and complexity, the involvement of government, the large number of contractual links and irregular intervals between projects, entrenched national interests, and the nature of work that is easily concealed (Transparency International 2005a).

Transparency International surveys business executives from around the world to estimate the prevalence of corruption. The data are published in the Bribe Payers Survey and used to generate two sector-specific rankings. The first ranks the bribery of public officials by sector; it measures the degree to which companies in each of 19 sectors are likely to bribe public officials. The second ranks state capture by sector; it measures the degree to which companies in each sector use contributions to politicians and political parties to achieve undue influence on government policy. The business executives who were contacted in 2008 indicated that the construction and public works sector is affected the most according to both rankings. The direct bribery of public officials is common relative to the situation in other sectors of the economy. Box 6.6 presents initiatives to tackle corruption at the corporate level.

**Box 6.6:** Initiatives to Prevent Corruption in Construction Projects

Transparency International (2005b) has developed a list of initiatives that an owner could take to reduce the risk of corruption in a construction project.

### Immediate actions

- Implement an internal anticorruption code of conduct and management program committing the owner to an anticorruption policy
- Prepare contractual documentation that includes adequate contractual safeguards, such as anticorruption warranties, termination, and compensation rights in the event of corruption
- Undertake greater due diligence focusing on the owner's staff in key posts and on agents
- Ensure that all prequalification, tendering, and project management procedures are fair, reasonable, objective, and transparent
- Report allegations of corrupt practices to the authorities and to any applicable trade or professional associations; corruption can only be prosecuted if it is reported
- Respect the minimum standards for public contracting (Transparency International 2005c)

### Medium-term actions

- Seek to contract only with companies that have implemented an internal anticorruption code of conduct and management program
- Support the introduction of an international externally audited ethical standard that companies can only attain and keep if they implement such an effective code and management program
- Require the appointment of an independent assessor who monitors the prequalification, tender, and execution of a project to ensure, as far as possible, that it is operated free of corruption
- Require the use of a project integrity pact for both tender and project execution; an independent assessor monitors compliance with the pact, which covers sanctions and arbitration mechanisms
- Develop a fair, proportionate, and transparent blacklisting procedure that bans companies from tendering for the owner's projects for a specified period of time after an offense

### *Removing rules and regulations that are unnecessarily trade restrictive*

The construction service sector is generally subject to a large number of regulations. These are partly in place to counteract negative externalities or common market failures that are associated with the supply of construction services and that affect third parties and society in general. Pollution of air and water and the generation of noise are examples of negative externalities in the construction process. The regulations are also in place to help tackle asymmetric information resulting from the fact that clients of construction services may know only vaguely what they want and rely on the expertise of the construction company to specify what needs to be done. Most regulations are nondiscriminatory, and the great majority of them are complied with during the application process for building and construction permits. But there are also regulations that explicitly target international contractors. Since commercial presence and the temporary movement of natural persons are the prevalent modes of delivery, trade restrictions are found in the regulation of the movement of capital and labor. Many of the identified restrictions may best be tackled at the multilateral level, while others can be pursued in bilateral or regional discussions.

### Identifying market access restrictions on commercial presence

Restrictions on the establishment and operation of commercial presence—Mode 3 trade—by foreign companies are common in the construction service sector (WTO 1998). Limitations on market access include restrictions on foreign investment, for example with regard to ownership rules (so that foreign companies are only allowed to hold minority posts in local commercial entities); on the type of legal entity that a foreign company is allowed to operate (rules may, for example, state that local incorporation is mandatory or prohibit the establishment of a branch office); on the number of suppliers that are allowed in a specific market; and on the value of transactions or assets (see tables 6.4 and 6.5). Several countries

**Table 6.4.** Commitments by WTO Members in Construction and Related Engineering Services
*percent*

| | Crossborder supply | | | Consumption abroad | | | Commercial presence | | | Presence of natural persons | | |
|---|---|---|---|---|---|---|---|---|---|---|---|---|
| | F | P | N | F | P | N | F | P | N | F | P | N |
| **Market access** | | | | | | | | | | | | |
| General construction work for building | 29 | 10 | 60 | 67 | 21 | 13 | 60 | 33 | 6 | 2 | 96 | 2 |
| General construction work for civil engineering | 27 | 12 | 61 | 61 | 20 | 18 | 51 | 43 | 6 | 4 | 94 | 2 |
| Installation and assembly work | 32 | 4 | 64 | 66 | 19 | 15 | 55 | 36 | 9 | 2 | 96 | 2 |
| Building completion and finishing work | 31 | 5 | 64 | 72 | 18 | 10 | 64 | 28 | 8 | 3 | 92 | 5 |
| Other | 24 | 18 | 58 | 27 | 58 | 15 | 27 | 64 | 9 | 0 | 97 | 3 |

*Source:* WTO (1998).
*Note:* F = full commitment; P = partial commitment; N = no commitment.

require international contractors to form joint ventures with local companies. The formation of a joint venture with a local company may be the most effective form of market entry, given the expertise of local companies in local market conditions and the regulatory environment. However, the requirement to form a joint venture is often imposed to seek transfers of technology and project management expertise, as well as to provide business opportunities to local companies.

There are also several restrictions on commercial presence that reflect a national treatment (WTO 1998). Table 6.5 shows that these include registration requirements, authorization requirements, performance requirements, and technology transfer requirements; licensing, standards, and qualifications; and nationality and residency requirements. Although the types of market access and

**Table 6.5.** Number of Measures in Construction and Related Engineering Services

| | Crossborder supply | Consumption abroad | Commercial presence | Presence of natural persons |
|---|---|---|---|---|
| **Market Access** | | | | |
| Limitations on | | | | |
| Number of suppliers | 1 | — | 5 | — |
| Value of transactions or assets | | — | 11 | — |
| Number of operations | — | — | — | — |
| Number of natural persons | — | — | — | 11 |
| Types of legal entity | — | — | 26 | — |
| Participation of foreign capital | | — | 16 | — |
| Other measures n.e.c. | 8 | 3 | 28 | 32 |
| **National Treatment** | | | | |
| Tax measures, subsidies, and grants | — | — | — | 9 |
| Nationality and residency requirements | — | — | 12 | 14 |
| Licensing, standards, and qualifications | — | 3 | 7 | 39 |
| Registration requirements | — | 3 | 7 | 3 |
| Authorization requirements | 4 | — | 5 | 5 |
| Performance requirements | — | 3 | 3 | 3 |
| Technology transfer requirements | — | — | 1 | — |
| Other | 5 | — | 8 | 6 |

*Source:* WTO (1998).

*Note:* — = not available; n.e.c. = not elsewhere classified. The number of other measures n.e.c. is large because many entries in the schedules could not be classified into one of the distinct categories of limitations. In some cases, this is the result of a lack of specificity in the descriptions of the measures, while, in other cases, it is because the measure itself does not correspond to any of the categories.

national treatment regulations may be horizontal rather than sector specific, they still affect the operational flexibility of international contractors, including the exposure of these contractors to risk and the possibilities for making profits and repatriating earnings to headquarters. The prospect of operating an entity without full control reduces the prospective gains from competition by foreign companies. Finally, market access is only allowed in some countries if the appropriate resources and input materials are inaccessible on the local market.

Table 6.5 shows the frequency of measures related to market access and national treatments. While crossborder supply and consumption abroad are relatively unaffected by restrictions, commercial presence (particularly for market access) and the presence of natural persons (particularly for national treatment) are the main target modes of supply for restrictions. The key negotiating objectives for construction services as identified by WTO members in the Doha Round of multilateral trade negotiations include, for commercial presence, various foreign equity limitations, joint venture and joint operation requirements, discriminatory licensing and registration procedures, and restrictions on the types of projects that can be undertaken by foreign suppliers of services (WTO 2005). Policy makers in developing countries may scrutinize their commitments in WTO and assess which of these restrictions are deemed effective and least trade restrictive in terms of the stated purposes.

### Identifying market access restrictions on temporary transfers of foreign project staff

In the construction service sector, with its intensive use of labor, the often stringent limitations on the temporary movement of natural persons are particularly serious impediments. These restrictions often disproportionally affect service providers from poor countries in which there is an abundant supply of low-skilled and medium-skilled construction workers willing to leave home and take up physically demanding jobs abroad. The restrictions are seldom part of official trade policy, but, rather, are formulated as part of labor market regulations and immigration policy. It is therefore especially challenging for policy makers to overcome these regulations through trade negotiations. It is also an area of political sensitivity.

The range of limitations on the temporary movement of natural persons is wide and covers measures from bans and quotas to economic needs tests and residency requirements. Even if workers fulfill the criteria for work permits, the administration of these documents for employees of international contractors can be bureaucratic and tedious to the extent that the administration delays projects, thereby increasing operating costs and making project execution unpredictable. In particular, new market entrants, without a local base of professionals, are dependent on the short-term circulation of managerial and professional staff and the medium-term circulation of builders, welders, crane operators, and so on.

In the adjacent engineering and architectural service sectors, which are frequently incorporated in-house in multinationals, the nonrecognition of professional qualifications may represent another barrier. Local labor policy may also impose rules on minimum-wage levels that are well above remuneration levels in the country of origin of the exporting company.

Trade-impeding regulations are not only imposed at the border. Domestic regulations affecting foreign providers of services can also have an adverse effect on trade and working conditions. For example, entities in the Persian Gulf region employ many millions of foreign construction workers. While the numbers may indicate an open door policy, local rules that regulate the stay of workers are prone to abuse (FIDH 2007). For example, temporary service providers who enter the Gulf countries can only obtain entry visas and residence permits if local citizens or local institutions employ them. The employer becomes a sponsor (*khafeel*) and signs a contract issued by the labor ministry. The contractual agreement essentially makes the sponsor legally and financially responsible for the service provider and ties the service provider to the sponsor (see Longva 1999, Baldwin-Edwards 2005).

Construction workers from low-income Arab, South Asian, or Southeast Asian countries often make huge financial sacrifices to move to the Persian Gulf, but they must leave the country if their contracts are refuted or broken. The responsibility of the sponsor to cover any prospective costs of repatriation has led to a common practice whereby sponsors confiscate the passports of service providers to control and circumscribe their ability to move. Longva (1999) has reported that any dispute with a sponsor leaves the service provider without legal residence, the possibility of working, or, effectively, the possibility of gaining legal redress. Bahrain recently abandoned this system, which, according to Crown Prince Salman, had, in effect, suppressed wages and often created abominable working conditions for foreign workers (de Boer and Kalkman 2007).

### Reviewing additional trade-distorting rules and regulations

Subsidies and other incentive schemes granted to domestic construction service suppliers in developed (and developing) countries can have a discriminatory effect on trade. They are provided in many countries for export promotion and to encourage the development of the domestic construction sector. If the subsidies are granted exclusively to local companies, they may be inconsistent with the national treatment obligations of WTO member states. Research and development are often supported by grants from governments that give companies in advanced markets a competitive edge through the use of information technology and other technologically advanced methods to improve quality, lower prices, and raise productivity (UNCTAD 2000a). Export credits may be offered for feasibility studies and to finance the operational costs of particular projects. Government guarantees are offered for private bank loans. Tied aid in bilateral development assistance is another measure that presents a barrier to companies operating in third countries, as well as to local construction companies, depending on the formulation in the tendering process.

The construction service sector is dependent not only on the movement of labor, but also on the movement of capital equipment and building materials. Restrictions that give rise to unnecessary costs for imports of construction machinery, such as slow or unpredictable customs services, can have a negative trade effect if local companies have easier access to imported equipment. Restrictions on land and real estate use or ownership are normally applied to all sectors, but they may have more impact on companies providing construction services. Geloso Grosso, Jankowska, and Gonzales (2008) note, for example, that foreign property developers may not be able to own real estate during the construction phase, but, rather, need to wait until the completion of the project. Teljeur and Stern (2002) also note that foreign companies seeking to enter the U.S. market need to register and be licensed in each individual state and face strict liability implications on, for instance, equipment failure. The U.S. issues are not discriminatory in their application, but they may have a negative impact on foreign direct investment from developing-country companies seeking entry into foreign markets.

### *Enhancing the competitiveness of domestic construction service companies*

If the market structure in many developing countries makes it difficult for homegrown small and medium-size enterprises to win larger contracts in competition with foreign multinationals, policy makers could facilitate the growth and relative strength of these enterprises through a number of measures. The implementation of some of them may be relatively straightforward, while the implementation of others may be significantly more complex and inherently risky. In general, these measures would be implemented unilaterally.

#### Addressing human resource shortages and transfers of technology and management expertise

Arguably, the most serious issue facing the construction service sector in many developing countries, particularly in the least developed countries, is the limited pool of trained personnel. This lack of adequate labor supply is hardly unique for the construction service sector. While the sector is an intensive user of low-skilled labor, it is also dependent on semiskilled or technical workers, as well as highly educated project managers and the like for larger and more sophisticated construction projects. The lack of adequate training facilities means that on-the-job training is a common way to develop expertise. This not only affects quality in the delivery of services, but it also often leads to weak organizational capacity and poor pricing and contract management (Mburu 2008). In countries in which the human resource pool is especially weak, the only option may be to bring in foreign contractors, including some of the labor force of these contractors.

Foreign companies can aid the process of capacity building by integrating local suppliers in their supply chains and by nurturing local talent. Much of this process is taking place naturally as a result of the industry's dependency on local production. Some countries legislate that market access by foreign providers is contingent on the formation of joint ventures with local partners and the hiring of local management. Joint ventures are common because of domestic regulatory considerations, but also because of the synergies or complementarities in terms of financing and transfers of technology and expertise (Nielson and Taglioni 2004). Such partnerships have, for example, raised the expertise in Mauritius among local contractors and helped the country become an exporter of construction services (UNCTAD 2000b).

There are plenty of success stories despite the significant challenges faced by developing-country contractors. While developing countries enjoy comparative labor cost advantages, many of the companies in developing countries have dramatically improved management and project execution, and they can increasingly tap into local talent across the skill spectrum, from builders and carpenters to architects, information technology specialists, environmental analysts, and civil engineers (Nielson and Taglioni 2004). Particularly in Asia and Latin America, companies are nowadays offering a wide range of construction services, including postconstruction operations and maintenance services based on tailored software solutions. Box 6.7 provides examples of companies successfully exporting construction services.

### Integrating local product standards and building codes with international good practice

Construction service companies must generally conform to numerous regulations. These may, for example, include rules regarding the use of land, building regulations and codes, technical requirements, and product standards. Companies may need to obtain building permits; comply with environmental, safety, and licensing regulations; deal with service inspectors; register proprietors, contractors, and professionals; and fulfill minimum criteria of solvency (WTO 1998).

**Box 6.7:** Homegrown Champions Exporting Construction Services

There are several successful exporters based in developing countries, particularly in East Asia and the Middle East. Larsen & Toubro is India's largest international contractor in the construction sector. The company is established in some 20 countries, including in Africa and the Middle East. Its US$1 billion in exports in 2007 covered turnkey projects in market segments such as power, industry, petroleum, transport, and general building construction. The project portfolio includes the design and engineering of power plants and the building of football stadiums and airport-terminal complexes.

Enka Construction & Industry Company is Turkey's leading exporter of construction services, with US$2.1 billion in exports in 2007. The company is involved in large transportation, petrochemical, and general building projects in Africa, Eastern Europe, the Middle East, and Central Asia. It has constructed high-rise buildings and commercial and business centers in Russia, highways in Eastern Europe, petrochemical plants in Central Asia, and industrial plants in countries such as Algeria, Ethiopia, and Russia.

Lebanon's Arabian Construction Company exported construction services worth US$1.1 billion in 2007. Its areas of expertise include telecommunications, in which it offers complete solutions in radio and fiber-optic communications systems. It also provides integrated information systems and information centers; the design, supply, installation, and maintenance of power systems; site preparation for computer and control rooms; electromechanical projects; and standby power backup for high-technology equipment. Some of the tallest towers in Dubai have been built by the company.

The largest developing-country exporter of construction services is China Communications Construction Company. In 2007, it exported construction services and designs for transport infrastructure, dredging, and port machinery manufacture worth US$4.2 billion. It is the third largest dredging company in the world and the world's largest container-crane manufacturer.

These requirements are often more stringent in developed countries than in developing countries, and they may be applied at the national and regional levels. The administration of standards and certifications and the recognition of qualifications are often delegated to professional bodies or private sector associations. But, aside from the benefits they may entail in terms of safety and quality assurance, they can be significant hurdles and sources of learning costs for companies wishing to enter a foreign market.

The implementation of international or regional product standards and building codes that comply with international good practice strengthens the local sector in two ways. First, it reduces transaction costs by removing the need for foreign companies to change their production processes at the same time as it provides more incentives for international contractors to integrate local suppliers in supply chains. Harmonized technical requirements, building codes, and product standards provide economies of scale in the procurement of materials, tools, and equipment and less need to invest in reeducation. Second, because they expose local companies to international standards and good practice in building codes, the companies become more well equipped to compete in foreign markets in which the same standards, codes, and so on are employed.

Yet, importing wholesale standards from abroad does not necessarily bring any benefits. Standards need to suit the local environment, and regional cooperation may well be the most useful way forward. In addition, in countries with limited government capacity, it makes sense to invest effort in harmonizing or reforming standards if they are likely to be implemented or followed by the sector. Policy makers should therefore consult with construction companies and other interest groups about the usefulness of prospective reforms to standards and building codes. It is also important to recognize the risk in poorly governed countries that government agencies with power to inspect and enforce sometimes unclear regulations may simply undertake rent-seeking activities that produce additional challenges rather than reducing transaction costs and raising quality and safety standards. For example, the World Bank (2007) reports on a Chinese construction company that pays an annual fee of US$20,000 for a license to operate in Tanzania. Whatever the value of the certification, the fee will always be covered by the Tanzanian clients.

The willingness to adapt the local sector to international good practice will eventually lead beyond product standards and building codes. For example, in Mauritius, local policy makers have sought to implement international standards and to support the development of new standards in areas such as registration, licensing and certification, procurement policies, liability, and copyrights (UNCTAD 2000b). The strong links between construction services and professional services such as engineering and architectural services may also convince policy makers, particularly policy makers in middle-income countries, to take a broader view of the issues, such as the problems associated with the nonrecognition of qualifications for foreign professionals, which creates difficulties in importing and exporting countries.

The institutions that are most well suited to address these issues and that can help upgrade local capacity are domestic or regional industry associations and standards bodies. Such institutions should promote the progressive implementation of international standards and building codes whenever these are applicable to the domestic environment, and developing countries can approach international donors who provide technical assistance and capacity building in these areas. Depending on the regulatory framework, the work laid out for policy makers may include modifying existing regulations, but also introducing regulations in countries in which none are available. For instance, the portfolio on building construction of the International Organization for Standardization covers standards for construction equipment; concrete, timber, and metal structures;

masonry; elements of buildings; and buildings and structures of buildings in general.[5] The construction service sector is in need of regulation, for example to uphold minimum safety and environmental standards. The objective of reform is, first and foremost, to make sure that these rules and regulations are appropriate and, second, to design them so that they are no more trade restrictive than necessary.

### Strengthening local competitiveness by fostering an environment of local cooperation

A common weakness of the construction service sector in developing countries is market fragmentation. Domestic companies lack the size and experience to take on large projects. This is not necessarily an issue if large international contractors are present and can provide the project management, financial solutions, and experience that are necessary to undertake big construction projects. However, the lack of permanently based companies can reduce competition for projects and result in poorly functioning markets. While this absence of large actors may be natural for a given market, policy makers may seek to nurture an environment that allows for cooperation among companies, while carefully avoiding policies that would facilitate cartel-style collusion.

Local companies have two essential strategies in competing for larger projects. First, they can establish a construction consortium with local competitors or companies with complementary capacity and expertise. This will allow local companies to obtain the project management experience necessary to move up the value chain. Both horizontal and vertical consortia can prove pivotal in building the necessary expertise and capacity to take on major construction projects. Second, by forming joint ventures with international contractors, local companies can complement the expertise of these contractors by adding knowledge of local market conditions and building practices and can leverage their access to human resources with the financial strength, technical expertise, and experience of the international contractors in managing large projects. Consortia or partnership agreements and strategic alliances are not unique to efforts at cooperation among companies from developing and developed countries; they are common in the industry generally (UNCTAD 2000b).

A large share of construction service companies are run by families that are often unwilling to dilute their control in exchange for debt financing. The role of the policy maker is to facilitate cooperation, and this can be done by ensuring that the formulation of tendering requirements is friendly to smaller players in government procurement. The rules for the slicing and packaging of large contracts are vital if consortia are to be able to compete for business effectively. Governments will also manage smaller contractors by requiring less stringent credit allowances and by making sure that these contractors pay their bills on time.

## Which Issues Warrant the Attention of Stakeholders?

Our discussion touches on a number of issues that merit the attention of policy makers as they advance the trade-integration agenda for construction services. Table 6.6 presents a checklist of questions that might help structure the reflections and ensure a comprehensive approach to reform.

**Table 6.6.** A Checklist of Questions on Trade-Related Aspects of Construction Service Reform

**Streamlining the administration of construction permits**

1. How does the local application process for construction permits compare with the process in other countries in terms of the number of administrative steps involved, the average processing time for applications, and associated fees and costs?
2. Are there significant differences in administrative performance across different regions within the country or across different types of contractors? If so, why?
3. Are there unnecessary steps in the process that can be shortened or eliminated? Are there bottlenecks that can be addressed? Can the number of required documents and signatures be reduced by centralizing the application process (for example, by providing a one-stop shop or a single window environment)?
4. Is the decision-making process transparent, and does it involve consultation with other interested parties? If not, what can be done to increase transparency and predictability in the process?
5. Are there prohibitively high fees or taxes involved in the application process? Can the application process be made less expensive, while still taking into account safety, health, zoning, and other important considerations?
6. Is there any government body to which a decision can be appealed?

**Ensuring a fair and transparent government procurement process**

1. What are the minimum criteria that bidding companies must fulfill in terms of solvency, proven expertise, and in-house capacity? Are the criteria in line with regional or international good practices or are they more or less stringent?
2. Does government procurement of infrastructure projects allow for subcontracting to stimulate backward links to local small and medium-size enterprises?
3. Are government contracts advertised in easily accessible media or gazettes? Do government agencies allow for sufficient time in the advertisement process?
4. Are winning bids announced to the public?
5. Is there any dispute resolution body available to resolve issues in the procurement process?
6. Do local authorities offer preference margins to local contractors? If so, what are the margins, and does this help raise participation by local contractors? If local contractors already dominate the market, do these preference margins squeeze out prospective foreign competitors?
7. Do government entities tend to pay their contractors according to agreed deadlines? If not, what can be done to improve timely payments to contractors?

(*Table continues on the following pages.*)

**Table 6.6.** A Checklist of Questions on Trade-Related Aspects of Construction Service Reform (*continued*)

8. Do local or foreign contractors follow any of the anticorruption guidelines provided by, for example, Transparency International?

   Does local government have an anticorruption strategy in place for government procurement? Would the country benefit from signing the WTO Agreement on Government Procurement?

**Facilitating commercial presence**

1. Are there legal restrictions to market entry through commercial presence by foreign contractors? If so, what types of restrictions are there, and what are their impact on foreign direct investment? What is the motivation for imposing the restrictions?
2. Is there a requirement for foreign contractors to form joint ventures with local contractors? Have such joint ventures been successful and fulfilled the prospective motivation of fostering the transfer of technology and management knowledge? Have they helped build local expertise in the industry?
3. Are potential restrictions to commercial presence compliant with the country's prospective WTO commitments?
4. How does competition law deal with cartels?
5. Do foreign contractors need to register and obtain licenses that are different (for example, in terms of costs) from the licenses required of local contractors?
6. Are there staffing requirements for the establishment of branch offices? Are there requirements that foreign contractors must hire local executives?
7. Can the policy rationale of restrictions be addressed through other, less trade-restrictive means?

**Facilitating the temporary movement of service providers**

1. What types of restrictions exist on foreign providers of services? Does the country impose bans, quotas, economic needs tests, or other impediments to the movement of project staff?
2. If a quota system is in place, does the labor quota change frequently?
3. Are the rules different for intracorporate transferees and contractual service providers?
4. Is there implicit or explicit discrimination with regard to the nationality of service providers?
5. Is the application process for business visas and work permits administered in a reasonably expedient and cost-effective way? Or is it opaque, slow, and cumbersome? What can be done to improve administrative efficiency in the application process?
6. Are there restrictions or other issues related to the nonrecognition of qualifications for construction workers at home or in major export markets?
7. Are there domestic regulations that have an adverse effect on foreign providers of services or that affect their welfare or the local labor market (for example, discriminatory remuneration and benefit structures)? Do local policies give rise to illegal migration?
8. What are the policy objectives of the restrictions? Can the policy rationale be addressed through other, less trade-restrictive means?

**Reviewing other trade-distorting rules and regulations**

1. What types of subsidies are provided to contractors operating in the local market? Are subsidies allocated in an equitable way or tied to specific criteria (if so, what are the criteria)?

2. What are the rules with regard to the ownership of land and real estate by foreign contractors? Are they different from the rules covering local investors? What effect do potential differences have on building activity?
3. Can foreign contractors bring in construction equipment for projects without the imposition of major taxes and waiting time at customs?
4. What types of margin preferences are provided to local contractors? How do these rules apply to exporters from developing countries?

**Integrating local product standards and building codes with international good practice**

1. Who establishes and monitors product standards and building codes in the industry?
2. What laws and regulations discipline construction companies? How are these enforced?
3. Are foreign contractors subject to different licensing conditions relative to domestic suppliers?
4. How effective are the practices of the local authorities who inspect the work of contractors? Is it a frequent or random process?
5. Do inspections tend to involve rent-seeking activity? Are foreign contractors particularly targeted?
6. Would it make economic sense and does the government have the necessary capacity to adopt any regional or international product standards or building codes that would facilitate the integration of the local market with international markets (in addition to maintaining or improving quality, health, safety, and other standards)?

*Source*: Authors' compilation.

## Conclusion

Few sectors of an economy are as prominent as the construction service sector in terms of value added and employment. This sector absorbs large numbers of low-skilled and medium-skilled workers and supports strong backward links to other parts of the economy, including suppliers of construction equipment and input materials, as well as architectural and engineering services. Construction services make up, on average, 6 percent of the GDP of countries, and the share increases to nearly 10 percent for the construction sector generally. The sector is also particularly pertinent in the daily lives of people as a provider of the physical infrastructure for personal shelter, sanitation, water, energy, schooling, health services, transportation, and private sector activities. The World Bank is a major financier of construction projects in the developing world, and the sector is one of the keys in helping achieve the World Bank's mission of eradicating poverty.

There are gains from the trade in construction service imports and exports, and open markets for construction services are therefore in the national interest of developed and developing countries alike. Open markets allow countries to specialize in what they do best, which expands the quality and quantity of goods and services that can be produced and consumed, thereby leading to the more efficient allocation of resources. The resulting gain in economic welfare helps raise overall living standards. The supply of construction services is local in nature, and commercial presence is consequently the most common mode of service delivery. The local production requirement helps allay the fears of prospective labor adjustments and favors increased openness to foreign direct investment. However, the other common mode of supply is the temporary movement of natural persons, which represents an advantage for some developing countries because of their relative abundance in labor. There are many millions of foreign construction workers imported to building sites, for example, within the OECD, the Persian Gulf region, and Russia. Openness to foreign guest workers has historically been politically sensitive despite the fact that the prospective benefits are significant.

The trade in construction services is growing in importance, and developing countries feature high on the list of major importers and exporters of these services. Firm-level data reveal that Chinese, Egyptian, Indian, Russian, Turkish, and Southeast Asian companies are some of the larger exporters. The sector is highly regulated in many countries, but most regulations are applied on a nondiscriminatory basis and are designed to uphold the safety of human life, protect the environment, and provide quality assurance and the orderly expansion of developed areas. The important question from a trade perspective is whether the rules and regulations are more trade restrictive than necessary to achieve the objectives. For example, the heterogeneity of standards, processes, and procedures that companies face in different export markets may not be discriminatory, but do give rise to increased transaction costs that may impede market entry. There is ample evidence that certain types of regulations are imposed mainly to prevent international contractors from providing competition in domestic markets.

Policy makers in developing countries may have significant scope to facilitate trade in construction services. Effective competition would generate gains among consumers and suppliers. This chapter identifies three main areas where policy makers could focus their attention in helping the domestic construction sector raise standards and thereby facilitate the sector's integration in international markets, as follows:

1. Policy makers could review domestic regulations and the implementation of these regulations to highlight reform needs. The administration of construction permits and the management of government procurement are two areas in which improved governance could greatly stimulate the sector and attract foreign investment. Effective measures to tackle the corruption that is common in construction and public works are of paramount importance not only in nurturing a healthy domestic construction sector, but also in attracting new, productive companies to enter the market.
2. Policy makers could aim to enhance the competitiveness of the domestic construction sector through the implementation, if feasible, of international or

regional standards in construction materials and good practices in building codes. This would lower transaction costs and facilitate imports and exports of construction services. Addressing human resource shortages and introducing incentives for cooperation and technology transfers between foreign and domestic contractors would strengthen the domestic sector.

3. Policy makers could seek to facilitate greater access to the domestic construction market by foreign construction companies and workers. This would stimulate competition and, by extension, save government resources and help improve access to key services by the poorest citizens. Policy makers could also seek improved market access for the domestic construction companies and workers of major trading partners. Facilitating the transfer of guest workers from developing countries would, in particular, help increase exports from poor countries with abundant endowments of unskilled and semiskilled labor.

A review of these various options, taking into consideration domestic conditions, would allow policy makers in developed and developing countries to harness trade opportunities and improve the workings of the domestic construction service sector.

## Notes

1. Based in a small and geographically isolated country, New Zealand's export-oriented construction service sector has, for example, specialized in the design of earthquake-resistant structures and the construction of dairy and meat facilities.

2. See http://www.wto.org/english/thewto_e/whatis_e/tif_e/agrm10_e.htm#govt.

3. In addition, advanced developing countries could contemplate signing the OECD Convention on Combating Bribery of Foreign Public Officials in International Business Transactions so as to increase pressure and create momentum to tackle graft in the industry.

4. See http://www.devbusiness.com/.

5. See building construction (TC 59) and building construction machinery and equipment (TC 195), respectively, at http://www.iso.org/iso/iso_catalogue/catalogue_tc/catalogue_tc_browse.htm?commid=49070&development=on and http://www.iso.org/iso/iso_catalogue/catalogue_tc/catalogue_tc_browse.htm?commid=54540&development=on.

## References

Baldwin-Edwards, Martin. 2005. "Migration in the Middle East and Mediterranean." Regional study, January, Mediterranean Migration Observatory, University Research Institute for Urban Environment and Human Resources, Panteion University, Athens.

Chen, Chuan. 2008. "Entry Mode Selection for International Construction Markets: The Influence of Host Country Related Factors." *Construction Management and Economics* 26 (3): 303–14.

CLR News. 2006. "Japan: What Can We Learn." CLR News 2/2006, CLR News, Brussels.

Corkin, Lucy, and Christopher Burke. 2006. *China's Interest and Activity in Africa's Construction and Infrastructure Sectors*. Stellenbosch, South Africa: Centre for Chinese Studies, Stellenbosch University.

de Boer, Kito, and Jaap B. Kalkman. 2007. "Meeting Bahrain's Challenges: An Interview with Crown Prince Salman bin Hamad Al-Khalifa." *McKinsey Quarterly*, January.

ENR (*Engineering News-Record*). 2008. "Top International and Global Contractors." Special report, August 18. http://enr.ecnext.com/coms2/summary_0271-52286_ITM.

FIDH (International Federation for Human Rights). 2007. "Egypt: Protection of the Rights of All Migrant Workers and Members of Their Families." Report to the United Nations Committee on the Protection of the Rights of All Migrant Workers and Members of Their Families, April, Egyptian Initiative for Personal Rights, Cairo, and International Federation for Human Rights, Paris. http://www.unhcr.org/refworld/docid/46f146900.html.

Geloso Grosso, Massimo, Anna Jankowska, and Frédéric Gonzales. 2008. "Trade and Regulation: The Case of Construction Services." Paper presented at the OECD's "Experts Meeting on Construction Services," Paris, December 11.

Human Rights Watch. 2009. *Russia: "Are You Happy to Cheat Us?"; Exploitation of Migrant Construction Workers in Russia.* New York: Human Rights Watch.

Longva, Anh Nga. 1999. "Keeping Migrant Workers in Check: The Kafala System in the Gulf." *Middle East Report* 211 (2): 20–22.

Mburu, Emily. 2008. "Construction Services: Contribution to Sustainable Development and Issues on Trade in Services." Paper presented at the International Centre for Trade and Sustainable Development, African Economic Research Consortium, and the Economic and Social Research Foundation, Tanzania, "Regional Dialogue for Eastern and Southern Africa on Trade in Services and Sustainable Development," Dar es Salaam, Tanzania, October 30–31.

Nielson, Julia, and Daria Taglioni. 2004. "Services Trade Liberalisation: Identifying Opportunities and Gains." OECD Trade Policy Working Paper 1, TD/TC/WP(2003)23/FINAL, Organisation for Economic Co-operation and Development, Paris.

Pietroforte, Roberto, and Tullio Gregori. 2003. "An Input-Output Analysis of the Construction Sector in Highly Developed Countries." *Construction Management and Economics* 21 (3): 319–27.

PovcalNet. World Bank, Washington, DC. http://go.worldbank.org/NT2A1XUWP0 (accessed September 2009).

Ratha, Dilip, and Zhimei Xu. 2008. *Migration and Remittances Factbook 2008*. Washington, DC: Development Prospects Group, World Bank.

Reyna, Peter. 2007. "Anti-Graft Efforts to Launch in Third World Construction." *Engineering News-Record* 259 (14): 17.

Ruddock, Les, and Jorge Lopes. 2006. "The Construction Sector and Economic Development: The 'Bon Curve.'" *Construction Management and Economics* 24 (7): 717–23.

Stansbury, Neil, and Catherine Stansbury. 2006. "Preventing Corruption on Construction Projects: Risk Assessment and Proposed Actions for Funders." Report, July, Transparency International and United Kingdom Anticorruption Forum, London.

Teljeur, Ethel, and Matthew Stern. 2002. "Understanding the South African Construction Services Industry: Towards a GATS Negotiating Strategy." Paper presented at the Trade and Industrial Policy Strategies' "Forum 2002: Global Integration, Sustainable Development, and the Southern African Economy," Muldersdrift, South Africa, January 1.

Transparency International. 2005a. *Global Corruption Report 2005; Special Report: Corruption in Construction and Post-Conflict Reconstruction*. London: Pluto Press.

———. 2005b. "Preventing Corruption on Construction Projects: Risk Assessment and Proposed Actions for Project Owners." Transparency International, Berlin. http://www.transparency.org/content/download/2229/13051/file/1_risk_assessment_owners.pdf.

———. 2005c. "TI's Minimum Standards for Public Contracting." Policy Positions 03/2005, Transparency International, Berlin.

Tulacz, Gary J. 2005. "World Construction Spending Nears $4 Trillion for 2004." *Engineering News–Record*, January 3. http://enr.construction.com/news/bizlabor/archives/050103-1.asp.

———. 2000a. "Regulation and Liberalization in the Construction Services Sector and Its Contribution to the Development of Developing Countries: Note by the UNCTAD Secretariat." Document TD/B/COM.1/EM.12/2 (September 12), Trade and Development Board, UNCTAD, Geneva.

———. 2000b. "Report of the Expert Meeting on National Experiences with Regulation and Liberalization: Examples in the Construction Services Sector and Its Contribution to the Development of Developing Countries." Document TD/B/COM.1/32 (December 18), Trade and Development Board, UNCTAD, Geneva.

World Bank. 2007. *Africa's Silk Road: China and India's New Economic Frontier*. Washington, DC: World Bank.

———. 2008. *Doing Business 2009*. Washington, DC: World Bank; New York: Palgrave Macmillan.

———. 2009a. "Dealing with Construction Permits in the Russian Federation." *Doing Business: Measuring Business Regulations*. World Bank, Washington, DC. http://www.doingbusiness.org/ExploreTopics/DealingLicenses/Details.aspx?economyid=159 (data as of January 2009).

———. 2009b. "Dealing with Construction Permits in Kenya." *Doing Business: Measuring Business Regulations*. World Bank, Washington, DC. http://www.doingbusiness.org/ExploreTopics/DealingLicenses/Details.aspx?economyid=101 (data as of January 2009).

WTO (World Trade Organization). 1991. "Services Sectoral Classification List: Note by the Secretariat." Document MTN.GNS/W/120 (July 10), WTO, Geneva.

———. 1998. "Construction and Related Engineering Services: Background Note by the Secretariat." Document S/C/W/38 (June 8), Council for Trade in Services, WTO, Geneva.

———. (2005), "Report by the Chairman to the Trade Negotiations Committee." Document TN/S/23 (November 28), Council for Trade in Services, Special Session, WTO, Geneva.

———. 2008. *International Trade Statistics 2008*. Geneva: WTO.

# 7

# EXPORTING INFORMATION TECHNOLOGY SERVICES: IN THE FOOTSTEPS OF INDIA

*Michael Engman*

## Introduction: Why Is Trade in Information Technology Services of Interest for Developing Countries?

Trade in information technology (IT) services is of interest for developing countries for several reasons.[1] First, with regard to essential supply-side requirements commensurate with factor endowments in many developing countries, the IT service sector makes intensive use of human capital, but is not particularly reliant on physical capital. An export-oriented IT service sector can thus thrive in a country with good technical education and limited infrastructure.

Second, widespread connectivity to international information and communication technology networks and inexpensive technical solutions for online collaboration and communication enable IT service entrepreneurs to compete for business independently of location. Electronic supply also reduces trade costs and allows companies to leverage local cost structures.

Third, a dynamic domestic market, while helpful, is not necessarily a prerequisite for success. As the Indian case proves, an IT service sector can be nurtured and thrive without significant local demand. Companies with the necessary talent can tap into international markets and grow on the back of foreign demand.

Fourth, software encompasses a wide array of products and technologies and is developed using different techniques such as programming languages, scripting languages, and microcode. Consequently, the IT service market consists of numerous subsectors and niche markets that IT service companies in developing countries can tap into. A country's social and economic ties are also key determinants of where IT service companies end up exporting. As a result, some countries have a language advantage, while other countries benefit from the availability of technical expertise or artistic talent. For example, Chinese IT service exports are mainly delivered to Japan, Czech exports to the European Union, Mauritian exports to France, Philippine exports to the United States, and Indian exports to the United States and the United Kingdom. Consequently, there are plenty of trade opportunities for companies across the world.

Fifth, the international market for IT services is growing rapidly. While most Fortune 500 companies are already procuring IT services from developing countries, more and more small and medium-size enterprises are outsourcing IT services, and so are large companies in non-English-speaking countries of the Organisation for Economic Co-operation and Development and in developing countries. New players will find plenty of business to contest in the future. From a gender perspective, the IT service occupation does not require any particular attributes that favor one gender over the other. It is therefore conducive to women's labor participation. Trade in IT services is also likely to increase skill premiums in developing countries and developed countries. Developed countries tend to outsource less skill-intensive IT services to developing countries, and these IT services tend to be relatively more skill intensive in developing countries (see Feenstra and Hanson 1996).

Among developed and developing countries alike, there are gains from trade in imports and exports, and open markets for IT services are therefore in the interests of these countries. Open markets allow countries to specialize in what they do best and expand the quality and quantity of goods and services produced and consumed. Open markets also lead to a more efficient allocation of resources. The resulting gain in economic efficiency helps raise overall living standards. While this chapter mainly covers IT service exports from developing countries, IT service imports are equally important in many low-income countries. The policy initiatives proposed in the following sections would aid the private sector as much in the import side as in the export side. In addition, intensive use of IT may result in considerable positive spillover effects that benefit domestic economies. A local buildup of IT expertise is likely to lead to increased IT diffusion in other sectors of the economy in developing countries. This may have positive effects on productivity and business innovation and, hence, lead to more broadbased economic growth. Software development is the foundation of the modern knowledge-based economy, and information and communication technology can be applied to tackle many of the social and economic challenges related to development (for a discussion, see UNCTAD 2004).

There are currently few policy-induced trade barriers affecting the IT service sector. It is arguably one of the sectors most open to international trade (see Ganguly 2005, Engman 2007, Kirkegaard 2008). The barriers that exist are predominantly associated with supply-side constraints. Some of these constraints are natural and arise because of the inherently complex task of delivering IT services through electronic supply. Other constraints are linked to shortages in human capital. In the next section, there is a brief overview of market fundamentals and the prospects for developing-country trade in IT services. In the subsequent section, we present a number of supply-side constraints and highlight priorities for policy makers in developing countries that may facilitate trade in the sector. The penultimate section summarizes some of the main issues that warrant the attention of stakeholders. The final section concludes.

## What Is the Situation of and What Are the Prospects for Trade in IT Services?

Trade in IT services—frequently referred to as the offshoring of IT services (see figure 7.1)—has grown rapidly and is expected to continue to grow rapidly, particularly in many developing countries. Formal data sources such as International Monetary Fund balance of payments statistics do not adequately record the international flows of IT services, and this leaves analysts dependent on estimates produced by market intelligence and consulting companies that track the industry.[2] In 2008, according to Willcocks, Griffiths, and Kotlarsky (2009), the global market for outsourced IT services was worth from US$220 billion to US$250 billion, and it is forecast to grow by 6–9 percent per year until 2013. The McKinsey Group estimates that, in 2007, the market for traditional IT services such as hardware and software maintenance, network administration, and help desk services was

**Figure 7.1.** Offshoring = International *In*sourcing + International *Out*sourcing

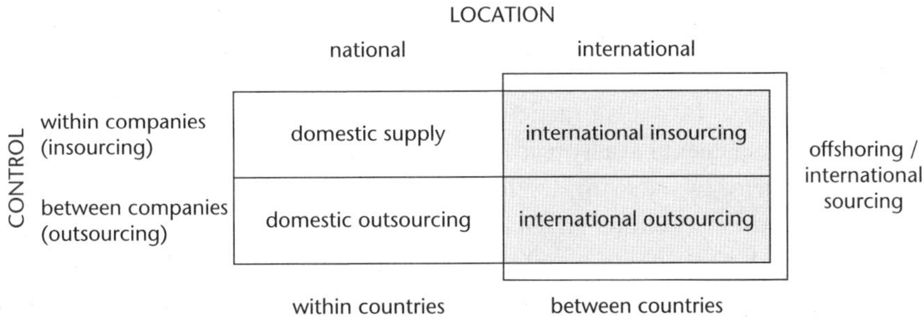


*Source:* Engman (2007).

worth about US$100 billion; system integration, US$50 billion; application development and maintenance, US$43 billion; embedded software services, US$40 billion; and consulting services, US$6 billion (see Dongier and Sudan 2009).

Developing countries captured approximately 14 percent of the global IT service market in 2007. The two leading exporters, India and Israel, exported IT and computer services worth roughly US$23.1 billion (in 2008) and US$5.3 billion (in 2006), respectively (Nasscom 2009). Chinese exports of IT services were worth an estimated US$1.2 billion in 2008 (Meyer 2009). Still, IT service exports are a fairly modest business activity in most developing countries. A large number of developing countries are enjoying the gains from trade in IT-enabled services, such as back-office support services and call centers, that are generally less skill intensive than the IT service sector itself. India is, so far, the only developing country that has created a sizable, export-oriented IT service sector. Table 7.1 shows that several other developing or emerging economies have significant exports. Argentina, Costa Rica, Malaysia, the Russian Federation, Sri Lanka, and Uruguay all made the list of major exporters put out by the World Trade Organization (WTO) in 2006. There are signs that the international market for IT services is becoming contested by companies in a growing number of countries, including large populous ones such as Brazil, China, the Arab Republic of Egypt, and Vietnam and small or less populous ones such as Mauritius and Romania. The McKinsey Group forecasts that developing-country exports will double and reach US$55 billion during 2010. Egypt, an emerging IT service location, is described in box 7.1.

*Demand* has been fueled by competition in international and maturing markets that compels companies to raise productivity and reduce the costs associated with the use of IT. Offshoring offers significant cost savings through labor-cost arbitrage and economies of scale in the delivery process. However, offshoring is associated with a number of other benefits that sometimes are more important than prospective cost savings. Offshoring can enable companies to offer their clients new, more flexible, and, often, higher-quality services. It may also offer reduced time to market, facilitate access to foreign markets, and create business opportunities for the development of new products for niche markets. International outsourcing allows companies to focus on what they do best, freeing up capital to be reinvested in research and development and more productive activities. Innovation in business practices, low productivity growth, and scarcity of local engineering talent have worked as drivers in many instances.

*Supply* is fueled by the many developing countries that have invested in education and are now able to offer an abundance of young, motivated, and technically adept graduates. Developing-country IT service exports are growing as delivery models mature and service providers become increasingly sophisticated. Offshoring has also been facilitated by economic integration—particularly through

**Table 7.1.** Major Exporters and Importers of Computer Services, 2006

| Rank | Exporters | Value (US$ millions) | Share in 15 economies (%) | Annual % change | Rank | Importers | Value (US$ millions) | Share in 15 economies (%) | Annual % change |
|---|---|---|---|---|---|---|---|---|---|
| 1 | European Union (27) | 60,398 | 59.5 | 14 | 1 | European Union (27) | 32,439 | 61.7 | 14 |
| | Extra–European Union (27) exports | 22,225 | 21.9 | 27 | | Extra–European Union (27) imports | 11,081 | 21.1 | 14 |
| 2 | India[a] | 21,061 | 20.7 | — | 2 | United States[b] | 10,522 | 20.0 | 24 |
| 3 | United States[b] | 6,208 | 6.1 | 8 | 3 | India | 1,979 | 3.8 | 61 |
| 4 | Israel | 5,289 | 5.2 | 17 | 4 | Brazil | 1,947 | 3.7 | 18 |
| 5 | Canada | 3,583 | 3.5 | 3 | 5 | Canada | 1,401 | 2.7 | 11 |
| 6 | Norway | 1,376 | 1.4 | 53 | 6 | Norway | 1,268 | 2.4 | 26 |
| 7 | Australia | 1,040 | 1.0 | 19 | 7 | Australia | 915 | 1.7 | 16 |
| 8 | Russian Federation | 576 | 0.6 | 54 | 8 | Malaysia | 518 | 1.0 | 37 |
| 9 | Malaysia | 572 | 0.6 | 31 | 9 | Russian Federation | 476 | 0.9 | 26 |
| 10 | Costa Rica | 371 | 0.4 | 46 | 10 | Korea, Rep. | 311 | 0.6 | — |
| 11 | Argentina | 342 | 0.3 | 48 | 11 | Hong Kong, China | 310 | 0.6 | −16 |
| 12 | Hong Kong, China | 301 | 0.3 | 45 | 12 | Argentina | 206 | 0.4 | 13 |
| 13 | Korea, Rep. | 182 | 0.2 | — | 13 | Colombia | 132 | 0.3 | 20 |
| 14 | Uruguay | 122 | 0.1 | 47 | 14 | Syrian Arab Republic | 95 | 0.2 | −5 |
| 15 | Sri Lanka | 98 | 0.1 | 19 | 15 | Philippines | 67 | 0.1 | 8 |
| | **Above 15** | **101,520** | **100.0** | — | | **Above 15** | **52,585** | **100.0** | — |

*Source:* WTO (2008).
*Note:* European Union (27) = member states of the European Union as of January 2007: Austria, Belgium, Bulgaria, Cyprus, the Czech Republic, Denmark, Estonia, Finland, France, Germany, Greece, Hungary, Ireland, Italy, Latvia, Lithuania, Luxembourg, Malta, the Netherlands, Poland, Portugal, Romania, the Slovak Republic, Slovenia, Spain, Sweden, and the United Kingdom. — = not available.
a. Estimate of the WTO secretariat.
b. Includes affiliated information service transactions.

**Box 7.1:** Egypt as an Emerging Offshore Location for IT Services

Egypt is rapidly emerging as the leading supply base for IT services in the Middle East and North Africa. A. T. Kearney (2007) estimates that, in 2008, Egypt's IT service exports were worth US$99 million and that they will reach US$150 million during 2010. Egypt is mainly used as a nearshoring (nearshore outsourcing) base for the region and for European Union markets. Egypt benefits from its proximity to wealthy Persian Gulf countries (in terms of geography, language, and culture) and Europe (in terms of geography and time zone). Several multinationals based in the West, including HP, IBM, and Microsoft, have established local software application development centers. Indian multinationals such as Infosys, Tech Mahindra, and Wipro have as well. Oracle and several leading telecommunications companies have established large technical support centers that serve foreign markets.

The key to Egypt's success in attracting foreign direct investment in the IT service sector lies in its endowment of technical personnel, its competitive cost structure, and its sustained political commitment to improve the local business environment. Egypt produces some 31,000 graduates annually in the technology, science, and engineering areas. Many graduates have multilingual skills, and the average compensation for IT programmers in Egypt is roughly a third of the compensation in Hungary, Poland, and Romania and somewhat lower than the compensation in India. The political commitment stems partly from the fact that Egypt's prime minister and three ministers in the government have a professional background in the IT sector.

The Ministry of Communication and Information Technology offers a range of customized support services to attract investment, for example in the areas of telecommunications, real estate, and training. In 2003, a technology park with modern infrastructure (referred to as a smart village business park) was established outside Cairo, and more are planned for Alexandria, Damietta, and New Cairo. In December 2004, an amendment to the investment law (Law 14/04) charged the General Authority for Investment and Free Zones as the sole authority to which investors need to turn for project approval, essentially introducing a one-stop shop with delegates from governmental agencies under a single roof. Streamlining administrative procedures has helped cut the time to register a company from four months to a maximum of three days. The authorities are also working to cut the administration associated with the process of registering a business, obtaining a tax card, getting industrial project approval, obtaining a building permit, obtaining an operating license, and clearing industrial registration. This initiative should reduce the total time from 277 days to 45 days.

In 2007, the country hosted 27 IT service companies with Capability Maturity Model and Capability Maturity Model Integration certification (described elsewhere below). Some of these companies had obtained Capability Maturity Model Integration level-5 certification, the highest possible level, in part through training and support offered through the government. The government has also launched initiatives to expand the supply of qualified staff in the information and communication technology sector, for example, in partnership with leading IT service companies and by improving computer-related training. One of the projects of the Ministry of Communication and Information Technology that is being implemented in collaboration with the Ministry of Higher Education is referred to as the Edu Egypt Initiative. Its objective is to equip undergraduates with more advanced software and language skills and technical training. A new university, Nile University, was opened in 2007 to raise local standards in applied IT research in close association with the private sector.

*Sources*: Marson and Blodgett (2007); Gott (2008); El Shenawi and Lanvin (2009); Willcocks, Griffiths, and Kotlarsky (2009); CyberMedia, CBC, and Global Services (2009).

liberalization in foreign direct investment—and by diaspora networks. For example, the Chinese and Indian professionals working in the IT sector in the United States either temporarily or as permanent immigrants have brought back best practices, reinvested in China and India, and facilitated investment by U.S. companies in the Chinese and Indian IT service sector. Many developing countries have targeted niche markets and benefited from IT-intensive local industries. For example, Israel has built a highly sophisticated software and service sector on the back of its national defense industry. Other countries hosting industrial leaders with in-house computer competence, such as Brazil's aviation industry or East Asia's hardware industry, have local clusters of IT service expertise that may have the potential to become large exporters. Mauritius and Singapore are both used as regional centers for disaster recovery for computer systems.

The IT service sector has greatly benefited from the improved capacity and reduced cost of information and communication technologies. Business process innovation has allowed the IT service value chain to be fragmented into small, well-defined tasks that can be traded at low transaction costs. In combination with the development of collaborative virtual work environments, the physical location of the service supplier has, in many instances, been rendered irrelevant. Customized software application development and maintenance are the types of task most commonly outsourced to developing countries. Web design and development represent another area in which entrepreneurs in developing countries have excelled. Systems integration and IT consulting may be reserved for technological leaders, but the remote management and maintenance of IT networks, including help desks, desktop support, data center services, mainframe support, and network operations, are increasingly outsourced to low-cost countries. The frantic pace of innovation in the IT service sector is constantly giving rise to new types of services that can be provided through electronic supply.

The terminology of the General Agreement on Trade in Services (GATS) of the WTO states that a service can be traded in four distinct ways.[3] *Developing-country imports* of IT services cover three of these ways: crossborder supply (that is, electronic delivery or Mode 1), commercial presence (Mode 3), and the temporary movement of natural persons (Mode 4). For example, if a Swiss insurance company instructs its Brazilian subsidiary to deliver IT services electronically to its headquarters or to another of its non-Brazilian subsidiaries, it is, in WTO terminology, engaged in Mode 1 trade. The same holds if the IT services are electronically delivered from any Brazilian company to a non-Brazilian company. If the Swiss insurance company establishes a commercial presence in Brazil to service the Brazilian IT service market, it is, in WTO terminology, involved in Mode 3 trade. Any IT professionals sent from Brazil to one of the Swiss company's non-Brazilian premises to deliver services are, in WTO terminology, engaged in Mode 4 trade.

However, service delivery through commercial presence is relatively unimpeded, and this is likely to imply that there is limited scope for trade liberalization. The multinationals that seek to enter a market or have already done so face few policy-induced restrictions. For this reason, this chapter is mainly focused on *developing-country exports* of IT services, which cover crossborder supply (Mode 1) and the temporary movement of natural persons (Mode 4). While a handful of the leading Indian IT service companies deliver a limited portion of their IT services through commercial presence (Mode 3), this mode of delivery represents only a tiny share of total developing-country exports of IT services.

As entrepreneurs in an increasing number of developing countries successfully contest the international market for IT services, policy makers may be excused for their enthusiasm about the prospect of helping to nurture a domestic export-oriented IT service sector. However, they need to have realistic expectations about the scope for generating IT service exports. While there is plenty of demand, relatively few developing countries have the supply capacity in terms of the quantity and quality of human resources and the sophistication of local companies to develop a sizable export industry in the short or medium term (see MGI 2005, Dongier and Sudan 2009). Even China and Eastern European countries that are relatively well endowed with technically skilled engineers face serious shortages of managers with industry-relevant experience who can manage the complex delivery process and engage in client-related activities. Most companies in countries with dynamic IT service sectors, including India, are struggling with staff attrition and salary inflation because of the limited number of adequately trained and experienced staff.

Dossani (2010) and others have concluded that the endowments of entrepreneurship and quality education are key in the IT service sector. Education and telecommunications policy are the two paramount issues in terms of policy fundamentals. Other privileges and targeted incentives such as tax breaks can help, but are not altogether critical. Policy makers should focus on helping to remove binding constraints to the industry, most of which are not unique to the IT service sector.

## What Can Be Done to Remove Binding Constraints and Harness Trade Opportunities?

There are several constraints that policy makers can address to help the private sector harness trade opportunities in the IT service sector. Effective strategies are likely to focus on initiatives that attract private investment from local and foreign investors (box 7.2), reward entrepreneurship by improving the business environment, and raise educational standards. In countries with weak infrastructure and poor business environments, a common approach is to let private real estate developers build software and high-technology parks near population centers

**Box 7.2:** The Value of Securing an Anchor Investor

Developing countries that, without national champions, seek to catch the attention of foreign multinationals in fiercely competitive markets for hardware, software, and related services often target a leading, high-profile anchor investor. The establishment of a leading multinational helps signal to other prospective investors that the country offers a business-conducive environment in which companies can prosper. A market leader transfers technology and management expertise. It can also provide the impetus for the creation of a local cluster of suppliers. Intel's decision to invest in Costa Rica in 1996 had an overwhelmingly positive impact on the country's economy, industry, and business culture (MIGA 2006). Costa Rica's investment in higher education helped attract Intel in the first place, and the company's establishment had a positive impact on higher education in turn. The anchor investment helped shape the country's investment promotion strategy and led to more investment in adjacent services. Other examples of middle-income countries attracting leading companies include the establishment by DHL of an IT service center in the Czech Republic in 2004 and IBM initiatives in Egypt, including investments in a nanotechnology research center and global service delivery center in 2005.

with engineering colleges and universities. These parks provide modern office facilities with a guaranteed supply of electricity and high-capacity broadband connectivity. By nurturing clusters, IT service companies can enjoy economies of scale in procuring input services and overcoming infrastructure bottlenecks. China, Egypt, India, and the Philippines are some developing countries that have successfully established such parks.

Some consulting companies assess and compare countries based on perceived attractiveness as offshore service locations. A. T. Kearney's global services location index is published twice a year and has developed into a widely studied benchmarking tool for the IT service sector and the IT-enabled service sector (figure 7.2 and table 7.2). It provides a useful starting point and offers a number of lessons for foreign investors who seek a new base for service delivery and local policy makers who seek to address supply barriers.[4] It is based on three pillars: financial attractiveness (cost and expense structures), people skills and availability (quality and quantity of human resources), and business environment (miscellaneous variables affecting the stability and time of supply).

The index provides a rather comprehensive coverage of issues, and the fact that foreign investors make use of it reinforces its importance and generates some traction in the efforts of governments at regulatory reform. It illustrates how different locations have different strengths that cater to the different needs of foreign clients. For some types of services, language skills are paramount in attracting business, while other companies are highly price sensitive. Many multinationals look for locations where they can rapidly scale up their operations by hiring hundreds or thousands of IT professionals without generating labor market disruptions. Developed

**Figure 7.2.** A. T. Kearney's Global Services Location Index

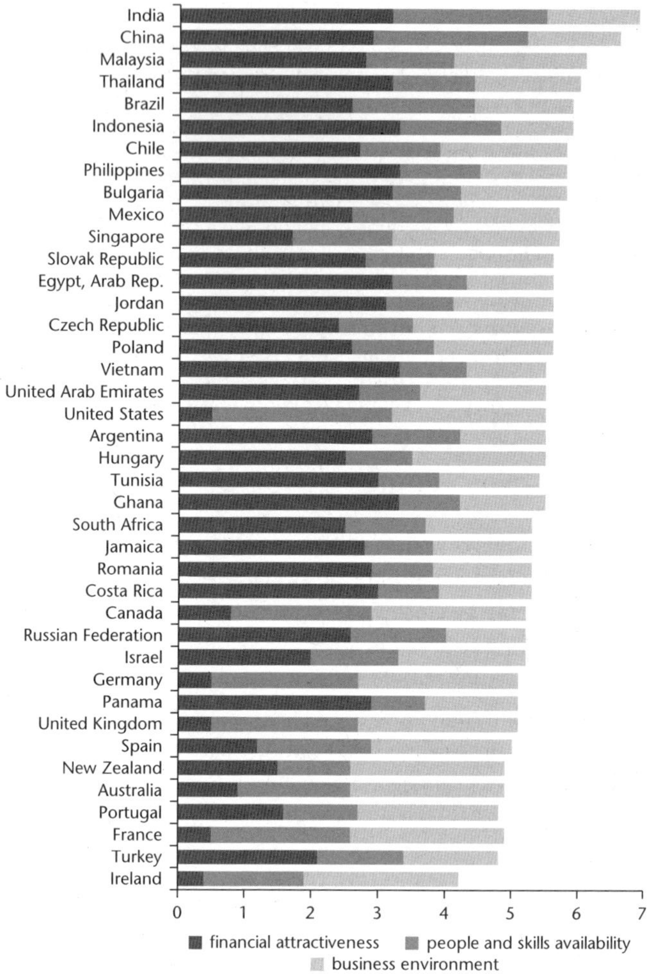


*Source:* A. T. Kearney (2007).

countries tend to have an advantage with regard to human capital and the business environment, while developing countries tend to rank high on local cost structures. China and India are the two developing countries that have high scores in human resources and in cost structures, and these two countries are most attractive overall according to A. T. Kearney's methodology. But several other developing countries in different parts of the world have high aggregate scores.

The focus hereafter is on some of the key initiatives that governments can undertake to remove common impediments in the international supply of IT services. These initiatives would not only benefit export-oriented IT service companies,

**Table 7.2.** A. T. Kearney's Index Metrics

----- FINANCIAL ATTRACTIVENESS (40%) -----

**(I) Compensation costs**

*Average wages*

*Median compensation costs*

**(II) Infrastructure costs**

*Rental costs*

*Commercial electricity rates*

*International telecom costs*

*Travel to major customer destinations*

**(III) Tax and regulatory costs**

*Relative tax burden*

*Corruption perception*

*Currency appreciation or depreciation*

----- PEOPLE SKILLS AND AVAILABILITY (30%) -----

**(I) Remote services sector experience and quality ratings**

*Size of existing IT and BPO sectors*

*Contact center and IT center quality certifications*

*Quality ratings of management schools and IT training*

**(II) Labor force availability**

*Total work force*

*University-educated work force*

*Work force flexibility*

**(III) Education & language**

*Scores on standardized education and language tests*

**(IV) Attrition risk**

*Relative IT and BPO sector growth and unemployment rates*

----- BUSINESS ENVIRONMENT (30%) -----

**(I) Country environment**

*Investor and analyst ratings of overall business and political environment*

*A.T. Kearney FDI Confidence Index*

*Security risk*

*Regulatory burden and employment rigidity*

*Government support for the ICT sector*

**(II) Infrastructure costs**

*Overall infrastructure quality*

*Quality of telecom, Internet, and electricity infrastructure*

**(III) Cultural exposure**

*Personal interaction score (A.T. Kearney Globalisation Index)*

**(IV) Security & intellectual property**

*Investor ratings of IP protection and ICT laws*

*Software piracy rates*

*Information security certifications*

*Source:* A. T. Kearney (2007).
*Note:* BPO = business process outsourcing; IP = intellectual property; ICT = information and communications technology.

but also local businesses in general. They include activities that would remove infrastructural bottlenecks, address weaknesses in the business environment, increase the number of graduates with adequate training, reduce barriers to labor mobility, and promote best practices in the IT service sector and, thereby, attract foreign investors.

### *Address the limitations in infrastructure and the business environment*

The IT service sector is not particularly dependent on inputs of external goods and services relative to the manufacturing sector or backbone service sectors such as transportation and telecommunications. Stable power and reliable telecommunications and Internet connectivity are the main critical inputs for production in the IT service value chain. While the installation of reliable broadband capacity may take considerable investment and years to achieve, small, dedicated power generators in countries with poor capacity or volatile distribution can provide adequate electricity. These generators often run on diesel fuel and may be noisy, environmentally unfriendly, and more expensive than the electricity provided by real power plants; yet, they do the job during power cuts. IT service exporters in developing countries generally operate in software and high-technology parks in which infrastructural bottlenecks and weaknesses in the local business environment can be overcome.

#### Internet bandwidth capacity: Critical for electronic supply

Table 7.3 presents information and communication technology performance indicators for regions (simple averages) and countries within those regions that show the lowest and highest reported costs for fixed residential broadband connections (see annex table 7A.2 for information on all countries). Residential broadband prices ought to be a good proxy for the prices that, in particular, small and medium-size enterprises are charged. The data reveal extreme differences within and across regions. Most notably, broadband is prohibitively expensive in many African countries and some countries in East Asia and the Pacific, as well as in Latin America and the Caribbean. The cost for a monthly residential broadband contract exceeds US$100 in purchasing power parity dollars in 39 of 171 countries and territories. In Burkina Faso, the Central African Republic, Cuba, Ethiopia, The Gambia, Guinea, Malawi, Nigeria, and Swaziland, it exceeds US$1,000 in purchasing power parity dollars. While these price levels may effectively shut out any export-oriented start-ups in the IT service sector, other factors are equally important. For example, the data do not reveal to what extent the broadband services are stable over time. Downtime is detrimental to companies that need to be able to access client data systems all the time or, at least, connect frequently throughout each day.

**Table 7.3.** Information and Communication Technology Performance Indicators

| | Internet users per 100 inhabitants | Fixed broadband subscribers per 100 inhabitants | Internet bandwidth per Internet user (bit/s) | Proportion of households with computer (%) | Proportion of households with Internet (%) | Monthly subscribers (US$) | Monthly subscribers (PPP$) |
|---|---|---|---|---|---|---|---|
| **Sub-Saharan Africa** | 4.2 | 0.5 | 891 | 5.9 | 2.5 | 322 | 692 |
| *South Africa* | 8.2 | 0.8 | 852 | 14.8 | 4.8 | 26 | 47 |
| *Swaziland* | 3.7 | — | 282 | 12.8 | 6.0 | 1,877 | 3,854 |
| **East Asia and Pacific** | 25.6 | 6.3 | 4,406 | 29.9 | 24.2 | 71 | 146 |
| *Taiwan, China* | 64.5 | 20.9 | 12,632 | 67.1 | 61.6 | 10 | 18 |
| *Lao PDR* | 1.7 | 0.1 | 1,880 | 6.7 | 1.8 | 268 | 772 |
| **Europe and Central Asia** | 26.7 | 5.9 | 6,107 | 27.2 | 20.1 | 27 | 43 |
| *Macedonia, FYR* | 27.3 | 4.9 | 61 | 25.0 | 15.5 | 15 | 30 |
| *Azerbaijan* | 10.9 | 0.1 | 6,475 | 10.1 | 9.3 | 85 | 167 |
| **Latin America and the Caribbean** | 20.5 | 2.9 | 7,906 | 18.7 | 9.0 | 96 | 69 |
| *Trinidad and Tobago* | 16.0 | 2.7 | 4,229 | 43.6 | 18.1 | 13 | 20 |
| *Cuba* | 11.6 | — | 162 | 2.3 | 1.8 | 1,630 | — |
| **Middle East and North Africa** | 23.6 | 5.1 | 3,214 | 29.8 | 22.3 | 41 | 82 |
| *Egypt Arab Rep.*[a] | 14.0 | 0.6 | 1,023 | 16.1 | 9.1 | 8 | 25 |
| *Yemen Rep.* | 1.4 | — | 1,969 | 2.6 | 2.0 | 226 | 525 |
| **South Asia** | 5.5 | 1.4 | 6,322 | 9.6 | 3.7 | 22 | 60 |
| *India*[b] | 6.9 | 0.3 | 441 | 3.7 | 3.0 | 6 | 16 |
| *Bangladesh* | 0.3 | — | 1,284 | 1.9 | 1.3 | 54 | 155 |
| **OECD countries** | 66.6 | 23.9 | 411,820 | 70.7 | 61.8 | 34 | 26 |
| *United States* | 72.5 | 24.0 | 15,341 | 70.2 | 61.7 | 15 | 15 |
| *Austria* | 67.0 | 19.4 | 30,116 | 71.0 | 60.0 | 61 | 46 |

*Source:* ITU (2009).
*Note:* PPP $ = U.S. dollars at purchasing power parity. — = not available.
a. Cap of 2 gigabytes.
b. Cap of 1 gigabyte.

The definition of broadband used by the International Telecommunication Union is 256 kilobits per second (kbps). This is far below the minimum requirement of a medium-size IT service company. Unless the telecommunications sector provides much more rapid connections, IT service companies may not have a reasonable chance to export through electronic supply (Mode 1). In 2006, fixed broadband was available in 30 of 53 African countries. Among these, the maximum speed was 256 kbps in five countries, 512 kbps in six countries, 1,024 kbps in nine countries, 2,048 kbps in nine countries, and over 2,048 kbps in one country (Touré 2007). For those countries in which much more rapid connections are offered to companies, price and reliability play crucial roles if foreign investors are to consider locating within the country or if local startups are to operate with efficiency.[5]

Eastern Europe and South Asia are two regions in which broadband access is often available at a relatively low price. The developing countries that host successful export-oriented IT service sectors or IT-enabled service sectors also tend to have low prices. For example, in China, Egypt, India, the Philippines, Russia, Singapore, and Taiwan, China, a fixed residential broadband connection costs less than US$24 a month. Dossani (2010) reports that, in Bangladesh and Sri Lanka, for instance, IT service companies are hampered by particularly high bandwidth costs as a result of only limited reform of telecommunications markets. In India, according to data provided by McKinsey Global Institute and cited by El Shenawi and Lanvin (2009), the annual cost of a 2 megabits per second leased line to the United States is US$72,000. In Bulgaria and Morocco, the equivalent line costs US$216,000 to US$220,000, and, in Egypt and the Philippines, the cost for such a line is US$42,000.

The data in annex table 7A.2 show large differences in terms of international Internet bandwidth per Internet user.[6] More than a third of the 152 countries that report this variable have less than 1 kilobits per Internet user per second. While India belongs to this low-capacity group, the country also has the world's lowest monthly fees and has managed to build a successful export-oriented IT service sector. The country's software and technology parks offer access to inexpensive, high-capacity bandwidth. Meanwhile, Africa's most populous nation, Nigeria, has some of the world's highest prices, but one of the world's lowest bandwidth capacities. According to Touré (2007), while Africa's international bandwidth capacity is low, the issue of Internet connectivity is worse than the data indicate. Over a third of Africa's international circuits (circuit equivalents of 64 kbps) are dedicated to voice-telephone traffic. In Europe, the equivalent share is 5 percent. The resulting capacity for transfers of nonvoice data is thus relatively lower in Africa than in other regions. In addition, while Europe had overcapacity of almost 100 percent in its Internet protocol circuits in 2005, thereby putting downward pressure on

**Box 7.3:** Raising Internet Connectivity in Africa

A number of investments are currently under way to improve Internet connectivity in Africa. Through the International Finance Corporation, the World Bank is participating in the East African submarine cable system, which is bringing together up to 28 telecommunications operators and a large number of sponsors.[7] The initiative involves the construction and operation of a submarine fiber-optic cable along the east coast of Africa to connect eight coastal countries and island nations—from South Africa to Sudan—to each other and to the rest of the world. The objectives are to provide high-speed broadband connectivity and to significantly reduce the currently prohibitive cost of telephone and Internet services in East and Southern Africa. The project is expected to raise regional competitiveness and growth and benefit educational and medical institutions. The cable will have an initial capacity of 20,000 megabits per second and an ultimate capacity at full upgrade of 320,000 megabits per second. In 2006, all of Africa had a capacity of 28,177 megabits per second, which is the equivalent of 3.5 percent of the capacity in Asia.

In separate projects, participants in the East African submarine cable system will build terrestrial connections to link landlocked countries to the cable, including Botswana, Burundi, Ethiopia, Lesotho, Malawi, Rwanda, Uganda, Zambia, and Zimbabwe. Among other large connectivity investments in Africa are the InfraCo Project, which will have connected Africa's west coast to the United Kingdom by the end of 2010, and the Seacom Project that is connecting East Africa, Southern Africa, Europe, and India via a 13,700 kilometer undersea cable (CyberMedia, CBC, and Global Services 2009).

prices, less than 2 percent of Africa's capacity was idle, on average. Consequently, surges in demand have a much more disruptive effect on quality transmission in Africa than in Europe. Box 7.3 discusses the issues involved in raising Internet connectivity in Africa.

The market for Internet services is relatively more open to competition than are the markets for fixed line and mobile telecommunications services (ITU 2007). High Internet prices are thus likely to arise more because of capacity shortages than because of a lack of competition. This issue ought to be one of the first priorities to be addressed by information and communication technology policy makers if their countries are to become IT service exporters or IT-enabled service exporters. The price, bandwidth capacity, and reliability of services are all equally important for companies seeking to export IT services through electronic supply. Accessibility is important, too, because broadband may only be available in capital cities or a few urban areas. It will take considerable investment, some of which is already online, to increase access to high-speed Internet services among households and companies in all developing countries.

The provision of IT services almost invariably involves intensive communication within project teams and between project team members and clients. Companies, particularly startups and small and medium-size enterprises, communicate by means of relatively simple software products such as messenger services and voice over Internet protocol services that allow free instant chat, voice, and videoconferencing. Consequently, regulators should think twice before banning any types of innovative Internet-based services. However, until recently, voice over Internet protocol services were banned in many developing countries (Touré 2007). In 2007, 36 African countries prohibited or allowed only monopoly incumbents to use such services, while seven countries (Algeria, Kenya, Mauritius, Somalia, South Africa, Tanzania, and Uganda) had legalized these services. In Egypt, voice over Internet protocol services are allowed only for business-to-business applications (El Shenawi and Lanvin 2009).

Policy makers in countries with particularly high broadband prices and low connectivity capacity should investigate local market conditions and assess whether capacity and prices are a result of the regulatory environment or the anticompetitive behavior of local providers. If necessary, they should then take action to improve competition or modify the rules and regulations that cover telecommunications and Internet broadband providers and thereby stimulate private investment. Policy makers in landlocked countries and countries that are far from the global arteries of fiber-optic cables should seek to work together with neighboring countries and connect to optical networks. For example, landlocked Bhutan and Nepal both enjoy relatively low prices thanks to their agreements with neighboring China and India. In contrast, the Lao People's Democratic Republic has a broadband price that is more than 1,500 percent higher than the price across the border in Vietnam. Developing-country policy makers can target international donors and investors in seeking to cofinance links to international fiber-optic networks, given the potential benefits from cost-effective Internet connectivity.

#### Providing a conducive infrastructure and business environment in high-technology parks

The poor supply of electricity, telecommunications-Internet broadband, and real estate services and weaknesses in the local business environment resulting from particularly burdensome regulation and government administration are common issues that entrepreneurs in many developing countries must deal with. To attract greenfield investment from foreign IT service companies, several developing countries have sought to overcome these constraints through software and high-technology parks. In the parks, export-oriented entrepreneurs enjoy dedicated infrastructure and streamlined administration for a fee. In China, the parks are referred to as software parks; in Egypt, the local IT sector increasingly operates in parks that are known as smart villages; in India, the parks have been named software technology parks; and, in the Philippines, they are called special economic zones.[8] The parks can be an effective way of pooling resources for investment in a limited area.

The key focus in high-technology parks is service provision. A streamlined interface with public authorities and ready-to-use facilities are the main attractions. IT service companies require reliable electricity and access to high-capacity information and communication technology networks. Many high-technology parks ensure full-time, year-round power generation by hosting their own power generators. They also link up to the global backbone of information and communication technology networks to ensure sufficient bandwidth capacity for clients. In addition, the parks are associated with real estate services and ancillary services such as transportation links, banking, restaurants, and hotel accommodation. Some high-technology parks are large enclaves located next to population centers, as in China, while other parks are located in small, individual office towers within city centers, as in the Philippines. There is no single best solution, and regulatory flexibility can allow real estate agents and park operators to experiment with marketable alternatives. High-technology park administrations are normally privately owned and operated for profit. They may offer expedient, single-window environments for incorporation, licenses, and other regulatory issues, thus allowing new entrants to focus on operations rather than on disentangling red tape and unnecessary bureaucracy.

Some high-technology parks offer fiscal incentives to export-oriented investors, such as time-limited income tax holidays, duty-free importation of capital goods, and grants to train new employees.[9] However, fiscal incentives are seldom necessary to attract investment in the first place, partly because subsidiaries of foreign multinationals operate as not-for-profit cost-recovering centers in these parks. Other types of common incentives include full equity ownership for foreign investors, the facilitated employment of foreign nationals in supervisory and technical positions, and domestic sales allowance equivalents as a share of total sales. The high-technology parks can aid in sheltering the IT service sector in countries that are affected by high levels of criminality and facilitate access to land in countries in which this access is a serious issue.

In addition, the labor legislation in some countries prohibits workers, especially women, from working evenings or on night shifts. This can have a negative effect on IT service companies with clients in different time zones. Work-time restrictions are more of an issue in the IT-enabled service sector, but certain types of IT services need to be provided during the operating hours of clients. Bangladesh and India are two examples of countries that have softened their labor legislation to allow certain companies to operate evening and night shifts, but only to meet the demands of clients in other time zones. By being sensitive to the needs of local and foreign investors, as well as local real estate companies, policy makers can stimulate investment in high-technology parks without committing public funds. Common issues include the opposition of electricity providers against independent power generation by park operators and protracted negotiations about the scope for fiscal incentives. As a rule, policy makers should focus on listening to the needs of the companies and providing flexible solutions and rapid services rather than offering fiscal incentives. If they are provided, fiscal incentives should be time limited and conform to WTO rules. (For an extensive discussion, see Creskoff and Walkenhorst 2009.)

### *Update technical education curricula, encourage students to learn languages, and support private technical colleges*

The IT service sector makes intensive use of engineering talent. Few countries produce enough IT talent to become significant exporters of IT services. There are great differences in terms of human resource endowments, but overall, the number of graduates in IT-related fields is growing rapidly. A career in the IT service sector is increasingly attractive. In South Asia, Sri Lanka produces roughly 3,500 graduates in IT-related fields every year. Bangladesh has 5,500 graduates; Pakistan has 20,000; and India has 350,000 (Dossani 2010).[10] Much of the growth in the number of engineering graduates in South Asia has been generated by the private provision of IT training. For example, in Pakistan, private higher education institutions train 80 percent of the local engineering graduates. The impact of private higher education in engineering science in India is also striking. In 1990, private education had a negligible market share, while, in 2005, more than three-fourths of engineering institutions were privately operated, and 95 percent of the increase in enrollments since 1997 has come from private colleges. Box 7.4 describes a private initiative to train personnel for IT careers.

The biggest challenge is to raise the quality and relevance of technical education. In 2005, the McKinsey Global Institute assessed the quantity and quality of young professionals (graduates with up to seven years of work experience) and their employability in multinationals in 36 developing countries (MGI 2005). Based on interviews and surveys of human resource managers employed by

**Box 7.4:** NIIT: A Private Initiative to Train Personnel for IT Service Careers

Established in 1981, NIIT Limited was originally set up to help India's nascent IT service sector overcome human resource shortages. With revenue exceeding US$2 billion, it has grown to become one of the world's leading private training institutes, offering learning solutions to individuals, companies, and educational institutions. It is active in some 40 countries, including 8 countries in Africa, 8 in the Americas, and 12 in Asia. According to the company's Web site, the company's training solutions in areas such as IT, business process outsourcing, and executive management education have provided computer-based learning to nearly 7.8 million students in over 9,500 schools.

multinationals, the institute found that, while the number of college-educated graduates in developing countries is growing quickly (over 5 percent annually), only a small fraction of the potential job candidates can successfully work in a multinational company. This shortcoming arises because of limited suitability (for example, the quality of the training and language and cultural issues), lack of accessibility (lack of mobility and dispersion of labor supply), and domestic competition for talent. Suitability rates in engineering vary greatly by country. In China and Russia, only 10 percent of the candidates would be suitable to work for a multinational. The corresponding numbers are 13 percent in Brazil, 20 percent in the Philippines, 25 percent in India, 35 percent in Malaysia, and 50 percent in the Czech Republic, Hungary, and Poland.

The IT service sector is entirely dependent on well-trained, technically adept personnel. Mastering the local language in the client country is a precondition in client-related roles and an advantage in other roles. Consequently, countries or regions that prohibit lecturing in foreign languages may, by extension, be removing themselves from the potential locations for the crossborder supply of IT services. The skill requirements in IT services, as in most other export-oriented services, are generally higher than those in manufacturing. A bachelor's of science degree is often the entry requirement for a young individual who seeks a career in the export-oriented IT service sector. Thus, investment in education is of paramount importance. As a high-income industry, private or public-private colleagues can increase access to technical training and, thereby, the supply of labor.

Policy makers in developing countries with capacity constraints in the provision of higher education services can learn from the experiences of private institutes in countries such as India and Pakistan in which the government's role increasingly involves providing effective regulation for quality assurance. Governments can facilitate access to finance for training institutes and students, work with the private sector to ensure the relevance of curricula, and help enhance governance in the education sector. Monitoring results and ensuring transparency are effective means to put positive pressure on training institutions.

### *Reduce barriers to labor circulation*

The global delivery model that has been championed mainly by India's exporters of IT services and, increasingly, by their foreign competitors is based on a combination of crossborder supply (Mode 1) and the temporary movement of natural persons (Mode 4). Rapidly improving global information and communication technology networks have brought down communication costs and spurred innovation in technology, and virtual work environments have allowed a growing number of IT professionals to stay in low-cost sites, such as India (*offshore*), and

**Figure 7.3.** Indian IT Workers in the United Kingdom

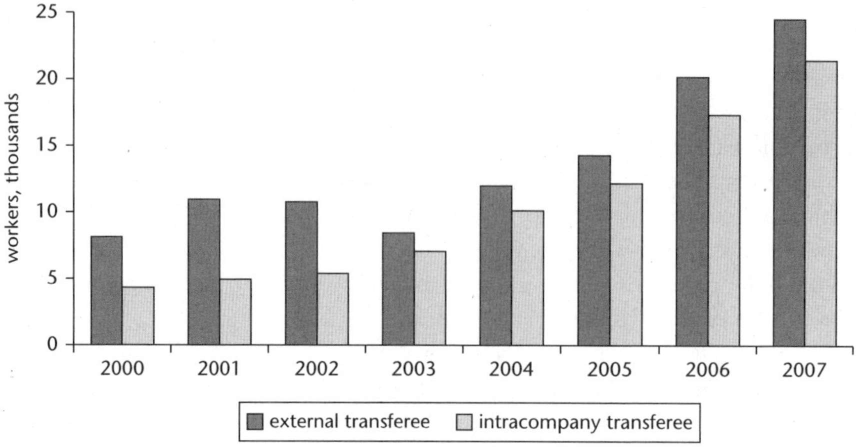


*Source:* U.K. Border Agency, cited in Engman (2009).

collaborate with colleagues at foreign client sites (*onsite*). The Indian professionals at the client site define project requirements, transfer knowledge and information, coordinate and monitor work, implement new software and solutions, train client staff, and provide rapid-reaction maintenance services. Their colleagues in India and elsewhere provide technical and database design, software programming, testing, documentation, and long-term maintenance services. It is a complex process, and the level of sophistication required to manage and execute these projects effectively has acted as an entry barrier to prospective competitors in many developing countries.

The Indian IT service sector exports IT services worth several billion U.S. dollars and annually applies for many thousands of business visas and work permits in core client countries; for example, figure 7.3 illustrates the growing stock of Indian IT workers based temporarily in the United Kingdom. According to the National Association of Software and Services Companies, the United Kingdom imports around one-fifth of Indian IT services (Nasscom 2009).

The process of applying for work permits in foreign markets is often a major impediment. At the heart of the problem is the fact that Mode 4 trade is affected more by immigration and labor market policies than by trade policy. And impediments to Mode 4 trade, by extension, reduce Mode 1 trade, given their complementary relationship. The regulatory restrictions and issues affecting Mode 4 trade in IT services can be divided into three distinctive groups, as follows:

- *Quantitative restrictions and prohibitions* include work permit quotas and economic needs test requirements.

- *Work permit and visa regulations* cover the criteria that a work permit applicant and the sending company must fulfill and the rules and regulations to which the work permit applicant must conform in the host country. These can, for example, include rules that limit mobility within countries and between clients, limitations on the duration of stay, minimum-wage parity requirements, biases against junior professionals, and minimum time of employment.
- *Consular and visa processing services* cover issues that a service provider faces at the consulate or public authority of the host country. The issues are mainly related to the capacity, transparency, professionalism, and efficiency of the consulates or public authorities offering business and work visa services.

Two types of restrictions have particularly negative effects on exports of IT services: (1) numerical limitations on work permits and (2) opaque, time-consuming, and cumbersome processing services for work permits. A work permit quota is applied in the United States to provide a ceiling on the number of external transferees (specialty occupations with H-1B permits) that are allowed to deliver services in the country. The quota acts as an absolute barrier to Mode 4 trade if demand exceeds supply. It introduces complexity and risk in the decision-making processes of companies with regard to human resource allocations. The random outcome of the U.S. quota allocation process—it currently organizes a lottery if demand exceeds supply—has serious productivity implications and impedes foreign IT service professionals from delivering their services to U.S. clients.

Slow, burdensome, and opaque consular services are, in most countries, a serious impediment to Mode 4 exports. They are also a source of frustration and sense of injustice. Small and medium-size enterprises without front-end operations in their client countries are particularly vulnerable. Companies are unable to allocate resources effectively if personnel are enmeshed in lengthy application processes. Arbitrary rejections are common. These issues lower labor productivity. If an exporter operates on a fixed-cost contract, the client may obtain services of lower quality. Another potential outcome is delays in service delivery. Slow and unpredictable visa-processing services cause damage such as lost business opportunities and strained client relations if project contracts and schedules need to be renegotiated.

In the case of many countries of the Organisation for Economic Co-operation and Development, Indian professionals go through an application process that takes four to six months. At some European consulates, the process can take up to nine months. Some countries require that documents be translated and notarized. Requirements also tend to change frequently, which makes it more difficult to plan work. But some countries have managed to handle the application process well. The process to obtain a U.K. work permit is widely considered rapid, transparent, fair, and efficient. Consular services tend to improve with time as trust is built between the companies and the consulate or visa-processing authority.

Economic needs tests are another common form of regulation affecting companies that seek to recruit foreign workers. The objective of an economic needs test is normally to restrict market access to foreign suppliers of services based on an assessment of the necessity of allowing entry into the host market. The test can be applied on an individual, case-by-case basis or on a more aggregate sectoral or occupational basis. There is no clear definition of an economic needs test; it may involve a requirement that the employer undertake a prior adequate search, a labor market test, a management needs test, human resource planning requirements, and so on (see UNCTAD 1999, Chanda 2005). Common complaints are that the tests are opaque and discretionary, which means that foreign companies face difficulties in planning the allocation of personnel.

Mode 4 trade liberalization has proven to be a complex and unsuccessful undertaking in most countries. There is only scope to facilitate Mode 4 trade if there is a political commitment to reform the process. Too often, political leaders ignore the constraints and, by extension, the possibilities of tapping into the associated gains from trade. The most obvious way to address this issue would be to streamline the application process and ensure that the rules with which applicants must comply are transparent and fair. A more expedient and predictable consular service would reduce information and transaction costs for all workers who need to move abroad for project-based assignments. The IT service sector would be one of the greatest beneficiaries. Such a reform would allow the IT service sector to allocate human resources more effectively. The client would gain from a more productive and predictable relationship with the supplier. The application process and all associated work permit rules should be made available on the Internet in an international language and with explanations and timely updates.

A streamlined process would cut out unproductive steps in the application process, while ensuring national security, and allow consular and visa-processing staff to focus on areas in which they add value. It would remove noncritical documentation requirements, including birth certificates (in cases where these are uncommon and passports have the same function), the collection and retention of payslips for many years, and the issuance of legally certified translations of all but the most critical documents. It would speed up operations and thereby increase the competitiveness of companies, particularly in developing countries.

While multilateral negotiations at the WTO have achieved only limited commitments, policy makers are increasingly turning to bilateral negotiations. Middle-income and high-income countries with relatively small populations, such as Chile and Singapore, have, through their preferential trade agreements, obtained concessions with regards to the U.S. H-1B work permit quotas. While the WTO and its multilateral GATS negotiations tend to be prolonged, they do offer an opportunity for developing countries to achieve Mode 4 market access commitments in return for market access commitments at home. Some of the current requests for Mode 4 market access include the removal of economic needs tests, numerical quotas on work permits, and wage parity requirements; enhanced transparency of Mode 4 commitments; and special provisions to facilitate the renewal of temporary work permits (see WTO 2005).

### *Establish a professional private industry association to promote the sector*

The international market for IT services is highly contested. Leading IT service multinationals from high-income countries, including Accenture, CapGemini, Deloitte, HP, IBM, and LogicaCGM, increasingly compete for business with predominantly Indian multinationals such as Infosys, TCS, and Wipro. There is also a host of companies headquartered in high-income countries with most of their human resources based in low-income countries, such as Cognizant, Lancesoft, and Syntel. In addition, a number of IT service companies in various emerging markets are starting to reach a respectable size, including China's Neusoft, Israel's Ness Technologies, and Russia's Luxoft. For companies in developing countries that have yet to establish themselves as international IT service providers, increased visibility and trust are key ingredients in raising interest and awareness and in attracting investment and business. An industry association can play a key role in this process by providing essential services such as the following:

- *Collecting and disseminating information about the sector* to increase transparency and provide vital market intelligence for media, prospective computer engineers, job seekers, local and foreign companies, and prospective clients
- *Organizing international trade fairs* to reach out to prospective clients, raise the industry profile, provide networking opportunities, and promote exports
- *Organizing workshops* to educate members and foster operational excellence
- *Promoting the use of professional certificates for IT staff* to raise quality standards and awareness among the professionals in the industry and make the staffs more attractive for prospective greenfield investments by leading foreign IT service companies
- *Promoting the use of international quality standards in project management* to aim for operational excellence and present objective benchmark indicators to foreign clients, who may doubt the maturity of the local industry. Software Engineering Institute–Capability Maturity Model Integration certification and International Organization for Standardization certification for data privacy and security are common yardsticks
- *Initiating public-private partnerships to promote improvements in technical training* to raise the quality and quantity of graduates with computer skills,

particularly in countries where recent graduates need to become better equipped to use modern technology effectively
- *Facilitating information exchange between the government and the private sector* in that the industry association should ideally be the counterpart that the government can consult on a regular basis to identify priorities on the policy agenda

India's National Association of Software and Services Companies is arguably the IT service sector's most successful industry association. It is a slim and professionally managed nonprofit organization that represents approximately 1,300 member companies (95 percent of the industry's revenue). It has flourished thanks to its leadership. The association enjoys broad support, and its executive council and team host top leaders from the industry's most influential companies. Several developing countries have sought to follow in the footsteps of this Indian association and develop a professional and well-supported association to raise the status and standards in the sector. For example, the national Ghana Association of Software and IT Services Companies has 50 members, and the Brazilian Association of Information Technology and Communication Companies, which is Brazil's equivalent software organization, covers 65 percent of the industry in terms of revenue.

The establishment of industry associations presents a number of challenges. First, a frequent problem is that several small rival associations compete for members, and the private IT service sector ends up without a leading voice or coherent message. This has previously been the case in, for example, the Philippines, although the Philippine Software Industry Association, under the umbrella organization, the Business Processing Association of the Philippines, now claims to have more than 110 members, ranging from multinationals to local small and medium-size enterprises that make up around 90 percent of the country's software sector. Second, in several countries, industry associations have been dependent on a single individual or a small team of enthusiasts that eventually discontinues operations because of a lack of funding or because of career changes, new priorities, and so on. Third, in some countries with authoritarian political systems, independent industry associations may be banned. For example, China does not allow an independent industry association to be formed in the IT service sector.

To be successful, an industry association should seek a balance among the members on its board. Foreign executives can bring necessary expertise and outside perspectives, but may only stay for limited periods and have less interest in promoting policies that lead to heightened competition for scarce local talent. Less senior members may have more time free for board meetings and outreach events, but carry less weight in promoting an agenda among political counterparts and stakeholders. A local industry association can be particularly potent if it has a mandate to promote an agenda that enjoys broad industry support, consists of a balanced board of senior managers, and is independently and professionally managed based on a long-term vision. Policy makers can help initiate the establishment of an industry association, facilitate international information exchange, and provide finance or collaboration between the country's export and investment promotion agencies, if they exist, and the local industry association.

### *Promote professional certificates and quality standards and protect data privacy and intellectual property rights*

Clients based in countries of the Organisation for Economic Co-operation and Development who look for partners in developing countries often have limited access to market intelligence about the maturity of local IT service companies and the quality of local IT professionals. They are also likely to be concerned about the record on intellectual property rights and protection in prospective client countries. To counteract these information asymmetries and build trust with prospective partners, IT service companies can raise their recognition internationally by promoting the use of professional certificates, conforming to international quality standards, and ensuring that they respect intellectual property rights and data privacy and security legislation. While the decision to adopt quality recognition certifications is taken on the firm level, there may be scope for policy makers to facilitate outreach events that disseminate information about the use of international certificates and standards. Policy makers are also responsible for enacting and enforcing legislation on intellectual property rights, as well as data privacy and security.

A company that seeks to source IT services from abroad may choose to establish a subsidiary to maintain full control of its work. Joint ventures and build-operate-transfer models are other sourcing strategies that offer a certain degree of control, although they are less commonly adopted. Yet, for local homegrown companies that are competing for foreign business, the use of quality recognition or professional certificates such as the Capability Maturity Model Integration certification from the Software Engineering Institute at Carnegie Mellon is not only a quality enhancement tool for operations, but also an important signaling device to prospective clients. The certification is neither inexpensive nor easy to obtain and caters mainly to medium and large companies. However, it is a quality mark that is frequently used for sales and marketing purposes. Many larger clients of IT services prefer to do business with suppliers that have obtained a Software Engineering Institute–Capability Maturity Model Integration certificate of at least a midlevel ranking. There are currently a large number of companies in developing countries that have obtained the top-level ranking.[11]

Data privacy and security concerns are related to the risk of data being lost, accessed by external parties, or misused by companies processing the information. Advanced technical solutions have been developed to address some of these IT security issues. Corporate procedures and ethics are paramount to ensure data privacy.[12] Leading IT service companies make the issue of data privacy and security a key priority since it is generally a requirement to attract foreign clients in the first place. A survey by Booz Allen Hamilton (2006) finds that information security is one of the three most important factors for U.S. companies in selecting an outsourcing partner. The survey also indicates that concerns about information security are related to the lack of trust in legal and regulatory environments. A country with a trusted legal and regulatory framework for data privacy and security issues may thus have a comparative advantage relative to other emerging markets.

In conjunction with legislation, there are several types of standards and guidelines that companies can adopt and conform to, including International Organization for Standardization–International Electrotechnical Commission 15504 (software process improvement and capability determination), International Organization for Standardization 17799 (for best practices in information security), International Organization for Standardization 27001 (for information security management systems), and COBIT (control objectives for business and related technology). However, the combined efforts to ensure high standards in the supply of IT services do not come cheap. Thus, Pai and Basu (2005) cite estimates in a TowerGroup study that show the costs of effective international outsourcing increasing by 7–9 percent in IT services for efforts to ensure due diligence and 3–5 percent for efforts at good risk management.

Despite the investment of service suppliers in robust systems, there is some fear that future legislation could erect barriers to crossborder supply. As a precaution against potential protectionism, more than 300 Indian IT-enabled service companies and IT service companies have established subsidiaries in Singapore, where they would be able to route data in case India were to be burdened by trade restricting legislation (Aron 2005). To counteract misuse during data handling, policy makers can establish a penal code for companies or individuals breaching the rules on data privacy. Equally important is the establishment of a penal code that protects intellectual property rights and the undertaking of initiatives to combat software piracy. Proper law enforcement is equally important for those countries that have enacted legislation.

## What Issues Warrant the Attention of Stakeholders?

The preceding discussion touches on a number of issues that merit the attention of policy makers as they advance the trade integration agenda for IT services. Table 7.4 shows a checklist of questions that might help structure the reflections and ensure a comprehensive approach to the removal of binding constraints and

**Table 7.4.** A Checklist of IT Service Questions for Policy Makers

**Improving the quality and quantity of the engineering talent pool**

1. Are fresh engineering and computer science graduates adequately trained? If not, where is the education failing? Are technical curricula up to date and in line with the demands of the IT service sector? What can be done to raise educational standards and the relevance of training? Are there any unnecessary restrictions or high tariffs associated with imports of technical and computer literature? Does the government have the capacity to enforce regulations for quality assurance?
2. Is the local education system producing enough computer science engineers to meet demand? If not, are there barriers to the private provision of training services in the IT field? If there are barriers, do they fulfill a prioritized objective? Do the barriers discriminate against foreign providers of training and technical education? If so, to what purpose? Is there scope for reforming these rules?
3. Are fresh graduates trained in international languages? Are there rules that prohibit or discourage teaching in international languages? If so, what are the objectives of such prohibitions, and can the same goals be reached while still allowing increased flexibility?
4. Are postgraduate courses offered in computer science and related engineering fields? If not, is there scope for initiating collaboration with the private sector to finance and design such programs and also help sponsor students?
5. Are there any particular barriers against women students of computer science and engineering or are there issues that reduce the desire of such women to join the industry? If so, what are they and how can they be removed?

**Addressing weaknesses in Internet connectivity and associated telecommunication regulation**

1. How do local broadband connectivity, reliability, and prices compare with these areas in other countries in the region and the world? Are there any local rules and regulations that hold back investment in network capacity?
2. Are high prices a result of a lack of competition? If so, what anticompetitive action can the government undertake to liberalize the market and increase investment?
3. Are there barriers to market access for foreign providers of Internet services and telecommunications services? If so, what purpose do they have? Can foreign providers provide the necessary investment and competition to improve connectivity and capacity?
4. Are tariffs imposed on the importation of the physical equipment for Internet connectivity? If so, to what extent are the tariffs likely to raise prices and reduce investment in broadband infrastructure?
5. Is the country's connectivity dependent on a single-source cable? If so, would more points of connection raise reliability and network capacity? Could negotiations with neighboring countries help address some of the capacity issues?
6. Are consumers prohibited from using voice over Internet protocol services? If so, does the prohibition serve a meaningful purpose? Who benefits from the restriction, and can negotiations reform the current framework?

**Facilitating the commercial presence of foreign IT service providers**

1. Are there legal restrictions to market entry through commercial presence for foreign companies?

(*Table continues on the following pages.*)

**Table 7.4.** A Checklist of IT Service Questions for Policy Makers (*continued*)

2. If so, what type of restrictions exist and what purpose do they serve? What is their impact on foreign direct investment? Can the policy rationale of restrictions be addressed through other, less-trade-restrictive means? Can full ownership of local subsidiaries be allowed in high-technology parks for export-oriented activities?
3. Are foreign suppliers required to establish locally through a particular legal form? If so, which one(s)? Are restrictions to commercial presence compliant with the country's prospective WTO commitments?
4. Is the local IT service sector controlled by public ownership? Do these links give rise to market distortions at home and hold back expansion abroad? If so, what is the strategic value if the government maintains a stake in the IT service sector?

**Facilitating the temporary movement of IT professionals**

1. What type of restrictions affect labor migration in client countries? Do major export markets impose quotas, economic needs tests, or other impediments to the movement of project staff?
2. Do local consulates of foreign countries provide expedient, fair, and streamlined application procedures for business visas and work permits? If not, what is the scope for local policy makers to approach these consulates to build trust and seek facilitated procedures?
3. What concerns do foreign consulates have, and what can policy makers and local IT service companies do to address these concerns? Do the country's IT service professionals have a poor record in obeying work permit rules in client countries? If so, what can policy makers do to make the IT service sector improve the record in this area?
4. At home, is the application process for business visas and work permits administered in a reasonably expedient and cost-effective way? Or is it opaque, slow, and cumbersome? What can be done to improve administrative efficiency in the local application process?
5. Are there restrictions or other problem issues related to the nonrecognition of qualifications for IT workers at home or in major export markets?
6. Can temporary movement be facilitated through bilateral, regional, or multilateral negotiations? Does the country have a clear vision of what it wants to obtain in the GATS negotiations? How does it communicate this vision?

**Other issues that can impede or stimulate trade**

1. What is the situation in the overall business environment and investment climate in the country? What effort has the government taken to remove binding constraints and ease the regulatory footprint on businesses? If infrastructure is underdeveloped and improvements in the local business environment are elusive, would private sector investment in a software and high-technology park be a solution? Is there demand for such a park? If so, are there rules or regulations that have impeded the related investments?
2. Does the country have an information technology law that protects the privacy of data and an intellectual property law that protects IT service companies from software piracy? If so, how are these laws enforced? If not, would prospective increases in the IT service trade warrant the effort to enact such laws? Would other sectors and citizens benefit from such laws?
3. Are taxes, tariffs, and customs fees on IT equipment high? If so, what impact do they have on the development of a local IT service sector and the development of the local use of IT? Can the revenue from such products be obtained in a less-growth-impeding manner?

4. Does the country's power sector generate sufficient electricity? If not, are companies allowed to establish their own power generation capacity? What are the import duties on the associated equipment?
5. Do local labor regulations impede IT professionals from working at odd hours? If so, what purposes do these regulations serve, and can the concerns be addressed in a more flexible way?
6. Does the country have taxation agreements with prospective client countries that avoid double taxation? If not, in which countries would such agreements make the most sense?
7. Does a local professional industry association promote the local IT service sector abroad and act as interlocutor with the government? If not, is there demand for one and could local policy makers help initiate one?

*Source:* Authors' compilation.

the promotion of trade. Most of these public interventions to promote the IT service sector are essentially no-regrets initiatives that carry little risk (for a discussion, see Dongier and Sudan 2009).

## Conclusion

Trade in IT services is a fairly modest activity in most developing countries. Several countries are enjoying the gains from trade in IT-enabled services, but only a handful of countries, including China, India, and Israel, have developed a sizable, export-oriented IT service sector. The international market for IT services is nevertheless increasingly contested by companies based in developing countries, and there are many reasons why these countries are gaining market share. Essential supply-side requirements in the IT service sector match factor endowments in many developing countries. Widespread connectivity to international information and communication technology networks enables IT service entrepreneurs to compete for business independently of location. A dynamic domestic market, while helpful, is not a prerequisite for success: companies with the necessary talent can tap into international markets and grow on the back of foreign demand. In addition, the IT service market consists of numerous subsectors and niche markets, and the trade in IT services is growing rapidly. By 2007, developing countries had captured approximately 14 percent of the global IT service market. Their IT service exports are expected to have doubled and reached US$55 billion in 2010.

The intensive use of IT may result in considerable spillover effects that help raise productivity and business innovation. There are currently few policy-induced trade restrictions affecting the IT service sector, and it is one of the sectors most open to international trade. The potential gains from trade from further trade liberalization are thus relatively limited. The barriers that exist are primarily associated with supply-side constraints. Some of these constraints are natural and caused by the inherently complex task of delivering IT services through electronic supply; others are linked to shortages of human capital. Policy makers can alleviate some of these constraints to help the private sector harness trade opportunities in the IT service sector. Effective strategies are likely to focus on initiatives that help attract private investment from local and foreign investors, reward entrepreneurship by improving the business environment, and raise educational standards.

In countries with weak infrastructure and poor business environments, a common approach is to permit private real estate developers to build software and high-technology parks near population centers with engineering colleges. These parks provide modern office facilities with a guaranteed power supply and Internet broadband connectivity. By nurturing clusters, IT service companies can enjoy economies of scale in procuring input services and overcoming infrastructure bottlenecks. There is no single best solution, and regulatory flexibility can allow park operators to experiment with marketable alternatives. The key focus in the parks is service provision. A streamlined interface to public authorities and ready-to-use facilities are the main attractions. Some high-technology parks offer fiscal incentives to their export-oriented investors, such as time-limited income tax holidays, the duty-free importation of capital goods, and grants for training new employees. However, fiscal incentives are seldom necessary to attract investment in the IT service sector. Essential incentives include full equity ownership for foreign investors and the facilitated employment of foreign nationals in supervisory and technical positions.

Inadequate Internet connectivity is one of the key supply constraints to trade through electronic supply. Data show that many countries, particularly in Africa, are restricted in their participation in the international IT service market because of expensive, unreliable, and low-capacity Internet connectivity. Policy makers in such countries should investigate local market conditions and assess whether poor capacity and high prices may be a result of the regulatory environment or the anticompetitive behavior of local providers. If necessary, they should take action to improve competition or modify the rules and regulations that cover telecommunications and Internet broadband providers and thereby stimulate private investment. Policy makers should also reassess local labor market policies and telecommunications policies, for example, with regard to restrictions on voice over Internet protocol services and night shifts, to ensure that the regulatory environment is conducive to IT service trade.

The greatest challenge in most developing countries revolves around raising the quality and relevance of technical education. India and Pakistan are two countries in which private colleagues have played a significant role in increasing access to technical training and thereby expanded the supply of labor for the IT service sector. In the education of IT professionals, the responsibility of these governments is increasingly associated with providing effective regulation to guarantee quality. Mastering the local language in the client country is a necessary precondition in client-related roles and an advantage in other roles. Consequently, countries or regions that prohibit teaching in international languages may remove the country or region from the list of potential locations for the crossborder supply of IT services.

In addition, there are several impediments to labor migration. The global delivery model that is increasingly used to deliver IT services to foreign markets is based on a combination of crossborder supply and the temporary movement of natural persons. The process of securing business visas and work permits for project managers in foreign markets has become a major impediment to trade in some countries. Quantitative restrictions and prohibitions, the restrictive regulation of work permit holders, and slow, opaque, and burdensome consular and visa-processing services are the main concerns that policy makers should address in their efforts to facilitate trade. Policy makers can also help kick-start an industry association that disseminates information, promotes the industry at home and abroad, and works to raise operational standards. The promotion of professional certificates and international quality standards and the enactment and enforcement of legislation protecting data privacy and intellectual property rights are other areas in which policy makers can play a constructive role in attracting investment and promoting trade.

## Annex 7A. Information and Communication Technology Services and Indicators

**Table 7A.1.** Computer and Related Services: UNCPC Descriptions of the GATS Sectoral Classification List Entries

| W/120[a] | UNCPC | UNCPC description |
|---|---|---|
| Ba | 841 | *Consultancy services related to the installation of computer hardware*: technical assistance services for clients in the installation of computer hardware and computer networks |
| Bb | 842 | *Software implementation services*: all services involving consultancy on and development and implementation of software; software is the sets of instructions required to make computers work and communicate, which may include a number of different programs developed for specific applications (application software) and situations in which the customer may have a choice of ready-made off-the-shelf programs (packaged software), specifically developed programs to meet specific needs (customized software), or a combination of the two; the subcategories are indicated hereafter under 8421–8425 |
| | 8421 | *Systems and software consulting services*: services of a general nature prior to the development of data processing systems and applications; they might be management services, project planning services, and so on |
| | 8422 | *Systems analysis services*: these include analyzing client needs, defining functional specifications, and setting up the team, as well as project management, technical coordination and integration, and the definition of systems architecture |
| | 8423 | *Systems design services*: these include technical solutions with respect to methodology, quality assurance, choice of equipment software packages or new technologies, and so on |
| | 8424 | *Programming services*: the implementation phase, that is, writing and debugging programs, conducting tests, and editing documentation |
| | 8425 | *Systems maintenance services*: consulting and technical assistance services for software products in using, rewriting, or changing existing programs or systems; maintaining up-to-date software documentation and manuals; and specialist work, such as conversions |
| Bc | 843/8431 | *Data processing services*: these are also called input preparation services and include data recording services such as key punching, optical scanning, or other methods for data entry |
| | 8432 | *Data processing and tabulation services*: these consist of services such as data processing and tabulation services, computer calculating services, and rentals of computer time |
| | 8433 | *Time-sharing services*: UNCPC states that there is no clear distinction between 8432 and 8433, noting that computer time only is bought; if it is bought from the customer's premises, telecommunications services are also bought; data processing or tabulation services may also be bought from a service bureau |

| | | |
|---|---|---|
| | 8439 | *Other data processing services*: these consist of services that manage the full operations of customer facilities under contract; they include computer-room environmental quality control services, management services of in-place computer equipment combinations, and management services of computer work flows and distributions |
| Bd | 844 | *Database services*: all services provided from primarily structured databases through a communication network; the UNCPC specifically excludes data and message transmission services, which it classifies under telecommunications services (as 7523), and it excludes documentation retrieval services, which it classifies as library services (as 96311) |
| Be | 849 | *Other computer services*: services for which UNCPC lists two subcategories, which are indicated as 8491 and 8499 |
| | 8491 | *Data preparation services*: services for clients not involving data processing services |
| | 8499 | *Other computer services n.e.c.*: training staff of clients and other professional services[b] |

*Source*: WTO (1998).
*Note*: UNCPC = United Nations Central Product Classification (see UN 1991).
a. W/120 = Services Sectoral Classification List (see WTO 1991).
b. n.e.c. = not elsewhere classified.

**Table 7A.2.** Information and Communication Technology Infrastructure Indicators

| | Use indicators (2007) | | Access indicators (2007) | | | Fixed broadband tariffs residential (2008) | | |
|---|---|---|---|---|---|---|---|---|
| Economy | Internet users per 100 inhabitants | Fixed broadband subscribers per 100 inhabitants | Internet bandwidth per Internet user (bit/s) | Proportion of households with computer (%) | Proportion of households with Internet (%) | Monthly subscribers (US$) | Monthly subscribers (PPP$) | Cap gigabyte |
| Albania | 18.5 | 0.3 | 1,164 | 9.5 | 7.8 | 31.4 | 53.1 | |
| Algeria | 10.3 | 0.9 | 857 | 8.3 | 6.8 | 17.3 | 30.8 | |
| Angola | — | — | — | — | — | 163.6 | 253.6 | |
| Argentina | 25.9 | 6.6 | 8,943 | 36.4 | 27.5 | 38.4 | 76.7 | |
| Armenia | 6.2 | 0.3 | 2,712 | 41.2 | 6.1 | 39.2 | 65.5 | |
| Australia | 69.0 | 23.3 | 8,035 | 73.0 | 64.0 | 27.5 | 21.0 | 12.0 |
| Austria | 67.0 | 19.4 | 30,116 | 71.0 | 60.0 | 60.9 | 46.0 | |
| Azerbaijan | 10.9 | 0.1 | 6,475 | 10.1 | 9.3 | 84.5 | 167.3 | |
| Bahrain | 33.2 | 9.1 | 7,660 | 50.7 | 34.1 | 26.7 | 40.2 | |
| Bangladesh | 0.3 | — | 1,284 | 1.9 | 1.3 | 54.0 | 155.1 | |
| Barbados | — | — | — | — | — | 49.4 | 80.1 | |
| Belarus | 29.0 | 0.9 | 427 | 24.9 | 12.1 | — | — | |
| Belgium | 67.0 | 26.0 | 37,831 | 67.0 | 60.0 | 30.5 | 22.3 | 1.0 |
| Belize | — | — | — | — | — | 89.5 | 146.5 | |
| Benin | 1.7 | — | 1,033 | 8.0 | 3.6 | 104.7 | 204.9 | |
| Bhutan | 4.6 | — | 1,125 | 13.7 | 6.1 | 24.3 | 64.6 | 0.5[a] |
| Bolivia | 10.5 | 0.4 | 398 | 18.0 | 5.9 | 33.5 | 95.3 | |
| Bosnia and Herzegovina | 26.8 | 2.2 | 1,896 | 35.6 | 25.8 | 14.8 | 24.7 | |
| Botswana | 5.3 | 0.2 | 810 | 4.5 | 0.1 | 29.6 | 65.3 | 3.0 |
| Brazil | 35.2 | 3.5 | 2,955 | 20.8 | 15.4 | 47.3 | 56.5 | |

| | | | | | | | | |
|---|---|---|---|---|---|---|---|---|
| Brunei Darussalam | 48.2 | 2.9 | 2,954 | 66.6 | 61.7 | — | — | |
| Bulgaria | 31.0 | 8.2 | 15,878 | 23.3 | 19.0 | 15.6 | 30.6 | |
| Burkina Faso | 0.7 | 0.1 | 2,170 | 3.0 | 1.8 | 1,861.0 | 4,098.5 | |
| Cambodia | 0.5 | 0.1 | 3,571 | 4.1 | 2.4 | 90.6 | 271.8 | 1.0 |
| Cameroon | 3.0 | — | 371 | 10.1 | 5.2 | 183.8 | 314.4 | |
| Canada | 73.0 | 27.6 | 22,250 | 79.1 | 72.1 | 19.8 | 16.5 | 1.0 |
| Cape Verde | 7.0 | 0.4 | 649 | 11.6 | 11.4 | 39.8 | 40.1 | 1.0 |
| Central African Rep. | — | — | — | — | — | 1,395.8 | 2,266.4 | |
| Chad | 0.8 | — | 61 | 2.0 | 0.1 | — | — | |
| Chile | 31.0 | 7.9 | 13,135 | 36.4 | 22.1 | 53.0 | 67.2 | |
| China | 16.0 | 5.0 | 1,735 | 39.1 | 16.4 | 18.5 | 36.8 | |
| Colombia | 26.2 | 2.6 | 3,528 | 27.4 | — | 36.3 | 59.9 | |
| Comoros | 2.6 | — | 317 | 4.3 | 1.0 | 449.8 | 646.4 | |
| Congo, Dem. Rep. | 0.4 | — | 43 | 0.3 | 0.2 | — | — | |
| Congo, Rep. | 2.6 | — | 10 | 5.0 | 1.4 | — | — | |
| Costa Rica | 33.6 | 3.0 | 2,440 | 31.6 | 11.8 | 17.0 | 31.6 | |
| Côte d'Ivoire | 2.3 | 0.4 | 689 | 6.2 | 3.6 | 46.5 | 68.8 | |
| Croatia | 43.6 | 8.5 | 7,553 | 34.7 | 29.5 | 20.9 | 24.8 | |
| Cuba | 11.6 | — | 162 | 2.3 | 1.8 | 1,630.0 | — | |
| Cyprus | 38.0 | 11.7 | 4,218 | 53.0 | 39.0 | 16.5 | 25.5 | |
| Czech Rep. | 49.0 | 12.9 | 14,649 | 43.0 | 35.0 | 28.9 | 33.3 | |
| Denmark | 81.0 | 36.0 | 42,752 | 83.0 | 78.0 | 30.4 | 17.4 | |
| Dominica | — | — | — | — | — | 47.8 | 84.2 | |
| Dominican Rep. | 17.2 | 1.6 | 894 | 12.5 | 5.7 | 28.0 | 50.8 | |
| Ecuador | 13.2 | 2.4 | 2,458 | 18.0 | 6.8 | 39.9 | 89.1 | |

(*Table continues on the following pages.*)

**Table 7A.2.** Information and Communication Technology Infrastructure Indicators (*continued*)

| | Use indicators (2007) | | Access indicators (2007) | | | Fixed broadband tariffs residential (2008) | | |
|---|---|---|---|---|---|---|---|---|
| Economy | Internet users per 100 inhabitants | Fixed broadband subscribers per 100 inhabitants | Internet bandwidth per Internet user (bit/s) | Proportion of households with computer (%) | Proportion of households with Internet (%) | Monthly subscribers (US$) | Monthly subscribers (PPP$) | Cap gigabyte |
| Egypt Arab Rep. | 14.0 | 0.6 | 1,023 | 16.1 | 9.1 | 8.3 | 24.9 | 2.0 |
| El Salvador | 11.1 | 1.3 | 157 | 8.6 | 3.6 | 18.0 | 34.5 | |
| Eritrea | 2.5 | — | 100 | 0.3 | 0.2 | — | — | |
| Estonia | 64.0 | 20.8 | 18,722 | 57.0 | 53.0 | 38.5 | 46.3 | |
| Ethiopia | 0.4 | — | 842 | 0.2 | 0.1 | 644.0 | 2,198.0 | |
| Fiji | 10.9 | 1.4 | 1,379 | 18.2 | 11.5 | 26.1 | 26.4 | 3.0 |
| Finland | 79.0 | 30.6 | 21,847 | 74.0 | 69.0 | 38.0 | 25.2 | |
| France | 64.0 | 25.2 | 46,086 | 62.0 | 49.0 | 38.0 | 27.4 | |
| Gabon | 6.2 | 0.2 | 2,439 | 4.3 | 3.6 | — | — | |
| Gambia, The | 5.9 | — | 618 | 4.0 | 2.0 | 383.8 | 1,051.8 | |
| Georgia | 8.2 | 1.1 | 9,103 | 12.6 | 2.4 | 47.6 | 84.5 | 2.5 |
| Germany | 72.0 | 23.7 | 35,487 | 79.0 | 71.0 | 38.1 | 28.3 | |
| Ghana | 3.8 | 0.1 | 565 | 5.1 | 1.8 | 64.4 | 114.7 | |
| Greece | 33.0 | 9.1 | 13,805 | 40.0 | 25.0 | 25.2 | 23.2 | |
| Grenada | — | — | — | — | — | 29.3 | 43.6 | |
| Guatemala | 13.1 | 0.6 | 1,429 | 13.6 | 1.8 | 34.0 | 61.1 | |
| Guinea | — | — | — | — | — | 800.0 | 1,897.3 | |
| Guinea-Bissau | 2.6 | — | 45 | 3.6 | 1.0 | — | — | |
| Guyana | — | — | — | — | — | 49.5 | 105.2 | |
| Haiti | 10.4 | — | 155 | 4.0 | 1.8 | — | — | |

| | | | | | | | | |
|---|---|---|---|---|---|---|---|---|
| Honduras | 6.0 | — | 4,081 | 10.1 | 3.3 | — | — | |
| Hungary | 52.0 | 14.2 | 9,203 | 54.0 | 38.0 | 24.8 | 29.5 | |
| Iceland | 90.0 | 32.5 | 8,121 | 89.0 | 84.0 | 57.0 | 38.7 | 4.0 |
| India | 6.9 | 0.3 | 441 | 3.7 | 3.0 | 6.1 | 16.4 | 1.0 |
| Indonesia | 5.6 | 0.1 | 923 | 8.1 | 6.9 | 21.7 | 42.5 | 1.0 |
| Iran, Islamic Rep. | 32.3 | 0.1 | 473 | 13.0 | 8.6 | 43.0 | 123.2 | 20.0 |
| Ireland | 57.0 | 18.7 | 27,122 | 65.0 | 57.0 | 38.1 | 25.2 | |
| Israel | 28.9 | 22.1 | 7,190 | 61.6 | 44.7 | — | — | |
| Italy | 38.0 | 18.4 | 27,339 | 53.0 | 43.0 | 25.8 | 19.5 | |
| Jamaica | 55.3 | 3.4 | 34,000 | 17.3 | 12.7 | 30.0 | 52.4 | |
| Japan | 68.9 | 22.1 | 5,415 | 85.0 | 62.1 | 31.6 | 28.0 | |
| Jordan | 19.0 | 1.5 | 831 | 25.1 | 10.5 | 30.9 | 54.7 | 3.0 |
| Kazakhstan | 12.3 | 1.8 | 1,052 | 15.6 | 13.9 | — | — | |
| Kenya | 8.0 | 0.1 | 112 | 5.5 | 2.2 | 167.8 | 318.6 | |
| Korea, Rep. | 76.3 | 30.5 | 1,353 | 80.0 | 94.0 | 20.3 | 26.6 | 2.0 |
| Kuwait | 31.6 | 2.5 | 2,577 | 34.1 | 29.1 | 46.3 | 58.1 | |
| Kyrgyzstan | 14.1 | 0.1 | 796 | 8.6 | 3.6 | — | — | |
| Lao PDR | 1.7 | 0.1 | 1,880 | 6.7 | 1.8 | 268.3 | 772.0 | |
| Latvia | 55.0 | 6.4 | 6,428 | 49.0 | 51.0 | 26.0 | 34.0 | |
| Lebanon | 31.5 | 4.9 | 289 | 40.0 | 38.0 | 23.0 | 39.7 | |
| Lesotho | 3.5 | 0.1 | 171 | 6.8 | 0.9 | 48.9 | 101.5 | |
| Libya | 4.7 | 0.2 | 1,064 | 6.3 | 4.3 | — | — | |
| Lithuania | 49.0 | 15.0 | 9,461 | 46.0 | 40.3 | 15.9 | 22.2 | |
| Luxembourg | 78.0 | 27.5 | 9,617,645 | 80.0 | 75.0 | 44.3 | 31.4 | 2.0 |
| Macedonia, FYR | 27.3 | 4.9 | 61 | 25.0 | 15.5 | 14.7 | 30.2 | |
| Madagascar | 0.6 | — | 1,240 | 12.8 | 1.0 | 120.1 | 262.4 | |
| Malawi | 1.0 | — | 480 | 4.0 | 1.4 | 900.0 | 2,674.3 | |
| Malaysia | 55.7 | 3.8 | 1,791 | 35.9 | 20.0 | 20.5 | 37.7 | |

*(Table continues on the following pages.)*

**Table 7A.2.** Information and Communication Technology Infrastructure Indicators (*continued*)

| | Use indicators (2007) | | Access indicators (2007) | | | Fixed broadband tariffs residential (2008) | | |
|---|---|---|---|---|---|---|---|---|
| Economy | Internet users per 100 inhabitants | Fixed broadband subscribers per 100 inhabitants | Internet bandwidth per Internet user (bit/s) | Proportion of households with computer (%) | Proportion of households with Internet (%) | Monthly subscribers (US$) | Monthly subscribers (PPP$) | Cap gigabyte |
| Maldives | 10.8 | 3.6 | 37,576 | 28.9 | 9.0 | 9.4 | 14.6 | 1.0 |
| Mali | 0.8 | — | 2,130 | 1.0 | 0.5 | 58.2 | 101.6 | |
| Malta | 45.0 | 20.4 | 12,817 | 63.0 | 54.0 | 21.2 | 22.1 | 25.0 |
| Mauritania | 1.4 | 0.2 | 4,889 | 2.0 | 1.0 | 62.4 | 127.1 | |
| Mauritius | 27.0 | 4.9 | 840 | 27.8 | 19.1 | 50.6 | 88.2 | |
| Mexico | 22.4 | 4.3 | 784 | 22.1 | 12.0 | 37.0 | 53.6 | |
| Micronesia, Fed. Sts. | — | — | — | — | — | 40.0 | 52.8 | |
| Moldova | 18.5 | 1.2 | 5,061 | 23.0 | 16.0 | 23.2 | 43.7 | |
| Mongolia | 12.0 | 0.3 | 938 | 12.5 | 7.7 | — | — | |
| Montenegro | — | — | — | — | — | 21.4 | 33.0 | 1.0 |
| Morocco | 21.1 | 1.5 | 3,808 | 17.2 | 7.0 | 20.0 | 31.1 | |
| Mozambique | 0.9 | 0.4 | 360 | 3.8 | 0.9 | 100.1 | 203.8 | 7.0 |
| Myanmar | 0.1 | — | 2,350 | 1.8 | 1.8 | — | — | |
| Namibia | 4.9 | — | 554 | 11.2 | 3.3 | 46.1 | 78.8 | 1.0 |
| Nepal | 1.4 | — | 350 | 2.8 | 1.0 | 22.8 | 60.6 | |
| Netherlands | 84.0 | 33.5 | 92,832 | 86.0 | 83.0 | 38.2 | 28.2 | |
| New Zealand | 70.0 | 20.4 | 6,569 | 75.7 | 65.9 | 30.7 | 25.9 | 3.0 |
| Nicaragua | 3.1 | 0.6 | 4,697 | 7.8 | 3.6 | 30.0 | 79.6 | |
| Niger | 0.4 | — | 2,826 | 1.0 | 0.2 | 58.2 | 111.4 | |
| Nigeria | 6.8 | — | 69 | 5.1 | 3.6 | 690.1 | 1,122.9 | |

| | | | | | | | | |
|---|---|---|---|---|---|---|---|---|
| Norway | 85.0 | 30.6 | 31,726 | 82.0 | 78.0 | 57.0 | 33.5 | |
| Oman | 13.1 | 0.8 | 1,088 | 29.5 | 17.0 | 31.3 | 51.6 | |
| Pakistan | 10.7 | — | 404 | 8.1 | 1.1 | 18.5 | 56.5 | |
| Panama | 22.3 | 4.3 | 71,616 | 16.9 | 8.9 | 15.0 | 28.8 | |
| Papua New Guinea | 1.8 | — | 104 | 3.0 | 2.0 | 19.5 | 35.6 | 0.2[b] |
| Paraguay | 8.7 | 0.8 | 1,886 | 10.4 | 4.0 | 35.0 | 65.7 | |
| Peru | 27.4 | 2.0 | 9,877 | 13.8 | 5.6 | 36.4 | 67.3 | |
| Philippines | 6.0 | 0.6 | 1,887 | 18.3 | 12.3 | 23.4 | 45.0 | |
| Poland | 44.0 | 9.0 | 6,251 | 54.0 | 41.0 | 27.0 | 31.0 | |
| Portugal | 40.0 | 14.4 | 11,960 | 48.3 | 39.6 | 30.2 | 28.4 | |
| Qatar | 41.8 | 8.4 | 6,624 | 34.2 | 33.8 | — | — | |
| Romania | 24.0 | 9.1 | 12,335 | 34.0 | 22.0 | 22.7 | 27.9 | |
| Russian Federation | 21.1 | 2.8 | 2,712 | 16.2 | 9.5 | 13.9 | 21.1 | |
| Rwanda | 2.1 | — | 780 | 0.3 | 0.1 | 91.8 | 231.0 | |
| São Tomé & Principe | — | — | — | — | — | 273.5 | 521.7 | |
| Samoa | — | — | — | — | — | 33.9 | 50.0 | 0.2[c] |
| Saudi Arabia | 25.8 | 2.5 | 1,932 | 43.2 | 35.6 | 39.7 | 57.7 | |
| Senegal | 6.6 | 0.3 | 2,079 | 7.8 | 1.0 | 29.1 | 48.4 | |
| Serbia | — | — | — | — | — | 9.0 | 14.7 | |
| Seychelles | — | — | — | — | — | 50.7 | 114.1 | |
| Singapore | 68.0 | 20.2 | 34,655 | 79.0 | 74.0 | 21.9 | 29.0 | |
| Slovak Republic | 56.0 | 8.8 | 9,932 | 55.0 | 46.0 | 28.5 | 35.0 | 2.0 |
| Slovenia | 53.0 | 17.2 | 12,784 | 66.0 | 58.0 | 27.5 | 27.8 | |
| South Africa | 8.2 | 0.8 | 852 | 14.8 | 4.8 | 26.3 | 47.2 | |
| Spain | 52.0 | 18.2 | 21,456 | 60.4 | 45.0 | 28.8 | 25.4 | 2.0 |
| Sri Lanka | 4.0 | 0.3 | 3,072 | 7.8 | 4.1 | 21.0 | 53.4 | |

(*Table continues on the following pages.*)

**Table 7A.2.** Information and Communication Technology Infrastructure Indicators (*continued*)

| | Use indicators (2007) | | Access indicators (2007) | | | Fixed broadband tariffs residential (2008) | | |
|---|---|---|---|---|---|---|---|---|
| Economy | Internet users per 100 inhabitants | Fixed broadband subscribers per 100 inhabitants | Internet bandwidth per Internet user (bit/s) | Proportion of households with computer (%) | Proportion of households with Internet (%) | Monthly subscribers (US$) | Monthly subscribers (PPP$) | Cap gigabyte |
| St. Lucia | — | — | — | — | — | 55.2 | 96.7 | |
| St. Vincent and the Grenadines | — | — | — | — | — | 55.2 | 92.4 | |
| Sudan | 9.1 | 0.1 | 3,800 | 4.3 | 1.0 | 29.2 | 51.8 | |
| Suriname | — | — | — | — | — | 95.0 | 153.0 | |
| Swaziland | 3.7 | — | 282 | 12.8 | 6.0 | 1,877.5 | 3,854.1 | |
| Sweden | 80.0 | 36.0 | 62,484 | 83.0 | 79.0 | 32.3 | 22.0 | |
| Switzerland | 77.0 | 31.8 | 38,541 | 78.1 | 77.5 | 32.2 | 20.6 | |
| Syrian Arab Republic | 17.4 | — | 304 | 35.0 | 30.0 | 51.3 | 114.3 | |
| Taiwan, China | 64.5 | 20.9 | 12,632 | 67.1 | 61.6 | 10.3 | 17.6 | |
| Tajikistan | 7.2 | — | 516 | 1.0 | 0.1 | — | — | |
| Tanzania | 1.0 | — | 250 | 2.3 | 0.6 | 68.0 | 194.1 | 1.0 |
| Thailand | 21.0 | 1.4 | 1,645 | 27.2 | 7.3 | 18.0 | 36.1 | |
| Togo | 5.2 | — | 84 | 3.5 | 1.0 | 105.9 | 202.6 | |
| Tonga | — | — | — | — | — | 109.8 | 157.3 | |
| Trinidad and Tobago | 16.0 | 2.7 | 4,229 | 43.6 | 18.1 | 12.7 | 19.6 | |
| Tunisia | 16.7 | 1.1 | 1,800 | 9.6 | 2.9 | 12.7 | 25.7 | |
| Turkey | 16.2 | 6.1 | 8,390 | 28.5 | 18.9 | — | — | |
| Turkmenistan | 1.4 | — | 3,414 | 1.0 | 0.5 | — | — | |

| | | | | | | | |
|---|---|---|---|---|---|---|---|
| Uganda | 3.6 | — | 306 | 5.1 | — | 170.0 | 412.9 |
| Ukraine | 21.6 | 1.7 | 956 | 16.2 | 6.8 | 20.8 | 45.2 |
| United Arab Emirates | 51.6 | 8.7 | 5,380 | 43.3 | 40.4 | 21.5 | 32.4 |
| United Kingdom | 72.0 | 25.7 | 55,281 | 75.0 | 67.0 | 29.5 | 22.5 |
| United States | 72.5 | 24.0 | 15,341 | 70.2 | 61.7 | 15.0 | 15.0 |
| Uruguay | 29.0 | 4.9 | 3,102 | 27.0 | 13.5 | 24.3 | 33.7 |
| Uzbekistan | 4.4 | — | 199 | 2.4 | 0.8 | — | — |
| Vanuatu | — | — | — | — | — | 450.0 | 787.2 |
| Venezuela, R.B. de | 20.7 | 3.1 | 3,016 | 11.9 | 3.0 | 31.3 | 45.8 |
| Viet Nam | 20.5 | 1.5 | 704 | 10.1 | 5.0 | 17.0 | 53.2 |
| West Bank and Gaza | 9.5 | 1.5 | 3,376 | 32.5 | 15.9 | — | — |
| Yemen, Rep. | 1.4 | — | 1,969 | 2.6 | 2.0 | 225.7 | 525.1 |
| Zambia | 4.2 | 0.1 | 74 | 4.3 | 1.8 | 91.5 | 116.1 |
| Zimbabwe | 10.1 | 0.1 | 42 | 7.8 | 1.8 | — | — |

*Source:* ITU (2009).
*Note:* PPP$ = U.S. dollars at purchasing power parity. — = not available.
a. Additional gigabyte = US$72.80.
b. Additional gigabyte = US$156.
c. Additional gigabyte = US$169.

## Notes

1. A generic definition of IT services is provided in Gartner (2004), which states that IT services refer to the application of business and technical expertise to enable organizations in the creation, management, optimization of or access to information and business processes. The Services Sectoral Classification List of the General Agreement on Trade in Services (GATS) includes computer services as a subsector (designated 1B) of business and professional services (see WTO 1991). The subsector covers five subcategories: consultancy services related to the installation of computer hardware, software implementation services, data processing services, database services, and other. The subcategories, which are outlined in annex table 7A.1, are defined in greater detail in the corresponding items of the Provisional Central Product Classification (UN 1991). According to this classification, software implementation services include systems and software consulting services, systems analysis services, systems design services, programming services, and systems maintenance services. Most IT service exports from developing countries fall under the software implementation services item.

2. The reader should thus interpret the trade data presented here with caution and as rough estimates, given the differences in definitions and in coverage across the available data sources. The information is often collected from industry associations or through targeted surveys. For the balance of payments statistics of the International Monetary Fund, see http://www.imf.org/external/np/sta/bop/bop.htm.

3. The GATS recognizes four modes of service delivery. Mode 1 refers to crossborder supply, Mode 2 to consumption abroad, Mode 3 to commercial presence, and Mode 4 to the temporary movement of natural persons.

4. See also McKinsey's locational readiness index, Hewitt's international benchmarking model, and Gartner's 10 criteria. The common approach is to rank countries based on a number of variables, including the price, quality, and accessibility of necessary inputs such as labor and capital. International benchmarking exercises are subject to criticism, and this may be their main strength: many industry representatives and policy makers care passionately about their relative ranking and strive to improve their results. In general, simplicity is inversely related to objectivity, and results should be interpreted with caution. For example, movements in foreign exchange rates can have a strong impact on measures of cost and therefore lead to significant shifts in relative rankings from year to year.

5. Satellite connections exist, but are not cost-effective options for IT service exporters.

6. The OECD average is highly inflated because of Luxembourg, while the South Asia average is highly inflated because of the Maldives.

7. See http://go.worldbank.org/GKHOFFDJB0.

8. See http://www.stpi.in/, http://www.peza.gov.ph/, and http://www.smart-villages.com/docs/front.aspx.

9. The plurilateral Information Technology Agreement of the WTO covers 97 percent of the trade in IT products and has reduced the attraction of duty-free imports of IT products in the 72 countries and customs territories in which duties on IT equipment have been reduced to zero. See http://www.wto.org/english/tratop_E/inftec_e/inftec_e.htm.

10. IT-related fields include computer science, computer engineering, electrical engineering, electronics engineering, communications, and IT.

11. See http://sas.sei.cmu.edu/pars/pars.aspx for published appraisal results by company name.

12. OECD (2006) provides a more extensive overview of data security and privacy issues.

## References

Aron, Ravi. 2005. "Move Over, India: The Shifting Geography of Offshore Outsourcing Creates New Challengers." *India Knowledge@Wharton*, January 14, Wharton School, University of Pennsylvania, Philadelphia. http://knowledge.wharton.upenn.edu/india/article.cfm?articleid=4035.

A. T. Kearney. 2007. "Offshoring for Long-Term Advantage: The 2007 A.T. Kearney Global Services Location Index." A.T. Kearney, Inc., Chicago.

Booz Allen Hamilton. 2006. "Information Security Risk a Top Concern among Outsourcing Executives." Report, March 23, Booz Allen Hamilton, McLean, VA.

Chanda, Rupa. 2005. "Trade in Services and South Asia: An Aggressive Agenda." In *South Asian Yearbook of Trade and Development 2005: Mainstreaming Development in Trade Negotiations; Run Up to Hong Kong*, ed. Centre for Trade and Development, 105–208. New Delhi: Centre for Trade and Development.

Creskoff, Stephen, and Peter Walkenhorst. 2009. "Implications of WTO Disciplines for Special Economic Zones in Developing Countries." Policy Research Working Paper 4892, World Bank, Washington, DC.

CyberMedia, CBC (Commonwealth Business Council), and Global Services. 2009. "Outsourcing to Africa: A Relative Ranking of 15 Country Locations." Report, CyberMedia, Gurgaon, India.

Dongier, Philippe, and Randeep Sudan. 2009. "Realizing the Opportunities Presented by the Global Trade in IT-Based Services." In *Information and Communications for Development 2009: Extending Reach and Increasing Impact*, ed. World Bank, 103–24. Washington, DC: World Bank.

Dossani, Rafiq. 2010. "Software Production: Globalization and Its Implications for South Asia." In *The Service Revolution in South Asia*, ed. Ejaz Ghani, chap. 4. New York: Oxford University Press.

El Shenawi, Nagwa, and Bruno Lanvin. 2009. "How Outsourcing Can Help Mobilize Talents Globally: Egypt's Success Story." In *The Global Information Technology Report 2008–2009: Mobility in a Networked World*, ed. Soumitra Dutta and Irene Mia, 113–22. Geneva: World Economic Forum.

Engman, Michael. 2007. "Expanding International Supply Chains: The Role of Emerging Economies in Providing IT and Business Process Services." OECD Trade Policy Working Paper 52, Organisation for Economic Co-operation and Development, Paris.

———. 2009. "Circular Labour Migration and Offshoring of IT Services: The Case of India." Working Paper (September), Groupe d'Economie Mondial, Sciences Po, Paris.

Feenstra, R. C., and G. H. Hanson. 1996. "Globalization, Outsourcing, and Wage Inequality." *American Economic Review Papers and Proceedings* 86 (2): 240–45.

Fink, Carsten, Aaditya Mattoo, and Randeep Rathindran. 2003. "An Assessment of Telecommunications Reform in Developing Countries." *Information Economics and Policy* 15 (4): 443–66.

Ganguly, Debjani. 2005. "Barriers to Movement of Natural Persons: A Study of Federal, State and Sector-Specific Restrictions to Mode 4 in the United States of America." ICRIER Working Paper 169 (September), Indian Council for Research on International Economic Relations, New Delhi.

Gartner. 2004. "Worldwide IT Services Market Definitions Guide, 3Q03." Gartner Dataquest Guide 13 (January), Gartner, Inc., Stamford, CT.

Gott, Johan. 2008. "The Advantage of Egypt as a Location for Offshore Services." Presentation, Information Technology Industry Development Agency, Giza, Egypt.

ITU (International Telecommunication Union). 2007. "Telecommunication/ICT Markets and Trends in Africa." Report, ITU, Geneva.

———. 2009. *Measuring the Information Society: The ICT Development Index 2009*. Geneva: ITU.

Kirkegaard, Jacob Funk. 2008. "Distance Isn't Quite Dead: Recent Trade Patterns and Modes of Supply in Computer and Information Services in the United States and NAFTA Partners." Working Paper 08–10, Peterson Institute for International Economics, Washington, DC.

Marson, Tony, and Mindy Blodgett. 2007. "Is the Future Bright for Outsourcing IT Services to Egypt?" Yankee Group Report, May, Yankee Group, Boston.

Meyer, Thomas. 2009. "Offshoring to China: From Workbench to Back Office?" *Economics* 68 (January 13), Deutsche Bank Research, Frankfurt.

MGI (McKinsey Global Institute). 2005. *The Supply of Offshore Talent in Services*. Part II of *The Emerging Global Labor Market*. San Francisco: McKinsey & Company.

MIGA (Multilateral Investment Guarantee Agency). 2006. "The Impact of Intel in Costa Rica: Nine Years after the Decision to Invest." Investing in Development Series, MIGA, World Bank, Washington, DC.

Nasscom (National Association of Software and Services Companies). 2009. "Indian IT-BPO Industry 2009: NASSCOM Analysis." Indian IT-BPO Industry Factsheet, February, Nasscom, New Delhi. http://nasscom.in/upload/5216/IT_Industry_Factsheet-Mar_2009.pdf.

OECD (Organisation for Economic Co-operation and Development). 2006. *OECD Information Technology Outlook 2006*. Paris: OECD.

———. 2008. *OECD Information Technology Outlook 2008*. Paris: OECD.

Pai, Arjun K., and Subhajit Basu. 2005. "Offshore Outsourcing: Weighing the Risks of Data Protection and Security." Paper presented at the "20th Annual British and Irish Legal Education and Technology Conference," Queen's University, Belfast, April 6–7.

Touré, Hamadoun I. 2007. "Competitiveness and Information and Communication Technologies (ICTs) in Africa." In *The Africa Competitiveness Report 2007*, ed. World Economic Forum, 87–109. Geneva: World Economic Forum.

UN (United Nations). 1991. "Provisional Central Product Classification (Provisional CPC)." Document ST/ESA/STAT/SER.M/77, Economic Statistics and Classifications Section, Statistics Division, Department of Economic and Social Affairs, United Nations, New York. http://unstats.un.org/unsd/class/family/family2.asp?Cl=9.

UNCTAD (United Nations Conference on Trade and Development). 1999. "Lists of Economic Needs Tests in the GATS Schedules of Specific Commitments." Document UNCTAD/ITCD/TSB/8 (September 6), UNCTAD, Geneva.

———. 2004. "ICT as an Enabler for Growth, Development, and Competitiveness: Implications for National and International Policies and Actions." Interactive Thematic Session at the UNCTAD XI Conference, São Paulo, June 13–18. http://www.unctadxi.org/templates/Event____69.aspx.

Willcocks, Leslie, Catherine Griffiths, and Julia Kotlarsky. 2009. "Beyond BRIC: Offshoring in Non-BRIC Countries: Egypt, a New Growth Market." LSE Outsourcing Unit Report (January), London School of Economics and Political Science, London.

WTO (World Trade Organization). 1991. "Services Sectoral Classification List: Note by the Secretariat." Document MTN.GNS/W/120 (July 10), WTO, Geneva.

———. 1998. "Computer and Related Services: Background Note by the Secretariat." Document S/C/W/45, Council for Trade in Services, WTO, Geneva.

———. 2005. "Communication from Bolivia, Chile, Colombia, Dominican Republic, Guatemala, India, Indonesia, Mexico, Pakistan, Peru, Philippines, and Thailand: Assessment of Mode 4 Offers of Members; Review of Progress as Established in Paragraph 15 of the Guidelines and Procedures for the Negotiations on Trade in Services (S/L/93)." Document JOB(05)131 (June 30), Special Session, Council for Trade in Services, WTO, Geneva.

———. 2008. *International Trade Statistics 2008*. Geneva: WTO.

8

# ACCOUNTING SERVICES: ENSURING GOOD GOVERNANCE, FINANCIAL STABILITY, AND ECONOMIC GROWTH THROUGH TRADE

*Olivier Cattaneo and Peter Walkenhorst*

## Introduction: Why Is Trade in Accounting Services of Interest for Developing Countries?

Accounting services can be defined as services that focus on the preparation and analysis of the financial information reported to internal and external users via financial statements. Auditing services involve evaluations of the reliability and credibility of financial information, as well as "the systems and processes responsible for recording and summarizing that information" (Messier, Glover, and Prawitt 2006, 5–6). Accountants analyze, record, quantify, accumulate, summarize, classify, report, and interpret numerous financial events and their cumulative effect on an organization. Their activities are not confined to bookkeeping, that is, the measurement and recording of financial flows; they also include tax preparation and auditing, that is, the certification of the accuracy of the financial position of an enterprise.

Accounting services are vital for transparency, financial integrity, and good governance, and they may accordingly provide considerable benefits for developing countries. This is especially the case insofar as the major international accounting firms rely on local members in developing countries to understand the language, rules, and operating procedures of individual markets. As a consequence, developing countries may be able to take advantage of training programs, knowledge transfers, software applications, and timely staff support (World Bank 2007).

The accounting profession is highly integrated internationally. The "big four" accounting firms (Deloitte Touche Tomatsu, Ernst & Young, KPMG, and PricewaterhouseCoopers) play a dominant role globally and account for more than three-quarters of the profession's revenues in many countries.[1] Moreover, the growing implementation of internationally recognized accounting standards and laws helps countries instill confidence in commercial transactions and facilitates trade and investment. This credibility-enhancing effect is particularly important for developing countries that are striving to attract foreign capital.

This chapter synthesizes background information on the accounting profession and discusses policy initiatives that decision makers interested in developing the profession can undertake to improve regulatory conditions at home and gain access to potential export markets. The first section provides an overview of the accounting profession and illustrates the extent and benefits of trade in accounting services. Initiatives to pursue a policy dialogue at the national and regional levels to identify trade-related issues and constraints are then discussed, and potential policy initiatives to build professional value and improve market access abroad are presented.

## What Is the Situation of and What Are the Prospects for Trade in Accounting Services?

While it is difficult to obtain comprehensive data for developed and developing countries, it can be seen in figure 8.1 that, in 2006, total revenue generated in the global accounting market amounted to US$215 billion, with annual growth rates

**Figure 8.1.** The Rising Global Revenues of Accounting Firms

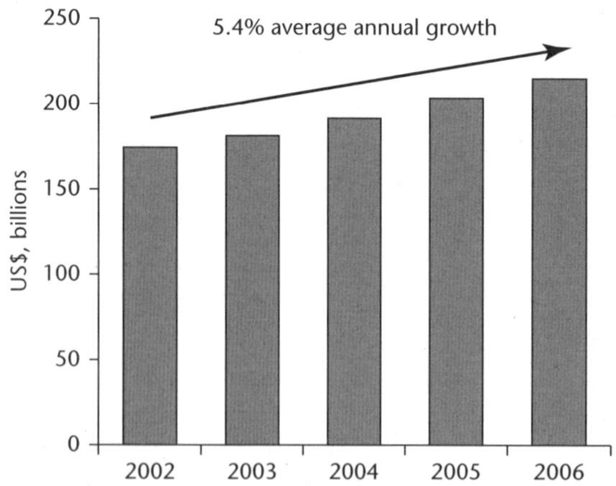


*Source:* Datamonitor (2007).

exceeding 5 percent. Privatization programs, increased attention to accurate financial statements, and the adoption of international accounting standards can be expected to continue to propel growth in the sector, which will entail expanded employment and offer new opportunities for professionals and university graduates with the appropriate credentials.

A good example is Tunisia, which experienced a 50 percent increase in employment in the accounting profession between 1997 and 2004 after the country had established a well-defined accounting framework requiring professionals to ensure that public and corporate reports accurately reflected the economic situation of the organizations examined (World Bank 2008).

While detailed data on the exports of accounting services are scarce, the available information suggests that a broad range of countries participate in the trade in accounting services. Some middle-income countries, such as Cyprus, the Czech Republic, and Hungary, generate substantial income from accounting service exports (table 8.1).

**Table 8.1.** Exports of Accounting and Consulting Services, 2007

| Country | Exports (US$ millions) | Country | Exports (US$ millions) |
|---|---|---|---|
| Albania | 0.309 | Latvia | 14.400 |
| Armenia | 1.561 | Lithuania | 14.291 |
| Austria | 81.248 | Macedonia, FYR[a] | 20.369 |
| Azerbaijan | 1.630 | Madagascar[b] | 0.090 |
| Bangladesh | 1.046 | Moldova | 1.350 |
| Belarus[b] | 1.000 | Mozambique[b] | 8.505 |
| Bulgaria | 18.702 | Netherlands Antilles | 15.497 |
| Cyprus | 475.351 | Norway | 125.279 |
| Czech Republic | 203.909 | Pakistan | 12.000 |
| Estonia | 9.381 | Portugal | 581.341 |
| Finland | 35.213 | Romania | 45.000 |
| Georgia | 0.521 | Russia | 232.900 |
| Guinea | 0.150 | Serbia | 33.716 |
| Hungary | 333.658 | Sierra Leone[c] | 0.018 |
| India[a] | 194.812 | Slovak Republic | 40.700 |
| Italy | 381.259 | Sweden | 485.584 |
| Jamaica | 0.240 | Tajikistan | 1.208 |
| Kazakhstan | 24.258 | Tonga | 0.287 |
| Korea, Rep. | 69.600 | | |

*Source:* International Monetary Fund balance of payments statistics, http://www.imf.org/external/np/sta/bop/bop.htm.
a. 2006.
b. 2005.
c. 2003.

### *Trade in accounting services occurs through several channels*

The accounting profession uses a variety of means to trade services. Accounting firms deliver services online, serve foreign investors in domestic markets, and follow clients overseas by establishing offices abroad or by visiting their clients abroad regularly (box 8.1). The trade in accounting services is the sum of these activities.

There are, unfortunately, no disaggregated data available on trade in accounting services broken down according to the individual General Agreement on Trade in Services (GATS) modes. Even the most detailed balance of payments information subsumes accounting services in the broader category of business services, which also include, among other services, legal, engineering, and management consulting services.

**Box 8.1:** The Four Modes of Supply of Accounting Services

The General Agreement on Trade in Services (GATS) of the World Trade Organization (WTO) defines four modes of supply in the service trade. The modes of supply have been identified to help trade negotiators determine commitments in trade agreements. Essentially, the modes are a construct for trade negotiations and aim to reflect how businesses operate. Most firms use a combination of some or all the modes of supply to conduct business. The modes focus on definitions related to the location of the service provider and the location of the service consumer. They are defined in the GATS as follows:

- Mode 1, crossborder supply: Nonresident service suppliers provide services across borders in a client's territory. This includes, typically, the international outsourcing of services. For example, a Moroccan firm keeps the accounts of a client operating in France.
  *Mode 1 trade may be inhibited, for instance, by restrictions on Internet use or by weak telecommunications infrastructure.*
- Mode 2, consumption abroad: A country's residents purchase services in the territory of another country. For example, a French firm established in Morocco hires a local accountant to keep its accounts.
  *Mode 2 trade may be inhibited, for instance, by excessively restrictive capital controls.*
- Mode 3, commercial presence: Foreign suppliers of services establish, operate, or expand their commercial presence into a client's territory such as through a branch, agency, or wholly owned subsidiary. For example, a Moroccan accounting firm establishes a front office in France.
  *Mode 3 trade may be inhibited, for instance, by arduous qualification requirements and licensing procedures and by equity limitations.*
- Mode 4, the movement of natural persons: The entry and temporary stay in a client's territory of foreign individuals to supply a service. For example, a Moroccan accountant visits a client in Tunisia to prepare an acquisition.
  *Mode 4 trade may be inhibited, for instance, by excessively restrictive visa fees or unpredictable and time-consuming work permit procedures.*

Analysts and policy makers can use the modes of supply to identify constraints on growth in the accounting service trade. This understanding can then inform policy decisions on the expansion of the trade and the promotion of exports.

### *Links to large accounting firms play a prominent role in trade*

Accounting firms frequently use a combination of affiliations and alliances to leverage the specialized expertise of accounting professionals to serve the international needs of clients. A typical organizational structure consists of an alliance in which each firm is treated as a member of the umbrella organization, while operating as a separate and independent legal entity. In an international context, this model makes it possible for each individual partner firm to benefit from transfers of knowledge and professional standards within the alliance, while complying with the legal and regulatory requirements of the country in which the firm is located.

Four large accounting alliances dominate the global market and influence the structure of service provision in many developing countries. The global accounting leaders derive approximately 65 percent of their income from work outside their home countries and are present in 140 to 150 different markets (table 8.2). The big four firms have 550,000 employees among them and combined revenues of about US$90 billion.

These four international accounting giants retain a partnership model that relies on local members and their professionals to understand the language, rules, and operating procedures of the respective market (box 8.2).[2] For example, several Moroccan firms have affiliated themselves with the big four. In exchange for royalties of about 10 percent of output, they can use the global firm's name and take advantage of its training, knowledge transfers, software applications, and timely staff support (World Bank 2007). Similarly, in Tunisia, the big four have been instrumental in raising accounting standards and training local accountants (World Bank 2008).

### *Offshoring offers export opportunities for developing countries*

Offshore outsourcing, that is, the outsourcing of services abroad, is often included in the global strategic plans of companies. Accounting services, along with many other business services, are now facing worldwide competition through new

**Table 8.2.** The Big Four Global Accounting Firms, 2007

| Big four | Headquarters | Employees | International presence | Revenues (US$, billions) |
|---|---|---|---|---|
| Deloitte Touche Tohmatsu | United States | 150,000 | 150 countries | 23.1 |
| Ernst & Young International | United States | 130,000 | 140 countries | 21.1 |
| KPMG International | Netherlands | 123,000 | 148 countries | 19.8 |
| PricewaterhouseCoopers | United States | 146,000 | 150 countries | 25.2 |

*Source:* Company Web sites.

**Box 8.2:** Affiliations of Developing-Country Accounting Firms with the Big Four

None of the big four accounting firms is a single firm. Each is a network of firms, owned and managed independently, that have entered into agreements with other member firms in the network to share a common name, brand, and quality standards. Each network has established an entity to coordinate the activities of the network. These entities do not themselves practice accounting and do not own or control the member firms.

In most cases, each member firm practices in a single country and is structured to comply with the regulatory environment in that country. However, in 2007, KPMG announced a merger of four member firms (in Germany, Liechtenstein, Switzerland, and the United Kingdom) to form a single firm.

There are many examples of affiliations of developing-country accounting firms with one of the global alliances. Selected cases are as follows:

### Arab Republic of Egypt

- Hazem Hassan: member of KPMG
- Mansour & Co.: member of PricewaterhouseCoopers
- Saleh, Barsoum, Abdel Aziz & Co.: member of Deloitte Touche Tohmatsu
- Hafez Rageb: member of Ernst & Young

### India

- C. C. Chokshi & Co., S. B. Billimoria Co.: affiliates of Deloitte Touche Tohmatsu
- Bharat S. Raut & Co. (BSR & Co.): affiliate of KPMG
- Lovelock & Lewes & RSM & Co., Dalal & Shah: affiliates of PricewaterhouseCoopers
- S. R. Batliboi & Co., S. R. Batliboi & Associates: affiliates of Ernst & Young–Indonesia
- KAP Purwantono, Sarwoko, Sandjaja: affiliate of Ernst & Young
- KAP Osman Bing Satrio: affiliate of Deloitte Touche Tohmatsu
- KAP Sidharta, Sidharta, Widjaja: affiliate of KPMG
- KAP Haryanto Sahari: affiliate of PricewaterhouseCoopers

### Pakistan

- A. F. Fergusons: member of PricewaterhouseCoopers
- Ford Rhodes Sidat Hyder & Co.: member of Ernst & Young
- Tasir Hadi Khalid & Co.: member of KPMG International
- M. Yousuf Adil Salim & Co.: member of Deloitte Touche Tohmatsu

### The Philippines

- Isla Lipana & Co.: affiliate of PricewaterhouseCoopers
- Manabat Delgado Amper & Co.: affiliate of Deloitte Touche Tohmatsu
- Sycip Gorres Velayo & Co. (SGV & Co.): affiliate of Ernst & Young
- Manabat Sanagustin & Co.: affiliate of KPMG

technologies. India is the most well known example of successful positioning in the offshoring market. Growth has actually been slower than many expected in the early 2000s, but significant potential remains.

The accounting profession is partially protected from offshoring by domestic regulations on liability insofar as a local accountant is liable for the delivery of certain services. Nonetheless, many upstream activities can be outsourced, particularly those that have low local knowledge content and require lower qualifications. Typically, bookkeeping, account management, billing services, payroll, tax planning and returns, and the preparation of financial statements are accounting services that can be outsourced. Outsourcing can be undertaken within a firm (with locations in different countries) or with a contracted service provider. An accounting firm can also use resources located outside a client's country whether or not the resources are part of a global network. For instance, some accountants in France have partnerships with Tunisian firms to second them in periods of high demand. Thus, the client could be a company or another accounting firm. There are, accordingly, a significant number of possible business models involving outsourcing and offshoring. Some examples of offshore accounting services are indicated in table 8.3.

The level of outsourcing opportunities for accounting firms will depend on international relationships, language ability, and professional expertise, as well as access to a quality communications infrastructure. Knowledge of international accounting standards is essential, and most firms engaged in this form of trade will seek certification through the International Organization for Standardization.

Technologies profoundly affect the accounting business. Good accounting software increases productivity in accounting firms, while requiring robust information and communications infrastructure and professional training. Software is widely used in the industry for accounting transactions and tax preparation. From a trade standpoint, policy makers can determine if tariffs, inadequate infrastructure, or limited educational opportunities are inhibiting domestic firms from deploying technology and competing on a global basis. They can adjust rules and regulatory oversight to ensure that accounting professionals have access to robust information technology systems. On the other hand, some accounting firms engaged in the offshoring business have expressed fears that the diffusion of this software would suppress the need for many of the outsourced services. Thus, the prospects for offshoring could be overestimated.

**Table 8.3.** Examples of Offshored Accounting Services

| Commoditized transactions | Value added | High value added |
|---|---|---|
| Invoice processing | Auditing | Financial planning |
| Expense processing | Financial statements | Financial analysis |
| Accounts receivable | Quarterly reports | Tax compliance |

*Source:* O'Sullivan (2008).

## What Can Be Done to Harness Trade Opportunities?

### *Promoting regulations at home and abroad that are less trade restrictive*

Accounting is a highly regulated profession. Regulations aim to protect against market failures, ensure good corporate behavior, and achieve societal objectives. Regulations can be the result of public policy processes and reflect sound policy objectives. For example, rules to protect against market imperfections include qualification requirements and technical standards in professional service sectors, prudential regulations in the financial sector, and performance requirements in the telecommunications sector. Regulations may also seek to achieve societal objectives. For instance, competition policy can prohibit anticompetitive practices that are detrimental to consumers. Investment policy can promote job creation. Universal service rules can ensure access to telecommunications, energy, and transportation.

Regulations can have a substantial impact on the way firms operate and trade. See box 8.3 for examples of domestic regulations that may impede trade in accounting services.[3] International trade arrangements therefore recognize the importance of regulations and seek to ensure that rules are not trade restrictive. For example, the GATS states that World Trade Organization (WTO) members recognize "the right of Members to regulate, and to introduce new regulations, on the supply of services within their territories in order to meet national policy objectives" (WTO 1993, 285). Rules are assessed according to their influence on trade rather than the underlying validity of their purpose. The challenge for policy makers is to ensure that professional rules achieve policy objectives and are crafted to be no more trade restrictive than necessary. In sum, it is important to improve regulation, not increase it.

The government is not the only regulator intervening in the profession. Professional bodies and oversight entities play an important role in the industry. From country to country, the organization of powers and responsibilities among the different regulators varies. The level of independence of professional bodies also varies. Oversight may touch on certification for professionals, licensing requirements for firms, and standards for accounting processes, as well as standards for the final service such as financial reports and income statements (WTO 2001).

The organization of powers and responsibilities sometimes makes it difficult for the government or professional bodies to adopt rules that are no more trade restrictive than necessary. In some countries, professional bodies are the main promoters of trade liberalization. In other countries, they represent the vested interests of the profession and oppose any kind of market liberalization. It is the role of the government to ensure that the interests of users are equitably represented. Regulatory entities can also improve the good governance of the sector and facilitate trade by providing inquiry points online and facilitating access to

**Box 8.3:** Examples of Domestic Regulations That May Impede Trade in Accounting Services

Rules are categorized to determine their potential impact on the trade in services. Rules that potentially may inhibit market access can be categorized as follows:

- Quantitative limitations on services providers, services, operations, and output: for example, limitations on the number of auditors or accountants
- The value of service transactions or assets: for example, the value of foreign subsidiaries is limited to a certain share of the total domestic assets of the sector
- Constraints on the type of legal entity or joint venture: for example, prohibitions on partnerships and constraints on the establishment of joint ventures
- Rules on the participation of foreign capital

Rules that potentially distort competition and deny national treatment include measures such as the following:

- Subsidy measures: for example, eligibility for subsidies is reserved to nationals
- Tax measures: for example, foreign firms are assessed discriminatory excise taxes
- Nationality requirements: for example, managers, accountants, and auditors must be citizens
- Licensing and qualification requirements: for example, licensing and qualification are reserved for citizens; professionals must be graduates of national universities; an in-country professional practice is required
- Registration requirements: for example, foreign companies are required to have an office registered in the country

Trade negotiations have prompted governments to reexamine such rules, their purpose, and their impact on service markets. As a consequence, policy makers may refine such rules to facilitate trade. For instance, they may lift quantitative limitations on service providers, loosen joint venture requirements, or raise foreign capital ceilings. Policy makers might also find alternatives for nationality requirements, streamline licensing and qualification requirements, and make registration requirements more transparent. Policy makers may make these changes as a reflection of market conditions at home and in export markets of interest. Regulations administered with integrity and restraint provide predictability and confidence in market operations for investors and service industry users.

information about administrative procedures and processes. For instance, robust electronic government is a useful tool to enable access to information and provide procedural transparency. In some countries, price controls may be applied in accounting services, possibly with detrimental effects (box 8.4).

The accounting profession does not operate in a vacuum. A number of regulations that apply to all sectors (in the business environment) affect the trade in accounting services. For example, the access to new clients in neighboring markets can be restricted because of constraints on financial transactions. Several countries, including Algeria, Libya, Mauritania, Morocco, and Tunisia, restrict capital flows and, in some cases, require central bank approval for transactions. Crossborder

**Box 8.4:** Price Controls: Legitimate Policy Objectives and Adverse Effects

A number of countries maintain a certain control over the prices of audits and other accounting services. The objective is to ensure that all businesses can afford an accountant to keep their accounts in good order and satisfy legal obligations pertaining to reporting and tax filing. Without access to affordable accounting services, a number of businesses would presumably move to the informal sector. The objective of the measure therefore appears to be legitimate.

Price controls are perceived by many, however, as a serious obstacle to trade and competition. The cost and the quality of the service provided vary from firm to firm. The complexity of the work also varies with the size of the client and the type of operations. Fixed prices can act as a market barrier to the larger firms that provide the highest quality services. Thus, in a few countries in which prices are fixed too low, the big four do not provide auditing services, but focus on consultancy instead. Meanwhile, at the other end of the spectrum, some accountants may charge prices that are higher than they would be in a more competitive market. Fixed prices do not always encourage the appropriate range in quality services.

There are a number of intermediate solutions between full liberalization and full control. In countries reluctant to remove price controls completely, regulations could apply only on a limited number of services: for example, only audit, or ceilings only in the case of smaller businesses, distinctions between simple and complex services, and so on.

credit operations are strictly controlled in some instances and also require central bank approval (Tahari et al. 2007).

Governments have a number of venues to negotiate trade liberalization, including bilateral, regional, and multilateral forums. A multilateral agreement can be considered the first-best solution and should therefore be encouraged. Table 8.4 gives some indication of the optimal levels of negotiations.

Among the regulatory issues to be considered, those pertaining to the movement of professionals are essential because of the structure of the accounting

**Table 8.4.** Optimal Levels of Negotiation for the Trade in Accounting Services

| Bilateral | Regional | Multilateral |
|---|---|---|
| • Mutual recognition agreements for diplomas and qualifications<br>• Reciprocal agreements on establishment<br>• Fast-track procedures for business visas | • Harmonization of accounting norms with neighboring countries<br>• Mutual recognition agreements for diplomas and qualifications<br>• Agreements on establishment and the movement of key personnel | • Consolidation of existing reforms in the GATS and negotiation of market access<br>• Negotiations on horizontal issues |

*Source:* World Bank (2007).

service market and the predominance of global networks. The crossborder movement of professionals enables global networks to manage their human resources and expertise more effectively by authorizing the creation of multinational teams that work on common projects. The temporary movement of accountants is an answer to short-term expertise shortages that might occur in a profession that is largely cyclical. Negotiations on Mode 4 take place in the WTO, but progress has been limited so far. Here again, pragmatic solutions exist and could prevail, such as the case of the Institute of Chartered Accountants of Tunisia (Ordre des Experts Comptables de Tunisie), which negotiated with the French Consulate and the institute's members to centralize requests for short-term visas. Tunisian accountants can now submit their requests directly to the institute, which then obtains multiple-entry business visas in a timely manner (usually 24 hours). This procedure has the benefit of offering the consulate some guarantees with regard to applicants: members of the institute with a registered business are less likely to remain in France after their visas expire.

### *Adopting international accounting standards*

With a view to facilitating trade in accounting services, the members of the WTO adopted the Disciplines on Domestic Regulation in the Accounting Sector in 1998. The disciplines are useful in highlighting policies that influence the trade in accounting services. They provide useful guidelines for governments seeking to design and implement reforms. The disciplines focus on transparency, licensing requirements, licensing procedures, qualification requirements, qualification procedures, and technical standards (WTO 1998).

The disciplines indicate that governmental and nongovernmental entities responsible for accounting regulations or the licensing process among professionals or firms should make rules publicly available, provide a rationale for rules upon request, and allow public comment on new rules. The disciplines are specific and represent a useful tool to improve public policy processes that influence trade in the accounting profession. Careful consideration and implementation of the disciplines can help policy makers improve the market for accounting services. The disciplines are also illustrative of the common issues in professional service markets and, if examined carefully, can help the entities create a robust environment for professional service firms.

The overwhelming importance of accounting in corporate and institutional management and relationships has helped countries agree on accounting disciplines. The accounting profession is now one of the most advanced in terms of international cooperation and standard setting. International financial reporting standards (IFRSs) are used in many parts of the world, including prominent developing countries (see box 8.5). While IFRSs are widely used by listed companies (85 countries impose the IFRSs for such companies), 36 countries allow some or all nonlisted companies to use the IFRSs, and 48 countries require some or all nonlisted companies to use them. Table 8.5 provides information about the use of the IFRSs in selected developing countries.

Adopting international standards has benefits for the domestic profession and the economy more generally. It promotes trade integration, including through the facilitation of commercial transactions and capital movements (foreign investment). For the profession, the adjustment of training and qualifications to meet international standards (unilaterally and through mutual

**Box 8.5:** International Accounting and Auditing Standards

Globalization has prompted standard-setting bodies to assess differences in standards, principles, and practices. For example, the International Accounting Standards Board and the Financial Accounting Standards Board are working toward a more principle-based means of regulating through the convergence of the IFRSs and the generally accepted U.S. accounting principles and rules. Standard-setting bodies are working toward global standards that enable creditors, investors, and corporate managers realistically to assess the financial health of private and public entities.

### Accounting

- International public sector accounting standards are developed and issued by the International Public Sector Accounting Standards Board of the International Federation of Accountants.
- The international private sector accounting standards are the IFRSs. They are developed and issued by the International Accounting Standards Board.

### Auditing

- International public sector auditing standards are developed and issued by the Professional Standards Committee of the International Organization of Supreme Audit Institutions. The committee has merged the old and new standards and guidelines into a framework. The overall purpose of the framework is to give the members of the International Organization of Supreme Audit Institutions and other interested parties an overview and common understanding of the auditing standards and guidelines. International Standards of Supreme Audit Institutions is the name commonly used to refer to the body of documents on the responsibilities of supreme audit institutions.
- The International Auditing and Assurance Standards Board of the International Federation of Accountants develops private sector international auditing standards.

*Source:* http://www.worldbank.org/ifa/rosc_aa.html.

**Table 8.5.** Use of International Financial Reporting Standards, Selected Developing Countries

| Country | IFRSs not permitted | IFRSs permitted | IFRSs required for all | Audit report states compliance with IFRSs | Use of IFRSs by unlisted companies |
|---|---|---|---|---|---|
| Argentina | x | | | | IFRSs not permitted |
| Bangladesh | x | | | | |
| Benin | x | | | | IFRSs not permitted |
| Botswana | | | x | Yes | IFRSs permitted |
| Brazil | | | All listed companies and all financial institutions starting 2010; optional for listed companies prior to 2010 | Not yet announced | IFRSs not permitted |
| Burkina Faso | x | | | | IFRSs not permitted |
| Cambodia | No stock exchange in Cambodia | | | | IFRSs permitted |
| Chile | | | x starting 2009 | Yes | IFRSs required starting 2009 |
| China | x | | | | IFRSs not permitted |
| Ecuador | | | x 2008 | Yes | |
| Egypt, Arab Rep. | | | x | Yes | |
| Ghana | | | x | Yes | IFRSs required for unlisted banks, utilities, brokerage, insurance, government-owned businesses starting 2007; IFRSs required for all other unlisted entities starting 2009 |
| Haiti | | | x | Yes | IFRSs required for all |
| India | x[a] | | | | IFRSs not permitted |
| Indonesia | x | | | | IFRSs not permitted |
| Jordan | | | x | Yes | |
| Kenya | | | x | Yes | IFRSs required for all |
| Mali | x | | | | IFRSs not permitted |
| Mauritius | | | x | Yes | |
| Mexico | x | | | | IFRSs not permitted |
| Morocco | | x[b] | | Yes | |
| Niger | x | | | | IFRSs not permitted |
| Pakistan | x | | | | IFRSs not permitted |
| Saudi Arabia | x | | | | IFRSs not permitted |
| South Africa | | | x | Yes | |
| Tunisia | x | | | | IFRSs not permitted |
| Uganda | | x | | Yes | |
| Vietnam | x | | | | |
| Zambia | | x | | | |

*Source:* Mirza, Orrell, and Holt (2008).

a. India has announced a plan to adopt IFRSs as Indian Financial Reporting Standards effective 2011.

b. Listed companies other than banks and financial institutions may choose IFRSs or Moroccan generally accepted accounting principles. Banks and financial institutions must use the latter.

recognition agreements) and acquaintance with the most up-to-date accounting methods and standards are essential to becoming internationally competitive. This could occur as the result of technology and knowledge transfers through participation in international networks of accounting firms (for example, the big four) or as part of an effort to achieve such integration. Most listed companies and multinational companies need their accounts to be kept according to international standards. Accountants who are not qualified or acquainted with such standards do not have access to these important clients.

For the economy as a whole, the adoption of best practices and international standards facilitates integrity in the public and private sectors, instills confidence in business transactions, and facilitates the access of businesses to credit, among other advantages. Trade opening and domestic reforms should therefore be accompanied by increased international cooperation and standards harmonization. While a strong case can be made for the adoption of international standards by developing countries, there are some caveats worth noting. Thus, for the majority of firms in developing countries that are small and medium-size enterprises, international standards may constitute an unnecessary burden on the firms themselves and on the local accounting service markets that lack enough qualified professionals. The potential risk is that developing countries might reallocate all their efforts and resources solely to the production of accountants qualified to implement international standards at the expense of accounting technicians who could provide affordable and appropriate services to the majority of domestic firms; the countries would thereby leave a large portion of the domestic market underserved, even if the prospects for exports would be enhanced.

Simplified IFRSs for small and medium-size enterprises have been developed by the International Federation of Accountants. The extent to which countries adopt these IFRSs and create a corresponding accounting technician qualification that is recognized internationally could actually benefit the exporting of accounting services, particularly those related to the outsourcing of activities that require lower qualifications, such as bookkeeping, account management, billing services, and payroll. (Box 8.6 provides an example of a support program for standard compliance.)

### *Adapting the profession to international competition*

The existence and diffusion of international standards are a means to enhance the global integration of the accounting profession. The more uniform the standards, the more tradable the services of domestic accountants. This

**Box 8.6:** Reports on the Observance of Standards and Codes

Reports on the Observance of Standards and Codes (ROSC) is a joint International Monetary Fund–World Bank initiative that helps member countries strengthen their financial systems by improving compliance with internationally recognized standards and codes. The initiative was developed in the wake of the financial crises of the late 1990s as part of a series of measures to strengthen the international financial architecture. The global financial community considered that the implementation of internationally recognized standards and codes would provide a framework to strengthen domestic institutions, identify potential vulnerabilities, and improve transparency. Ultimately, the ROSC aims to enhance the resilience of countries to shocks, support risk assessments in these countries more effectively, and strengthen important pillars of the market economic system.

The focus of the initiative is 12 key areas, as follows:

- Accounting, with recognized international standards and codes
- Auditing, with recognized international standards and codes
- Anti–money laundering and countering the financing of terrorism
- Banking supervision
- Corporate governance
- Data distribution
- Fiscal transparency
- Insolvency and creditor rights
- Insurance supervision
- Monetary and financial policy transparency
- Payment systems
- Securities regulation

Reports summarizing findings of the exercises in the 12 areas are prepared and published at the request of the member countries. The World Bank ROSC accounting and auditing Web page makes available the published ROSC accounting and auditing reports and additional information (see the source below). The ROSC accounting and auditing review evaluates a country's accounting and auditing standards and practices, using the IFRSs and international standards on auditing as benchmarks. The review also analyzes the strengths and weaknesses of the institutional framework that underpins the accounting and auditing practices in the country. The review uses a diagnostic template developed by the World Bank to facilitate data collection, complemented by the findings of in-country due-diligence exercises conducted by the World Bank ROSC team. Following the completion of a ROSC accounting and auditing review, the country stakeholders, assisted by World Bank staff, develop a country action plan that forms the basis for accounting reform and development. The main objective of ROSC accounting and auditing reviews is therefore capacity building to strengthen the institutional underpinnings of corporate financial reporting in countries.

*Source:* http://www.worldbank.org/ifa/rosc_aa.html.

distinguishes the accounting profession from the legal profession, for instance, in which most of the legal corpus largely remains specific to each country. The more diffuse the international standards in the domestic accounting system (for example, for all listed companies or for all listed and unlisted companies), the more the profession is exposed to competition in an open trade environment. Thus, the adoption of international standards and trade integration create business opportunities and highlight areas in need of adjustment in the profession.

For trade purposes, it is essential that the education and training of accountants include exposure to international standards. In some countries, the profession has complete control of education and training, as well as the professional qualifications tests. In other countries, the government is involved. Frequent dialogue between the private and public sectors is needed to adjust curricula to the profession's needs. Unlike in many other professions, some international examinations exist that make mutual recognition of diplomas more straightforward. Students in developing countries can sit for the Association of Certified Chartered Accountants examination (160 examination centers in the world) and gain the associated accreditation without needing to attend a course in the United Kingdom or elsewhere. This diploma is recognized in most English-speaking countries. Pass rates depend on the quality of the education received locally, and it is therefore in a country's best interests to adjust curricula. (See box 8.7 for an example of a regional agreement on the mutual recognition of qualifications in the European Union [EU].)

It is important for countries to provide adequate training (quality) for an adequate number of professionals (quantity). Certification requirements vary among countries; generally, they may include a postsecondary degree, professional experience, and, in some instances, an examination. Licensing requirements are also often unique to each country. In some cases, the examinations are so burdensome that the country does not train enough professionals to meet its local or even its international needs. In Morocco, for instance, only three new accountants were admitted to the professional order between 1993 and 2002. This number was insufficient to allow for the development and renewal of the profession. The vested interests of a few already established professionals or entities obviously prevailed over the interests of consumers. The adoption of standard international qualifications ensures that these requirements are not used for anticompetitive purposes and are not more trade restrictive than necessary. In Tunisia, the passing rate on the accounting examination is only 3 percent. The length of study, including mandatory initial training, exceeds the length required in France and other countries for certification. The country nonetheless managed to double the number of practicing accountants between 1997 and 2004. A clear assessment of the economy's needs for accounting services should be made by the government and professional bodies to fine-tune the education system. Opening access to

**Box 8.7:** An Example of a Regional Agreement on the Mutual Recognition of Qualifications

The rights of EU citizens to establish themselves or to provide services anywhere in the EU are fundamental principles of EU law. Directive 2005/36/CE establishes a general system for the recognition of professional qualifications that regulates the establishment and the crossborder provision of services.[4]

The following conditions apply in the case of establishment in another member state:

- Professional qualifications gained in the home member state will be recognized by competent authorities in the host member state in which the professional wants to establish.
- Before reaching a decision on an application, the competent authority will compare the professional education and training in the home member state with that required in the host member state. If it finds that there are significant differences, it may make recognition conditional on the fulfillment of additional requirements. The applicant may be required to complete an adaptation period or an aptitude test in the host member state.
- Member states may stipulate an aptitude test where the knowledge of local laws and regulations in the host member state is essential to the proper delivery of the service. Under the regime of Directive 89/48, this system has been consistently applied to accountants and auditors by the competent authorities in each EU member state.

Under the new qualification directive, the following regime will apply in case of temporary and occasional provisions of services:

- The services must be provided under the title of the member state of establishment. The national competent authorities do not perform a preliminary check of the equivalence of qualifications. This regime does not apply to statutory audit.
- Member states may require automatic temporary registration with pro forma membership of a professional organization.
- The practitioner shall be subject to the professional rules of the member state in which services are provided and to the disciplinary provisions applicable in this member state.

*Source:* FEE (2008).

the profession too widely could lead to lower quality in the education provided, to greater unemployment, and to depressed wages. (Investing in education to meet international standards is described in the case of Zambia in box 8.8.)

The accounting profession has also pioneered in the field of ethics. It is the first profession to have adopted an international code of ethics. This code is maintained by the International Ethics Standards Board for Accountants (see IESBA 2009). The fundamental principles of the code address integrity, objectivity,

**Box 8.8:** Investing in Education to Meet International Standards: The Case of Zambia

A number of developing countries face an acute shortage of qualified accountants. Harnessing the benefits of increased trade in accounting services requires an investment in education to adjust the profession both quantitatively and qualitatively, that is, to train more accountants and include the study of international standards in the accounting curricula. The example of the Zambia Centre for Accounting Studies is often referred to as a best practice.

The center was established in 1988 with support from the EU. The establishment of the center enabled Zambia to introduce a national accounting qualification. The related examinations are internationally recognized and are part of a joint examination scheme with an accounting body in the United Kingdom. Students thus no longer need to go to the United Kingdom for training. It is estimated that this has saved Zambia over US$16 million in foreign exchange. Over 350 students attend courses at the center. The success rate of students is high: the average pass rate of 65 percent compares with 35 percent worldwide. In 1988, before the center had become operational, only four Zambians qualified as accountants. In 1994, the center produced 24 qualified accountants. Qualified Zambians are replacing expatriates in the workplace.

*Source:* http://www.zcas.ac.zm.

professional competence, due care, confidentiality and professional behavior. The adherence of domestic accountants to the code increases international credibility and tradability.

## What Questions Should Stakeholders Bear in Mind as They Advance Reforms?

Tables 8.6–8.8 bring together a number of considerations that are pertinent to a process of reform in accounting services. Table 8.6 provides a checklist of the influences on accounting firms and services that may affect success, the institutions that influence the accounting marketplace, and initiatives to enhance export growth and development. Table 8.7 draws on box 8.3 and the related discussion and provides a list of common restrictions to trade in accounting services and their impact on professionals in the marketplace. This list of restrictions may be useful to policy makers in assessing the impact of various restrictions and determining how they can be refined so that they are nondiscriminatory and no more trade restrictive than necessary. Table 8.8 provides a checklist that focuses on initiatives to build trade capacity by enabling policy makers to enhance the value of accounting professionals, help accounting firms improve access to clients, and work to facilitate trade.

**Table 8.6.** Influences on Accounting Firms and Services

| Main drivers and institutions in accounting services trade and development | |
|---|---|
| **Drivers and institutions** | **Initiatives** |
| Developing educational excellence<br>Colleges of accounting<br>Primary and secondary educational institutions | • Commission third-party audits of accounting curricula and professor-student ratios using international benchmarks<br>• Increase public profile of highly regarded accounting colleges through award programs, links with colleges abroad, links to primary and secondary institutions to draw students from the region |
| Promoting international quality standards<br>Professional organizations of accountants<br>National standards boards | • Underwrite investment in staff, technology, engagement in international bodies<br>• Underwrite investment in electronic tools to ensure publicly available and objective administration of rules and regulations<br>• Facilitate enforcement of professional and quality standards |
| Negotiating mutual recognition agreements<br>Professional bodies and associated regulatory entities | • Facilitate regional cooperation with counterparts in neighboring countries to share best practice, exchange information on respective rules and regulations, and, ultimately, to facilitate mutual recognition<br>• Consider potential for regional integration of professional organizations and standards boards where practicable and in light of limited resources over the long term |
| Adopting objective, transparent rules for procurement<br>Public and commercial entities procuring accounting services | • Encourage open procurement processes for public entities<br>• Require publication of the terms of procurement and procedural processes and adherence to definite timelines, as well as periodic audits and enforcement of procedural requirements<br>• Encourage commercial entities to conduct open bidding processes |
| Facilitating access to and use of new technologies<br>Customs authorities<br>Telecommunications authorities | • Ensure customs authorities facilitate trade in information technology products<br>• Ensure access to vibrant information and communication technology infrastructure with adequate bandwidth |
| Investing in human resources<br>Primary, secondary, tertiary educational institutions<br>Ministries that facilitate the temporary movement of professionals and students | • Maintain quality standards and encourage the acquisition of the languages spoken in export markets of interest<br>• Ensure that educational institutions are aware of accounting employment trends at home, in the regional market, and globally<br>• Engage early in discussions at the bilateral, regional, and multilateral levels to facilitate the temporary movement of accounting professionals and students<br>• Train immigration authorities and invest in technology at ports of entry |
| Developing an offensive trade policy and strategy | • Engage stakeholders to identify constraints in the domestic market to export expansion, as well as barriers in export markets of interest |

(*Table continues on the following pages.*)

**Table 8.6.** Influences on Accounting Firms and Services (*continued*)

| **Main drivers and institutions in accounting services trade and development** | |
|---|---|
| **Drivers and institutions** | **Initiatives** |
| Ministry of trade, commerce<br>Ministry of finance<br>Immigration authorities | • Increase flows of information about the accounting profession; for example, commission university studies, hold public-private forums, facilitate links with professional bodies<br>• Create materials targeted at ministry officials that explain the scope of the accounting profession and opportunities at home and abroad<br>• Identify for ministries specific restrictions in export markets of interest important to the accounting profession<br>• Facilitate capital flows and equitable tax treatment and ameliorate foreign investment restrictions, specifically equity limitations |

| **Potential regulatory restrictions to reform** | |
|---|---|
| **Potential restrictions** | **Reform initiatives** |
| Nationality and residency requirements | Identify presence in domestic and in export markets of interest; determine the purpose of such restrictions, in consultation with professional bodies and governmental authorities; propose alternative approaches that, for example, require local collaboration, bonding, or crossdisciplinary action |
| Procedures for the recognition of qualifications | The WTO disciplines on domestic regulation in the accounting sector provide guidance on ensuring that requirements are no more trade restrictive than necessary; policy makers can pursue transparent administrative procedures in applying requirements; policy makers can use the WTO disciplines to assess and refine:<br>• Licensing requirements<br>• Licensing procedures<br>• Qualification requirements<br>• Qualification procedures<br>• Technical standards |
| Equity limitations on foreign investors | Identify presence in domestic and in export markets of interest; determine the purpose of such restrictions, in consultation with professional bodies and governmental authorities; assess the impact of equity limitations on the ability of domestic firms to raise capital for export expansion; propose that equity limitations be lifted or scheduled for removal, at a minimum in certain geographic areas, by a particular date |
| Commercial presence requirements | Identify the scope of commercial presence requirements in the domestic and in export markets of interest; determine the purpose of such restrictions, in consultation with professional bodies and governmental authorities; develop |

| | |
|---|---|
| | alternative methods for achieving the same policy objectives: for example, online registration that provides specific data to meet policy objectives without requiring firms to establish a physical presence |
| Restrictions on the form of establishment | Identify the scope of constraints on the type of legal entity or joint venture at home and in export markets of interest; determine if such restrictions are discriminatory relative to national firms; assess the impact of such constraints on firm operations, financing options, employment practices, and so on; undertake consultations with professional bodies and government authorities to review the purpose of the restrictions and alternative approaches that are no more trade restrictive than necessary |
| Procedures for work permits and visas | Document processes at home and in export markets of interest; implement electronic systems to speed work permit and visa processes at home and request such initiatives in export markets of interest; train immigration authorities to facilitate the movement of professionals |
| Capital controls | Determine the scope of capital controls at home and in export markets of interest; assess the impact of such constraints on firm operations, financing options, ability to serve clients; engage in consultations with professional bodies and ministries of finance to ensure that controls are no more trade restrictive than necessary and do not hinder export expansion |
| Tax treaties | Identify current treaties; quantify the impact of double taxation on firms, in consultation with professional bodies; engage appropriate domestic ministries to promote tax treaties with markets of export interest |
| Restrictions on the use of brand names | Identify restrictions at home and in export markets of interest; collect data that determine the impact of such restrictions on domestic firms; undertake consultations with professional bodies and governmental authorities to lift such restrictions |
| Restrictions on marketing and advertising | Identify restrictions at home and in export markets of interest; collect data that determine the impact of such restrictions on domestic firms; undertake consultations with professional bodies and governmental authorities to lift such restrictions |
| Public procurement processes | Review public procurement processes in home markets and in export markets of interest; in consultation with professional bodies and governmental authorities, assess impacts on domestic firms; institute electronic government systems at home to promote objective, merit-based procurement processes; request transparent, objective, and competitive processes in export markets of interest |
| Prescribed fee schedules | Identify schedules in the home market and in export markets of interest; in consultation with professional bodies and governmental authorities, determine the purpose of such schedules; develop alternative approaches that are no more trade restrictive than necessary |

(*Table continues on the following page.*)

**Table 8.6.** Influences on Accounting Firms and Services (*continued*)

| Potential regulatory restrictions to reform | |
|---|---|
| **Potential restrictions** | **Reform initiatives** |
| Discriminatory treatment of nonnationals | Determine measures in the home market that distort competition relative to national and foreign firms; determine measures in export markets of interest that distort competition relative to national and foreign firms; in consultation with professional bodies and governmental authorities, assess the impact of such measures on business operations; refine such measures to ensure they are no more trade restrictive than necessary |

*Source:* Authors' compilation.

**Table 8.7.** Restrictions on the Trade in Accounting Services

| Restrictions | Impact on professionals | Influence in the marketplace |
|---|---|---|
| Nationality and residency requirements | Limits access to foreign accounting professionals with current technology and new expertise<br>Constrains the potential scope and expertise of practicing accountants in the domestic market<br>Inhibits practicing accountants from linking with international firms<br>Reduces ability to build commercial relationships with foreign firms<br>Minimizes export potential | Users of accounting services may lose access to higher-quality, lower-cost services<br>Nationality and residency requirements act as a cap on the productivity of commercial enterprises reliant on accounting services: for example, agricultural, industrial, and manufacturing production facilities<br>Reduces efficiencies in the public sector entities reliant on professional accounting services: for example, wastewater treatment, transportation systems, electricity grids, and so on |
| Opaque and cumbersome procedures for the recognition of qualifications | Delays or deters collaboration with foreign partners<br>Creates obstacles to participating in multicountry projects<br>Particularly detrimental to microfirms with limited resources | Creates a drag on productivity |
| Equity limitations on foreign investors | Restricts financing to domestic sources | Problematic if a shallow financial services market does not provide adequate credit or finance for accounting firms |

| | | |
|---|---|---|
| Commercial presence requirements as a prerequisite to conduct business | Reduces the potential for cooperation with foreign firms | Acts as a tax on accounting services for users |
| Restrictions on the form of establishment | Prescribed forms of establishment may reduce the type of personnel the firm can use and limit the flexibility to use more efficient and cost-effective structures | Users of accounting services may forgo the benefits of increased productivity that arise through other, more efficient forms of establishment |
| Opaque and cumbersome procedures for work permits and visas | Can impede the travel of foreign clients, investors, commercial contacts from abroad<br>Limits the base of accounting clients, potential investors, and new business opportunities<br>Limits accounting export potential by impeding the movement of people critical to accounting services<br>Particularly detrimental to microaccounting firms with limited resources | Reduces and delays accounting services for public sector and commercial users |
| Excessive capital controls | Deters commercial transactions between accounting firms and clients<br>Deters accounting firms from participating in regional or global projects for domestic accounting professionals | Deters exporting; reduces growth in the accounting profession; reduces opportunities for employment in accounting and those professions that support the delivery of accounting services at home and abroad |
| Opaque, distorted public procurement processes | Practicing accountants experience growing costs in doing business<br>Wastes the time, capital, management expertise of accounting firms<br>Creates difficulty in properly preparing for bids in terms of human resources and strategic alliances<br>Particularly detrimental to microaccounting firms with limited resources | Distorts the marketplace by subduing competition<br>Delays procurement<br>Increases the cost of public entities or commercial buyers<br>Reduces the integrity of the process; contributes to corruption; may result in inferior accounting services |

(*Table continues on the following page.*)

**Table 8.7.** Restrictions on the Trade in Accounting Services (*continued*)

| Restrictions | Impact on professionals | Influence in the marketplace |
|---|---|---|
| Absence of tax treaties | Accounting firms experience double taxation<br>Reduces the adequate returns on the investment necessary to undertake export expansion | Deters exporting; reduces the growth of the accounting profession; reduces the opportunities for employment in accounting and those professions that support the delivery of accounting services at home and abroad |
| Restrictions on the use of brand names | Deters the use by firms of primary assets earned through investment in professionals and performance | In decision making in the marketplace, limits the information on the quality and experience of accounting practitioners |
| Restrictions on marketing, advertising | Limits the ability of accounting firms to reach new clients through commercial channels | In decision making in the marketplace, limits the information going to accounting service users |
| Prescribed fee schedules | Deters accounting firms from reacting to the supply and demand for services | |
| Discriminatory treatment of nonnationals | Lowers the incentives for domestic accounting firms to invest in technology, to invest in a broader scope of services, and to compete at regional and international levels | Narrows the accounting services available in the marketplace |

*Source:* Authors' compilation.

**Table 8.8.** Initiatives to Improve the Environment for Accounting Firms

| Professional priorities of firms | Initiatives to build professional value |
|---|---|
| Exceptional expertise<br>Broad and evolving scope of expertise<br>Multijurisdictional knowledge<br>Effective oversight of professional standards and ethics<br>Well-qualified recruits | Firms and practitioners<br>• Facilitate online training, professional internships, exchange programs, and continuing adult education<br>• Facilitate on-the-job training with different firms<br>• Facilitate concentration and links with foreign firms<br>• Permit hiring of foreign practitioners<br>• Allow domestic practitioners to be employed in foreign firms<br>Professional bodies<br>• Facilitate cooperation with regional and international counterparts using exchange programs, forums on trends in the profession, professional development seminars with international partners<br>• Share best practices<br>• Invest in staff, technology, and international engagement |

| | |
|---|---|
| | Colleges of accounting<br>• Facilitate independent third-party audits of curricula and educational standards<br>• Provide assistance to raise standards and increase professor-student ratios<br>• Facilitate electronic partnerships with schools of accountancy abroad |
| | **Initiatives to improve access to clients** |
| Access to clients<br>Ability to attract, serve, and retain clients<br>Establishment of international networks | Reduce domestic restrictions<br>• Reassess marketing restrictions that inhibit the ability of firms to reach new clients at home and abroad<br>• Reduce capital controls that impede the ability of domestic firms to operate in neighboring and regional markets<br>• Review tax policy to reduce the incidence of double taxation<br>• Review restrictions on the number of partners in firms, the ability to hire foreigners, and flexibility in setting fee schedules<br>Improve the temporary movement of accounting professionals<br>• Simplify and speed visa procedures to facilitate the movement of accounting professionals to neighboring and regional markets on a reciprocal basis<br>• Train immigration authorities quickly and accurately to process the movement of accounting professionals on a reciprocal basis<br>Export promotion programs<br>• Enable firms to participate in trade exhibitions at home and abroad so as to introduce firms to potential partners and clients<br>Improve use of the Internet<br>• Help firms establish an online presence and online relationships with other firms to reach new clients |
| | **Initiatives to facilitate trade** |
| Recognition of qualifications | Pursue mutual recognition agreements<br>• Facilitate links between professional bodies and their counterparts in neighboring and regional markets<br>• Facilitate links between government regulatory entities and their counterparts in neighboring and regional markets |

(*Table continues on the following pages.*)

**Table 8.8.** Initiatives to Improve the Environment for Accounting Firms (*continued*)

| | **Initiatives to facilitate trade** |
|---|---|
| | • Facilitate links between colleges of accounting in neighboring and regional markets<br>• Facilitation activities include the following:<br>  ◦ Exchanging specialists with counterpart organizations<br>  ◦ Holding regional forums on professional trends<br>  ◦ Commissioning stakeholders to undertake regional studies<br>  ◦ Holding consultations on negotiating requests |
| Priority practice areas of accounting firms | Determine the priorities and restrictions and lower restrictions<br>• With practitioners, identify export markets of interest<br>• Determine nationality and residency restrictions in those markets<br>• Determine other barriers inhibiting trade (use of brand names, marketing, advertising, price setting, form of establishment, hiring practices, equity restrictions, capital controls, double taxation, opaque rules, discriminatory application of rules, and so on)<br>• Determine the scope of the regulatory authority of professional entities and complementary government authorities<br>• Determine the potential for the reciprocal reduction of nationality and residency requirements by the professional body and related government entities<br>• Determine the potential for alleviating restrictions through the professional body and related government entities<br>Assess ongoing negotiations at the bilateral and regional levels<br>Determine the objectives for commercial presence in the domestic market and in export markets of interest; consider the potential for lifting restrictions on the following:<br>• Equity<br>• Form of establishment<br>• Use of firm names<br>• Hiring practices<br>• Nationality and residency requirements<br>• Marketing, advertising, fixed fees[a]<br>Determine the possibility for specific provisions within the agreements to accomplish the following:<br>• Create an accounting working group to facilitate trade<br>• Proactively facilitate mutual recognition agreements<br>• Proactively facilitate the temporary movement of accounting professionals<br>• Adopt skill-transfer resolutions with regard to training, mentoring, accounting education[b]<br>Determine the possibility for transparency provisions requiring the publication of rules and regulations |

| | |
|---|---|
| Administrative procedures | Improve the administration of rules at home and abroad |
| Ability to understand qualification requirements, licensing procedures, and other rules influencing the practice of law<br>Ability to receive objective treatment under rules | • Facilitate the publication and administration of rules online at the regional level<br>• Underwrite technology and training for professional bodies and government entities that regulate legal services at the regional level<br>• Institute robust electronic government practices in professional bodies and government entities at the regional level |

*Source:* Authors' compilation.
a. Australian Permanent Mission to the WTO (2006).
b. Terry (2008).

## Conclusion

Accounting is an important part of the business sector of any modern economy. Information about a firm's financial accounts is essential for managers, owners, and creditors and is a key input for lender and investor decision making on whether, when, and how to provide financing to corporations. The growth of multinational enterprises generally and of multinational accounting firms in particular has focused attention on issues related to the international trade in accounting services.

The accounting profession is highly integrated internationally. The big four accounting firms (Deloitte Touche Tomatsu, Ernst & Young, KPMG, and PricewaterhouseCoopers) play a dominant role globally and provide more than three-quarters of the profession's revenues in many countries. Moreover, the increased implementation of internationally recognized accounting standards and legal codes helps countries instill confidence in commercial transactions and facilitates trade and investment. This credibility-enhancing effect is particularly important for developing countries that are striving to attract foreign capital.

In 2006, the total revenue generated in the global accounting market amounted to US$215 billion, with annual growth rates exceeding 5 percent. Privatization programs, increased attention to accurate financial statements, and the adoption of international accounting standards will continue to propel growth in the sector. Such economic expansion entails growth in employment and offers new opportunities for professionals and university graduates with the appropriate credentials.

The accounting profession uses a variety of means to trade services. Accounting firms deliver services online, serve foreign investors in the domestic market, and follow their clients overseas by establishing offices abroad or by visiting the clients temporarily. The trade in accounting services is the sum of these activities.

Accounting firms frequently use a combination of affiliations and alliances to leverage the specialized expertise of accounting professionals to serve the international needs of clients. A typical organizational structure consists of an alliance in which each firm is treated as a member of an umbrella organization, while operating as a separate and independent legal entity. In an international context, this model makes it possible for each individual partner firm to benefit from transfers of knowledge and professional standards within the alliance, while complying with the legal and regulatory requirements of the country in which the firm is located.

The outsourcing of services abroad is often included in the global strategic plans of companies. Accounting services, along with many other business services, are now facing worldwide competition through new technologies. In the early 2000s, a number of studies forecast dramatic growth in the trade in accounting services through the offshoring channel.

The accounting profession is a highly regulated profession. To facilitate trade in accounting services, the WTO and other international bodies have encouraged the adoption of international accounting standards, the adoption of consistent accounting curricula in business schools worldwide, and the continued promotion of policy integration and regulatory consistency among member countries.

## Notes

1. The next two largest firms are BDO and Grant Thornton, and they operate similarly to the big four.
2. In several countries, including Botswana, Mozambique, and South Africa, the local entity providing services is 100 percent foreign-owned and uses the name of the big four firm.
3. Gootiiz and Mattoo (2009) conducted a survey of actual or applied trade policies in services in 32 developing countries and 24 countries in the Organisation for Economic Co-operation and Development for the World Bank in 2007. The survey covered the four modes of supplying services and focused on five sectors, notably, financial services (banking and insurance), telecommunications, retail distribution, transportation, and professional services. Financial accounting and financial auditing are included in the professional service category. For each sector and mode of supply, the authors mapped the openness of policy toward foreign suppliers on a five-point scale, ranging from no restrictions to highly restricted. They aggregated the sector results across modes of supply based on weights reflecting judgments of the relative importance of the different modes. They then aggregated sector restrictiveness indexes using sector shares of gross domestic product, as well as country income group indexes using weights of gross domestic product for the component countries. The indexes for accounting and auditing provide indications of the openness of accounting services in the countries and regions covered in the study and may therefore be useful in assessing the need for policy reforms.
4. See http://eur-lex.europa.eu/LexUriServ/LexUriServ.do?uri=OJ:L:2005:255:0022:01:EN:HTML.

## References

Australian Permanent Mission to the WTO. 2006. "Collective Request: Legal Services." Australian Department of Foreign Affairs and Trade, Canberra.

Datamonitor. 2007. "Global Accountancy." Datamonitor Industry Market Research, London.

FEE (Federation of European Accountants). 2008. "Recognition of Professional Qualifications in the EU." FEE Fact Sheet FST005, FEE, Brussels.

Gootiiz, B., and A. Mattoo. 2009. "Services in Doha: What's on the Table?" Policy Research Working Paper 4903, World Bank, Washington, DC.

IESBA (International Ethics Standards Board for Accountants). 2009. *Code of Ethics for Professional Accountants*. New York: International Federation of Accountants.

Messier, William F., Steven M. Glover, and Douglas F. Prawitt. 2006. *Auditing and Assurance Services: A Systematic Approach*. New York: McGraw-Hill.

Mirza, Abbas A., Magnus Orrell, and Graham Holt. 2008. *Wiley IFRS: Practical Implementation Guide and Workbook*. New York: John Wiley & Sons.

O'Sullivan, Kate. 2008. "Offshoring Spreads Its Wings: From East Asia to Eastern Europe, Offshore Outsourcing Is Taking Off." *CFO Magazine*, March 1. http://www.cfo.com/article.cfm/10755461.

Tahari, A., P. Brenner, E. De Vrijer, M. Moretti, A. Senhadji, G. Sensenbrenner, and J. Solé. 2007. "Financial Sector Reforms and Prospects for Financial Integration in Maghreb Countries." IMF Working Paper 07/125 (May), International Monetary Fund.

Terry, Laurel S. 2008. "GATS, Legal Services, and Skills Transfer in Developing Jurisdictions." Presentation at the Third Annual International Bar Association Bar Leaders Conference, Amsterdam, May 14–15.

World Bank. 2007. "Morocco's Backbone Services Sectors: Reforms for Higher Productivity and Deeper Integration with Europe." Report 39755-MA, World Bank, Washington, DC.

———. 2008. *Tunisia's Global Integration: Second Generation of Reforms to Boost Growth and Employment*. Report 40129-TN, Washington, DC: Social and Economic Development Sector Unit, Middle East and North Africa Region, World Bank.

WTO (World Trade Organization). 1993. "General Agreement on Trade in Services." WTO, Geneva. http://www.wto.org/english/docs_e/legal_e/26-gats.pdf.

———. 1998. "Disciplines on Domestic Regulation in the Accountancy Sector." Document S/L/64 (December 17), Council for Trade in Services, WTO, Geneva.

———. 2001. *Guide to the GATS: An Overview of Issues for Further Liberalization of Trade in Services*. WTO Guide Series. London: Kluwer Law International.

9

# ENGINEERING SERVICES: HOW TO COMPETE IN THE MOST GLOBAL OF THE PROFESSIONS

*Olivier Cattaneo, Linda Schmid, and Michael Engman*

## Introduction: Why Is Trade in Engineering Services of Interest for Developing Countries?

Trade in engineering services is of interest to developing countries from an import and export perspective. Trade openness at home will lead to more choice in terms of price and quality, which benefits the families and the public and private sector clients that are dependent on engineering services in their daily lives and productive activities. The services, which predominantly focus on advisory, design, consulting, and project management functions, are key in upholding effective public services such as wastewater treatment, transportation systems, and electricity generation and transmission. They also contribute to a country's capacity to absorb and adapt new technology. Box 9.1 supplies a description of engineering services.

There are five main fields of expertise in engineering services, as follows:

- Civil engineering is instrumental in the construction of bridges, dams, and water, energy, and transportation systems, all which are crucial to developing countries that need to build or upgrade infrastructure.
- Mechanical engineering is critical in the mechanization of agricultural processes and in the industrialization of production processes.

**Box 9.1:** Definition of Engineering Services

The United Nations Provisional Central Product Classification list covers two relevant items on the four-digit level for engineering services (UN 1991):

*Engineering services (CPC 8672)*: covering (1) advisory and consultative engineering services, (2) engineering design services for the construction of foundations and building structures, (3) engineering design services for mechanical and electrical installations for buildings, (4) engineering design services for the construction of civil engineering works, (5) engineering design services for industrial processes and production, (6) engineering design services not elsewhere classified, (7) other engineering services during the construction and installation phase, and (8) other engineering services.

*Integrated engineering services (CPC 8673)*: covering (1) integrated engineering services for turnkey transportation infrastructure projects, (2) integrated engineering and project management services for turnkey water supply and sanitation works projects, (3) integrated engineering services for the construction of turnkey manufacturing projects, and (4) integrated engineering services for other turnkey projects.

- Electrical engineering is fundamental to the operation of public works, such as utilities, as well as commercial facilities and communication systems.
- Petroleum engineering is a primary input in some of the most productive sectors in oil-producing developing countries. These sectors account for up to 98 percent of exports in some developing countries (Sawinski and Mason 2007).
- Industrial engineering focuses on methods of production and efficiency and contributes to the overall productivity in the agriculture, manufacturing, and service sectors.

Consequently, for their welfare, citizens in developing countries have a significant interest in ensuring access to cost-competitive and high-quality engineering services.

Trade openness abroad is necessary so that engineering companies in developing countries may access foreign markets. Developing-country exports of engineering services are currently on the rise because new channels of electronic supply are creating new business opportunities and because the international sourcing of engineering services is becoming increasingly common. Several developing countries are large exporters of complementary services, such as construction services, and the provision of engineering services often represents a natural expansion for these companies in moving up the value chain. Engineering service exports may therefore provide many high-paying jobs to technicians and engineers in those developing countries that offer decent training opportunities.

In sum, trade liberalization in the engineering sector is in the interest of developing countries both at home and abroad. The next section addresses the issue of what can be done to harness trade opportunities by pursuing reforms in home markets, improving access to finance, promoting quality education and training in engineering, adopting an offensive (rather than defensive) trade strategy, and using trade negotiations to advance the interest in engineering exports. Then the role of engineers and professional bodies are considered, with special attention to designing business strategies to reinforce competitiveness, strengthening professional standards, meeting international standards, and promoting professional qualifications. The final section concludes by setting out the questions that stakeholders should bear in mind as they advance reforms. Tables are presented that identify initiatives to build trade capacity in engineering services by recognizing the dynamics in the marketplace and the common restrictions that affect the trade in engineering services.

## What Is the Situation of and What Are the Prospects for Trade in Engineering Services?

Global spending on engineering services constitutes roughly 2 percent of world income, and companies in developed countries are moving an increasing share of the supply of these knowledge-intensive services to developing countries. While labor costs remain an important motivation for this trade, access to local skills and markets is often driving the decisions by multinationals. It is estimated that the sector will grow by 2.4 percent on average until 2020 and create millions of high-income jobs in developing countries, many of which will be linked to exports. Of the industry's estimated US$1 trillion turnover in 2020, some 14–20 percent may be provided by emerging markets. This implies that the international supply by companies based in developing countries would double roughly every four years until 2020 (Booz Allen Hamilton 2006).

National trade statistics on engineering services are limited at best. Table 9.1 presents data on trade in architectural, engineering, and other technical services in 2006 for a number of markets. This broad category includes some services that are not covered in common definitions of engineering services, and our numbers here should therefore be interpreted with caution. The data reveal that emerging markets such as those of Brazil, India, the Republic of Korea, the Russian Federation, and Singapore are large exporters and that these countries, plus Kazakhstan, are also major importers. China would have been included among the top traders if data were available, and so would several Persian Gulf countries.

Rapid economic growth in countries such as China and India and in regions such as the Gulf and, until recently, Eastern Europe has led to greater demand for infrastructure. Aging infrastructure in developed economies also generates much demand for engineering services (Holloway 2007). The construction boom in the Middle East, particularly in resource-rich countries, has attracted plenty of

**Table 9.1.** Trade in Architectural, Engineering, and Other Technical Services, Selected Economies, 2006
*US$ millions*

| Exporters | | Importers | |
|---|---|---|---|
| European Union (27) | 39,212 | European Union (27) | 25,169 |
| Extra–European Union (27) exports | 22,657 | Extra–European Union (27) exports | 10,331 |
| India[a] | 7,360 | India[a] | 2,746 |
| United States[b] | 5,020 | Canada | 2,560 |
| Canada | 4,066 | Brazil | 1,708 |
| Brazil | 3,033 | Russian Federation | 1,616 |
| Norway | 2,144 | Kazakhstan | 1,289 |
| Russian Federation | 1,571 | Singapore | 977 |
| Singapore | 1,398 | Norway | 579 |
| Australia | 955 | Korea, Rep. | 531 |
| Korea, Rep. | 253 | Australia | 370 |
| Hong Kong, China | 162 | Croatia | 305 |
| Argentina | 77 | United States[b] | 281 |
| | | Hong Kong, China | 39 |

*Source:* WTO (2007).
a. Estimates of the World Trade Organization. Exports of "miscellaneous business, professional, and technical services, other" include information technology–enabled services.
b. Market research and public opinion polling are also included in "miscellaneous business, professional, and technical services, other."

foreign engineering service firms to the region. Large projects include, for example, Algeria's ambitious development program (including an east-west highway that is 1,216 kilometers long), Libya's new urban housing project, and various megaprojects in the Gulf, where more than 2,000 projects are either planned or under way. The value of the Gulf projects alone amounted to over US$1 trillion in 2006, with Saudi Arabia and the United Arab Emirates accounting for 20 and 29 percent, respectively (Buckley 2007).

In 2008, the top 500 global engineering design firms generated over US$80 billion in revenue. The bulk came from building, transportation, petroleum, waste, and energy projects (figure 9.1). If engineering service exports are counted together with architectural and other technical services, the European Union leads, followed by India, Canada, the United States, and Singapore (Tulacz 2008). The list of top exporters illustrates that some emerging economies have a comparative advantage in the production and delivery of engineering services. Engineering firms use a variety of means to deliver services internationally. The main channels are online service provision or interaction with clients in offices established

**Figure 9.1.** Top 500 Engineering Design Firms by Revenue and Type of Work, 2008

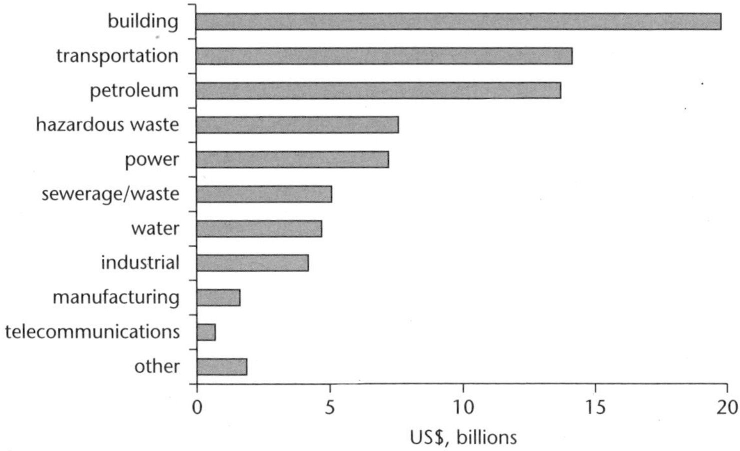


*Source:* Tulacz (2008).

abroad. Engineering firms also visit clients in their home markets to provide services (see box 9.2 for an overview).

Leading engineering firms provide integrated service packages to a broad range of clients, often using advanced technology (see table 9.2 for a list of leading firms). Joint ventures and partnership agreements are particularly common delivery platforms in developing countries. Leaders partner with local companies to leverage their expertise, skills, and connections. Engineering firms in developing countries use their commercial relationships with larger firms to take advantage of the global presence of the larger firms. Firms in developing countries also adopt international quality standards to position themselves advantageously relative to competitors. The international market for engineering services is large and employs a considerable number of qualified engineers and professionals. Several developing countries with adequate training capacity have been successful in creating a thriving engineering service sector based on exports to foreign markets.

Statistical accounts often treat engineering services and construction as distinct sectors. However, in the marketplace, many firms provide integrated packages to meet the demands of their clients. For example, CH2M Hill, an employee-owned professional engineering service firm, offers industrial engineering services in conjunction with construction, operations, project management, and

**Box 9.2:** The Four Modes of Supply of Engineering Services

The General Agreement on Trade in Services of the World Trade Organization defines four modes of supply in the trade in services. The modes of supply are identified to help trade negotiators determine trade commitments in trade agreements. Essentially, the modes are a construct for trade negotiations and seek to reflect how businesses operate. Most firms use a combination of some or all the modes of supply to conduct business. The modes focus on the location of the service provider and the location of the service consumer. They are defined in the general agreement as follows:

- Mode 1, *crossborder supply*: Nonresident service suppliers deliver services crossborder into a client's territory. For example, a Brazilian engineer sends sketches to a client in República Bolivariana de Venezuela. Mode 1 trade may be inhibited, for instance, by restrictions on Internet use and weak telecommunications infrastructure.
- Mode 2, *consumption abroad*: Residents in country A purchase services inside the territory of country B. For example, a U.S. oil company established in Nigeria buys services from a local engineering firm. Mode 2 trade may be inhibited, for instance, by excessively restrictive capital controls.
- Mode 3, *commercial presence*: Foreign suppliers of services establish, operate, or expand their commercial presence in a client's territory, such as a branch, agency, or wholly owned subsidiary. For example, a Tunisian engineering firm opens an office in Dakar to serve the Senegalese market. Mode 3 trade may be inhibited, for instance, by arduous qualification requirements and licensing procedures and by equity limitations.
- Mode 4, *the temporary movement of natural persons*: This involves the entry and temporary stay in a client's territory of foreign individuals to supply a service. For example, an Indian engineer supervises a construction project in Bangladesh. Mode 4 trade may be inhibited, for instance, by excessively restrictive visa fees or unpredictable and time-consuming work permit procedures.

Analysts and policy makers can use the modes of supply to identify constraints to growth in the engineering service trade. This understanding can then inform policy decisions to expand the trade in engineering services.

related technical services to public and private sector firms operating in the information technology, energy, life sciences, and advanced technology sectors around the world. Argentine (Techint), Brazilian (Andrade Gutierrez, Camargo Corrêa, Odebrecht, and Queiroz Galvão), and Mexican (ICA group) engineering and construction firms have also diversified into other industries and become large conglomerates (ECLAC 2007). The list of integrated service providers could be made long, and policy makers should therefore assess potential reforms in light of the commercial structure of the marketplace.

Growing international demand for engineering services in developed and developing countries creates employment opportunities for qualified professionals. However, engineering firms in a multitude of countries and sectors are experiencing shortages in skilled engineering professionals. For example, labor scarcity in the engineering and construction sectors has resulted in delays and

**Table 9.2.** Leading Engineering Firms, 2005

| Firm | Industry clients | Gross revenue, (US$, billions) | Employees | International presence |
|---|---|---|---|---|
| Vinci (France) | Transportation infrastructure, energy infrastructure, manufacturing, telecommunications | 25 (45% of revenue from outside France) | 142,500 (84,000 in France, 35,000 in the rest of Europe, 22,500 outside Europe) | 75 countries |
| Bouygues SA (France) | Transportation infrastructure | 32 | 115,411 (52,000 employed outside France) | 80 countries |
| Halliburton Co. (Kellogg, Brown, & Root [KBR] engineering division) (United States) | Civil engineering, nuclear engineering, weapons engineering, marine engineering, petroleum engineering | 12.5 (KBR division) | 60,000 (KBR division) | 43 countries (KBR division) |
| Bechtel Group (United States) | Transportation infrastructure, power plants, pipelines, telecommunications | 17.4 | 40,000 | 25 countries |
| Fluor Corporation (United States) | Petroleum engineering, industrial engineering, hazardous waste engineering | 9.4 | 35,000 | 25 countries |
| CH2M Hill Companies Limited (United States) | Water, transportation, environmental (including ecosystem management, human health, and ecological risk assessment), ground remediation services, nuclear engineering | 5.8 | 25,000 | 76 countries |

*Sources:* Sawinski and Mason (2007), http://www.ch2m.com/corporate/region_select.asp.

lost business opportunities in relation to some petrochemical projects in the Middle East in recent years (D'Amico 2008). Initiatives in developing countries to build engineering expertise are necessary to help close some of the gaps in skills.

Engaging effectively with global engineering leaders is an important means of business development for engineering firms at the local level. The top

**Box 9.3:** An Example of Trade Success: Tunisian Engineering Firms

Founded in 1970, STUDI, a Tunisian engineering service firm, employs more than 300 professionals. Exports represent about 75 percent of the firm's turnover. The firm has carried out more than 2,500 missions in some 38 countries. International expansion has resulted in subsidiaries in Algeria, Libya, Senegal, and the United Arab Emirates, as well as branch offices in 14 Sub-Saharan African countries.

Another Tunisian firm, SCET Tunisie, employs 200 professionals and has been exporting services to Sub-Saharan Africa for the last 30 years. The firm has a client portfolio spanning 26 countries. Exports represent 70 percent of the firm's turnover, and 40 percent of exports are absorbed by the Sub-Saharan African region. The firm was initially owned by Caisse des Dépôts et Consignations, a French company, but 95 percent of corporate equity is now owned by Tunisian citizens. The firm has acquired an engineering company in France and become established in Algeria (at the project level) and Senegal (partial participation).

A somewhat newer Tunisian engineering service firm, COMETE, was founded in 1987 and employs about 90 professionals. Export revenue represents 50 percent of the firm's turnover and has recently grown rapidly. The company aims to increase this share to at least two-thirds in the near future. The company operates in 16 countries and is becoming established in Algeria, Burkina Faso, and Saudi Arabia. The group is partly owned by Groupe Suez and Banque Tuniso-Koweïtienne de Développement.

*Source:* World Bank (2008).

200 international engineering design firms generated US$33 billion in revenue in 2006 from projects outside their respective home countries (ENR 2007). When involved in the design and construction of public works and commercial facilities in the Middle East or North Africa, for example, these firms may be headquartered in one country, assemble engineering specialists from several other markets, and use sources of materials and labor locally and from third countries (Nicholson 2007).

Several engineering firms in the developing world compete successfully on foreign markets with multinationals based in the countries of the Organisation for Economic Co-operation and Development. For example, Tunisia has a foothold in the engineering service market at a regional level. Tunisian engineering firms provide services through all four modes of supply, including the temporary movement of natural persons in Africa, the Middle East, and France (box 9.3). Despite their relatively limited size, many of these privately owned Tunisian firms are profitable.

## What Can Be Done to Harness Trade Opportunities?

The growth of trade in engineering services can be encouraged by a set of policies. First, policy makers, together with professional bodies, must assess the domestic regulatory environment and its effects on the development of engineering services.

Second, policy makers and professional bodies must examine whether there are other constraints that hinder the development of engineering services. In this regard, access to financing and policies relating to public procurement are particularly important in engineering services.

Third, trade barriers in engineering services go beyond issues of market access and national treatment. The quality of engineering services, including professional, process, and product standards, is determinant of trade opportunities. Policy makers ought to design ways to improve quality standards in engineering services in accordance with international standards and best practices.

Fourth, some trade and administrative barriers may be overcome through international cooperation. Policy makers must understand the role that trade and mutual recognition agreements can play in harnessing the trade in engineering services.

Finally, as in other professional services, the role that professional associations play in various policy areas must be addressed.

### *Pursuing reforms in home markets*

The engineering profession is subject to a variety of laws, regulations, and administrative rules at home and abroad that are administered by professional and government entities. These measures have a substantial impact on the way engineering firms operate. Legislation, regulations, and administrative rules shape the following:

- The organization of the firm
- The contours of the marketplace and the clients that firms may serve
- The ability to visit and establish in new markets
- The ability to move engineering equipment
- The cost of exporting
- The ability to undertake commercial transactions
- Employment practices
- Access to finance
- Insurance and bonding policies
- The potential return on investment

Policy makers can analyze how specific rules influence the engineering profession in a positive and negative manner. They can reexamine the purpose of such regulations, whether they are achieving this purpose, and if they are effectively administered. Policy makers can determine if other methods would achieve the same objectives. They can adjust such rules accordingly so as to strengthen the environment for the engineering profession.

Engineering standards set at the national level can have a significant influence on the competitive position of domestic firms. If national standards are not consistent with international expectations, domestic players may have difficulty competing in foreign markets. Foreign firms that operate using international standards will maintain a competitive advantage over domestic firms using outdated or subpar engineering standards. Policy makers can work with standards associations to ensure that national firms use international standards and can therefore compete in foreign markets more effectively.

National or subfederal rules that limit engineering firms to a particular type of legal entity or joint venture structure may influence a firm's financial options. Arbitrary equity limitations can also reduce the financing options available to engineering firms. Policy makers can examine why particular types of entities are required, the purpose of the rules, and whether the rules are achieving their objectives. They can investigate the impact of the rules on the ability of domestic engineering firms to compete at home and in foreign markets. Consultations with engineers and their professional associations would help inform such an assessment.

Policy makers can review rules governing nationality and residency requirements, engineering qualification and recognition procedures, equity limitations, investment limitations, and so on to determine their influence on the engineering profession at home and abroad. With a comprehensive assessment, policy makers can pursue unilateral reform, as well as bilateral, regional, and multilateral negotiations. (A full examination of such rules and their impact on engineering professionals in the marketplace is provided below.)

Policy makers can encourage professional bodies to collaborate with their counterparts in regional markets to promote professional exchanges, undertake analyses of different approaches to the profession, and investigate regulatory developments. They can support discussions among regulatory institutions in a region to address concerns with regard to procurement policies, nationality and residency restrictions, double taxation, and so on. They can facilitate the engagement of professional bodies and related government entities in discussions on cooperation to adjust rules so as to facilitate trade, thereby providing a greater flow of information about the engineering market, professional opportunities, and key drivers in the industry. They can commission studies of the engineering profession, hold public forums, and facilitate links with professional bodies. Each option will require investment in improved public policy processes.

### *Improving access to finance*

Engineering firms require financial services attuned to credit extension on the basis of forward contracts, intellectual property, and probable returns on investment rather than a concentration of physical assets. The engineering industry is a 3 to 4 percent margin business, creating a demand for competitive financing (Tulacz 2008). Engineering firms subject to double taxation, excessive capital controls, and limits on foreign equity face financial limitations.

Access to finance remains an issue in many developing countries, and the lack of access puts engineering firms at a competitive disadvantage. For example, in Tunisia, credit is limited to 5 percent of the output of the engineering firm, compared with 10 percent in other sectors such as tourism and manufacturing (World Bank 2007). Local financial institutions may have difficulty accurately assessing an engineering firm's potential returns on investment and may not have the capacity to value forward contracts, intellectual property, and professional expertise. They may rely too heavily on physical assets in determining credit extension.

Affirmative steps with local financial institutions that explore credit extension based on a variety of variables rather than a narrow reliance on physical assets may help improve the financial position of local engineering firms. Similarly, engineering trade associations can prepare financial proposals as a service to their engineering members. Such proposals would explain to financial institutions the financial model that engineering firms use. These steps can help improve the competitive position of engineering practitioners. Engineering firms and professionals also need access to adequate insurance. An underdeveloped insurance market may impede engineering professionals from obtaining the necessary scope of liability protection. Without this protection, the firms will be at a competitive disadvantage relative to firms with adequate insurance protection.

### *Administering public procurement policies*

Large infrastructure projects designed by governments and donors, as well as commercial contracts, represent a large share of the revenue of many engineering firms. Rules affecting public procurement, including the transparency of procedures, are therefore shaping the trade in engineering services. The engineering profession benefits from concerted attention on objective procurement policies in the public and private sectors. Administering well-defined and open procurement processes on all levels enhances the economic opportunities for productive business. Failure to act can prove costly: as much as 5 percent of Africa's gross domestic product may be squandered through graft in construction projects alone (Reyna 2007). In an environment of transparent procurement policies, practicing engineers can bid on projects at home and abroad from an informed position.

Without publicly available information about project requirements and the bidding process, engineering firms, particularly smaller ones, will face a greater challenge in competing in the procurement process. Ensuring the integrity and transparency of procurement processes is a challenge in many economies.

However, electronic means can support integrity and enhance transparency. Publicizing the terms of procurement initiatives and information on the related procedural aspects and timelines can provide a level playing field for bidders. Audit and enforcement can provide integrity. Eliminating bribes, political contributions, facilitation payments, gifts, hospitality, and expenses that influence procurement awards will lower the cost for engineering professionals to participate in the market. Correcting distorted administrative practices requires political commitment, possibly legislation, and enforcement capability. Initiatives to counter corruption that effectively address the public and private sectors can reduce distortions in the engineering service marketplace.

In addition, public procurement may be used as a means to advance specific social objectives. For example, according to Rustomjee (2007), in South Africa, public procurement is explicitly used to achieve the following:

- Safety: compulsory registration among the firms bidding in public service tenders
- Consumer protection: registration to ensure that engineers are qualified, perform with integrity, deliver quality, and allow redress
- Industry development: accreditation graded according to the capacity and track record of the respective firm
- Employment creation: uses structured progression from small contractors to larger corporate entities
- Empowerment of historically disadvantaged people

With a view to promote trade, policies to achieve these objectives can be designed to be nondiscriminatory and to advance the transfer of professional expertise. For example, occupational safety requirements should be made publicly available and applied consistently to local and foreign firms. Consumer protection rules that mandate indemnity requirements should be the same for local and foreign firms. The same should be true for technology transfer and training requirements. Policy makers can examine rules at home and abroad to determine if they distort the competitive position of foreign firms relative to local firms.

### *Promoting quality education and training in engineering*

A number of developing economies are poised to take advantage of the increasing demand for engineering professionals. For example, colleges of engineering in Morocco maintain high standards of educational excellence. Students experience a rigorous curriculum and take advantage of formal links with colleges in the region, in Europe, and in North America. Graduates obtain degrees that are highly regarded in export markets of interest. At the same time, only 4 students

**Figure 9.2.** Comparative Student Enrollments in Engineering, Selected Countries

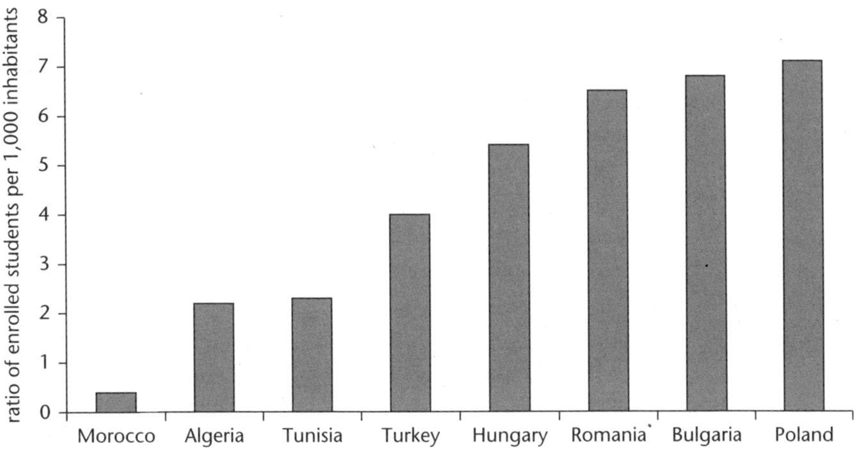


*Source:* UNESCO Institute for Statistics.
*Note:* The ratio is the number of students (tertiary) enrolled in engineering, manufacturing, and construction per 1,000 inhabitants. Data for Tunisia are from 2003.

per 10,000 inhabitants choose to study engineering in Morocco (figure 9.2). This ratio is lower than the ratios for Algeria and Tunisia, where it is approximately 20 per 10,000, and Eastern European countries, where it is 60 per 10,000 (World Bank 2007). Focusing attention on colleges of engineering in a region can leverage educational assets and help build a larger pool of qualified engineers in the region.

Colleges of engineering can work to improve the level of enrollment among qualified students from home and abroad. They can create educational outreach programs for primary and secondary educational institutions, which can adjust curricula to facilitate interest in the field of engineering. In other cases, improving curricula is critical in attracting students. For example, in Mozambique, an average engineering student requires eight years to complete the degree, which should normally take five years, thereby discouraging students to enroll in engineering studies. Moreover, because the quality of secondary education in Mozambique is poor, students do not have the skills, tools, and knowledge needed to pursue higher education. This has resulted in a low number of professionals in Mozambique in general. Therefore, reforming the secondary education system is also critical (Fernandes and Mattoo 2009).

From the standpoint of exports, highly regarded colleges of engineering can be marketed at the regional level to attract students from other developing countries interested in pursuing the engineering profession. In this respect, Morocco may be well positioned to export educational services by attracting foreign students. Given the employment opportunities at the global level, highly regarded colleges of engineering can actively work to raise enrollments, while maintaining high standards.

Professional bodies and trade associations can undertake to highlight the opportunities in the engineering profession to prospective students. For example, in Germany, engineering firms are offering discovery boxes filled with science experiments for 3-to-6-year-olds in kindergarten to excite interest in the field of engineering (Milne 2008). Professional bodies and engineering firms can facilitate internships for youth with engineering professionals. They can create links with secondary educational institutions through engineering competitions and award programs. Professional bodies and trade associations can circulate career guides and information on engineering employment trends to secondary educational institutions in a region. Such initiatives can leverage educational assets to increase employment in the growing engineering profession.

### *Adopting an offensive (rather than defensive) trade strategy*

Developing countries can institute a program to create a better environment for engineering professionals. An effective starting point is an engineering service policy dialogue at the national level to gather information on the engineering marketplace at home and abroad. Such a dialogue can create important information for decision makers and negotiators. This dialogue can provide information on the following:

- Employment in the engineering profession, the contribution of the profession to gross domestic product, growth trends
- Domestic engineering service firms operating at home and abroad
- Firm business models, areas of expertise, and export markets of interest
- Why certain markets are of particular interest in terms of exports
- Trade barriers in export markets of interest
- How restrictions impact the domestic engineering profession
- How restrictions impact the marketplace
- How firms are positioned within larger global networks of engineering firms

An engineering service trade dialogue can pinpoint restrictions in the domestic market and in export markets of interest. The engineering service dialogue creates a case for unilateral reform and negotiations at the bilateral, regional, and multilateral levels. If conducted rigorously, it can also create momentum for legislative, regulatory, and administrative changes at home. Stakeholders can support negotiations and the consequent tasks associated with implementing trade commitments.[1]

### *Using international negotiations to advance engineering export interests*

Trade negotiations can achieve national treatment and market access for engineering firms. For example, in regional markets, engineering firms reportedly encounter discriminatory treatment relative to national firms. In Europe, foreign engineering firms reportedly are subject to requirements that they establish local offices to practice, and they encounter discriminatory treatment relative to national and third-country firms (World Bank 2007). Tunisian engineering firms face double taxation because of a lack of bilateral and regional tax treaties (World Bank 2008). The absence of bilateral tax arrangements can reduce the returns on exports and make export prospects untenable.

Trade agreements at the bilateral, regional, or multilateral level can effectively improve the market environment at home. For example, Morocco has engaged in bilateral arrangements with provisions to facilitate trade in engineering. A recent free trade agreement contains substantial transparency provisions that require the establishment of contact points, the prompt publication of rules, and opportunity for comment on the rules. Crossborder trade provisions enable the parties to the agreement to pursue the mutual recognition of professional qualifications. Parties allow for the temporary admission of goods with regard to specialized equipment frequently used in engineering. Government procurement provisions require open procurement processes (Bennett 2004). Implementation requires investment in public policy procedures.

Engagement in service negotiations under the General Agreement on Trade in Services of the World Trade Organization also offers a vehicle to address barriers to trade in engineering services at a multilateral level. A review of the plurilateral requests on engineering services can help policy makers understand the parameters of negotiations. For example, the requests highlight the removal of nationality requirements, residency requirements, rules that restrict a particular type of legal entity, limitations on the participation of foreign capital, and joint ventures (International Trade Canada 2006). Engagement in negotiations can also expose World Trade Organization members to market concerns across the spectrum of economies. Engagement requires a comprehensive approach and an understanding of the potential trade-offs involved in each aspect of the Doha Round. Regional arrangements can also foster integration in the engineering service trade (box 9.4).

**Box 9.4:** The Contribution of Regionalism to Integration in the Engineering Service Trade

Deepening existing regional arrangements can facilitate trade. For example, the 1989 Treaty of the Arab Maghreb Union, which includes Algeria, Libya, Mauritania, Morocco, and Tunisia, was designed to integrate goods, service, capital, and labor markets. However, it only led to the establishment of a Bank for Investment and Foreign Trade to foster financial integration. Nonetheless, according to Tahari et al. (2007), all members have made tangible progress at strengthening the legal and regulatory framework governing financial systems. Policy makers can build on this momentum to revisit service provision within the union and, at a minimum, establish a working group on professional services. The working group could explore the establishment of regional vehicles for the mutual recognition of qualifications and for facilitating the temporary movement of professionals.

Created in 1981, the Gulf Cooperation Council has progressed toward monetary convergence. Members are contemplating a regional stock market (Tahari et al. 2007). Members are also interested in employment diversification. Establishing a working group on professional services under the auspices of the council is a means to explore vehicles to facilitate trade in legal, engineering, and accounting services at the regional level.

Regional agreements offer examples of provisions that facilitate trade in professional services. The recently concluded agreement between the Caribbean nations and the European Union, the CARIFORUM–European Union Economic Partnership Agreement, includes specific provisions on professional services. According to OTN (2008), the provisions on professional services will accomplish the following:

- Initiate consultations among professional bodies
- Enable professional bodies to make recommendations to a joint committee
- Ensure reviews of the progress on mutual recognition agreements
- Facilitate short-term visits for business purposes
- Establish inquiry points to provide regulatory information

Other arrangements such as the Caribbean Community, the Southern Cone Common Market, the North American Free Trade Agreement, and the European Union offer models for facilitating trade in professional services at the regional level (UNCTAD 2005).

Policy makers can balance increased market access and national treatment with complementary measures to enhance the environment for engineering services at home and to advance export opportunities. It is necessary to address the fears associated with the various measures (box 9.5).

## What Is the Role of Engineers and Professional Bodies?

### *Designing business strategies to reinforce competitiveness*

Local engineering firms can explore a variety of business strategies to improve their competitive position and capture greater market shares abroad. Engineering firms compete on the basis of technology, cost, scope of services, particular area of

**Box 9.5:** Addressing the Fears Associated with Trade Opening: Accompanying Measures

Proposed changes to laws, regulations, and administrative rules on a unilateral basis or as a result of trade negotiations may raise a host of concerns. Lifting nationality and residency requirements and lifting restrictions on commercial presence, which would allow foreign engineering professionals into once protected segments of the market, can raise anxiety about competition. Practicing engineers and engineering firms may fear the capabilities of new market entrants. Standards boards and associated regulatory agencies may be concerned about the poor quality of engineering services and poor liability protection. Lifting equity limitations may prompt concerns about renewed colonialism. A country's ministry of finance may oppose the loosening of capital controls and engagement in tax treaties. Implementing transparent and open processes for qualifications, registration, and procurement can reduce the authority of regulatory officials to make discretionary decisions.

Whether as a result of unilateral reform or trade negotiations, policy makers can undertake changes on a graduated basis in terms of geography, time, and scope to soften competition. Policy makers can also replace restrictive measures with rules that are no more trade restrictive than necessary. For example, to reduce the fears associated with increased competition and poor performance in the marketplace in professional services, policy makers can formulate measures in place of nationality and residency requirements. Policy makers can formulate requirements for "collaboration with locals, bonding requirements to ensure recourse and agreements on cross-disciplinary actions" (International Trade Canada 2006, 3). Policy makers can also use skill-transfer provisions that require foreign professionals to participate in training, mentoring, and education as a part of licensure requirements (Terry 2008).

Market opening can be balanced by investment in domestic institutions and engagement in mutual recognition agreements, as well as export promotion. The ability of professional bodies and associated regulatory agencies to oversee the market effectively in terms of quality, service delivery, and consumer protection can be strengthened. Invigorated oversight bodies can enforce important rules designed to protect consumers and ensure the delivery of quality services. Policy makers can help strengthen professional bodies, standards boards, and regulatory entities, as well as educational institutions, to enable professionals to engage effectively in the global market.

Market openings can also be matched by investment in export promotion. Countries with the resources to post commercial officers abroad and an adept ministry of commerce can provide direct assistance to engineering firms. Commercial officers abroad can help engineering firms navigate regulatory requirements in export markets of interest. They can actively facilitate the development of commercial relationships with potential clients and foreign engineering firms.

Policy makers can undertake specific initiatives to link domestic engineering professionals with each other. A country's ministry of commerce or export promotion agency can organize trade missions. Gathering engineering professionals to participate in trade missions can promote commercial relationships within the domestic profession. Increasing commercial links among engineering professionals can enable these professionals to offer a broader scope of services.

Increased links with universities can help engineering professionals obtain export market analysis, develop export strategies, and create business plans. Links with the business media can help engineering firms enhance their commercial profiles and can offer news about commercial developments, interviews, and success stories. Matching market opening with investment in domestic infrastructure and export promotion can help engineering firms compete.

expertise, quality of service, and delivery schedules, as well as postdelivery service. Engineering firms can therefore evaluate their internal structures and determine how to best choose, market, serve, and retain their clients. Elements of these strategies could include the following:

- Firms could invest in technology to capture a greater share of emerging and growing markets in maintenance, environment, and computer engineering and specialize in sophisticated, value added engineering services rather than in commoditized engineering projects procured primarily on the basis of cost.
- Firms could collaborate with other firms or international partners to offer a broader scope of services to access a greater client base. Although small service firms export in large numbers, microenterprises forgo the benefits of the economies of scale necessary to invest in technology, offer a broad scope of services, and execute marketing, export, and strategic plans. Encouraging firms to collaborate strategically can therefore improve their competitive position.
- Firms could expand their online presence and participate in export promotion missions abroad to develop commercial relationships and new business.

The expanding global delivery of engineering services places a premium on management skills. Mergers and acquisitions that create geographically dispersed firms also generate demand for astute engineering professionals. Engineering managers are often responsible for project delivery, as well as finance, business development, marketing, and maintaining the relationship with clients. The international market for engineering services thus requires that engineering professionals have complementary business and language skills. Box 9.6 outlines the strategies that can be applied at the firm and market levels.

### *Strengthening professional bodies*

Building the competence and external relationships of professional bodies can improve conditions for engineering firms at home and in neighboring markets. Effective professional bodies can help engineering firms improve their market knowledge and operations. Without healthy professional bodies, engineering firms are disadvantaged because of limitations in the professional support that supplies commercial information, analysis of regional trends in the market, and professional exchange opportunities.

Professional engineering bodies may have a limited scope for service to their members. Engineering bodies may not have the resources to conduct outreach, engage internationally, or discipline professionals. They may also be dominated by

**Box 9.6:** Articulating Microstrategies and Macrostrategies

Policy makers can focus on recognizing and promoting the commercially valuable attributes of engineering firms and positive conditions in the market generally.

Policy makers can reinforce the commercially valuable attributes at the firm level through the following:

- Establishment of a quality reputation because of successful service delivery
- Ability to compete on price, while delivering quality
- International Organization for Standardization certification

Policy makers can reinforce commercially valuable attributes at the market level through the following:

- Employment of engineering professionals with bilingual language ability
- Educational standards consistent with international expectations
- Access to joint degrees at educational institutions abroad
- Ability to engage with foreign practitioners so as to allow the transfer of skills
- Ability to employ foreign practitioners so as to allow a broad scope in engineering services
- A domestic financial regulatory framework that allows relatively free capital flows
- Regional transit policies that welcome the movement of professionals

a particular segment of the profession. To broaden the perspective of professional bodies, the government of South Africa has, for example, mandated public participation in the governing bodies of professional associations (Rustomjee 2007).

Underwriting investment in the staff, technology, and services of professional governing bodies for engineering services may help microengineering firms collaborate, share technology, share market information, and execute advertising, marketing, and export plans. Facilitating links between professional bodies and counterparts in regional markets can improve the potential for collaboration, help engineering firms navigate external markets, and promote mutual recognition agreements. For example, the Engineering Council of South Africa is active at the regional level in strengthening sister organizations in neighboring countries to improve services to members and raise standards in the profession (Rustomjee 2007).

### *Meeting international standards*

The engineering field is subject to quality standards set at the national and international levels. Generally at the national level, standards boards or institutes formulate standards, in conjunction with the private sector. Most participate in the International Organization for Standardization, which is a forum for national standards institutes from 157 countries, as well as trade associations. In cooperation with the private sector, the International Organization for Standardization has created more than 17,000 standards in, for example, infrastructure, engineering technologies, transport, material technologies, and construction. Stakeholders remain engaged to avoid the use of standards as industrial policy or discriminatory trade barriers.

Engineering firms that are focused on quality and building their reputations seek to adhere to such standards and achieve International Organization for Standardization certification for process regularity and product specifications (Sawinski and Mason 2007). For example, a number of Moroccan engineering firms are certified, and Morocco's Service de Normalisation Industrielle Marocaine is a member of the International Organization for Standardization (World Bank 2007). National standards boards can actively engage in the International Organization for Standardization, encourage engineering firms to invest in certification, and actively disseminate developments in engineering standards to industry as a means to invigorate the engineering profession.

### *Promoting the recognition of professional qualifications*

Professional qualification requirements are fundamental drivers in the industry. Countries use different models of registration and licensing to oversee the profession. Government entities may offer licenses according to specific qualifications, or professional societies may offer licenses. In some instances, the licensing and registration systems are in their infancy. From a trade standpoint, clear licensing and registration procedures should be established, and information on them should be made publicly available. They should also be associated with clear processes and timelines.

Engineering is a pioneer profession; it has relied on multilateral accords since 1989 to facilitate the mutual recognition of qualification requirements. These accords represent agreements among agencies responsible for accreditation or the recognition of tertiary-level engineering qualifications within their jurisdictions (IEA 2007). They encourage licensing authorities to provide the same rights and privileges to graduates in the recognized programs as those afforded in the home country. The Dublin, Sydney, and Washington Accords cover different engineering professions and work to facilitate mutual recognition.

Engineering institutions that invest in raising standards and apply the accords can provide a competitive advantage to their engineering professionals. Institutional engagement in the accords facilitates recognition for engineers seeking to practice their profession abroad. The agreements can also be replicated at a regional level. Engagement in existing accords and the development of like agreements at the regional level can expand the commercial horizon for practicing engineers. The best practices in business services that rely on applying mutual recognition agreements to engineering are listed in table 9.3.

**Table 9.3.** Best Practices in Business Services: Mutual Recognition Agreements in Engineering

| Agreement | Scope | Members |
|---|---|---|
| **Washington Accord (1989)** | Substantial equivalence in the accreditation of qualifications in professional engineering | Engineering institutions in Australia; Canada; Hong Kong, China; Ireland; Japan; Korea, Rep.; New Zealand; Singapore; South Africa; Taiwan, China; United Kingdom (new members may apply) |
| **Sydney Accord (2001)** | Equivalence of accredited engineering technology education programs | Engineering institutions in Australia; Canada; Hong Kong, China; Ireland; New Zealand; South Africa; United Kingdom (new members may apply) |
| **Dublin Accord (2002)** | Equivalence of the educational base for engineering technicians | The founding institutional members are from Canada, Ireland, South Africa, United Kingdom |
| **APEC Engineer Agreement (1999)** | Equivalence at the level of practicing engineers<br>Allows minimal assessment prior to obtaining registration in countries party to the agreement<br>Members maintain registers of engineers | Institutional members originate in Australia; Canada; Hong Kong, China; Indonesia; Japan; Korea, Rep.; Malaysia; New Zealand; Philippines; Singapore; Taiwan, China; Thailand; United States |
| **Engineers Mobility Forum Agreement (2001)** | Members maintain registers of professional engineers | Institutional members originate in Australia; Canada; Hong Kong, China; Ireland; Japan; Korea, Rep.; Malaysia; New Zealand; Singapore; South Africa; Sri Lanka; United Kingdom; United States |
| **Engineering Technologist Mobility Forum Agreement (2003)** | Members maintain international engineering technologist registers<br>Receive credit when seeking registration or licensure in the jurisdiction of another member | Member institutions originate in Canada; Hong Kong, China; Ireland; New Zealand; South Africa; United Kingdom |

*Source:* Authors compilation based on http://www.washingtonaccord.org/.

## Conclusion

Engineering services are a knowledge-intensive industry essential to the productivity and sustainability of various other economic activities such as manufacturing and construction. The services are predominantly advisory, design, consulting, or project management services and are input services in both the public and private sectors. Worldwide spending on engineering services has been estimated at US$750 billion in 2004 and is projected to exceed US$1 trillion by 2020. The expansion of the sector is likely to create millions of high-income jobs in developing countries, many of which will be linked to trade.

Rapid economic growth in many emerging markets and upgrades in aging infrastructure in developed economies are driving the demand for engineering services. Rules affecting public procurement, including the transparency of procedures, are shaping trade in the profession. Administering well-defined and open procurement procedures enhances the economic opportunities for productive business. Technology is an integral part of engineering services, and it influences business operations and service delivery. The Internet has facilitated the globalization of the engineering industry and allowed additional fragmentation in the value chain and trade in the various parts of the production process.

Engineering standards set at the national level can have a significant influence on the competitive position of domestic firms. If national standards are inconsistent with international expectations, domestic players may have difficulty competing in foreign markets. Policy makers can institute programs to create a better environment for engineering professionals. An engineering service trade dialogue can identify restrictions in the domestic market and in export markets of interest. International negotiations can improve market access for engineering firms. Building the competence and external relationships of professional bodies can improve conditions for engineering firms at home and in neighboring markets.

The engineering industry is instrumental in the productivity and export potential of many other economic sectors. For example, agricultural producers, manufacturers, and telecommunications service providers each rely on a variety of engineering services to store, produce, and deliver their products. Policy makers can take specific steps to improve the environment for engineering services and increase export potential.

Policy makers can work to build professional value, help engineering firms improve access to clients, and facilitate trade. Regarding professional value, specific initiatives that could be considered encompass the promotion of online training, engineering internships, exchange programs, and continuing adult education and the fostering of links with foreign engineering firms, including hiring foreign engineering practitioners and allowing domestic engineering practitioners to be employed in foreign firms.

Access to clients can be improved by designing a tax policy to reduce the incidence of double taxation and cooperate with trading partners to facilitate the temporary movement of engineering professionals. Among the most relevant measures that could be undertaken to facilitate trade in engineering services are the implementation of mutual recognition agreements and improved access to information and communication technology infrastructure, as well as cooperation with trading partners to ameliorate the administration of the rules and regulations that affect trade in engineering.

Finally, policy makers, in collaboration with professional bodies and leading engineering firms, can define work programs to identify domestic regulatory reforms, improve professional qualifications, and pursue international cooperation, including international negotiations at the regional, bilateral, and multilateral levels. The aim would be to reduce the regulatory burden faced by service providers and eliminate trade barriers, such as nationality and residency requirements that affect the establishment of commercial presence.

This chapter covers several issues that merit the attention of policy makers as they advance a trade-integration agenda in engineering services. To address these issues, a public-private partnership that includes all relevant stakeholders is necessary. This partnership can build a work program that reflects the issues identified in this chapter. Table 9.4 contains a list of possible items that could be included in this work program and that aim at improving the regulatory environment and creating trade opportunities for the engineering profession. The checklist of questions may not be exhaustive, but still helps provide structure to the issues and ensures a comprehensive approach to reform.

**Table 9.4.** A Checklist of Questions on Trade-Related Aspects of Engineering Service Reform

| **Facilitating commercial presence** |
|---|
| 1. Are there legal restrictions on market entry through commercial presence for foreign engineering firms? If so, what type of restrictions are there, and what is their impact on flows of foreign direct investment? Are they discriminatory relative to the restrictions imposed on domestic firms, and are they compliant with prospective commitments of the World Trade Organization? What is the rationale for imposing the restrictions? |
| 2. If there is a requirement for foreign engineering firms to form joint ventures with local contractors, have such joint ventures been successful and fulfilled the prospective motivations of transferring technology and management knowledge? Have they helped build local expertise? |
| 3. Do foreign engineering firms need to register and obtain licenses that are different (for example, in terms of cost) from the licenses domestic firms need? Are there any capital control requirements that may have a negative impact on trade? |
| 4. Are there any particular staffing requirements for the establishment of branch offices? Do foreign branches need to hire local executives or board members? Are there residency requirements? To what extent does this impact the investment and business decisions of firms? |
| 5. Can the policy rationale of restrictions be addressed through other, less-trade-restrictive means? |

(*Table continues on the following page.*)

**Table 9.4.** A Checklist of Questions on Trade-Related Aspects of Engineering Service Reform (*continued*)

**Facilitating the temporary movement of engineering professionals**

1. What type of restrictions exist on foreign engineers serving in the domestic market? Does the country impose bans, work permit quotas, economic needs tests, or other impediments to the movement of project staff? Are rules different for intracorporate transferees and contractual service providers?
2. Is there implicit or explicit discrimination with regard to the nationality of service providers? How do such restrictions affect competition?
3. Is the business visa and work permit application process administered in a reasonably expedient and cost-effective way? Or is it opaque, slow, and cumbersome? What can be done to improve administrative efficiency in the application process? Is there scope for bilateral or regional agreement on this issue?
4. Are there issues related to the nonrecognition of qualifications for engineers at home or in major export markets?
5. What are the policy objectives of the restrictions? Can the policy rationale be addressed through other means that are less trade restrictive and more competition friendly?

**Reviewing other trade-distorting rules and regulations**

1. Are there any types of subsidies provided to domestic engineering service firms? Are subsidies allocated in an equal way, or are they tied to specific criteria? If they are so tied, what are the ties?
2. Can foreign firms import engineering equipment for projects without the imposition of major taxes and waiting time at customs? Is the country a signatory of the Information Technology Agreement of the World Trade Organization, which eliminates tariffs on information technology products?
3. Are government contracts advertised in easily accessible media or gazettes? Do government agencies allow sufficient time for the advertisement process? Are winning bids announced to the public? Is there a dispute resolution mechanism to resolve issues in the procurement process?
4. Do local authorities offer preference margins to domestic firms? If so, what are the margins and how much do they help raise participation by domestic engineering service firms? If domestic firms already dominate the market, do these preference margins hamper foreign competition?
5. Are there any other barriers inhibiting trade in engineering services that can be removed, such as restrictive rules on the use of brand names, marketing, advertising, price setting, hiring practices, and so on?
6. Does the country operate treaties that solve issues of double taxation?

**Integrating local engineering practices with internationally accepted good engineering standards and practices**

1. Is there (a) a professional body for engineers, (b) a national standards board, and (c) an industry association promoting the interests of engineering firms?
2. If so, do these associations have sufficient power or too much power for the good of the domestic market? Are concerns about foreign firms addressed by these associations? What role can these associations play in strengthening the sector?
3. To what extent is there a regional dimension in the work agendas of these associations?

*Source:* Authors compilation.

## Note

1. Trade commitments may require investment in public policy mechanisms, the creation of independent regulatory authorities, inquiry points, and changes in legislation, regulation, or administrative rules and practices.

## References

Bennett, B. Timothy. 2004. "The U.S.-Morocco Free Trade Agreement." Report of the Industry Sector Advisory Committee on Services for Trade Policy Matters, April 6, Office of the United States Trade Representative, Washington, DC.

Booz Allen Hamilton. 2006. *Globalization of Engineering Services: The Next Frontier for India*. New Delhi: National Association of Software and Services Companies.

Buckley, Bruce. 2007. "Rapid Global Development Fueling Greater Demand for Rail and Transit: Major Cities in Key Markets Planning Major Systems or Upgrades." *Engineering News-Record* 259 (23).

D'Amico, Esther. 2008. "Talent Management: Skilled Worker Demand Outweighs Supply." *Chemical Week* 170 (11): 22–23.

ECLAC (United Nations Economic Commission for Latin America and the Caribbean). 2007. *Foreign Investment in Latin America and the Caribbean, 2006*. Santiago, Chile: ECLAC.

ENR (*Engineering News-Record*). 2007. "The Top 200 International Design Firms." 259 (23).

Fernandes, Ana Margarida, and Aaditya Mattoo. 2009. "Professional Services and Development: A Study of Mozambique." Policy Research Working Paper 4870, World Bank, Washington, DC.

Helgren, Dale E. 2006. "Trends in Engineering." *Marketplace* 18 (3): 42.

Holloway, James. 2007. "Playing the Global Infrastructure Boom." *The Outlook*, September 11, Standard & Poor's, New York.

IEA (International Engineering Alliance). 2007. "International Educational Accords: Rules and Procedures." International Engineering Alliance Secretariat, Institution of Professional Engineers New Zealand, Wellington, New Zealand. http://www.ieagreements.org/Rules_and_Procedures.pdf.

International Trade Canada. 2006. "Collective Request: Architectural, Engineering and Integrated Engineering Services." Department of Foreign Affairs and International Trade, Ottawa.

Milne, Richard. 2008. "German Groups Seek Next Crop of Engineers in the Kindergarten." *Financial Times*, June 17.

Nguyen-Hong, Duc. 2000. "Restrictions on Trade in Professional Services." Productivity Commission Staff Research Paper 1638, AusInfo, Canberra. http://papers.ssrn.com/sol3/papers.cfm?abstract_id =270787.

Nicholson, Tom. 2007. "Expansion of Market Spurs Firms to Adopt Coherent Global Approach." *Engineering News-Record* 259 (23).

OTN (Office of Trade Negotiations). 2008. "The Treatment of Professional Services in the EPA." OTN, Caribbean Community Secretariat, Bridgetown, Barbados. http://www.sice.oas.org/TPD/CAR_EU/Studies/CRNM_professionalservices_e.pdf.

Reyna, Peter. 2007. "Anti-Graft Efforts to Launch in Third World Construction." *Engineering News-Record* 259 (14): 17.

Rustomjee, Zavareh. 2007. "Engineering Services Trade: The Case of South Africa." Paper presented at the Organisation for Economic Co-operation and Development and the World Bank, "Sixth Services Experts Meeting on Domestic Regulation and Trade in Professional Services," Paris, February 15–16.

Sawinski, Diane M., and Wendy H. Mason, eds. 2007. "Engineering Services." In *Encyclopedia of Global Industries*, ed. Diane M. Sawinski and Wendy H. Mason, e-book ed., 709–14. Amenia, NY: Grey House Publishing.

Tahari, A., P. Brenner, E. De Vrijer, M. Moretti, A. Senhadji, G. Sensenbrenner, and J. Solé. 2007. "Financial Sector Reforms and Prospects for Financial Integration in Maghreb Countries." IMF Working Paper 07/125 (May) International Monetary Fund, Washington, DC.

Terry, Laurel S. 2008. "GATS, Legal Services, and Skills Transfer in Developing Jurisdictions." Presentation at the Third Annual International Bar Association Bar Leaders Conference, Amsterdam, May 14–15.

Tulacz, Gary J. 2008. "The Top 500 Design Firms: Watching for Signs of a Market Slowdown." *Engineering News-Record* 260 (13).

UN (United Nations). 1991. "Provisional Central Product Classification (Provisional CPC)." Document ST/ESA/STAT/SER.M/77, Economic Statistics and Classifications Section, Statistics Division, Department of Economic and Social Affairs, United Nations, New York. http://unstats.un.org/unsd/class/family/family2.asp?Cl=9.

UNCTAD (United Nations Conference on Trade and Development). 2005. "Report of the Expert Meeting on Trade and Development Aspects of Professional Services and Regulatory Frameworks." Report TD/B/COM.1/EM.25/3 (March 2), UNCTAD, Geneva. http://www.unctad.org/en/docs/c1em25d3_en.pdf.

World Bank. 2007. "Morocco's Backbone Services Sectors: Reforms for Higher Productivity and Deeper Integration with Europe." Report 39755-MA, World Bank, Washington, DC.

———. 2008. *Tunisia's Global Integration: Second Generation of Reforms to Boost Growth and Employment*. Report 40129-TN, Washington, DC: Social and Economic Development Sector Unit, Middle East and North Africa Region, World Bank.

WTO (World Trade Organization). 2007. *International Trade Statistics 2007*. Geneva: WTO.

10

# UNDERSTANDING TRADE IN ENVIRONMENTAL SERVICES: KEY ISSUES AND PROSPECTS

*Nora Carina Dihel*

## Introduction: Why Is Trade in Environmental Services of Interest for Developing Countries?

Environmental development is essential for long-term economic growth and improvements in the quality of life (box 10.1). Developing countries face significant needs to improve environmental infrastructure, protect scarce resources, and address the legacy of pollution and its impact on health. But a huge gap looms between the environmental needs faced by developing countries and the resources that are available to them to address these needs. In light of this gap, international cooperation and trade in environmental goods and services are key factors in enabling developing countries to build up their environmental sector.

The potential direct and indirect gains of developing countries from liberalizing environmental services are considerable. The main benefits are expected on the import side through increased efficiency because of competition and investment, which will lead to the greater availability of environmental infrastructure services for the benefit of the environment and the health of the population. Liberalization can also open up the economy to foreign capital and technological expertise in environmental management, thereby helping domestic sectors with limited investment in clean research and development and increasing access to advanced management skills and the latest technology. This can foster innovation and the provision of improved services and new technologies. For example,

**Box 10.1:** What Do Environmental Services Cover?

The businesses that make up the environmental industry offer products and services that help measure, prevent, limit, or correct environmental problems. The producers of environmental goods and equipment, as well as water supply companies, environmental consultancy services, and developers of clean technology, are all part of the environmental sector. Environmental services are thus one segment of the environmental industry. The classification of environmental services has been the object of intense debate in developing and developed countries. At this stage, there is no agreement on a common classification. Several classification lists have been used in service negotiations.

The World Trade Organization classification, which is largely based on the United Nations Provisional Central Product Classification (UN 1991), categorizes environmental services into (1) sewerage services, (2) refuse disposal services, (3) sanitation and similar services, and (4) other (cleaning services for exhaust gases, noise abatement services, nature and landscape protection services, and other environmental services not elsewhere classified). There is recognition that the World Trade Organization classification reflects a rather traditional view of the industry. Given the new regulatory requirements related to the emergence of the private sector in environmental initiatives, the growing public awareness of and sensitivity about environmental problems, and the shift in environmental regulatory approaches from end-of-pipe pollution control to pollution prevention, as well as intersectoral problems (many environmental services fall within the scope of other sectors such as business, construction, education, tourism), alternative frameworks for classifying environmental services have been developed in regional, intergovernmental, and international forums such as Eurostat, the Organisation for Economic Co-operation and Development, and the United Nations Conference on Trade and Development (UNCTAD).

The Organisation for Economic Co-operation and Development–Eurostat classification list includes the following broad groups of services: (1) pollution management, (2) cleaner technologies and products, and (3) resource management.

UNCTAD classifies environmental services into four segments: (1) environmental infrastructure services (for example, water and waste management), (2) noninfrastructure and commercial environmental services (for example, site clean-up and remediation, the cleaning of exhaust gases, noise abatement, and nature and landscape protection), (3) remediation services with environmental end use (for example, construction or engineering services), and (4) support services.

Commercial classifications categorize environmental services on the basis of market structure and behavior, technological development, and regulatory frameworks that distinguish among the following services categories: (1) infrastructural goods and services, including household, industrial, and hazardous solid waste disposal, potable water, sewerage system management, and recycling, and (2) pollution management, which comprises air and water pollution treatment and control, noise abatement, soil and water remediation, consulting, engineering, instruments and information systems, testing and analysis, and industrial processes and product designs to prevent pollution.

In the classification debate, one relevant issue involves ensuring that the classification adopted reflects the actual structure and state of the environmental industry. Generally, the division among infrastructural, commercial, and supporting environmental services can be useful for this purpose.

In addition, the distinction between environmental goods and environmental services continues to be a matter of disagreement in international trade talks. Environmental services are often supplied through goods, and the separation of goods and services in an environmental activity is difficult because of this integrated nature. Despite the disconnect in environmental goods and service negotiations, the reform of environmental services should be undertaken in coordination with environmental goods reform and liberalization.

*Sources:* Claro et al. (2007), Geloso Grosso (2004).

British investors in Peru's waste treatment facilities in Lima are leveraging carbon bond technology in Peruvian landfills (*Business News Americas* 2008a). There would be additional external benefits in terms of improvement in environmental quality, more cost effective and environmentally sound approaches to resource use in a number of industrial activities that can reduce costs and prices in associated commodity markets, and greater resource efficiency for the economy generally. In addition to the effect on economic prosperity, widespread access to environmental services has a strong impact on human health and well-being, especially in low-income countries that lack basic environmental services such as access to clean water, sewerage systems, and garbage disposal.

Furthermore, the growth of the environmental service sector and the trade in environmental services can generate employment opportunities for unskilled and skilled labor in developing countries. For example, the South African firm EnviroServ, which provides services in integrated waste reduction, management, reuse, treatment, and disposal in Mozambique, Namibia, and South Africa and which has over 1,000 permanent employees in sanitation, technical, and supervisory positions, has set aside funds for skills development.[1]

Given that environmental services are typically provided in conjunction with other products or services, the expansion of the environmental service sector would generate demand in other sectors, including engineering, design, construction, research and development, training, and consulting. Environmental services are vital for sustaining revenue from the tourism sector, which is a primary service export in many developing countries. In 2007, travel receipts in developing countries reached US$285 billion, around 33 percent of the total exports in commercial services of these countries (WTO 2008). The least developed countries have experienced a 13 percent annual growth rate in tourism since 2000 (WTO 2008). A robust environmental service industry would assist developing countries in managing the environmental impact of the tourism industry. For example, the tourism industry in Cancun, Mexico, generates substantial waste; yet, "treatment plants do not clean sewage enough to make it safe for coral," one of the main attractions for visiting tourists (Lange 2008).

Importing environmental services enhances domestic capacity, which can, in turn, lead to the development of export capacity and broader economic benefits. On the export side, several developing countries are already benefiting from export opportunities in environmental services, particularly via Mode 4. Cuba, for instance, has developed a comparative advantage in environmental studies, assessments, and consultancy services and has exported such services to Brazil, the Dominican Republic, Haiti, Mexico, Nicaragua, Spain, and República Bolivariana de Venezuela. The provision of consultancy services through Mode 1 could also provide opportunities for developing countries to export environmental services.

The magnitude and risks associated with the severe environmental challenges faced by developing countries require firm action to avoid reversals of the development progress. The environmental industry is also important to the health and well-being of citizens in developing countries. Strengthening the environmental service industry is thus critical in managing the consequences of economic growth and development, and international cooperation and trade in environmental goods and services are key factors in achieving this goal. In the context of the current debate on tackling climate change and competitiveness, the global trade in environmental goods and services will play a critical role.

While the liberalization of imports of environmental services and access to new environmental export markets are clearly important, they are only part of the equation. Liberalization needs to be a component of a strategy that emphasizes competition, sound regulation, and policies to widen access to services, that enhances the capacity to design and implement appropriate regulations, and that improves the business climate. What are the elements of successful reform in environmental services?

This chapter presents broad guidance on how to design the necessary reforms and liberalization strategies in environmental services. The next section describes why trade in environmental services is of interest for developing countries. The subsequent section considers the situation of the trade in environmental services and the prospects for this trade, the extent to which environmental service markets are emerging in developing countries, the evolving trade and investment patterns in environmental services, and the factors influencing the competitive positions of developing countries. The following section addresses what can be done to harness trade opportunities for environmental services, focusing on the importance of environmental standards in driving the growth of the industry, the role of government procurement policies regarding environmental services, and the components of an offensive (rather than defensive) strategy for promoting trade in environmental services. The penultimate section poses the questions that stakeholders should bear in mind as they advance the reform of environmental policies for trade and development. The final section summarizes.

## What Is the Situation of and What Are the Prospects for Markets and Trade in Environmental Services?

The environmental sector is going through important structural changes (for example, privatization, consolidation), output-related changes (for example, from end-of-pipe technology to cleaner technology), and regulatory changes (for example, from compliance with environmental regulations to policies that encourage improvements in resource productivity). This generates a number of issues related to the factors that are driving the evolution of environmental markets, with significant implications for the composition and direction of the trade in environmental services.

### *The environmental market*

The global market for environmental services is growing rapidly because of environmental awareness and market demand. In 2006, the global market for environmental goods and services stood at US$690 billion, with an expected increase to around US$780 billion in 2010 (Sinclair-Desgagné 2008).

Within the environmental industry, environmental services represent the most important component. The services accounted for over 65 percent of total environmental market value in 2002 (table 10.1). The largest segment in terms of value is solid waste management, followed at a distance by wastewater treatment. Smaller, but still substantial sectors include environmental consulting and engineering, remediation and industrial services, hazardous waste management, and environmental testing and analysis services.

Currently, developing countries have a small share of the environmental market. In 2006, only 14 percent of total environmental revenues were generated by developing countries (including transition economies) (table 10.2). This appears to be low, but the magnitude of environmental services in developing countries is probably underestimated because of statistical reporting problems.

Table 10.2 also shows that developing countries represent the greatest growth market. Many developing countries recorded dynamic (often double-digit) growth rates over 2000–06. It is estimated that the market in the developing countries has grown by over 10 percent during the last six years, compared with a 4 percent

**Table 10.1.** The Global Environmental Industry, by Segment, 2002

| Segment | US$, billions |
|---|---|
| Environmental products | 187 |
| Environmental services | 376 |
| Solid waste management | 141 |
| Wastewater management | 80 |
| Water distribution | 89 |
| Consulting and engineering | 32 |
| Remediation services | 30 |
| Analytical services | 4 |

*Source:* Geloso Grosso (2004), derived from data of Environmental Business International.

**Table 10.2.** Evolution of the Global Environmental Industry, by Region or Country, 2000–06

| Region or country | 2000 (US$, billions) | 2006 (US$, billions) | 2000 (%) | 2006 (%) | Compound annual growth rate, 2000–06 (%) |
|---|---|---|---|---|---|
| United States | 197.7 | 271.2 | 37.9 | 39.2 | 5.41 |
| Western Europe | 156.0 | 189.1 | 29.9 | 27.3 | 3.26 |
| Japan | 90.7 | 102.6 | 17.4 | 14.8 | 2.08 |
| Australia, New Zealand | 8.5 | 10.8 | 1.6 | 1.6 | 4.07 |
| Canada | 13.6 | 18.9 | 2.6 | 2.7 | 5.64 |
| ***Developed countries*** | ***466.5*** | ***592.6*** | ***89.3*** | ***85.7*** | ***4.07*** |
| Central and Eastern Europe | 9.4 | 15.7 | 1.8 | 2.3 | 8.93 |
| Mexico | 2.3 | 5.1 | 0.4 | 0.7 | 14.19 |
| Rest of Latin America | 9.4 | 14.0 | 1.8 | 2.0 | 6.86 |
| Rest of Asia | 24.6 | 46.7 | 4.7 | 6.8 | 11.27 |
| Middle East | 6.6 | 11.3 | 1.3 | 1.6 | 9.38 |
| Africa | 3.4 | 6.5 | 0.7 | 0.9 | 11.41 |
| ***Developing countries*** | ***55.7*** | ***99.3*** | ***10.7*** | ***14.4*** | ***10.12*** |
| **Total** | **522.2** | **691.8** | 100.0 | 100.0 | 4.80 |

*Source:* Data of Environmental Business International.

average growth rate recorded by developed countries. This evolution can be explained, on the one hand, by the maturity of environmental markets in developed countries and, on the other hand, by the state of environmental degradation, the move toward efficiency in energy and resource use, and the implementation of better environmental regulation in developing countries (box 10.2).

Driven mainly by the need for massive investments to improve environmental infrastructure, developing countries are expected to enjoy high rates of growth in areas such as water and wastewater treatment, waste management, air pollution control, and environmental monitoring and instrumentation. As these economies grow and become more advanced, there will be additional demand for cleaner technologies, renewable energy, the remediation of contaminated land, and environmental consultancy.

Developed countries are expected to see higher growth rates in areas such as cleaner technologies and processes, renewable energy, energy management, waste management, and environmental consulting services. The main driver of this development is the shift in policy toward encouragement for integrated pollution control techniques rather than reliance on end-of-pipe solutions, and there is also recognition of the need for a fundamental step in resource productivity to address global environmental issues such as climate change, resource depletion, and waste generation.

## Box 10.2: Explaining the Growth Potential of Environmental Markets: The Environmental Market Development Model

The environmental market development model provides a useful framework for analyzing environmental markets in different countries or regions. The model links environmental market growth to the stage of development of an economy, its infrastructure, and its regulatory framework (figure 10.1).

**Figure 10.1.** Position of World Regions or Countries in the Environmental Market Development Model, 2000

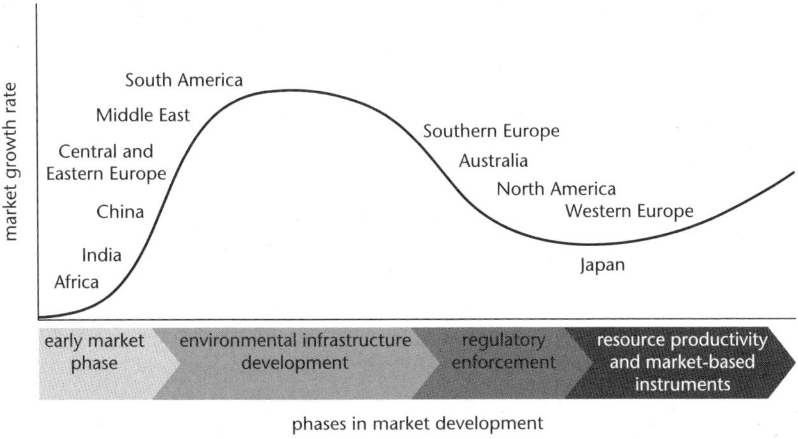


The first phase is the early market phase, when environmental investments are limited; work on identifying environmental priorities for such investments is only beginning to emerge. Many parts of Africa and several South Asian countries are still at this level.

The second phase is the environmental infrastructure development phase. As economies develop, they invest heavily in environmental infrastructure (for example, water, wastewater, and waste management infrastructure) to address basic environmental problems and the health impacts of pollution. This phase is characterized by a surge in the growth rate of environmental markets. Several Asian and Latin American countries are currently in this phase.

Once basic environmental infrastructure and operations are in place, governments typically shift their focus to the development and enforcement of environmental regulations. This is sometimes called the regulatory enforcement phase. This drives investment in industrial environmental management and pollution control. The growth rates in environmental markets during this phase are still relatively high, but generally lower than the growth rates during the second phase.

The final phase is the resource productivity and market-based instruments phase, in which many developed countries are located. Governments introduce fiscal and economic incentives for environmental improvement and greater resource productivity through, for example, landfill taxes and tax incentives for cleaner technologies. Integrated cleaner processes and activities such as recycling and renewable energy are also developed during this stage.

The providers of environmental infrastructure undergo a major growth surge during the second phase of development, while companies involved in pollution control and in monitoring the environment see more steady growth in the third phase. During the last phase, renewable energy providers and companies focusing on developing more innovative ways of providing environmental services record considerable expansion.

*Source:* JEMU (2002).

### *Trade in environmental services*

Reform in environmental regulation, greater public awareness, and growing private participation are contributing to the development of the environmental sector, but also to the increase in the international trade in environmental services. In trading internationally, environmental firms may deliver remote monitoring services electronically and provide consulting services online. An example of crossborder trade (Mode 1) is offered by a Brazilian firm that electronically monitors wastewater in Peru from a facility in Brazil. Firms may also serve foreign investors in the domestic market. For example, a Brazilian environmental testing firm might consult with a visiting Peruvian executive (consumption abroad). Environmental service firms often establish offices abroad. Thus, for example, a Brazilian firm provides hazardous waste management to a Peruvian plant in Peru (commercial presence). Firms might also visit clients in the home market to provide services. For example, a Brazilian environmental analyst might travel to assess a Peruvian facility in Peru (the movement of natural persons). Given the largely physical nature of the industry, the primary means of trade is commercial presence (Mode 3), but there is also substantial cross-border movement of environmental professionals (Mode 4) (USITC 2004).

Statistics on trade in environmental services are scarce. Using various commercial statistical sources and anecdotal evidence, we derive a broad picture of the trade in environmental services, emphasizing the variation between developing and developed countries and the variations across the segments of the industry.

#### Evolution and current situation

Data limitations do not permit an exact estimation of the volume of trade in environmental services. Rough estimates indicate that global exports of environmental goods and services reached US$79 billion in 2002.[2] The European Union, Japan, and the United States were the leading exporters that year, together accounting for approximately 90 percent of total environmental exports.

According to Geloso Grosso (2004), based on information from Environmental Business International, developing countries are net importers of environmental services, though their exports are increasing. Currently, the exports of developing countries tend to be oriented mainly toward regional markets. (For example, see the case of Mexico in box 10.3.)

In the middle of this decade, UNCTAD, the United Nations Development Programme, and the Organisation for Economic Co-operation and Development each carried out surveys of environmental markets, in total covering 17 developing or emerging economies (Kennett and Steenblik 2005).[3] Many of the studies attempted to quantify the exports and imports of environmental goods and services. The results of these reports have confirmed some of the broad statistics presented here. The studies indicate that imports of environmental goods and services account for 5–10 percent of total goods and service imports in the countries examined, and imports and

**Box 10.3:** Case Study: Trade in Environmental Services, Mexico, 2001–06

Environmental services represent almost 50 percent of the environmental market in Mexico, which hosts more than 2,600 environmental service companies, which in turn represent 60 percent of all environmental companies in the country. Despite the growing importance of environmental services in the Mexican environmental market, exports of environmental services registered a relatively modest performance (table 10.3). In 2006, exports of environmental services were slightly above 30 percent of total Mexican environmental exports (down from more than 40 percent in 2001) and showed lower average growth rates over 2001–06 than all other environmental segments. In contrast, imports of environmental services recorded the highest average growth rates across all segments, with water treatment works and solid waste management accounting for the biggest shares of environmental service imports.

**Table 10.3.** Trade in Environmental Services, Mexico, 2001–06

| Segment | Environmental exports, 2001 (US$ billions) | Environmental imports, 2001 (US$ billions) | Environmental exports, 2006 (US$ billions) | Environmental imports, 2006 (US$ billions) | Compound annual growth exports, 2001–06 (%) | Compound annual growth imports, 2001–06 (%) |
|---|---|---|---|---|---|---|
| **Total equipment** | **0.019** | **0.56** | **0.04** | **0.75** | **16.05** | **6.02** |
| **Services** | | | | | | |
| Solid waste management | 0.004 | 0.11 | 0.006 | 0.22 | 8.45 | 14.87 |
| Hazardous waste management | 0.000 | 0.03 | 0.001 | 0.04 | — | 5.92 |
| Consulting and engineering | 0.002 | 0.05 | 0.003 | 0.09 | 8.45 | 12.47 |
| Remediation/ industrial services | 0.006 | 0.17 | 0.01 | 0.21 | 10.76 | 4.32 |
| Analytical services | 0.000 | 0.01 | 0.001 | 0.01 | — | 0.00 |
| Water treatment works | 0.009 | 0.22 | 0.005 | 0.64 | −11.09 | 23.81 |
| **Total services** | **0.021** | **0.59** | **0.026** | **1.21** | **4.36** | **15.45** |
| **Total resources** | **0.007** | **0.48** | **0.014** | **0.9** | **14.87** | **13.40** |
| **Total** | **0.05** | **1.6** | **0.079** | **2.9** | **9.58** | **12.63** |

*Source:* Ferrier (2008).
*Note:* — = not available.

foreign investments are expected to rise in real terms and in relation to total imports in coming years. According to the regional distribution, most imports have originated from France, Germany, Japan, or the United States. Latin American countries show a preference for imports from the United States, while Asian countries seem to prefer Japanese products. On exports of environmental goods and services, the summary paper indicates that almost every country asserts that export capacity and overseas sales have been increasing and will continue to do so. Interestingly, among the study countries, only the Czech Republic report highlights the substantial barriers that exporters have faced and the problems associated with the lack of capital and the inaccessibility of export credits, suggesting that exports of environmental goods and services may only be a problem for developing countries in a more advanced stage of development.

According to UNCTAD, the largest environmental firms are still concentrated in developed countries. However, a recent UNCTAD study shows that the participation of developing countries in infrastructure and noninfrastructure environmental services is increasing. This is the case of a number of Asian and Latin American companies that have acquired technological and service capacities, partly through joint ventures in the environmental sector in their home countries (UNCTAD 2003).

Box 10.4 documents several cases of environmental service transactions involving firms in developing countries. The determinants and underlying factors in this trade are highlighted.

**Box 10.4:** The Participation of Developing Countries in Environmental Services

Economic growth in Asia has boosted the trade in environmental services. Industrial waste management service revenues in Malaysia, the Philippines, and Singapore amounted to US$255 million in 2006 and are expected to grow to US$378 million in 2013 (*Asia Pulse* 2007). This growth is attributed to rising populations and industrial growth (*Asia Pulse* 2007).

Financial conditions in the home market can help environmental service firms succeed in exporting. For example, a Colombian utility that provides water and sanitation services is planning to expand into rural markets in Bolivia, Ecuador, Honduras, Nicaragua, and Peru. The utility plans to use direct investment and acquisition as part of its international strategy. The utility's comfortable financial position at home will enable it to expand abroad (*Business News Americas* 2008b).

Firms in developing countries engage in trade across a variety of environmental service segments. The South African firm EnviroServ has experienced a significant increase in revenue in recent years from its operations in domestic waste collection services in Angola, Mozambique, and Namibia (Mokopanele 2008).

In developing countries, the enforcement of environmental rules is pushing firms to become more sophisticated. South African regulations that require the reduction of waste generation and disposal have catalyzed EnviroServ to expand its services higher up the waste hierarchy (EnviroServ 2003). As a consequence, EnviroServ offers services to promote waste avoidance, minimization, reuse, recycling, treatment, and disposal in all its markets (EnviroServ 2003).

Firms in developing countries are anticipating growth in export markets of interest because of the adoption of more stringent regulations in many countries. Thus, the Chilean firm Manantial already offers domestic and industrial wastewater treatment services in Argentina and Peru and is contemplating expansion into Cuba and Ecuador. Determining factors are the legal framework in export markets, as well as familiarity with market conditions (*Business News Americas* 2008c).

### Expected trends in the environmental service trade

In terms of imports of environmental services, it is expected that the current and future investment needs of developing countries, combined with the saturation of environmental markets in the developed countries, will push mature environmental firms in more advanced economies to seek export opportunities in developing countries. Privatization and the deregulation of utilities in developing countries are expected to increase the opportunities for foreign participation. Thus, the share of the trade in environmental services (imports by developing countries), though small in the worldwide trade in services today, is set to expand significantly. Recent examples of such Mode 3–related trade are presented below.

Joint ventures are a common way of providing environmental services in developing countries. In Uganda, a waste management business recently opened as a result of a joint venture between Ugandans and a Danish firm (Ssonko 2008). In the Middle East, partnerships permeate the environmental service landscape. Peru's solid waste treatment market is attracting investors from Brazil who use advanced technology (*Business News Americas* 2008d). Wholly owned subsidiaries are also found in developing countries. Table 10.4 offers several examples of collaborative arrangements.

**Table 10.4.** The Operation of Environmental Service Firms Abroad

| Country or region | Sector | Firm | Arrangements |
|---|---|---|---|
| Qatar | Water treatment and distribution, wastewater collection and treatment, solid waste collection and treatment | Suez Environment (French) (49%), Qatari Diar Real Estate Investment Company (51%) | Joint venture in the form of a shareholding limited liability company[a] |
| Middle East and North Africa | Wastewater collection and treatment | Veolia Environment (French) (51%), Mubadala (Abu Dhabi, United Arab Emirates) (49%) | Joint venture[b] |
| United Arab Emirates | Waste management services | SLR Consulting (United Kingdom), Edessa environmental and engineering firm (Lebanon) | Collaboration agreement[c] |
| Peru | Environmental remediation services | Hazco (Canada) | Wholly owned subsidiary[d] |
| Brazil, Chile, Kazakhstan, Mexico, South Africa | Environmental planning, management, regulatory compliance | Ecology and Environment, Inc. (United States) | Over 29 subsidiary entities operating abroad[e] |

*Sources:* a. *Middle East Company News* (2008). b. Euclid Infotech (2008). c. TradeArabia News Service (2008). d. *Business News Americas* (2008e). e. Standard & Poor's (2008).

The developing world's capacity to export environmental infrastructure services is limited, and the business is dominated by firms from developed countries. Except for a few advanced developing countries, a similar trend is expected in the future. For most developing countries, noninfrastructure environmental services and environmentally preferable services, such as ecotourism, present some opportunities, although a number of barriers, such as those hindering the temporary movement of people, remain to be tackled. According to Geloso Grosso (2007), the greatest export niche for developing countries is represented by a group of noninfrastructure environmental services that includes professional and other support services, such as engineering, testing and analysis, research and development, and specialized consultancy. This export capacity depends on strong domestic policies that favor the development of the environmental sector, the integration of the sector with the world economy, and the existence of educational institutions that can fulfill the demand for environmental service professionals.

Developing countries are currently net importers of environmental services. Particularly important are environmental infrastructure imports; this mirrors the stage of development of the environmental service markets in these countries. This trend is expected to continue, given the needs of developing countries and the saturation of environmental infrastructure markets in developed countries. However, a number of developing countries are beginning to develop export potential in noninfrastructure environmental services and ecotourism. The greatest export niches for developing countries seem to be in environmental engineering, testing and analysis, research and development, and specialized consultancy.

## What Can Be Done to Harness Trade Opportunities?

Traditionally, the environmental industry has not been trade oriented. This is because (1) many services have been provided mainly by municipalities; (2) for a long time, local demand has provided enough business; (3) small and medium-size companies, which account for half of the market in developing and developed countries, have little inclination and limited capacity to export; and (4) specific expertise linked to local environmental problems and conditions is often required. The recent structural and regulatory developments faced by the sector are making the environmental service industry more trade oriented, and developing countries are starting to participate in crossborder transactions.

However, the liberalization of environmental services is not uncontroversial. There has been much debate about the potential conflict between efficiency and the equity induced by liberalization disciplines. For example, there are concerns that the disciplines of the General Agreement on Trade in Services of the World Trade Organization have the potential to affect the ability of governments to regulate the water industry in the pursuit of social objectives (Lang 2004). Furthermore, (foreign) private participation in water and sanitation services raises concerns relating to price increases and the fear that poor people will not be able to afford water because of the lack of incentives from private firms to manage natural resources in a sustainable way (Cossy 2005). These views seem to be supported by a number of high-profile failures in privatization operations. For example, in Argentina, private participation through concession proved an unsuccessful experience, leaving many stakeholders dissatisfied. The Organisation for Economic Co-operation and Development and the World Bank note that this represents a case in which the granting of a concession to manage water services was not supported by an independent regulatory framework (OECD and World Bank 2006). Many analysts underline that liberalization disciplines need to be preconditioned or complemented by regulatory reforms that increase access to essential facilities and quality services.

Policy makers in developing countries may have significant scope to facilitate trade in environmental services. They have to be guided by a strategic vision of the sector and its role in overall economic, social, and ecological development. Although the benefits of liberalization can be important in terms of increased efficiency and service access and affordability, experience has shown that reforms must be appropriately designed and supported by a strong regulatory framework. More competition and better regulation are vital for the development of the environmental sector in developing countries. Trade reform then needs to be integrated into an open and transparent process of regulatory reform in which decisions on the nature and pace of reform are supported by careful analysis and an understanding of best practices.

### *Establishing a good regulatory environment*

The regulatory reform discussion differentiates between environmental infrastructure services and noninfrastructure environmental services because of the different types of market and regulatory failures that need to be addressed in these two segments of the industry.

#### Ensuring that effective competition delivers efficiency and low prices to consumers

In environmental infrastructure and noninfrastructure services, effective competition is essential to increasing efficiency. However, several environmental infrastructure services exhibit natural monopoly characteristics that can pose special and significant challenges for trade policy making. Given that there are strong economies of scale or scope in many environmental infrastructure segments, the costs of provision are minimized if only one supplier is servicing the market; in such cases, there are risks that this supplier may abuse its monopoly power. Recently, however, competition has been introduced in several segments, such as solid waste management services or sewerage treatment, which do not face cost constraints related to network duplication. For example, Geloso Grosso (2004, 18) indicates that in developing and developed countries "much of the waste generated by food retailers, shopping centres, restaurants and office buildings is collected by private waste collection and disposal service providers." It is important to continue to separate those segments in which competition can develop and those segments in which natural monopoly elements remain. Yet, it is equally important that foreign entry leads to more competition and improved service and not merely to a transfer of ownership from a public authority to a private firm or from a national monopoly to a foreign one.

If competition *in* the market is not possible, it is possible to introduce competition *for* the market through monopoly franchises or licenses. Many countries have used innovative strategies such as public-private partnerships to facilitate private participation in environmental infrastructure services. Public-private partnerships can take different forms, ranging from service and management contracts to concessions, build-operate-transfer contracts, and dispossession. *Service contracts* grant private companies, through a competitive bidding process, the right to execute technical tasks for a short period, while responsibility for investment remains with the public sector. *Management contracts* transfer responsibility for operating and maintaining government business to the private sector, while responsibility for capital investment remains with the public sector. *Concessions* transfer the responsibility for operating and maintaining assets and for investment to private stakeholders. A build-operate-transfer concession is a particular form of concession whereby ownership of a constructed operating asset effectively remains with the operator for a fixed term and is then transferred to the public authority for an agreed sum. In the short to medium term, it has the character of a privatization. Finally, *dispossession* transmits full responsibility for operations, maintenance, and investment to the private sector.

In addition to such large-scale contracts, there are a number of local-level, small-scale independent providers who complement public authorities and large concessionaires and service consumers who have been left off the network (OECD and World Bank 2006).

The experience with such contracts is mixed. In general, they have raised coverage (and sometimes prices), but have not spread the service as widely as they could have. For example, private participation in the operation of water utilities in Senegal through a contract that created financial incentives for the participating private company to serve poor households has resulted in better services. Eight years after the signing of the contract, there has been a 20 percent increase in the amount of services supplied, and the number of connected customers has increased by 35 percent. Other case studies (for example, the water and wastewater concessions in Buenos Aires) show that most gains have accrued to already-connected consumers and that the results are more limited in extending coverage to the poorest. The poorest remain the most disadvantaged in terms of access and cost. Analysts point out that the main strategic error in this case has been the award of the concession to the lowest tariff bidder, while retaining a high connection charge for the unserved. In general, the main conflict in these concession contracts is between keeping prices down and extending provision. Expanding access remains the most critical issue.

#### Ensuring access to basic environmental services

To achieve access to essential services in this new environment, developing countries can impose universal access obligations on all new entrants in a nondiscriminatory way. A common measure aimed at extending access to a service is the inclusion of network-expansion obligations in contracts with private providers. Governments have also used various forms of subsidies paid in kind (free tranches of water for households, for example) or in cash (deductions on consumer bills) directed at poorer groups in society. Subsidies can, alternatively, be targeted at operators to create incentives to extend access into otherwise unprofitable areas (Geloso Grosso 2004). Still, effective targeting remains a challenge. Experience shows that, in targeting, subsidies for connection are more cost effective than subsidies for consumption.

### *Ensuring that effective and transparent procurement policies play an important role*

Despite some controversies as to whether public-private partnerships can be viewed as government procurement, environmental service firms in the infrastructure and noninfrastructure segments can benefit from concerted attention to objective procurement policies in the public and private sectors. Government agencies, municipalities, and donors represent a significant proportion of all environmental service consumers. Rules affecting procurement, including administrative transparency, therefore shape the trade in environmental services. Achieving clearly defined, open procurement processes in domestic and regional markets can enhance the opportunities for environmental firms and reduce corruption.

If procurement policies are transparent, environmental firms can bid on projects at home and abroad from an informed position. For example, the wastewater management and remediation subsidiary of WWE Holdings Bhd of Malaysia provides services to government agencies and the private sector in China, Indonesia, Malaysia, Singapore, and Thailand (ISI Emerging Markets 2008a). Without publicly available and timely procurement information, environmental firms, particularly smaller ones, will face a greater challenge organizing for the procurement process. Ensuring the integrity and transparency of procurement processes is a challenge in many economies.

Electronic communications can support the integrity and transparency of public procurement processes. Publicizing the terms of procurements, the procedural processes, and the timelines can open the process. Audit and enforcement can provide integrity. Eliminating the bribes, political contributions, facilitation payments, gifts, hospitality, and expense accounts that influence procurement awards will lower the costs faced by environmental firms participating in the market. Correcting distorted administrative practices requires political commitment, possibly legislation, and enforcement capability. Initiatives to counter corruption that effectively address the public sector and the private sector can therefore reduce distortions in the environmental service marketplace.

#### Using standards and market-based instruments to strengthen the environmental service industry

In several environmental infrastructure and noninfrastructure services, standards that specify result requirements (for example, requirements on service quality, reliability, and continuity) or input requirements (for example, requirements related to the materials or procedures that the operators must use) are necessary to deal with negative externalities. For example, in infrastructure, environmental service standards play an important role in ensuring the access of the poor to water. Also, standards can prevent the contamination of underground water or the degradation of natural resources because of the otherwise inadequate disposal of untreated wastewater, or they can prevent the appearance of health issues related to the illegal discharge or inadequate treatment of waste. In services for monitoring and controlling the emission of pollutants, standards are important in preventing negative public health consequences or damage to the environment because of inadequate air pollution monitoring and control. In other (mainly noninfrastructure) services, the adoption and enforcement of standards can help developing countries benefit from trade opportunities. Also, given that the delivery of such noninfrastructure environmental services typically involves the movement of skilled labor, the mutual recognition of qualifications and skills becomes an issue (Geloso Grosso 2007).

International and national standards drive the growth of the environmental service industry. Which standards are appropriate for strengthening the environmental service industry and increasing trade opportunities? Are such standards national or international? And which are the appropriate instruments to implement such standards?

Harmonized international environmental management standards, such as those maintained by the International Organization for Standardization, can increase the trade opportunities in environmental services. Industries use environmental services to meet these standards, which are required by many buyers abroad. For example, Tunisie Lait, based in Sousse, Tunisia, implements International Organization for Standardization 14001 standards in managing the impact of its production facilities on the environment (ISI Emerging Markets 2008b). Furthermore, firms adhere to such standards to meet licensing requirements in export markets of interest. For example, the waste management company Sancon Resources Recovery adheres to International Organization for Standardization 14001 standards and offers services in Australia and China (AllBusiness 2008). Policy makers can promote standards and facilitate private sector engagement through the International Organization for Standardization. They can ensure financing initiatives for small and medium-size enterprises that include environmental service firms.

In contrast, in environmental infrastructure services, several examples demonstrate that, particularly in developing countries, national standards with high domestic relevance have the potential to ensure that important access and safety goals are ensured. In Bolivia, flexible national standards that provide jointly owned connections to water and wastewater services at lower cost using smaller pipes in underground trenches under patios and pavements (instead of the prevalent custom connections inside homes) have enabled the expansion of water services at an affordable price to the poorest part of El Alto and La Paz. The technology has been approved by the Bolivia Institute for Norms and Technical Standards. Developing countries are encouraged to introduce such flexible local regulations that encourage operators to meet service standards and ensure that important goals set by authorities are not compromised (Geloso Grosso 2007).

In terms of instruments, the implementation of environmental regulation and legislation is the main driver in environmental service markets and trade. At the national level, laws and regulations are the primary drivers for key environmental service industries. The establishment of regulatory authorities, the promulgation of legislation, and enforcement actions influence the development of environmental services. Policy makers can recognize the economic and environmental value of supporting environmental institutions that promulgate and enforce regulations. However, environmental improvement and development can be achieved in a more efficient way through economic instruments—such as environmental charges and taxes, tradable permits, emission fees and tradable emission allowances, and environmental subsidies—because these provide incentives for companies to meet environmental targets.

To implement the reform process, it is essential to establish efficient regulatory agencies and competition authorities. The role of these authorities is to ensure that the interests of consumers are protected against potential abuse by private companies operating in an uncompetitive environment. To be effective, such authorities should be guided by the principles of coherence, independence, accountability, transparency, predictability, and capacity.

### Enhancing the competitiveness of domestic firms

Environmental service firms in developing countries face a variety of challenges in the domestic market (box 10.5). These firms would benefit from well-informed policy makers who are knowledgeable about how the industry operates. Firms require access to financing, progressive landfill policies that will enhance technological development, and incentives to enter important subsidiary businesses that can generate additional revenue streams, such as waste-to-energy systems and recycling.

Policy makers can undertake specific initiatives to improve the conditions for environmental service firms at home. To reduce domestic restrictions on export expansion, policy makers might do the following:

- Review tax policy to reduce the incidence of double taxation
- Reduce capital controls that impede the ability of domestic firms to transact business in neighboring and regional markets

**Box 10.5:** Market Challenges Faced by Environmental Service Firms at Home

Environmental service firms in developing countries face the following challenges:

- Adequate financing for capital investment, transport costs, energy costs
- Technical expertise of clients purchasing services
- Informed policies governing landfills: tipping fees, facility requirements
- Availability of incentives for waste-to-energy systems (incineration and gas capture)
- Access to technology as a consequence of the tariff treatment of technological equipment
- A public informed about how and what to recycle
- Potential for partnerships with international firms, along with adequate legal representation
- Information management and monitoring systems to ensure the ability of firms to adjust to changes in waste production
- Professional capacity with regard to management and environmental expertise
- Relationship with local authorities and communities
- Bilateral tax arrangements
- Less than stringent enforcement of environmental regulations

*Source:* Motalaote (2005).

- Encourage domestic firms to hire foreigners to facilitate knowledge transfer
- Enhance public accessibility to environmental service rules, regulations, and specifications.

### *Pursuing an offensive (rather than defensive) trade strategy*

#### National dialogue and sector assessment

Developing countries can work to create better conditions for trade in environmental services and closely coordinate their trade strategy with domestic regulatory reform in the sector. An effective starting point is an environmental service policy dialogue at the national level to gather information on the environmental marketplace at home and abroad. Consumer education and client knowledge play an important role in the success of recycling enterprises and in establishing astute environmental service procurement and forward-looking regulation. A national dialogue can therefore draw attention to the industry and create important information for policy makers at home.

A national environmental service dialogue can provide information on the following:

- Employment in the environmental industry, the contribution to gross domestic product, growth trends
- The number and size of domestic environmental service firms operating at home and abroad
- The business models, areas of expertise, and export markets of interest for firms
- Why certain export markets are of particular interest
- Trade barriers in export markets of interest
- How restrictions impact domestic environmental firms
- How restrictions impact the marketplace
- How firms are positioned within larger global networks of environmental firms

Policy makers can use this information to refine domestic rules and regulations. The environmental service dialogue also creates a case for unilateral reform and trade negotiations. If it is conducted rigorously, a national dialogue can create momentum for legislative, regulatory, and administrative changes at home. Stakeholders can also support the tasks associated with implementing trade commitments.[4]

An environmental service trade dialogue can help negotiators pursue specific market-opening objectives in multilateral, regional, and bilateral trade negotiations. Consultation with environmental service firms, regulatory agencies, and environmental service users can determine specific barriers that should be removed.

### Addressing explicit trade barriers

Policy makers can identify explicit barriers to the trade in environmental services according to the modes of supply described in an earlier section on the situation and prospects in environmental services.

The major share of the international trade in environmental services takes place through commercial presence. Thus, most restrictions faced by environmental exporters will relate to Mode 3. Examples of typical restrictions affecting commercial presence in environmental services include the following:

- An economic needs test for the approval of foreign investment in solid waste management services, air pollution services, and technical testing and analysis services
- Numerical quotas on the number of operating licenses available to providers of industrial wastewater treatment services that apply to local and foreign investors
- A joint venture requirement for the supply of environmental, architectural, construction, and related engineering services
- Regulation of contracts by value and number through an annual licensing system in the construction and engineering segment
- Nationality or residency requirements for foreign establishment for companies operating public utilities, for example, or to gain the right to open a practice in professional services, such as architectural engineering
- A requirement that foreign businesses hire specific ratios of domestic staff to foreign staff
- A reservation of some service sectors or activities for nationals or residents

The supply of environmental services through Mode 3 will often be accompanied by Mode 4 supply to provide skilled and professional services directly to projects and to maintain local offices. Environmental service firms use a variety of professionals, such as scientists, ecologists, and specialized technicians. The deployment of these professionals for temporary assignments in export markets as a complement to foreign direct investment is common in the industry. The movement of natural persons is a sensitive issue in many countries because of illegal immigration and security concerns. Restrictions on Mode 4 may also arise from a country's overall immigration policy or specific labor market conditions. Common examples of specific conditions for the approval of the entry of service suppliers include the following:

- Labor market testing
- Residency requirements for intracorporate transferees and a requirement that the foreign company employ specific numbers of local staff

- Authorization subject to the nonavailability of locals
- Authorization subject to performance requirements (employment creation, the transfer of technology, the ongoing level of investment)

Finally, trade in selected environmental services, such as environmental consultancy services, can be provided via Mode 1 by using mass communications systems (post, fax, telephone, Internet). The principal restrictions on the crossborder supply of environmental services are the requirements that the services be certified by locally registered service providers and the requirements that crossborder service providers already have a commercial presence in the importing country.

### Liberalization: Nondiscriminatory and multilateral, or preferential and bilateral or regional?

Trade negotiations can achieve national treatment and market access for environmental firms in export markets of interest. Engagement in service negotiations under the General Agreement on Trade in Services offers a vehicle for addressing barriers to trade in environmental services in a nondiscriminatory way.

Policy makers can work on a regional and bilateral basis to improve the market for environmental services by engaging in deeper cooperation. They can facilitate discussions among regional professional bodies and government entities associated with environmental services. They can also pursue the reduction of nationality and residency requirements for professionals such as the scientists, engineers, and technicians who are important in the delivery of environmental services.

In regional and bilateral negotiations, policy makers can focus on regulatory issues and create provisions within agreements to achieve the following:

- Enforce or harmonize standards and undertake capacity building
- Create an environmental service working group to facilitate trade
- Proactively facilitate the temporary movement of environmental professionals such as scientists, environmental engineers, and technicians
- Adopt a resolution on the transfer of environmental service skills that addresses training, mentoring, and professional education (Terry 2008)
- Adopt transparency provisions to improve procurement and qualification processes

Regional arrangements that strengthen environmental protection agencies and enforcement may also support the development of environmental services.

Effective refinements of regulations that influence the environmental service industry originate from a robust information base gathered at the national level with contributions from industry, the users of environmental services, and associated environmental regulatory agencies. Changes in domestic rules and trade negotiations at the bilateral, regional, and multilateral levels can help improve the environmental service market.

### Export promotion

Governments can use a variety of export promotion programs to increase the trade in environmental services. For example, the World Bank has found that well-financed and appropriately staffed export agencies can have "a strong and statistically significant impact on exports" (Lederman, Olarreaga, and Payton 2006, 1). To understand and promote environmental services, export promotion agencies will find it useful to track national statistics on the number of employees in the industry by jurisdiction, the sectoral contribution to gross domestic product, and growth trends. They should maintain close relationships with firms to understand business models, the services offered, and export markets of interest. Export promotion agencies may also examine how firms are positioned within larger global networks of service producers and suppliers to determine competitive strengths and weaknesses. Many export promotion agencies work to understand the complex barriers that firms face in export markets, how those barriers impact business operations, and whether firms face discriminatory treatment in foreign markets relative to national firms or other foreign firms in these markets. This information will resonate with the government officials responsible for supporting export agencies and ameliorating trade obstacles in foreign markets.

A robust environmental service industry can help developing countries manage the consequences of industrial growth and development. With the aid of investment, technology, and the enforcement of environmental regulations, environmental service firms can expand operations and services. A reduction in market restrictions at home and in export markets of interest can facilitate trade in environmental services and offer greater opportunities for employment. State-of-the-art environmental services can also help developing countries sustain revenue from the tourism sector. Environmental service firms in developing countries are following the trajectory of the global industry into subsidiary operations such as recycling, waste-to-energy systems, and participation in the cap-and-trade system. Policy makers can take decisive steps to advance this progression in the context of unilateral regulatory reform, as well as multilateral, regional, and bilateral trade arrangements.

The priority areas for reforming and liberalizing environmental services in developing countries are identified as follows:

1. In environmental infrastructure and noninfrastructure services, effective competition is essential to increasing efficiency. Effective competition *in* the

market or, in infrastructure segments that have natural monopoly characteristics, effective competition *for* the market (such as bids for concession contracts) can be ensured through sound procurement policies, privatization, and public-private partnerships. Furthermore, for several basic environmental services, such as water and sanitation, universal access is a priority. Wider access to basic environmental services can be ensured by an incentive framework aimed at consumers or at private actors involved in the provision of these services. While targeting remains a challenge, experience shows that the most effective way to target services involves subsidies for connection rather than subsidies for consumption. In several environmental infrastructure and noninfrastructure services, standards that specify result requirements (for example, requirements on service quality, reliability, or continuity) or input requirements (for example, requirements related to the materials or procedures that the operators must use) are necessary to deal with negative externalities. Policy makers could strengthen environmental services by using appropriate standards and implementing these standards through market-based instruments.

2. Trade reform then needs to be integrated into an open and transparent process of regulatory reform whereby decisions on the nature and pace of reform are supported by careful analysis and an understanding of best practices. At the multilateral level, policy makers could lock in or seek further access for foreign environmental companies on a nondiscriminatory basis. Investment in environmental infrastructure and noninfrastructure services is likely to generate significant gains for developing countries. At the regional level, policy makers could engage in deeper cooperation on issues such as capacity building and the enforcement or harmonization of standards. At the bilateral level, policy makers from developing countries could engage in discussions on the movement of the workforce relevant to noninfrastructure environmental service exports such as personnel in environmental engineering, testing and analysis, research and development, and consulting where these have a potential comparative advantage. Finally, policy makers can use a variety of export promotion programs to increase the trade in environmental services.

## What Questions Should Stakeholders Bear in Mind as They Advance Reform?

The checklist in table 10.5 summarizes the main points that deserve the attention of policy makers in preparing the reform and liberalization agenda in environmental services.

**Table 10.5.** A Checklist of Questions on Trade-Related Aspects of Environmental Service Reform

***Establishing the regulatory agenda***

1. Which authorities are in charge of adopting and implementing regulations on environmental services?
2. Must the authorities follow detailed standards or rules in setting prices for environmental utilities? What is the price mechanism used (for example, price cap or cost-plus)?
3. What measures (at which level) and mechanisms are in place to assure universal access to basic environmental services? In which subsectors? Are they objective and transparent? Are foreign suppliers of services subject to different or additional conditions relative to domestic suppliers in terms of public service obligations?
4. Which regulations are in place to ensure environmental service quality? Which technical standards apply? Are they transparent? Have alternative, more efficient ways to meet the standards been considered?
5. How is uncompetitive behavior, such as the abuse of monopoly power, addressed?
6. Are institutions independent of the government? How is accountability ensured?
7. Are price changes phased in? Is the public informed about the reasons for the changes?
8. Are there any programs in place to promote the participation of consumers and other stakeholders in regulation?

***Ensuring a fair and transparent government procurement process***

1. What procurement procedures are applied for environmental services (for example, tendering)? Under what circumstances are different procedures used?
2. How are intended procurements publicized?
3. Are there registration, residency, or other requirements for potential suppliers?
4. Is procurement subject to (a) local content, (b) technology transfer, (c) local employment, and (d) investment or local presence in the importing country?
5. Do procuring entities grant price advantages to domestically owned companies relative to foreign companies?
6. Are there lists of approved suppliers? If so, what are the procedures for checking the capability of firms applying for inclusion on tenderer lists?
7. What criteria are taken into account in the award of tenders? Are the criteria for the award of contracts made available in advance to potential suppliers? How are tenders received, registered, and opened?
8. Are entities required to publish details of the contracts awarded or notify unsuccessful tenderers? Are entities required to publish or provide to unsuccessful bidders information on the pertinent reasons why their bids were rejected?
9. What, if any, are the procedures available for parties, domestic and foreign, to lodge complaints about the awarding of contracts?
10. Does the procurement regime distinguish between the procurement of environment-related goods and services? If so, what rules apply in cases of joint procurement involving both goods and services?

**Table 10.5.** *(continued)*

*Facilitating commercial presence*

**Private participation**

1. Is there a government monopoly in the environmental service sector such that private investment is not permitted? If so, in which subsectors?
2. For environmental infrastructure services, how is private participation allowed (concessions, build-operate-transfer concessions, and so on)?
3. How is it regulated at the central and local levels? What are the procedures and criteria used? Is preference given to any particular enterprise or group of enterprises? Is it a transparent process?

**Foreign ownership**

1. In which segments is foreign ownership allowed in the provision of environmental services?
2. When laws restrict foreign shareholdings in local environmental companies, what is the maximum foreign equity permitted or the minimum local shareholding?

**Screening laws**

1. Are proposed foreign investments in the environmental sector subject to screening by a specialized authority in the host state?
2. Are there economic needs tests for the approval of foreign investment? If so, in which subsectors? Are these tests transparent?
3. Are there nationality or residency requirements for foreign investment for establishment (for example, to gain the right to practice environment-related professional services such as engineering)?
4. Which authorities are charged with investment screening?
5. Which criteria apply in evaluating applications for approval?
6. Are investors offered rights of judicial review against unfavorable decisions by the screening authorities? Are clear administrative guidelines issued from which investors can reasonably predict the responses of host state authorities to investment proposals?

**Legal and joint venture requirements**

1. Are environmental firms required to establish locally through a particular legal form of establishment (that is, subsidiary, branch, or representative office)?
2. Are established foreign companies subject to specific performance requirements, including (a) licensing requirements and technology transfer rules, (b) remittance and foreign exchange restrictions limiting external financial transfers, and (c) local hiring and sourcing requirements?
3. Is entry of the foreign environmental firm conditional on the substantial involvement of local participants in the ownership and management of the investment project (joint venture requirement)?
4. Is local control (for example, 51 percent or more of the equity contribution) required for (equity, contractual) joint ventures? Does the law provide for a progressive increase in the control over such ventures?
5. Are there requirements regarding the composition of the board of directors?
6. What is the prescribed legal form of a joint undertaking (general partnership, professional corporation, or limited liability company)?

**Measures relating to licensing**

1. What laws and regulations govern the licensing of environmental activities?
2. What types of licenses and regimes apply in different segments? What is the rationale for such licensing?

*(Table continues on the following page.)*

**Table 10.5.** A Checklist of Questions on Trade-Related Aspects of Environmental Service Reform (*continued*)

3. Who issues and monitors licenses?
4. Are licenses automatic or not automatic?
5. Are licenses open ended or time limited?
6. What licensing procedures are applied (for example, application or bidding procedures)? Under what circumstances are different procedures used?
7. What provisions apply in the modification, termination, and revocation of licenses?

*Facilitating the temporary movement of service providers*

1. How are entry and work permits obtained?
2. Are there any restrictions on the movement of intracorporate transferees? What about contractual service suppliers? For the latter, do the same restrictions apply to employees of firms and to independent professionals?
3. Do the restrictions apply to natural persons seeking long-term establishment or to individuals traveling for business purposes for short periods of time?
4. Is the entry of foreign experts subject to economic needs tests? Are such tests transparent?
5. Are there residency or nationality requirements with respect to certain categories of personnel employed by locally established environmental or environment-related firms?
6. Are equivalent professional qualifications for environmental support services that have been obtained abroad recognized in the importing country?
7. Are there prior experience requirements or postqualification experience attached to the granting of visas?

*Reviewing other trade-distorting rules and regulations*

**Temporary entry for trade in service-related tools?**

1. Are there any restrictions on the temporary entry of trade in service-related tools (for example, construction equipment, technical and training material, or engineering software and design tools)?
2. Do restrictions apply to the temporary intrafirm transfer of service-related equipment?
3. Do restrictions on trade in service-related tools apply to contractual service suppliers?
4. Do customs procedures exist in the importing country allowing for duty-free temporary admission of trade in service-related tools?

**Other relevant measures**

1. Are there subsidies for environmental service providers? In which segments?
2. Are there laws or regulations on intellectual property rights that may inhibit the transfer of environmentally sound technology?

**Preferential liberalization**

1. Are there any preferential agreements affecting the supply of environmental and support services? Which measures are subject to preferential treatment? Do preferential measures also apply to the movement of natural persons?
2. What conditions must foreign suppliers of environmental support services fulfill to meet the requirements of existing mutual recognition agreements to which host country providers are parties?
3. Does the importing country maintain preferential access arrangements for developing-country service providers?

*Source*: Adapted from Geloso Grosso (2004).

## Conclusion

The magnitude and risks associated with the severe environmental challenges faced by developing countries require firm action to avoid reversals in the progress of development. The environmental industry is also important to the health and well-being of citizens in developing countries. Strengthening the environmental service industry is thus critical in managing the consequences of economic growth and development. In the context of the current debate on tackling climate change and competitiveness, the global trade in environmental goods and services will likewise play a critical role. However, there is a huge gap between the environmental needs faced by developing countries and the resources that are available to them to address these needs. In light of this gap, international cooperation and trade in environmental goods and services are key factors in enabling developing countries to build up the environmental sector.

The potential direct and indirect gains of developing countries from the liberalization of environmental services are considerable. The main benefits are expected on the import side through increased efficiency because of competition and investment, leading to the greater availability of environmental infrastructure services for the benefit of the environment and the health of populations. Liberalization can also provide capital and technological expertise in environmental management, thereby increasing access to advanced management skills and the latest technology. Furthermore, the growth of the environmental service sector and the trade in environmental services can generate employment opportunities for unskilled and skilled labor in developing countries. There could also be positive spillover effects in export-oriented sectors like tourism and in related sectors such as engineering and design, construction, research and development, training, and consulting. Finally, environmental service imports often enhance domestic capacity, which can, in turn, lead to the development of export capacity and broader economic benefits.

Developing countries are net importers of environmental services at this stage. Mirroring the development stage of their environmental service markets, environmental infrastructure imports are particularly important to developing countries. This trend is expected to continue given the needs of these countries for massive investments to improve environmental infrastructure and given the saturation of environmental infrastructure markets in developed countries. As developing countries grow and become more advanced, there will be additional demand for trade in cleaner technologies, renewable energy, the remediation of contaminated land, and environmental consultancy. Several developing countries are beginning to develop export potential in environmental services. The best export niches for developing countries seem to be in environmental engineering, testing and analysis, research and development, specialized consultancy, and ecotourism.

It should be noted, however, that the liberalization of environmental services is not without controversy. There has been much debate about the potential conflict between efficiency and the equity induced by liberalization disciplines. Recent high-profile failures of efforts at privatization in water services have fueled this debate and strengthened opposition groups. In this context, many analysts underline that liberalization disciplines need to be preconditioned or complemented by regulatory reforms that increase access to essential facilities and quality services.

The chapter identifies priority areas for reforming and liberalizing environmental services in developing countries, as follows:

1. In environmental infrastructure and noninfrastructure services, effective competition is essential to increase efficiency. Effective competition *in* the market or, in infrastructure segments that have natural monopoly characteristics, effective competition *for* the market (such as bids for concession contracts) can be ensured through sound procurement policies, privatization, and public-private partnerships. Furthermore, in several basic environmental services such as water and sanitation, universal access is a priority. Wider access to basic environmental services can be ensured by an incentive framework aimed at consumers or at the private actors involved in the provision of these services. While targeting remains a challenge, experience shows that the most effective way to target involves subsidizing connection to infrastructure rather than subsidizing more consumption of the associated goods or service. In several environmental infrastructure and noninfrastructure services, standards that specify results-based requirements (for example, requirements on service quality, reliability, and continuity) or input requirements (for example, requirements related to the types of materials or procedures that the operators must use) are necessary to deal with negative externalities. Policy makers could strengthen environmental services by using appropriate standards and implementing them through market-based instruments.
2. Trade reform then needs to be integrated into an open and transparent process of regulatory reform in which decisions on the nature and pace of reform are supported by careful analysis and an understanding of best practices. At the multilateral level, policy makers could lock in or seek greater access for foreign environmental companies on a nondiscriminatory basis. Investment in environmental infrastructure and noninfrastructure services is likely to generate significant gains for developing countries. At the regional level, policy makers could engage in deeper cooperation on issues such as capacity building or the enforcement or harmonization of standards. At the bilateral level, policy makers from developing countries could engage in discussions on the movement of the personnel relevant to noninfrastructure environmental service exports,

such as personnel in environmental engineering, testing and analysis, research and development, and consulting, where these segments have a potential comparative advantage. Finally, policy makers can use a variety of export promotion programs to increase the trade in environmental services.

## Notes

1. http://www.enviroserv.co.za/pages/.
2. Data, taken from Geloso Grosso (2004), were based on the best estimates derived from interviews conducted by Environmental Business International with companies, researchers, and government agencies.
3. The economies examined are Brazil, Chile, China, Cuba, the Czech Republic, the Dominican Republic, Guatemala, Honduras, Israel, Kenya, the Republic of Korea, Mexico, Nicaragua, Pakistan, Panama, Thailand, and Vietnam.
4. Trade commitments may require investment in public policy mechanisms, the creation of independent regulatory authorities and inquiry points, and changes in legislation, regulation, or administrative rules and practices.

## References

AllBusiness. 2008. "New Recycling Law in China Positions Sancon Resources Recovery for Strong Growth." *Business Wire*, October 14, AllBusiness, San Francisco.

*Asia Pulse*. 2007. "Industrial Waste Management Services Markets in Southeast Asia." November 2. http://www.asiapulse.com/.

*Business News Americas*. 2008a. "British Firms Interested in Environment Sector: Peru." September 22.

———. 2008b. "EPM to Invest US$2.2 Billion from 2009–11: Launches New International Division." October 9.

———. 2008c. "Manantial Eyes Ecuador, Cuba as Part of International Expansion." October 16.

———. 2008d. "Pro Inversion: Brazilian Firms Aim to Invest around US$2.5 Billion." September 22.

———. 2008e. "Canadian Investors See 'Enormous' Potential in Environment Sector." April 21.

Claro, E., N. Lucas, M. Sugathan, M. Marconini, and E. Lendo. 2007. "Trade in Environmental Goods and Services and Sustainable Development: Domestic Considerations and Strategies for WTO Negotiations." Policy Discussion Paper, December, International Centre for Trade and Sustainable Development, Geneva.

Cossy, Mereille. 2005. "Water Services at the WTO." In *Fresh Water and International Economic Law*, ed. Edith Brown Weiss, Laurence Boisson de Chazournes, and Nathalie Bernasconi-Osterwalder, 117–42. London: Oxford University Press.

EnviroServ. 2003. *Annual Report 2003*. Germiston, South Africa: EnviroServ.

Euclid Infotech. 2008. "United Arab Emirates: Mubadala, Veolia in Water Treatment JV." *Euclid Infotech–Utilities News*, October 7, Euclid Infotech, Mumbai.

Ferrier, Grant. 2008. "The Evolution of the Environmental Services Industry in Mexico 1995–2005." Paper presented at the Commission for Environmental Cooperation (Canada) "Fourth North American Symposium on Assessing the Environmental Effects of Trade," Phoenix, April 23.

Geloso Grosso, Massimo. 2004. "Managing Request-Offer Negotiations under the GATS: The Case of Environmental Services." OECD Trade Policy Working Paper 11, Trade Directorate, Organisation for Economic Co-operation and Development, Paris.

———. 2007. "Regulatory Principles for Environmental Services and the General Agreement on Trade in Services." Trade in Services Series, Issues Paper 6, International Centre for Trade and Sustainable Development, Geneva.

ISI Emerging Markets. 2008a. "WWE Holdings Berhad (Malaysia) Company Profile." Company report, ISI Emerging Markets, New York.

———. 2008b. "Tunisie Lait Company Profile." Company report, ISI Emerging Markets, New York.

JEMU (Joint Environmental Markets Unit). 2002. "Global Environmental Markets and the UK Environmental Industry: Opportunities to 2010." Report URN 02/534, JEMU, London.

Kennett, Maxime, and Ronald Steenblik. 2005. "Environmental Goods and Services: A Synthesis of Country Studies." OECD Trade and Environment Working Paper 2005–03, Organisation for Economic Co-operation and Development, Paris.

Lang, A. 2004. "The GATS and Regulatory Autonomy: A Case Study of Social Regulation of the Water Industry." *Journal of International Economic Law* 7 (4): 801–38.

Lange, Jason. 2008. "Pollution Killing World's Coral Reefs." Reuters, September 30.

Lederman, Daniel, Marcelo Olarreaga, and Lucy Payton. 2006. "Export Promotion Agencies: What Works and What Does Not." Trade Note 30 (September 30), International Trade Department, World Bank, Washington, DC.

*Middle East Company News*. 2008. "Qatari Diar, Barwa and GDF SUEZ Group to Establish Multi-utility Company in Qatar." October 15.

Mokopanele, Thabang. 2008. "Stricter Waste Laws Benefit EnviroServ." *Business Day* (Johannesburg), September 12.

Motalaote, Seteng. 2005. "Cleaning Up: Environmental Services in Botswana." International Trade Forum 4/2005, International Trade Centre, Geneva.

OECD (Organisation for Economic Co-operation and Development) and World Bank. 2006. *Liberalisation and Universal Access to Basic Services: Telecommunications, Water and Sanitation, Financial Services, and Electricity*. OECD Trade Policy Studies. OECD and World Bank. Paris: OECD.

Sinclair-Desgagné, Bernard. 2008. "The Environmental Goods and Services Industry." *International Review of Environmental and Resource Economics* 2 (1): 69–99.

Ssonko, Kiganda. 2008. "New Garbage Firm Starts Operations." *All Africa*, October 5. http://allafrica.com/stories/200810060120.html.

Standard & Poor's. 2008. "Ecology and Environment, Inc." Company description, January 26, Standard & Poor's, New York.

Terry, Laurel S. 2008. "GATS, Legal Services, and Skills Transfer in Developing Jurisdictions." Presentation at the Third Annual International Bar Association Bar Leaders Conference, Amsterdam, May 14–15.

TradeArabia News Service. 2008. "Edessa Ropes in UK Consulting Firm." TradeArabia, September 24, Al Hilal Publishing and Marketing Group, Manama, Bahrain.

UN (United Nations). 1991. "Provisional Central Product Classification (Provisional CPC)." Document ST/ESA/STAT/SER.M/77, Economic Statistics and Classifications Section, Statistics Division, Department of Economic and Social Affairs, United Nations, New York. http://unstats.un.org/unsd/class/family/family2.asp?Cl=9.

UNCTAD (United Nations Conference on Trade and Development). 2003. "Environmental Services." In *Energy and Environmental Services: Negotiating Objectives and Development Priorities*, ed. UNCTAD, 285–420. Document UNCTAD/DITC/TNCD/2003/3. Geneva: UNCTAD.

USITC (United States International Trade Commission). 2004. *Solid and Hazardous Waste Services: An Examination of U.S. and Foreign Markets*. Investigation 332–455, Publication 3679 (April). Washington, DC: USITC.

Wilkinson, I. F., L.-G. Mattsson, and G. Easton. 2000. "International Competitiveness and Trade Promotion Policy from a Network Perspective." *Journal of World Business* 35 (3): 275–99.

WTO (World Trade Organization). 2008. *International Trade Statistics 2008*. Geneva: WTO.

# INDEX

*Boxes, figures, notes, and tables are indicated by italic b, f, n, and t following the page numbers.*


## A

Accenture, 241
access to health services, 103–12
accounting services, 2, 263–91
  bilateral trade agreements for, 272–73, 272*t*
  current environment for, 264–69, 264*f*, 265*t*
  exports of, 265*t*, 267–69, 269*t*
  horizontal integration in, 70
  large accounting firms, role of, 267, 267*t*, 268*b*
  multilateral trade agreements for, 272–73, 272*t*
  recommendations for, 270–80, 281–89*t*
  regulatory environment, 270–73, 271–72*b*, 282–84*t*
  in RTAs, 272–73, 272*t*
  standards for, 273–76, 274*b*, 275*t*, 277*b*, 279–80*b*
  supply channels for, 266, 266*b*
Acumen Fund, 107
adjustment costs, 11–12, 149–51
Afghanistan
  construction services in, 192
  legal services trade in, 74
Africa. *See also specific countries*
  distribution services in, 146*b*
  Internet connectivity in, 232, 233, 233*b*
  legal services in, 70*b*
Agreement on Government Procurement (WTO), 198, 198*b*
Agreement on Trade-Related Aspects of Intellectual Property Rights (WTO), 137
agriculture, 60, 150
air pollution control, 324
Albania-Greece labor agreement, 60
Aldi (multinational corporation), 148*b*
Algeria
  accounting services in, 271
  construction services in, 186, 186*f*
  engineering services in, 296, 300*b*, 305, 305*f*, 308*b*
  health services trade agreements, 134
  legal services in, 77
  VOIP services legalized in, 234
anchor investors, 227*b*
ancillary services and products, 113, 118*b*
Andrade Gutierrez (engineering firm), 298
Angola
  construction services in, 182, 198*b*
  distribution services in, 146*b*
  environmental services in, 328*b*
APEC Engineer Agreement (1999), 312, 313*t*
Arabian Construction Company, 208*b*
Arab Maghreb Union, 308*b*
Arab Republic of Egypt. *See* Egypt
Argentina
  construction services in, 184, 184*f*
  distribution services in, 145, 153
  engineering services in, 298
  environmental services in, 328*b*, 331
  health services imports, 132*b*
  IT services in, 222
  labor migration agreements, 65*n*9
  legal services in, 79, 79*f*
Arkell, Julian, 141
Armenia
  construction services in, 184, 184*f*
  legal services in, 79*f*
artisans, 56
association agreements, 45

Association of Certified Chartered Accountants, 278
Association of Southeast Asian Nations (ASEAN)
  construction services in, 185, 186*f*
  distribution services agreements, 165
  medical travel and, 117, 118*b*
  RTAs, 50, 51–53*t*, 54, 56
Auchan (multinational corporation), 148*b*, 148*t*
Australia
  bilateral labor agreement with China, 60, 61
  environmental services in, 335
  health services in, 108*b*, 119
  labor mobility in RTAs, 50–54, 51–53*t*, 55*f*, 64–65*n*4
Australian Productivity Commission, 128
Azerbaijan, construction services in, 182

## B

back-office functions, 7, 80, 110
Bahrain, construction services in, 205
Baker & McKenzie law firm, 69
Bangladesh
  construction services in, 177
  Internet connectivity in, 232
  IT services in, 235, 236
Bank for Investment and Foreign Trade, 308*b*
bankruptcy laws, 164, 172
Banque Tuniso-Koweïtienne de Développement (engineering firm), 300*b*
Barbados, bilateral labor agreement with Canada, 58, 58*t*, 59
Basu, Subhajit, 244
BDO (accounting firm), 290*n*1
Bhutan, Internet connectivity in, 234
big four accounting firms, 18, 264, 267, 267*t*, 268*b*, 289. *See also specific firms*
bilateral labor agreements (BLAs), 15, 27, 57–61, 58*t*
bilateral trade agreements
  for accounting services, 272–73, 272*t*
  for distribution services, 165–66, 172
  for engineering services, 307
  for environmental services, 339–40
  for health services, 134–35, 136*t*
biodiversity, 150
BMI Healthcare, 131*b*
Bolivia
  environmental services in, 328*b*, 335
  labor migration agreements, 65*n*9
Bolivia Institute for Norms and Technical Standards, 335
Booz Allen Hamilton, 244
Bosnia and Herzegovina, construction services in, 184, 184*f*
Botswana
  accounting services in, 290*n*2
  bilateral labor agreement with South Africa, 60
  distribution services in, 146*b*
  Internet connectivity in, 233*b*
  legal services in, 70*b*
Boylaud, Olivier, 156–57*b*
Bracero Program (U.S.), 57
Brazil
  construction services in, 178*b*, 184, 184*f*, 185, 186*f*, 192
  distribution services in, 145, 153
  engineering services in, 295, 298
  environmental services in, 321, 329
  health services in, 132*b*
  IT services in, 222, 225, 237
  legal services in, 79, 79*f*
  service exports, 3, 10
Brazilian Association of Information Technology and Communication Companies, 242
Bribe Payers Survey, 200
bribery. *See* corruption
broadband capacity. *See* Internet
Brunei Darussalam, RTA with New Zealand, 50, 51–53*t*
building codes, 207–10, 213*t*
building permits. *See* construction permits
build-operate-transfer models, 243
Bulgaria
  bilateral labor agreements, 60
  Internet connectivity in, 232
Burkina Faso
  engineering services in, 300*b*
  Internet connectivity in, 230
Burundi, Internet connectivity in, 233*b*
Business Processing Association, 242
business visitors and salespersons (BVs), 37, 38, 44, 54

## C

Caisse des Dépôts et Consignations (engineering firm), 300*b*
Camargo Corrêa (engineering firm), 298
Canada
  bilateral labor agreements, 58–59
  engineering services in, 296
  health services in, 108*b*, 119, 120, 121*t*
  labor mobility in RTAs, 38–44, 42–43*t*, 54–56, 55*f*
Capability Maturity Model Integration certification, 19, 224*b*, 241, 243
capacity building
  in accounting services, 277*b*
  in construction services, 207
  in distribution services, 150, 167
  in environmental services, 339
  in health services, 110
  in Internet connectivity, 230–34, 231*t*
  in legal services, 87

cap-and-trade system, 340
CapGemini, 241
Caribbean Community (CARICOM)
  engineering services in, 308*b*
  health services in, 135
  RTAs, 45, 56
CARIFORUM-EU EPA, 45, 46–47*t*, 55, 308*b*
Carrefour (multinational corporation), 148*b*, 148*t*
cartelization of legal services, 81*b*
Cattaneo, Olivier, 1, 67, 99, 263, 293
Central African Republic, Internet connectivity in, 230
Central America. *See also specific countries*
  distribution services in, 145
  guest workers from, 177
  RTA negotiations, 56
certification standards
  for accounting services, 278
  for IT services, 243–44
  for services, 14, 18–20
CET Tunisie (engineering firm), 300*b*
Chen, Chuan, 182
child labor, 163
Chile
  association agreement with EU, 45, 46–47*t*
  bilateral trade agreements, 39, 40–43*t*, 44
  distribution services in, 10, 145, 153
  health services imports, 132*b*
  labor migration agreements, 65*n*9
  RTAs with, 45, 48–49*t*, 50, 51–53*t*, 54
China
  bilateral labor agreements, 58*t*, 59, 60
  construction services in, 177, 178*b*, 182, 185, 186*f*, 187, 192, 198*b*, 208*b*, 214
  distribution services in, 145, 146*b*, 153, 160
  engineering services in, 295
  environmental services in, 334, 335
  health services in, 120
  high-technology parks in, 21, 227, 234, 235
  Internet connectivity in, 232
  IT services in, 220, 222, 225, 228, 237, 242
  legal services in, 70*b*, 74
  remittances to, 36
  RTAs with, 51–53*t*, 54, 56
  service exports, 3, 9, 10
China Communications Construction Company, 208*b*
China National Electronics Import & Export Corporation, 178*b*
CH2M Hill (engineering firm), 297, 299*t*
civil engineering, 293. *See also* engineering services
COBIT standards, 244
Cognizant, 241
Colombia
  bilateral labor agreements, 58, 58*t*, 59
  bilateral trade agreements, 39, 42–43*t*, 44
  construction services in, 197*b*
  environmental services in, 328*b*
  RTAs with, 55, 56, 65*n*7
COMETE (engineering firm), 300*b*
commercial presence (Mode 3)
  in accounting services, 266*b*
  in construction services, 181, 202–3*t*, 202–4, 212*t*
  defined, 8*t*
  in distribution services, 169–70
  in engineering services, 298*b*, 315*t*
  in environmental services, 326
  in health services, 100, 101*t*, 104*t*, 107
  in IT services, 225, 245–46*t*
  in legal services, 72*b*, 73–74, 74*t*, 93–94*t*
  restrictions on, 13
commission agents, 142*b*
competition law enforcement, 17, 161
competitiveness of domestic firms
  construction services, 206–10, 208*b*
  engineering services, 308–10
  environmental services, 336–37, 336*b*
concessions agreements, 332
construction permits, 17, 159, 188–96, 189–91*f*, 193–95*t*, 197*b*, 200, 211*t*
construction services, 2, 177–217
  characteristics of, 177–81, 178*b*, 179*f*, 180*b*
  competitiveness of domestic firms, 206–10, 208*b*
  construction permits, 17, 159, 188–96, 189–91*f*, 193–95*t*, 197*b*, 200, 211*t*
  corruption in, 196, 200–201, 201*b*, 215*n*3
  current environment for, 181–87
  exports of, 182–85, 183*t*, 184*f*, 208*b*
  imports of, 182–85, 183*t*
  market access issues, 202–3*t*, 202–4, 212*t*
  multinational firms in, 185–87, 186*f*
  product standards in, 207–10, 213*t*
  public procurement process, 196–99, 199*b*, 211–12*t*
  recommendations for, 187–210, 211–13*t*
  regulatory environment, 188–201
  temporary transfers of foreign labor in, 204–5, 212*t*
  trade restrictive regulations, 201–6, 212–13*t*
  WTO commitments in, 202, 202*t*
consular services, 239
consumer protection, 172, 304
consumption abroad (Mode 2)
  in accounting services, 266*b*
  in construction services, 202–3*t*, 202–4
  defined, 8*t*, 9
  in engineering services, 298*b*
  in health services, 100, 101*t*, 104*t*, 105–7
  in legal services, 72*b*, 73–74, 74*t*
contract support, 80, 80*t*
contractual services suppliers (CSSs), 37, 45, 54

Convention on Combating Bribery of Foreign Public Officials in International Business Transactions (OECD), 215*n*3
corporate social responsibility, 162–63
corruption
  in construction services, 196, 200–201, 201*b*, 215*n*3
  in engineering services procurement, 304
  in environmental services procurement, 334
  in public procurement process, 20
Costa Rica, IT services in, 222, 227*b*
costs
  of construction permits, 191*f*, 192
  of health services, 118–19, 119*t*
  of health services education, 107
  of legal services, 85–86, 85*t*, 86*b*
  transaction costs, 17, 167, 208, 209, 215, 225
  welfare costs, 154
Croatia and health services trade agreements, 134
crossborder supply (Mode 1)
  accounting services, 266*b*
  construction services, 202–3*t*, 202–4
  defined, 8–9, 8*t*
  distribution services, 170–71
  engineering services, 298*b*
  environmental services, 326
  health services, 100, 101*t*, 104, 104*t*
  IT services, 225, 226, 237
  legal services, 72*b*, 73–74, 74*t*, 93*t*
cross-subsidization in distribution services, 149
Cuba
  environmental services in, 321, 328*b*
  health services exports, 131, 132*b*, 133, 134
  Internet connectivity in, 230
customs practices, 7, 167
Cyprus
  accounting services in, 265
  service exports, 10
Czech Republic
  accounting services in, 265
  environmental services in, 328
  IT services in, 220, 227*b*, 237
  service exports, 10

D

data privacy protection, 241, 243–44
Deloitte Consulting, 99, 112, 113, 241
Deloitte Touche Tomatsu, 264, 267*t*
Denton Wilde Sapte law firm, 70*b*
Dihel, Nora Carina, 319
direct marketing, 160, 172
Disciplines on Domestic Regulation in the Accounting Sector (WTO), 273
distribution services, 2, 141–76
  bilateral trade agreements on, 165–66, 172
  current environment for, 147–53
  economic scope of, 143*b*
  exports, 152–53
  governmental policies for, 163–67, 171–72
  imports, 147–49, 148*b*
  internationalization trends, 151–52
  market access issues, 158–63, 168–69
  market liberalization, 149–51, 163–67
  principal activities in, 142*b*
  reform recommendations, 153–58, 156–57*b*, 167–72
  in RTAs, 165–66, 172
  trade facilitation for, 167
  WTO Doha development agenda for, 166–67
*Doing Business 2009* (World Bank), 188
Dominican Republic
  bilateral labor agreement with Spain, 60
  environmental services in, 321
  RTA negotiations with Canada, 56
door-to-door direct selling, 160
Dossani, Rafiq, 226, 232
double taxation, 307, 314, 336
DR-CAFTA, 39, 40–41*t*
Dubai, health services in, 108*b*
Dublin Accord (2002), 312, 313*t*

E

East African submarine cable system, 233*b*
economic needs tests, 240, 338
Economic Partnership Agreement (EPA), 45, 135
ecotourism, 165
Ecuador
  bilateral labor agreement with Spain, 59–60
  environmental services in, 328*b*
  labor migration agreements, 65*n*9
  legal services in, 77
  RTA negotiations with EU, 56
education
  accounting services, 278, 280*b*
  engineering services, 304–6, 305*f*, 309*b*
  environmental services, 339
  health services, 107, 123–25, 124*b*, 135
  IT services, 226, 227, 227*b*, 236–37, 236*b*, 248
  legal services, 85–88, 85*t*, 86*b*, 88*t*
  service sectors, 20–21
Edu Egypt Initiative, 224*b*
Egypt, Arab Republic of
  accounting services in, 268*b*
  bilateral labor agreement with Greece, 60
  construction services in, 177, 178*b*, 182, 184, 185, 186*f*, 197*b*, 214
  distribution services in, 146*b*, 166
  health services exports, 105–6*b*
  high-technology parks in, 21, 227, 234
  Internet connectivity in, 232
  IT services in, 222, 224*b*, 227*b*
  regional trade agreement with EU, 44
  service exports, 9, 10
  VOIP services in, 234

Ehrbeck, Tilman, 115, 116
electrical engineering, 294. *See also* engineering services
electricity supply, 147, 230
El Shenawi, Naqwa, 232
emergency care, 116
employment. *See* labor and employment
Engineering Council of South Africa, 311
engineering services, 2, 293–318
  competitiveness of domestic firms, 308–10
  current environment for, 295–300, 296*t*, 297*f*, 299*t*
  defined, 294*b*
  education in, 304–6, 305*f*
  exports of, 296*t*
  finance, access to, 302–3
  home market reforms, 301–2
  imports of, 296*t*
  mutual recognition agreements, 312, 313*t*
  offensive trade strategies for, 306–7
  professional organizations for, 310–11
  public procurement policies, 303–4
  recommendations for, 300–308, 309*b*, 311*b*, 315–16*t*
  regional agreements in, 307–8, 308*b*
  standards for, 311–12
  supply channels for, 298*b*
  training in, 304–6, 305*f*
Engineering Technologist Mobility Forum Agreement (2003), 312, 313*t*
Engineers Mobility Forum Agreement (2001), 312, 313*t*
Engman, Michael, 1, 177, 219, 293
Enka Construction & Industry Company, 208*b*
Environmental Business International, 326, 347*n*2
Environmental Market Development Model, 325*b*, 325*f*
environmental services, 2, 319–48
  bilateral trade agreements, 339–40
  competitiveness of domestic firms, 336–37, 336*b*
  current environment for, 322–30, 323–24*t*, 325*b*
  defined, 320*b*
  efficiency improvements, 331–33
  exports, 340–41
  market access issues, 333, 339–40, 343*t*
  multilateral trade agreements, 339–40
  offensive trade strategies for, 337–41
  pricing improvements via competition, 331–33
  public procurement policies for, 333–37, 342*t*
  recommendations for, 330–41, 342–44*t*
  regulatory framework for, 331–33, 342*t*
  in RTAs, 339–40
  standards for, 334–36
  temporary movement of service providers in, 344*t*
  trade in, 326–30, 327*b*, 328*b*, 329*t*, 338–39
  trends in, 329–30
EnviroServ, 321, 328*b*
EPA (Economic Partnership Agreement), 45, 135
Ernst & Young, 264, 267*t*
ethics in accounting services, 279
Ethiopia, Internet connectivity in, 230, 233*b*
Euro-Mediterranean Partnership, 135
European Free Trade Association, 65*n*7
European Retail Round Table, 148*b*, 148*t*
European Society for Quality in Healthcare, 128
European Union (EU)
  construction services in, 182, 187
  distribution services in, 148*b*
  engineering services in, 296, 308*b*
  environmental services in, 326
  health services trade in, 113, 135
  IT services in, 220
  labor mobility in RTAs, 44–45, 46–47*t*, 54–56, 55*f*
  legal services regulation in, 81–82
  service exports, 3
Eurostat, 320*b*
expatriates, 115
exports
  accounting services, 265*t*, 267–69, 269*t*
  construction services, 182–85, 183*t*, 184*f*, 206, 208*b*
  distribution services, 152–53
  engineering services, 296*t*
  environmental services, 340–41
  health services, 112–25, 114*b*, 114*f*, 115*b*, 116–17*f*, 119*t*, 121*t*, 122*b*, 124*b*
  incentive credits for, 206
  IT services, 223*t*, 224*b*
  service sector, 9–10

F

fast-track visa procedures, 89*b*
FDI. *See* foreign direct investment
fiber-optic networks, 234
Financial Accounting Standards Board, 274*b*
financing
  access to, 153, 164
  construction services, 213
  engineering services, 302–3
Fink, M., 81
fisheries, bilateral labor agreements for, 60
foreign direct investment (FDI)
  distribution services, 143*b*, 146*b*, 149
  health services, 103–4, 108–9*b*
  IT services, 224*b*
  legal services, 70*b*
foreign legal consultants, 78*b*

Former Yugoslav Republic of Macedonia. *See* Macedonia
Forrester Research, 79
France
  accounting services in, 269
  bilateral labor agreements, 58*t*, 59
  construction services in, 185, 186*f*
  environmental services in, 327
  IT services in, 220
  remittances from, 36
franchising service suppliers, 142*b*, 147
free trade agreements (FTAs), 38. *See also* bilateral trade agreements; multilateral trade agreements; regional trade agreements (RTAs)
front-office functions, 80

## G

Gambia, Internet connectivity in, 230
Gartner, Inc., 260*n*1
GATS. *See* General Agreement on Trade in Services
GATT (General Agreement on Tariffs and Trade), 137, 167
Geloso Grosso, Massimo, 206, 326, 330, 332
gender equality, 145, 220
General Agreement on Tariffs and Trade (GATT), 137, 167
General Agreement on Trade in Services (GATS)
  on construction services trade, 181
  on health services trade, 137
  on labor mobility, 30
  modes of supply defined in, 72*b*
  scope of, 7–8, 7*t*
  Services Sectoral Classification List, 260*n*1
General Healthcare Group, 131*b*
Germany
  bilateral labor agreements, 58*t*, 59
  construction services in, 185, 186*f*
  distribution services in, 143*b*
  engineering services in, 306
  environmental services in, 327
  health services trade agreements, 134
  remittances from, 36
Ghana
  distribution services in, 146*b*
  health services labor from, 120
  legal services in, 70*b*
  service exports, 10
Ghana Association of Software and IT Services Companies, 242
Global Forum on Migration and Development (2007), 58
global services location index, 227–29, 228*f*, 229*t*
Gonzales, Frédéric, 206
Gootiiz, B., 290*n*3
government procurement. *See* public procurement process
graduate trainees, 45
Grant Thornton (accounting firm), 290*n*1
Greece, bilateral labor agreements of, 60
Griffiths, Catherine, 221
Groupe Suez (engineering firm), 300*b*
Grupo Cubanacan, 132*b*
Guevara, Ceani, 115, 116
Guinea
  construction services in, 186, 186*f*
  Internet connectivity in, 230
Gulf Cooperation Council, 15, 56, 308*b*
Guyana
  distribution services in, 146*b*
  remittances to, 36

## H

Haiti
  construction services in, 192
  environmental services in, 321
health and safety regulations, 161
health insurance portability, 113, 117, 134
Health Insurance Portability and Accountability Act of 1996 (U.S.), 115*b*
health services, 2, 99–140
  bilateral agreements for, 134–35, 136*t*
  business strategies for, 130–31, 131–32*b*
  domestic regulatory framework for, 128–30, 129*b*
  exports of, 112–25, 114*b*, 114*f*, 115*b*, 116–17*f*, 119*t*, 121*t*, 122*b*, 124*b*
  imports of, 103–12, 104*t*, 105–6*b*, 108–9*b*
  institutional framework reforms, 131–33
  multilateral agreements for, 135–38
  as public good, 22–23
  recommendations for, 125–38
  regional agreements for, 134–35
  supply channels for, 100, 101*t*
Herman, Lior, 113
high-technology parks, 21, 234–36
HLL Lifecare Limited, 107
Hochtief AG, 178*b*
Honduras
  environmental services in, 328*b*
  remittances to, 36
horizontal integration, 70, 133
hospitals, 108–9*b*
HP, 241
Hufbauer, Gary, 29
Human Resources and Skills Development Canada, 59
Hungary
  accounting services in, 265
  IT services in, 224*b*, 237
  service exports, 10

## I

IBM, 227*b*, 241
ICA Group (engineering firm), 298
ICTs. *See* intracorporate transferees
IFRSs. *See* international financial reporting standards
Immigration Act of 2002 (South Africa), 60
immigration policies and labor migration, 238
imports
  construction services, 182–85, 183*t*
  distribution services, 147–49, 148*b*
  engineering services, 296*t*
  health services, 103–12, 104*t*, 105–6*b*, 108–9*b*
  IT services, 223*t*
incentive schemes
  in construction services, 205
  in IT services, 235
  in temporary labor migration, 15
independent professionals (IPs), 37, 38, 44, 45
India
  accounting services in, 268, 268*b*
  bilateral labor agreement with UK, 60
  construction services in, 177, 178*b*, 182, 185, 186*f*, 192, 208*b*, 214
  distribution services in, 145, 146*b*, 148*b*, 153, 165
  engineering services in, 295, 296
  health services in, 99, 102, 105–6*b*, 107, 108–9*b*, 119*t*, 120, 134
  high-technology parks in, 21, 227, 234
  Internet connectivity in, 232
  IT services in, 14, 220, 222, 224*b*, 225, 228, 235–38, 248
  legal services in, 70*b*, 79, 79*f*
  remittances to, 36
  RTA negotiations, 56
  service exports, 3, 9, 10
Indonesia
  construction services in, 177, 184
  distribution services in, 145, 146*b*
  environmental services in, 334
  health services in, 111
  RTA with Japan, 48–49*t*, 50, 56
industrial engineering, 294. *See also* engineering services
informal sector in construction services, 179*b*
information security, 244. *See also* data privacy protection
information technology (IT) services, 2, 219–62
  certification and quality standards, 243–44
  current environment for, 221–26, 221*f*, 250–51*t*
  data privacy protection, 241, 243–44
  in distribution sector, 143, 145, 164
  exports of, 223*t*, 224*b*
  high-technology parks for, 21, 227, 234–36
  infrastructure limitations, 230–36, 231*t*, 233*b*, 245*t*, 252–59*t*
  intellectual property rights, 243–44
  labor circulation barriers, 237–41, 238*f*, 245–46*t*
  professional industry associations for, 241–43
  recommendations for, 226–44, 228*f*, 229*t*, 245–47*t*
  technical education curricula for, 236–37
Infosys, 241
InfraCo Project, 233*b*
infrastructure
  construction services for, 178*b*, 179*b*, 184, 187, 198*b*
  distribution services needs for, 147, 152, 160, 171
  engineering services for, 295, 303
  environmental services needs for, 340–41, 346
  IT services needs for, 21, 230–36, 231*t*, 233*b*, 234, 245*t*, 252–59*t*
innovation
  in health services, 130–31
  in legal service business process, 78
installers, 54, 56
Institute of Chartered Accountants of Tunisia, 273
Institute of Hospital Quality Improvement and Accreditation, 118*b*
institutional framework reforms, 131–33
Intel Corporation, 227*b*
intellectual property rights, 19, 156, 164, 172, 243–44
International Accounting Standards Board, 274*b*
International Auditing and Assurance Standards Board, 274*b*
International Ethics Standards Board for Accountants, 279
International Federation of Accountants, 274*b*
International Finance Corporation, 233*b*
international financial reporting standards (IFRSs), 274, 274*b*, 275*t*, 276
International Labour Organization, 58, 65*n*8
international law, 67
International Lawyers Network, 77
International Monetary Fund (IMF), 143*b*, 167, 182, 221, 277*b*
International Organization for Migration, 58
International Organization for Standardization
  accounting services certification, 269
  construction services standards, 209–10
  distribution services standards, 161
  engineering services certification, 311–12
  environmental services standards, 335
  health services standards, 128, 137
  IT services certifications, 241, 244
International Organization of Supreme Audit Institutions, 274*b*

International Public Sector Accounting Standards Board, 274*b*
International Society for Quality in Health Care, 128
International Telecommunication Union, 232
Internet
  bandwidth capacity, 230–34, 231*t*, 233*b*, 245*t*, 248
  legal services trade and, 78
intracorporate transferees (ICTs), 8, 37, 38, 44, 54, 338
IPs. *See* independent professionals
Iraq and health services exports, 105–6*b*
Islamic states, legal services in, 70*b*
ISO. *See* International Organization for Standardization
Israel
  construction services in, 178*b*, 182
  IT services in, 222, 225
  service exports, 9, 10
IT. *See* information technology services
Italy
  bilateral labor agreements, 58*t*, 59
  construction services in, 185, 186*f*, 200
  remittances from, 36

J
Jamaica
  bilateral labor agreement with Canada, 58*t*, 59
  construction services in, 197*b*
Jankowska, Anna, 206
Japan
  bilateral labor agreement with China, 60, 61
  construction services in, 182, 186, 186*f*, 187
  distribution services in, 143*b*
  environmental services in, 326, 327
  IT services in, 220
  labor mobility in RTAs, 45–50, 48–49*t*, 54–56, 55*f*
  legal services in, 85
Joint Commission International, 128
Joint Initiative on Priority Skills Acquisition Act of 2004 (South Africa), 60
joint ventures
  in construction services, 207
  in engineering services, 297
  in environmental services, 329, 338, 343*t*
  in IT services, 243
Jordan
  bilateral labor agreement with China, 60
  health services trade agreements, 134
  legal services in, 78*b*
  RTAs with, 44, 56
just-in-time logistics systems, 143

K
Kalirajan, Kaleeswaran, 157*b*
Karsenty, Guy, 31*b*
Kazakhstan
  construction services in, 182
  engineering services in, 295
  legal services in, 79*f*
Kearney, A. T., 224*b*, 227–28, 228*f*, 229*t*
Kenya
  construction services in, 192, 195*t*, 197*b*
  distribution services in, 145, 146*b*, 150, 153
  service exports, 10
  VOIP services legalized in, 234
Korea, Republic of
  Australia RTA negotiations with, 56
  bilateral labor agreements, 39, 60
  construction services in, 185, 186*f*
  distribution services in, 145, 153
  engineering services in, 295
  RTAs with, 56
Kotlarsky, Julia, 221
KPMG International, 264, 267*t*
Kuwait, construction services in, 178*b*, 185, 186*f*
Kyrgyz Republic, construction services in, 184, 184*f*, 197*b*

L
labor and employment
  accounting services, 265
  construction services, 181
  distribution services, 147, 149, 173
  engineering services, 304
  environmental services, 321, 337
  legal services, 69*b*, 70, 85–86, 85*t*, 86*b*
  professional services, 11–12
labor circulation. *See* temporary labor migration
labor mobility, 15, 29–66. *See also* temporary labor migration
  in bilateral trade agreements, 57–61, 58*t*
  concept of, 30–32
  economic gains from, 32, 33–35*t*
  immigration policies and, 238
  recommendations for promoting, 61–64
  remittances and, 32–37
  in RTAs, 38–56, 40–43*t*, 46–49*t*, 51–53*t*, 55*f*
  trade agreements, categories of labor for, 37–38
labor shortages, 39, 56, 63, 298
Lancesoft, 241
land ownership and use restrictions, 155, 159, 160, 171
Lanvin, Bruno, 232
Lao People's Democratic Republic, Internet connectivity in, 234
large accounting firms, 267, 267*t*, 268*b*
Larsen & Toubro (construction firm), 208*b*

Lebanon, construction services in, 178*b*, 185, 186*f*, 208*b*
legal services, 2, 67–97
- channels for trade in, 71–77, 72*b*, 73–74*t*
- cooperative arrangements for, 77–78
- current environment for, 69–70*b*, 69–71
- domestic regulatory environment and, 80–85, 81*b*, 82, 83–84*t*
- foreign legal consultants, 78*b*
- process outsourcing as export opportunity, 78–80, 79*f*, 80*t*
- recommendations for, 88–90, 89*b*, 93–95*t*
- skill base enhancement for domestic firms, 85–88, 85*t*, 86*b*, 88*t*
- Uruguay Round commitments on, 90, 91–92*t*

Legal Services Act 2007 (UK), 84
Lesotho
- bilateral labor agreement with South Africa, 60
- Internet connectivity in, 233*b*
- remittances to, 36

Lewis, James, 200
Lex Africa law community, 77
Liberia
- construction services in, 197*b*
- health services labor from, 120

Libya
- accounting services in, 271
- engineering services in, 296, 300*b*, 308*b*
- health services in, 102, 134

licensing
- for accounting services, 271, 278
- for distribution services, 158–59, 168–69
- for legal services, 81, 94*t*
- for services, 18–20

litigation support, 80, 80*t*
LogicaCGM, 241
logistics systems, 143, 145
Longva, Anh Nga, 205
Lowell, B. Lindsay, 38
Luxoft (technology firm), 241

## M

Macedonia, Former Yugoslav Republic of, construction services in, 178*b*, 184, 184*f*, 185, 186*f*
Madagascar, distribution services in, 146*b*
Malawi
- bilateral labor agreement with South Africa, 60
- Internet connectivity in, 230, 233*b*
- legal services in, 74
- service exports, 10

Malaysia
- construction services in, 182, 184
- distribution services in, 145, 146*b*, 150
- environmental services in, 328*b*, 334
- health services in, 99, 108*b*, 118*b*, 119
- IT services in, 222, 237
- RTA negotiations with Australia, 56
- service exports, 9, 10

Maldives, distribution services in, 145
Malta and health services exports, 117–18
management expertise, 145, 206–7
Manantial (environmental services firm), 328*b*
Mango, Paul D., 115, 116
market access issues
- construction services, 177, 180, 187–88, 202–3*t*, 202–4, 212*t*
- distribution services, 158–63, 168–69
- environmental services, 333, 339–40, 343*t*
- labor mobility of professional workers and, 61
- legal services, 88–90, 89*b*, 93–95*t*

Martin, Susan, 38
Mattoo, Aaditya, 107, 290*n*3
Mauritania
- accounting services in, 271
- bilateral labor agreement with Spain, 60
- engineering services in, 308*b*

Mauritius
- bilateral labor agreements, 58*t*, 59, 60, 61
- construction services in, 207, 209
- distribution services in, 146*b*
- health services in, 108*b*, 119
- IT services in, 220, 222, 225
- legal services in, 70*b*
- VOIP services legalized in, 234

Mburu, Emily, 179*b*
McKinsey Global Institute, 113, 221, 222, 232, 236
MDGs. *See* Millennium Development Goals
mechanical engineering, 293. *See also* engineering services
medical tourism, 100, 102, 112, 115–19, 128
medical transcription services, 115*b*
medical travel, 115–16, 116–17*f*
mergers and acquisitions in health services, 119, 120*f*
Metro (multinational corporation), 148*b*, 148*t*
Mexico
- association agreement with EU, 45
- bilateral labor agreements, 57, 58*t*, 59
- construction services in, 177, 178*b*
- distribution services in, 10, 143, 145, 153
- engineering services in, 298
- environmental services in, 321, 327*b*
- health services in, 120, 132*b*
- labor migration agreements, 65*n*9
- remittances to, 36
- RTA with Japan, 45, 48–49*t*

Middle East and North Africa region. *See also specific countries*
- engineering services in, 295–96, 299
- environmental services in, 329
- legal services trade in, 74

migrants. *See* labor mobility; temporary labor migration
Millennium Development Goals (MDGs)
  education-related, 6
  health-related, 6, 23, 100, 139*n*1
minimum wage levels, 163
Mode 1. *See* crossborder supply
Mode 2. *See* consumption abroad
Mode 3. *See* commercial presence
Mode 4. *See* movement of natural persons
Moldova, remittances to, 36
monopolies, 16, 163
Morocco
  accounting services in, 267, 271, 278
  bilateral labor agreements, 39, 40–41*t*, 60
  engineering services in, 304, 305*f*, 306, 307, 308*b*
  health services in, 122, 135, 136*t*
  Internet connectivity in, 232
  legal services in, 75–76*t*, 77, 78*b*
  RTA with EU, 44, 46–47*t*
  SWOT analysis for health services trade, 127*b*
movement of natural persons (Mode 4). *See also* temporary labor migration
  accounting services, 266*b*, 273
  categories of, 37
  construction services, 181, 202–3*t*, 202–4, 212*t*
  defined, 8*t*
  distribution services, 170
  engineering services, 298*b*, 316*t*
  environmental services, 326, 344*t*
  health services, 100, 101*t*, 104*t*, 107–10
  IT services, 225, 226, 237, 246*t*
  labor mobility and, 30–31, 31*b*
  legal services, 72*b*, 73–74, 74*t*, 93–94*t*
  restrictions on, 14–15
Mozambique
  accounting services in, 290*n*2
  bilateral labor agreement with South Africa, 60
  distribution services in, 146*b*
  engineering services in, 305
  environmental services in, 321, 328*b*
multilateral trade agreements
  accounting services, 272–73, 272*t*
  engineering services, 307
  environmental services, 339–40
  health services, 135–38
multinational corporations, 64, 71, 185–87, 186*f*
mutual recognition agreements
  engineering services, 301, 312, 313*t*, 315
  legal services, 74, 87*b*
  for services, 18–20
Myanmar, construction services in, 184

**N**

NAFTA. *See* North American Free Trade Agreement
Namibia
  distribution services in, 146*b*
  environmental services in, 321, 328*b*
National Accounts Main Aggregates Database (UN), 174*n*1
National Association of Software and Services Companies, 238, 242
National Committee for Quality Assurance, 128
Nepal, Internet connectivity in, 234
Ness Technologies, 241
Netcare (holding company), 131*b*
Netherlands, health services labor in, 120
Neusoft (technology firm), 241
New Zealand
  construction services in, 215*n*1
  labor mobility in RTAs, 50–54, 51–53*t*, 54–56, 55*f*
NGOs (nongovernmental organizations), 152
Nguyen-Hong, Duc, 81
Nicaragua, environmental services in, 321, 328*b*
Nicoletti, Giuseppe, 156–57*b*
Niger, construction services in, 192
Nigeria
  distribution services in, 146*b*
  Internet connectivity in, 230, 232
  legal services in, 77
NIIT Limited, 21, 236*b*
Nile University, 224*b*
nongovernmental organizations (NGOs), 152
Nordås, Hildegunn Kyvik, 151
North American Free Trade Agreement (NAFTA), 38, 42–43*t*, 308*b*
North-South trade
  in distribution services, 152
  in health services, 102, 116
Norway, health services trade agreements, 134

**O**

Odebrecht (engineering firm), 298
OECD countries
  construction services in, 182, 185, 186*f*
  distribution services in, 145, 148*b*, 154, 156–57*b*, 161
  law firms in, 70
  legal services regulation in, 81*b*
Office of Trade Negotiations (OTN), 308*b*
official development assistance, 179*b*
offshoring of IT services, 221–26, 221*f*. *See also* information technology (IT) services
Ogus, A., 81
Oman
  health services imports, 102, 105, 105–6*b*, 110
  legal services in, 78*b*

One District, One Doctor Project (Thailand), 124*b*
opening hours for retail stores, 160–61
Organisation for Economic Co-operation and Development (OECD). *See also* OECD countries
anti-corruption program, 215*n*3
distribution services capacity building assistance from, 167
environmental market survey, 326
environmental services classification, 320*b*
regulatory principles, 25, 26*t*
on trade restrictions in health services, 128
Organization for Security and Co-operation in Europe, 58
Organization of Eastern Caribbean States, 58*t*, 59
Outsource Transcription Philippines, Inc., 115*b*

## P

Pai, Arjun K., 244
Pakistan
accounting services in, 268*b*
construction services in, 178*b*, 185, 186*f*
distribution services in, 145
health services in, 105–6*b*
IT services in, 236, 248
legal services in, 74, 77, 79*f*
Panama
bilateral trade agreement with U.S., 39
legal services in, 79, 79*f*
RTA negotiations with Canada, 56
Papua New Guinea, legal services in, 77
Paraguay, distribution services in, 153
Paralegal Advisory Service, 74, 77
partnerships
in construction services, 210
in distribution services, 152
in engineering services, 297
in environmental services, 332, 341
in IT services, 241–42
patent support services, 80, 80*t*
Paterson, I., 81
permits
construction permits, 17, 159, 188–96, 189–91*f*, 193–95*t*, 197*b*, 200, 211*t*
for distribution services, 158–59, 168–69
work permits, 15, 159, 204, 238, 239
Peru
bilateral trade agreements, 39, 40–41*t*, 42–43*t*, 44
environmental services in, 328*b*, 329
labor migration agreements, 65*n*9
RTAs of, 55, 56
petroleum extraction
construction services for, 179*b*, 179*f*
engineering services for, 294
P4 (Trans-Pacific Strategic Economic Partnership Agreement), 50, 51–53*t*
Philippines
accounting services in, 268*b*
bilateral labor agreement with UK, 60
distribution services in, 145, 146*b*
environmental services in, 328*b*
health services in, 105–6*b*, 113, 115*b*, 120, 123, 134
high-technology parks in, 21, 227, 234, 235
Internet connectivity in, 232
IT services in, 220, 237
labor migration agreements, 65*n*9
remittances to, 36
RTA with Japan, 48–49*t*, 50, 56
service exports, 10
Philippine Software Industry Association, 242
Poland, IT services in, 224*b*, 237
pollution control, 324
portability of health insurance, 113, 115*b*, 117, 134
port management, 167
power supply, 147, 230
predatory pricing, 161
price controls
for accounting services, 271, 272*b*, 283*t*
for distribution services, 145, 149, 157*b*, 161, 164
PricewaterhouseCoopers, 264, 267*t*
private sector. *See also* public-private partnerships
accounting services role of, 6, 278
in distribution services, 149, 162
in environmental services, 341, 343*t*
in health services, 101, 108*b*
in IT services, 21, 236–37, 236*b*, 242
and labor mobility, 39
in legal services, 6
private technical colleges, 236–37, 236*b*
privatization
accounting services role in, 265, 289
of utilities, 329, 331, 341, 346
process outsourcing of legal services, 78–80, 79*f*, 80*t*
procurement. *See* public procurement process
product standards. *See* standards
professional industry associations
accounting services, 270
engineering services, 306, 310–11
IT services, 241–43
legal services, 81*b*, 82, 82*b*
recommendations for, 22
project financing, 70*b*
Provisional Central Product Classification, 260*n*1, 294*b*, 320*b*
public international law, 67

public-private partnerships
in environmental services, 332, 341
in IT services, 241–42
public procurement process
construction services, 179*b*, 196–99, 198*b*, 199*b*, 211–12*t*
corruption in, 200
engineering services, 303–4
environmental services, 333–37, 339, 342*t*
transparency in, 20, 27
public sector. *See also* state-owned enterprises
accounting services education, role in, 278
construction services for, 179*b*, 184
health services, role in, 101, 124*b*

## Q

Qatar, construction services in, 186, 186*f*
Queiroz Galvão (engineering firm), 298

## R

Rathindran, Randeep, 107
recycling, 337, 340
regional trade agreements (RTAs)
accounting services, 272–73, 272*t*
distribution services, 165–66, 172
engineering services, 307–8, 308*b*
environmental services, 339–40
health services, 134–35
labor mobility and, 30, 38–56, 40–43*t*, 46–49*t*, 51–53*t*, 55*f*
regulatory framework
accounting services, 270–73, 271–72*b*, 282–84*t*
construction permits, 188–96, 189–91*f*, 193–95*t*, 197*b*, 211*t*
corruption and, 200–201, 201*b*
distribution services, 144–45, 158–63, 171–72
environmental services, 331–33, 342*t*
health services, 100, 128–30, 129*b*
legal services, 80–85, 81*b*, 82, 83–84*t*
public procurement process, 196–99, 199*b*, 211–12*t*
reform strategy for, 23–25, 24*t*
retail sector reforms, 156–57*b*
service sector, 10–11, 16–20
trade restrictive regulations, 201–6, 212–13*t*
remittances, 32–37, 64*n*1, 119, 185
renewable energy technologies, 324
Reports on the Observance of Standards and Codes (ROSC), 277*b*
República Bolivariana de Venezuela. *See* Venezuela
Republic of Korea. *See* Korea
Republic of Yemen. *See* Yemen
retail distribution. *See also* distribution services
defined, 142*b*
economic scope of, 143*b*
promotion of, 164–65
regulatory environment, 160–63
retraining, 154, 155, 164, 171. *See also* training
Rewe-Zentral (multinational corporation), 148*b*, 148*t*
Reyna, Peter, 200
Rizvi Isa Afridi & Angell law firm, 74
Romania
bilateral labor agreement with Spain, 60
IT services in, 222, 224*b*
Russian Federation
construction services in, 178*b*, 182, 184, 184*f*, 185, 186*f*, 192, 193–95*t*, 214
distribution services in, 145
engineering services in, 295
Internet connectivity in, 232
IT services in, 222, 237
legal services in, 79, 79*f*
service exports, 9
Rustomjee, Zavareh, 304
Rwanda, Internet connectivity in, 233*b*

## S

Sáez, Sebastián, 1, 65*n*5
safety regulations, 161
Sancon Resources Recovery, 335
Saudi Arabia
construction services in, 178*b*, 185, 186*f*
engineering services in, 296, 300*b*
health services in, 108*b*, 119, 121
legal services in, 70*b*, 78*b*
remittances from, 36
Schmid, Linda, 293
Seacom Project, 233*b*
Seasonal Agricultural Worker Program (Canada), 59
Senegal
bilateral labor agreement with Spain, 60
engineering services in, 300*b*
environmental services in, 332–33
Serbia, construction services in, 178*b*
service contracts, 332
Service de Normalisation Industrielle Marocaine, 312
Services Sectoral Classification List (GATS), 260*n*1
Sharia law, 70*b*
Sierra Leone, construction services in, 197*b*
Singapore
bilateral trade agreement with U.S., 39, 40–41*t*
construction services in, 192
engineering services in, 295, 296
environmental services in, 328*b*, 334
health services in, 99, 108*b*, 118*b*, 119, 119*t*
Internet connectivity in, 232
IT services in, 225
RTAs with, 50, 51–53*t*, 56

skill-transfer provisions, 309*b*
Slovenia and health services trade agreements, 134
smart villages. *See* high-technology parks
Software Engineering Institute, 19, 241, 243
software parks. *See* high-technology parks
solid waste management, 323. *See also* environmental services
Somalia, VOIP services legalized in, 234
South Africa
  accounting services in, 290*n*2
  bilateral labor agreements, 58*t*, 59, 60, 61
  construction services in, 192
  distribution services in, 10, 143, 145, 146*b*, 153
  engineering services in, 304, 311
  environmental services in, 321
  health services in, 125, 131, 131*b*
  legal services in, 70*b*, 79
  VOIP services legalized in, 234
Southern Cone Common Market
  engineering services in, 308*b*
  RTA negotiations with EU, 56
South Korea. *See* Korea, Republic of
South-South trade
  in distribution services, 143, 152–53, 166
  in health services, 102, 116
  in legal services, 74
Spain
  bilateral labor agreements, 58*t*, 59, 60
  construction services in, 185, 186*f*
  environmental services in, 321
  health services trade agreements, 134
special economic zones. *See* high-technology parks
Sri Lanka, IT services in, 222, 232, 236
standards
  accounting services, 273–76, 274*b*, 275*t*, 277*b*, 279–80*b*, 290
  construction services, 207–10, 213*t*
  distribution services, 144, 150–51
  engineering services, 309*b*, 311–12, 314
  environmental services, 334–36, 346
  IT services, 241, 243–44
  legal services, 82, 86
  service sector, 10, 18–20
state-owned enterprises, 16, 163, 198*b*
Stephenson, Sherry, 29
Stern, Matthew, 206
Stern, Robert M., 1
STUDI (engineering firm), 300*b*
subsidies
  for accounting services, 271
  for construction services, 205
  for distribution services, 164, 171
  for environmental services, 16, 333, 341
  for health services, 16
Sudan, health services exports, 105–6*b*
supply channels. *See also specific modes*
  for accounting services, 266, 266*b*
  for engineering services, 298*b*
  for health services, 100, 101*t*
  for legal services, 71–77, 72*b*, 73*t*, 74*t*
  modes of, 8, 8*t*
Swaziland
  bilateral labor agreement with South Africa, 60
  distribution services in, 146*b*
  Internet connectivity in, 230
Switzerland, remittances from, 36
SWOT (strengths, weaknesses, opportunities, threats) analysis, 126, 127*b*
Sydney Accord (2001), 312, 313*t*
Syntel, 241
Syrian Arab Republic, regional trade agreement with EU, 44

# T

Taiwan
  construction services in, 178*b*
  distribution services in, 145
  Internet connectivity in, 232
Tajikistan, remittances to, 36
Tanzania
  construction services in, 192, 198*b*
  distribution services in, 146*b*
  legal services in, 70*b*
  VOIP services legalized in, 234
tariffs, 7
tax incentives
  for accounting services, 271
  for construction services, 205
  for distribution services, 164
  for engineering services, 307, 314
  for environmental services, 336
TCS (technology firm), 241
Techint (engineering firm), 298
technical colleges, 227, 236–37, 236*b*
technological expertise, 1, 206–7
telecommunications, 147, 226, 230, 232, 245*t*
telemedicine, 100, 104
Teljeur, Ethel, 206
temporary labor migration. *See also* labor mobility; movement of natural persons (Mode 4)
  for construction services, 204–5, 212*t*
  for distribution services, 159–60, 170
  for environmental services, 344*t*
  extent of, 31*b*
  for IT services, 237–41, 238*f*, 245–46*t*
Tesco (multinational corporation), 148*b*, 148*t*

Thailand
construction services in, 182, 184
distribution services in, 145, 146*b*
environmental services in, 334
health services in, 99, 111, 114*b*, 115, 118*b*, 119*t*, 123, 124*b*, 133
legal services in, 77
service exports, 9, 10
Touré, Hamadoun I., 232
tourism promotion, 164–65
town planning. *See* zoning
trade policy
for construction services, 201–6, 212–13*t*
for distribution services, 167
for engineering services, 306–7
for environmental services, 337–41
for health services, 128
for services, 12–15, 28*n*2
Trade-Related Aspects of Intellectual Property Rights Agreement (WTO), 137
training
in accounting services, 278
in distribution services, 145, 164, 171
in engineering services, 304–6, 305*f*, 309*b*
in environmental services, 339
in health services, 107, 135
in legal services, 85–88, 85*t*, 86*b*, 88*t*
transaction costs
in construction services, 17, 208, 209, 215
in distribution services, 167
in IT services, 225
transcription services, 110, 115*b*
Trans-Pacific Strategic Economic Partnership Agreement (P4), 50, 51–53*t*
transparency
accounting services and, 263, 271
in engineering services procurement, 303–4
in environmental services procurement, 333–37, 339
in government procurement process, 196–99, 199*b*
in IT services, 241
in public procurement process, 20, 27
Transparency International, 200, 201*b*
transportation networks, 147, 179*b*, 179*f*
Trinidad and Tobago and bilateral labor agreement with Canada, 58*t*, 59
Tunisia
accounting services in, 265, 267, 269, 271, 278
construction services in, 184, 184*f*
engineering services in, 300, 300*b*, 303, 305, 305*f*, 308*b*
health services in, 102, 111, 120–21, 122*b*, 128, 129*b*, 134
legal services in, 78*b*, 83–84*t*, 89*b*
regional trade agreement with EU, 44
service exports, 10
Tunisie Lait (environmental services firm), 335
Turkey
construction services in, 177, 178*b*, 182, 184, 184*f*, 185, 186*f*, 200, 208*b*, 214
regional trade agreement with EU, 44, 46–47*t*
service exports, 9


## U


UAE. *See* United Arab Emirates
Uganda
distribution services in, 146*b*, 153
environmental services in, 329
Internet connectivity in, 233*b*
legal services in, 70*b*
VOIP services legalized in, 234
UK. *See* United Kingdom
Ukraine, legal services in, 77
unemployment benefits, 154, 164, 171
Union for the Mediterranean, 135
United Arab Emirates (UAE)
bilateral labor agreement with China, 60–61
construction services in, 178*b*, 185, 186, 186*f*
engineering services in, 296, 300*b*
health services imports, 110
health services in, 108*b*, 119
legal services in, 74
United Kingdom (UK)
bilateral labor agreements, 58*t*, 59, 60
distribution services in, 143*b*
health services in, 108*b*, 118, 119, 120, 131*b*, 134
IT services in, 220, 238
legal services in, 74, 74*t*, 79, 81*b*, 84
United Nations Conference on Trade and Development, 119, 196
distribution services capacity building assistance from, 167
environmental market survey, 326, 328
environmental services classification, 320*b*
United Nations Development Programme, 326
United States
bilateral labor agreements with Mexico, 57
construction services in, 182, 185, 186*f*, 187
distribution services in, 143*b*, 148*b*
engineering services in, 296
environmental services in, 326, 327
health services in, 99, 107, 108*b*, 119, 119*t*, 120, 121*t*, 130, 135, 136*t*
IT services in, 220
labor mobility in RTAs, 14, 38–44, 40–41*t*, 54–56, 55*f*, 64–65*n*4
legal services in, 71, 74, 74*t*
medical tourists from, 112
medical transcription needs in, 115*b*
remittances from, 36
service exports, 3

Uruguay
distribution services in, 153
IT services in, 222
utility companies, 329, 331, 341, 346

V

Venezuela, República Bolivariana de
environmental services in, 321
health services imports, 132*b*
vertical integration in distribution services, 155
Vietnam
distribution services in, 145, 148*b*
IT services in, 222, 234
legal services in, 77
voice over Internet protocol (VOIP) services, 234

W

wage differentials, 32
Walkenhorst, Peter, 67, 263
Washington Accord (1989), 312, 313*t*
waste management, 323–24, 328*b*
waste-to-energy systems, 340
water and wastewater treatment, 324, 331
welfare costs, 154
WHO (World Health Organization), 115
wholesale distribution services, 142*b*. *See also* distribution services
Willcocks, Leslie, 221
Wipro (technology firm), 241
women
in health services, 145
in IT services, 220
working conditions, 155, 163, 235
work permits, 15, 159, 204, 238, 239
World Bank
accounting standards initiative, 277*b*
construction services financing by, 213
on construction services regulatory reforms, 197*b*, 199*b*
distribution services capacity building assistance from, 167
on export promotion, 340
health services FDI from, 108*b*
Internet connectivity in Africa project, 233*b*
legal reforms promoted by, 67
on trade restrictiveness in health services, 128
World Customs Organization, 167
World Health Organization (WHO), 115
World Trade Organization (WTO). *See also* General Agreement on Tariffs and Trade (GATT); General Agreement on Trade in Services (GATS)
Agreement on Government Procurement, 198, 198*b*
commitments in construction services, 202, 202*t*
Disciplines on Domestic Regulation in the Accounting Sector, 273
distribution services capacity building assistance from, 167
Doha development agenda, 90, 137, 166–67, 204
Information Technology Agreement, 260*n*9
Uruguay Round commitments, 90, 91–92*t*
WWE Holdings Bhd, 333

Y

Yemen, Republic of, construction services in, 177, 184

Z

Zafar & Mandviwalla Law Associates, 74
Zambia
accounting services, 280*b*
distribution services in, 146*b*
Internet connectivity in, 233*b*
legal services in, 70*b*
Zambia Centre for Accounting Studies, 280*b*
Zimbabwe
construction services in, 192
distribution services in, 146*b*
Internet connectivity in, 233*b*
zoning, 155, 160

**ECO-AUDIT**

*Environmental Benefits Statement*

The World Bank is committed to preserving endangered forests and natural resources. The Office of the Publisher has chosen to print ***International Trade in Services*** on recycled paper with 30 percent postconsumer fiber in accordance with the recommended standards for paper usage set by the Green Press Initiative, a nonprofit program supporting publishers in using fiber that is not sourced from endangered forests. For more information, visit www.greenpressinitiative.org.

Saved:
- 12 trees
- 3 million BTUs of total energy
- 861 lb. of net greenhouse gases
- 4,147 gal. of waste water
- 252 lbs. of solid waste

green press INITIATIVE